BASIC LEGAL RESEARCH

ASPEN COURSEBOOK SERIES

BASIC LEGAL RESEARCH

TOOLS AND STRATEGIES

FIFTH EDITION

AMY E. SLOAN

Professor of Law
University of Baltimore School of Law

 Wolters Kluwer
Law & Business

Published by Wolters Kluwer Law & Business in New York.

Wolters Kluwer Law & Business serves customers worldwide with CCH, Aspen Publishers, and Kluwer Law International products. (www.wolterskluwerlb.com)

To contact Customer Service, e-mail customer.service@wolterskluwer.com, call 1-800-234-1660, fax 1-800-901-9075, or mail correspondence to:

> Wolters Kluwer Law & Business
> Attn: Order Department
> PO Box 990
> Frederick, MD 21705

Printed in the United States of America.

1 2 3 4 5 6 7 8 9 0

ISBN 978-1-4548-0847-3

Library of Congress Cataloging-in-Publication Data

Sloan, Amy E., 1964-
   Basic legal research : tools and strategies / Amy E. Sloan.—5th ed.
      p. cm.—(Aspen coursebook series)
   Includes index.
   "Appendix: Selected Internet Research Resources.
   ISBN 978-1-4548-0847-3
1. Legal research-United States.   I. Title.

KF240.S585 2012
340.072'073—dc23

2012015980

About Wolters Kluwer Law & Business

Wolters Kluwer Law & Business is a leading global provider of intelligent information and digital solutions for legal and business professionals in key specialty areas, and respected educational resources for professors and law students. Wolters Kluwer Law & Business connects legal and business professionals as well as those in the education market with timely, specialized authoritative content and information-enabled solutions to support success through productivity, accuracy and mobility.

Serving customers worldwide, Wolters Kluwer Law & Business products include those under the Aspen Publishers, CCH, Kluwer Law International, Loislaw, Best Case, ftwilliam.com and MediRegs family of products.

CCH products have been a trusted resource since 1913, and are highly regarded resources for legal, securities, antitrust and trade regulation, government contracting, banking, pension, payroll, employment and labor, and healthcare reimbursement and compliance professionals.

Aspen Publishers products provide essential information to attorneys, business professionals and law students. Written by preeminent authorities, the product line offers analytical and practical information in a range of specialty practice areas from securities law and intellectual property to mergers and acquisitions and pension/benefits. Aspen's trusted legal education resources provide professors and students with high-quality, up-to-date and effective resources for successful instruction and study in all areas of the law.

Kluwer Law International products provide the global business community with reliable international legal information in English. Legal practitioners, corporate counsel and business executives around the world rely on Kluwer Law journals, looseleafs, books, and electronic products for comprehensive information in many areas of international legal practice.

Loislaw is a comprehensive online legal research product providing legal content to law firm practitioners of various specializations. Loislaw provides attorneys with the ability to quickly and efficiently find the necessary legal information they need, when and where they need it, by facilitating access to primary law as well as state-specific law, records, forms and treatises.

Best Case Solutions is the leading bankruptcy software product to the bankruptcy industry. It provides software and workflow tools to flawlessly streamline petition preparation and the electronic filing process, while timely incorporating ever-changing court requirements.

ftwilliam.com offers employee benefits professionals the highest quality plan documents (retirement, welfare and non-qualified) and government forms (5500/PBGC, 1099 and IRS) software at highly competitive prices.

MediRegs products provide integrated health care compliance content and software solutions for professionals in healthcare, higher education and life sciences, including professionals in accounting, law and consulting.

Wolters Kluwer Law & Business, a division of Wolters Kluwer, is headquartered in New York. Wolters Kluwer is a market-leading global information services company focused on professionals.

For Bebe

SUMMARY OF CONTENTS

Contents

PREFACE

The fifth edition of *Basic Legal Research: Tools and Strategies* is completely revised. The advent of new research platforms has revolutionized legal research, and students need instruction in the new platforms. At the same time, research process remains fundamentally a problem solving process, and instruction on research requires continued focus on the analytical nature of the research task.

In response to the changes in legal research, this new edition redefines the central metaphor that describes the research process. It does so in a way that encompasses both the traditional sources of legal research and the new research platforms. It describes research not as a process of gathering source material, but rather, as a process of narrowing the field of all legal information to the subset of authority necessary to analyze a legal issue. This narrowing process can occur before a search begins by selecting a source to search (a source-driven approach) or by filtering results after a search for information on a topic is executed (a content-driven approach). By explaining various approaches to research using a common metaphor, the text helps students learn to make informed choices about the best way to accomplish any given research task. Incorporating this material required both adding material and reorganizing portions of the text.

More specifically, the fifth edition contains the following changes:

New research process material—Chapter 1, Introduction to Legal Research, introduces source- and content-driven searching and provides a more detailed overview of the research planning process than in prior editions.

New material on generating search terms—Chapter 2, Generating Search Terms, contains a new section on how to prioritize search terms depending on the nature of the research project and the knowledge a researcher brings to the project.

A new chapter on evaluating research options—Chapter 3, Evaluating Search Options, is a new chapter that describes how source- and content-driven searching works. It uses a research example to illustrate how each process leads to relevant authority and how to evaluate which approach is best for a particular research task.

Updated explanation of electronic search techniques—Chapter 10, Electronic Legal Research, has been completely revised to include explanations of different types of word searching and the use of Boolean searching to narrow search results. It uses a research example to illustrate how and why the results of an electronic search will differ depending on the provider and search method used.

Coverage that reflects both teaching needs and actual practice—The fifth edition places greater emphasis on electronic research than prior editions of the text. The increased emphasis on electronic research reflects the introduction of WestlawNext, Lexis Advance, Google Scholar, the Federal Digital System and other services, as well as reduced print collections at many law libraries. At the same time, the fifth edition maintains coverage of print sources necessary to give students a strong foundation in print research. Each chapter is organized to allow professors to tailor the degree of print and electronic coverage to fit their pedagogical approach.

To accommodate coverage of new products without increasing the length of the text, the fifth edition reduces coverage of sources not typically covered in the first-year curriculum. Specifically, the fifth edition does not cover Shepard's in print, nor does it cover the CIS print and microfiche sets for legislative history research. The chapter devoted to subject-matter (looseleaf) services has been omitted, with limited coverage of BNA, CCH, and other subject-specific publishers included in Chapter 10, Electronic Legal Research.

Fully updated sample pages and research explanations—All sample pages have been updated. All explanations of research sources have been updated for current coverage. Coverage of Westlaw and Lexis includes both the traditional and new versions of both services. Specific changes include the following:

- Chapter 4 (Secondary Source Research) has been reorganized so that the descriptions of commonly used secondary sources are separate from the explanations of the print and electronic research processes.
- Chapter 5 (Case Research) includes discussion of Google Scholar.

- Chapter 6 (Research with Citators) includes a research example that allows students to evaluate the editorial characterization of the treatment of a case in Shepard's and KeyCite.
- Chapter 8 (Federal Legislative History Research) and Chapter 9 (Federal Administrative Law Research) include coverage of the Federal Digital System (FDSys), which has replaced GPO Access.

The philosophy and the format of the fifth edition remain the same as those of earlier editions. The genesis of this book was a conversation I had with Todd Petit, a student in my Lawyering Skills class at Catholic University, in the fall of 1994. Todd was working on a research project, and he came to me in frustration and bewilderment over the research process. Over the course of the year, Todd ultimately mastered the skill of legal research. Nevertheless, our conversation that fall caused me to start thinking about how I could teach research more effectively, a process that ultimately culminated in this book.

I do not believe Todd's experience was unique. Mastering a skill is a form of experiential learning—learning that can be done only by doing. And the "doing" aspect necessarily involves periods of trial and error until a person grasps the skill. It is not surprising that this can be frustrating and even bewildering at times.

Having said that, however, even experiential learning has to be built on a base of information. My goal with this book is to provide two kinds of information necessary for students to learn the process of legal research: basic information about a range of research sources and a framework for approaching research projects.

This text provides instruction in a variety of legal research sources, including secondary sources, cases and digests, citators, statutes, federal legislative history, and federal administrative regulations. Each of these sources is described in a separate chapter that includes the following components:

- introductory information about the source
- step-by-step instructions for print research
- an explanation of electronic research tools available for the source
- an explanation of citation rules for the source
- an annotated set of sample pages and screen shots illustrating the research process for the source
- a checklist summarizing both the research process and the key features of the source.

The range of material in each of these chapters is intended to accommodate a variety of teaching and learning styles. These chapters contain textual explanations, charts, and checklists that can be used for in-class discussions and for out-of-class reference as students are conducting research.

In addition, the sample pages and screen shots illustrating the research process provide both instructional material and a useful summary synthesizing the information on the source from the rest of the chapter.

This text does more, however, than simply explain the bibliographic features of various research sources. It also provides instruction in research as a process, and it does this in two ways. First, Chapter 1 provides an overview of research sources and the research process. By providing a framework for understanding the relationships among different types of legal authority, this chapter sets the stage for a process-oriented introduction to research instruction. Second, Chapter 11 provides a framework for creating a research plan. By setting out a process based on a series of questions students can ask to define the contours of any type of research project, it provides a flexible approach that can be adapted to a variety of assignments. Although Chapter 11 is the last chapter in the text, it can be used whenever students are required to develop a strategy for approaching a research project.

Of course, a comprehensive understanding of legal research requires students to be familiar with both print and electronic research sources. This text explains electronic research in a way that will allow students to develop their electronic research skills regardless of whether they learn about electronic research along with print research or as a separate component of the curriculum. Each chapter devoted to an individual research source includes information on the types of electronic research options available for that source. General techniques for conducting electronic research, however, appear in a separate chapter, Chapter 10. This chapter can be used in conjunction with other chapters at any point in the course when students begin learning about electronic legal research.

Moreover, the text provides instruction in a wide range of electronic research sources. It discusses research using commercial services such as Westlaw and Lexis. But it also covers a range of other electronic research options, including subscription services and material available for free via the Internet. As part of this instruction, the text discusses cost considerations in a way not addressed in other texts so that students can learn to make informed decisions about when to use electronic sources and how to select the best electronic source for any research project.

This text seeks to provide students with not only the bibliographic skills to locate the legal authorities necessary to resolve a research issue, but also an understanding of research process that is an integral component of students' training in problem-solving skills. I hope this text will prove to be a useful guide to students as they undertake this intellectual challenge.

Amy E. Sloan

April 2012

Acknowledgments

Many people contributed to the fifth edition of this book. My thanks here will not be adequate for the assistance they provided. I want to thank my research assistant, Jamie Cosloy, and the reference librarians at the University of Baltimore Law Library, especially Joanne Dugan. A number of my colleagues at other schools contributed to this project by sharing their experiences in teaching with earlier editions, both by communicating with me directly and through anonymous reviews. I am especially indebted to Jan Levine and Melanie Oberlin for their suggestions.

The people at Aspen Publishers have been incredibly generous with their time and talents. Carol McGeehan, Richard Mixter, Christine Hannan, and their colleagues provided everything from moral support to editorial advice to production assistance. Their guidance and expertise contributed greatly to the content, organization, and layout of the text, and I am grateful for their assistance. I very much appreciate Troy Froebe's skill and patience in the production process.

I want to thank my family and friends for their support, especially Peggy Metzger and Jack and Drew Metzger-Sloan.

I would be remiss if I limited my acknowledgments to those who assisted with the fifth edition of the text because much of what appears here originated in the earlier editions. In particular, I would like to acknowledge Diana Donahoe, Susan Dunham, Lauren Dunnock, Lynn Farnan, Susan B. Koonin, Carli Masia, Herb Somers, Jessica Thompson, Robert Walkowiak III, and Michelle Wu for their work on earlier editions of the text.

I would also like to acknowledge the publishers who permitted me to reprint copyrighted material in this text:

Figure 4.1 Am. Jur. 2d main volume entry under False Imprisonment Reprinted with permission from Thomson Reuters/West, *American Jurisprudence*, 2d Series, Vol. 32 (2007), p. 46. © 2007 Thomson Reuters/West.

Figure 4.2   Treatise main volume entry for False Imprisonment
Reprinted with permission from Thomson Reuters/West. Dan B. Dobbs, *The Law of Torts* (2001), p. 67. © 2000 by Thomson Reuters/West.

Figure 4.3   LegalTrac citation list
From Gale. *LegalTrac* ©, a part of Cengage Learning, Inc. Reproduced by permission. www.cengage.com/permissions.

Figure 4.4   Introductory page of an A.L.R. Annotation
Reprinted with permission from Thomson Reuters/West, *American Law Reports*, 4th Ser., Vol. 20 (1983), p. 823. © 1983 Thomson Reuters/West.

Figure 4.5   Later page of an A.L.R. Annotation
Reprinted with permission from Thomson Reuters/West, *American Law Reports*, 4th Ser., Vol. 20 (1983), p. 831. © 1983 Thomson Reuters/West.

Figure 4.6   Section 35 of the *Restatement (Second) of Torts*
© 1965 by The American Law Institute. Reproduced with permission. All rights reserved. *Restatement (Second) of the Law of Torts*, 2d ed., Vol. 1, § 35 (1965), p. 52.

Figure 4.7   Appendix Volume, *Restatement (Second) of Torts*
© 2005 by The American Law Institute. Reproduced with permission. All rights reserved. *Restatement (Second) of the Law of Torts*, 2d ed., Appendix through June 2004, §§ 1-309 (2005), p. 119.

Figure 4.8   ULA entry for the Uniform Single Publication Act
Reprinted with permission from Thomson Reuters/West and National Conference of Commissioners on Uniform State Laws (NCCUSL), *Uniform Laws Annotated*, Vol. 14 (2005), pp. 471-472. ULA © 2005 Thomson Reuters/West. The text of the Act and any comments are copyright 1952 by NCCUSL.

Figure 4.9   HeinOnline display of a legal periodical article
From HeinOnline. © 2012 HeinOnline. Reproduced with permission.

Figure 4.11   Index to Am. Jur. 2d
Reprinted with permission from Thomson Reuters/West, *American Jurisprudence*, 2d Series, General Index (2011 edition), p. 389 © Thomson Reuters/West.

Figure 4.12   Am. Jur. 2d main volume entry under False Imprisonment
Reprinted with permission from Thomson Reuters/West, *American Jurisprudence*, 2d Series, Vol. 32 (2007), p. 46. © 2007 Thomson Reuters/West.

Figure 4.13   Am. Jur. 2d pocket part entry for False Imprisonment
Reprinted with permission from Thomson Reuters/West, *American Jurisprudence*, 2d Series, Vol. 32 Cumulative Supplement (2011), p. 2. © 2011 Thomson Reuters/West.

Figure 4.14 A.L.R. Index
Reprinted with permission from Thomson Reuters/West, *American Law Reports*, Index F-H, p. 30. © 2008 Thomson Reuters/West.

Figure 4.15 A.L.R. Annotation
Reprinted with permission from Thomson Reuters/West, *American Law Reports*, 4th Ser., Vol. 20 (1983), pp. 823-825 & 831. © 1983 Thomson Reuters/West.

Figure 4.16 Pocket part accompanying an A.L.R. volume
Reprinted with permission from Thomson Reuters/West, *American Law Reports Supplement*, 4th Ser., Insert in Back of Vol. 20 (2011), pp. 94-95. © 2011 Thomson Reuters/West.

Figure 4.17 Section of Am. Jur. 2d in Lexis.com
Section of Am Jur. 2d in Lexis.com, Copyright 2012 LexisNexis, a division of Reed Elsevier Inc. All Rights Reserved. LexisNexis and the Knowledge Burst logo are registered trademarks of Reed Elsevier Properties Inc. and are used with the permission of LexisNexis.

Figure 4.18 Analytical materials search results
Lexis Advance Search Results, Copyright 2012 LexisNexis, a division of Reed Elsevier Inc. All Rights Reserved. LexisNexis and the Knowledge Burst logo are registered trademarks of Reed Elsevier Properties Inc. and are used with the permission of LexisNexis.

Figure 4.19 Selected search option in WestlawNext
WestlawNext search options © 2012 Thomson Reuters/West. Reproduced with permission.

Figure 4.20 Portion of an A.L.R. Annotation in Westlaw.com
A.L.R. Annotation in Westlaw.com © 2012 Thomson Reuters/West. Reproduced with permission.

Figure 5.2 Excerpt from *Popkin v. New York State*
Reprinted with permission from Thomson Reuters/West, West's *Federal Reporter*, 2d Ser., *Popkin v. New York State*, 547 F.2d 18-19 (2d Cir. 1976). © 1976 Thomson Reuters/West.

Figure 5.3 Beginning of the West topic for "Abandoned and Lost Property"
Reprinted with permission from Thomson Reuters/West, *West's Federal Practice Digest*, 4th Ser., Vol. 1 (2006), p. 1. © 2006 Thomson Reuters/West.

Figure 5.4 Case summary under the "Abandoned and Lost Property" topic, key number 2
Reprinted with permission from Thomson Reuters/West, *West's Federal Practice Digest*, 4th Ser., Vol. 1 (2006), p. 6. © 2006 Thomson Reuters/West.

Figure 5.9   Excerpt from the Descriptive-Word Index
Reprinted with permission from Thomson Reuters/West, *West's Federal Practice Digest*, 4th Ser., Descriptive-Word Index, Vol. 97 (2002), p. 1. © 2002 Thomson Reuters/West.

Figure 5.10   Interim pamphlet closing table
Reprinted with permission from Thomson Reuters/West, *West's Federal Practice Digest*, 4th Ser., October 2011 Pamphlet, inside cover. © 2011 Thomson Reuters/West.

Figure 5.11   Example of a case in Westlaw.com
Reprinted with permission of Thomson Reuters/West, from Westlaw, 729 F. Supp. 2d 231. © 2012 Thomson Reuters/West.

Figure 5.12   Example of a case in WestlawNext
Reprinted with permission of Thomson Reuters/West, from Westlaw, 729 F. Supp. 2d 231. © 2012 Thomson Reuters/West.

Figure 5.13   Example of a case in Lexis.com
Copyright 2012 LexisNexis, a division of Reed Elsevier Inc. All Rights Reserved. LexisNexis and the Knowledge Burst logo are registered trademarks of Reed Elsevier Properties Inc. and are used with the permission of LexisNexis, 636 F. Supp. 2d 23.

Figure 5.14   Example of a case in Lexis Advance
Copyright 2012 LexisNexis, a division of Reed Elsevier Inc. All Rights Reserved. LexisNexis and the Knowledge Burst logo are registered trademarks of Reed Elsevier Properties Inc. and are used with the permission of LexisNexis, 636 F. Supp. 2d 23.

Figure 5.16   Descriptive-Word Index
Reprinted with permission from Thomson Reuters/West, *West's Federal Practice Digest*, 4th Ser., Vol. 97 (2002), p. 1. © 2002 Thomson Reuters/West.

Figure 5.17   Key number outline, "Abandoned and Lost Property" topic
Reprinted with permission from Thomson Reuters/West, *West's Federal Practice Digest*, 4th Ser., Vol. 1 (2006), pp. 1-2. © 2006 Thomson Reuters/West.

Figure 5.18   Case summaries under "Abandoned and Lost Property" topic
Reprinted with permission from Thomson Reuters/West, *West's Federal Practice Digest*, 4th Ser., Vol. 1 (2006), pp. 6-7. © 2006 Thomson Reuters/West.

Figure 5.19   Digest volume, pocket part
Reprinted with permission from Thomson Reuters/West, *West's Federal Practice Digest*, 4th Ser., Pocket Part, Vol. 1 (2011), p. 1. © 2011 Thomson Reuters/West.

Figure 5.20 Noncumulative interim pamphlet
Reprinted with permission from Thomson Reuters/West, *West's Federal Practice Digest*, 4th Ser., October 2011 Pamphlet, p. 1. © 2011 Thomson Reuters/West.

Figure 5.21 Results of word search with West key number system
WestlawNext search results © 2012 Thomson Reuters/West. Reproduced with permission.

Figure 5.22 Results of a word search in Lexis Advance
Lexis Advance search results. Copyright 2012 LexisNexis, a division of Reed Elsevier Inc. All Rights Reserved. LexisNexis and the Knowledge Burst logo are registered trademarks of Reed Elsevier Properties Inc. and are used with the permission of LexisNexis.

Figure 5.23 *Hunt v. DePuy Orthopaedics, Inc.*, 729 F. Supp. 2d 231 (D.D.C. 2010)
Reprinted with permission from Thomson Reuters/West, West's *Federal Supplement,* 2d Ser., Vol. 729 (2010), pp. 231-233. © 2010 Thomson Reuters/West.

Figure 6.1 Shepard's® Entry Excerpt for 165 Ohio App. 3d 699 in Lexis.com
Copyright 2012 LexisNexis, a division of Reed Elsevier Inc. All Rights Reserved. LexisNexis and the Knowledge Burst logo are registered trademarks of Reed Elsevier Properties Inc. and are used with the permission of LexisNexis. Shepard's entry for 165 Ohio App. 3d 699.

Figure 6.2 Shepard's® Entry Excerpt for 165 Ohio App. 3d 699 in Lexis Advance
Copyright 2012 LexisNexis, a division of Reed Elsevier Inc. All Rights Reserved. LexisNexis and the Knowledge Burst logo are registered trademarks of Reed Elsevier Properties Inc. and are used with the permission of LexisNexis. Shepard's entry for 165 Ohio App. 3d 699.

Figure 6.4 Citing decisions grid view in Lexis Advance
Copyright 2012 LexisNexis, a division of Reed Elsevier Inc. All Rights Reserved. LexisNexis and the Knowledge Burst logo are registered trademarks of Reed Elsevier Properties Inc. and are used with the permission of LexisNexis. Shepard's Entry for 165 Ohio App. 3d 699.

Figure 6.5 Headnote 9 from the original case, *Uddin v. Embassy Suites Hotel*
Copyright 2012 LexisNexis, a division of Reed Elsevier Inc. All Rights Reserved. LexisNexis and the Knowledge Burst logo are registered trademarks of Reed Elsevier Properties Inc. and are used with the permission of LexisNexis. LexisNexis, from LexisNexis 165 Ohio App. 3d 699.

Figure 6.6 SHEPARD'S® entry for *Uddin v. Embassy Suites Hotel*
Copyright 2012 LexisNexis, a division of Reed Elsevier Inc. All Rights Reserved. LexisNexis and the Knowledge Burst logo are registered trademarks

of Reed Elsevier Properties Inc. and are used with the permission of LexisNexis. From Lexis, Shepard's entry for 165 Ohio App. 3d 699.

Figure 6.19   KeyCite Display
Reprinted with permission from Thomson Reuters/West, from Westlaw, KeyCite entry for 165 Ohio App.l 3d 699.   © 2012 Thomson Reuters/West.

Figure 7.2   18 U.S.C.A. § 2725
Reprinted with permission from Thomson Reuters/West, *United States Code Annotated*, Title 18 (2000), p. 340. © 2000 Thomson Reuters/West.

Figure 7.4   Chapter outline in Title 18
Reprinted with permission from Thomson Reuters/West, *United States Code Annotated*, Title 18 (2000), p. 331.   © 2000 Thomson Reuters/West.

Figure 7.5   Excerpt from the U.S.C.A. General Index
Reprinted with permission from Thomson Reuters/West, *United States Code Annotated*, 2011 General Index J-R, p. 453. © 2011 Thomson Reuters/West.

Figure 7.7   Annotations accompanying 18 U.S.C.A. § 2725
Reprinted with permission from Thomson Reuters/West, *United States Code Annotated*, Title 18 (2000), p. 340. © 2000 Thomson Reuters/West.

Figure 7.8   Pocket part update for 18 U.S.C.A. § 2725
Reprinted with permission from Thomson Reuters/West, *United States Code Annotated*, 2011 Cumulative Annual Pocket Part, Title 18, p. 128. © 2011 Thomson Reuters/West.

Figure 7.9   Driver's Privacy Protection Act entry, popular name table
Reprinted with permission from Thomson Reuters/West, *United States Code Annotated*, 2011 Popular Name Table, p. 939. © 2011 Thomson Reuters/West.

Figure 7.10   Conversion table entry for Pub. L. No. 106-346
Reprinted with permission from Thomson Reuters/West, Tables Vol. II, *United States Code Annotated*, 2011, p. 1457. © 2011 Thomson Reuters/West.

Figure 7.11   Excerpt from 18 U.S.C.A. § 2725 in Westlaw.com
Reprinted with permission from Thomson Reuters/West, from Westlaw, 18 U.S.C.A. § 2725. © 2012 Thomson Reuters/West.

Figure 7.12   Excerpt from 18 U.S.C.A. § 2725 in WestlawNext
Reprinted with permission from Thomson Reuters/West, from Westlaw, 18 U.S.C.A. § 2725. © 2012 Thomson Reuters/West.

Figure 7.13   Westlaw.com U.S.C.A. Statutes Index Search Screen
Reprinted with permission from Thomson Reuters/West, from Westlaw, U.S.C.A. Statutes Index search screen. © 2012 Thomson Reuters/West.

Figure 7.14   WestlawNext U.S.C.A. table of contents and search options
Reprinted with permission from Thomson Reuters/West, from Westlaw, U.S.C.A. Table of Contents screen. © 2012 Thomson Reuters/West.

Figure 7.15   Excerpt from 18 U.S.C.S. § 2725 in Lexis.com
Copyright 2012 LexisNexis, a division of Reed Elsevier Inc. All Rights Reserved. LexisNexis and the Knowledge Burst logo are registered trademarks of Reed Elsevier Properties Inc. and are used with the permission of LexisNexis. From Lexis, 18 U.S.C.A. § 2725.

Figure 7.16 Excerpt from 18 U.S.C.S. § 2725 in Lexis Advance
Copyright 2012 LexisNexis, a division of Reed Elsevier Inc. All Rights Reserved. LexisNexis and the Knowledge Burst logo are registered trademarks of Reed Elsevier Properties Inc. and are used with the permission of LexisNexis. From Lexis, 18 U.S.C.A. § 2725.

Figure 7.17   Lexis.com U.S.C.S. search screen
Copyright 2012 LexisNexis, a division of Reed Elsevier Inc. All Rights Reserved. LexisNexis and the Knowledge Burst logo are registered trademarks of Reed Elsevier Properties Inc. and are used with the permission of LexisNexis. From Lexis, U.S.C.S. search screen.

Figure 7.18   Excerpt from U.S.C.A. General Index
Reprinted with permission from Thomson Reuters/West, *United States Code Annotated*, 2011 General Index J R, p. 453. © 2011 Thomson Reuters/West.

Figure 7.19   Outline of Chapter 123
Reprinted with permission from Thomson Reuters/West, *United States Code Annotated*, Title 18 (2000), p. 331. © 1998 Thomson Reuters/West.

Figure 7.20   18 U.S.C.A. § 2725
Reprinted with permission from Thomson Reuters/West, *United States Code Annotated*, Title 18 (2000), p. 340. © 2000 Thomson Reuters/West.

Figure 7.21   Pocket part entry for 18 U.S.C.A. § 2725
Reprinted with permission from Thomson Reuters/West, *United States Code Annotated*, 2011 Cumulative Annual Pocket Part, Title 18, pp. 128-129. © 2011 Thomson Reuters/West.

Figure 7.22   Vernon's Texas Statutes and Codes Annotated Index
Reprinted with permission from Thomson Reuters/West, from Westlaw, Statutory Index for Vernon's *Texas Statutes and Codes Annotated*. © 2012 Thomson Reuters/West.

Figure 7.23   Texas Civil Practice and Remedies Code § 96.001
Reprinted with permission from Thomson Reuters/West, from Westlaw, Vernon's *Texas Codes Annotated*, Civil Practice and Remedies Code § 96.001. © 2012 Thomson Reuters/West.

Figure 7.24 Outline of Chapter 96, Texas Civil Practice and Remedies Code
Reprinted with permission from Thomson Reuters/West, from Westlaw, Vernon's *Texas Codes Annotated*, Civil Practice and Remedies Code, Chapter 96 table of contents. © 2012 Thomson Reuters/West.

Figure 7.25 Lexis Advance search results
Copyright 2012 LexisNexis, a division of Reed Elsevier Inc. All Rights Reserved. LexisNexis and the Knowledge Burst logo are registered trademarks of Reed Elsevier Properties Inc. and are used with the permission of LexisNexis. From Lexis Advance, statutory search results.

Figure 7.26 Texas Civil Practice and Remedies Code § 96.002
Copyright 2012 LexisNexis, a division of Reed Elsevier Inc. All Rights Reserved. LexisNexis and the Knowledge Burst logo are registered trademarks of Reed Elsevier Properties Inc. and are used with the permission of LexisNexis. From Lexis Advance, Texas Annotated Statutes, Texas Civil Practice and Remedies Code § 96.002.

Figure 8.1 How a Bill Becomes a Law
Reprinted with permission from Guide to Congress, CQ Press, 6th ed. (2007), p. 1303. Copyright © 2008 CQ Press, an imprint of SAGE Publications, Inc.

Figure 8.2 Excerpt from annotations accompanying 18 U.S.C.A. § 2441
Reprinted with permission from Thomson Reuters/West, *United States Code Annotated*, Vol. 18 (2000), p. 14. © 2000 Thomson Reuters/West.

Figure 8.3 Starting page, House Judiciary Committee Report on the War Crimes Act of 1996
Reprinted with permission from Thomson Reuters/West, *United States Code Congressional and Administrative News*, 104th Congress-Second Session 1996, Vol. 5 (1997), p. 2166. © 1997 Thomson Reuters/West.

Figure 8.7 HeinOnline Sources of Compiled Legislative Histories Entry
Reproduced with permission of HeinOnline. © 2012 HeinOnline.

Figure 8.8 Search Options for Congressional Publications in ProQuest Congressional
Reprinted with permission of ProQuest, ProQuest Congressional search options. © 2012 ProQuest Congressional.

Figure 9.2 Annotations to 42 U.S.C.S. § 1751
Copyright LexisNexis, a division of Reed Elsevier, Inc. All rights reserved. *United States Code Service*, Title 42 The Public Health and Welfare §§ 1561-1860 (1990), p. 153.

BASIC LEGAL RESEARCH

Introduction to Legal Research

- A. Introduction to the legal system
- B. Introduction to the process of legal research
- C. Introduction to research planning
- D. Introduction to legal citation
- E. Overview of this text

What is legal research and why do you need to learn about it? Researching the law means finding the rules that govern conduct in our society. To be a successful lawyer, you need to know how to research the law. Lawyers are often called upon to solve problems and give advice, and to do that accurately, you must know the rules applicable to the different situations you and your clients will face. Clients may come to you after an event has occurred and ask you to pursue a remedy for a bad outcome, or perhaps defend them against charges that they have acted wrongfully. You may be asked to help a client accomplish a goal like starting a business or buying a piece of property. In these situations and many others, you will need to know your clients' rights and responsibilities, as defined by legal rules. Consequently, being proficient in legal research is essential to your success in legal practice.

As a starting point for learning about how to research the law, it is important to understand some of the different sources of legal rules. This chapter discusses what these sources are and where they originate within our legal system. It also provides an introduction to the process of legal research, an overview of some of the research tools you will learn to use, and an introduction to legal citation. Later chapters explain how to locate legal rules using a variety of resources.

A. INTRODUCTION TO THE LEGAL SYSTEM

1. SOURCES OF LAW

There are four main sources of law, which exist at both state and federal levels:

- constitutions;
- statutes;
- court opinions (also called cases);
- administrative regulations.

A constitution establishes a system of government and defines the boundaries of authority granted to the government. The United States Constitution is the preeminent source of law in our legal system, and all other rules, whether promulgated by a state or the federal government, must comply with its requirements. Each state also has its own constitution. A state's constitution may grant greater rights than those secured by the federal constitution, but because a state constitution is subordinate to the federal constitution, it cannot provide lesser rights than the federal constitution does. All of a state's legal rules must comport with both the state and federal constitutions.

Since grade school, you have been taught that the U.S. Constitution created three branches of government: the legislative branch, which makes the laws; the judicial branch, which interprets the laws; and the executive branch, which enforces the laws. State governments are also divided into these three branches. Although this is elementary civics, this structure truly does define the way government authority is divided in our system of government.

The legislative branch of government creates statutes, which must be approved by the executive branch (the president, for federal statutes; the governor, for state statutes) to go into effect. The executive branch also makes rules. Administrative agencies, such as the federal Food and Drug Administration or a state's department of motor vehicles, are part of the executive branch. They execute the laws passed by the legislature and create their own regulations to carry out the mandates established by statute.

The judicial branch is the source of court opinions. Courts interpret rules created by the legislative and executive branches of government. If a court determines that a rule does not meet constitutional requirements, it can invalidate the rule. Otherwise, however, the court must apply the rule to the case before it. Court opinions can also be an independent source of legal rules. Legal rules made by courts are called "common-law" rules. Although courts are empowered to make these rules, legislatures can adopt legislation that changes or abolishes a common-law rule, as long as the legislation is constitutional.

FIGURE 1.1   BRANCHES OF GOVERNMENT AND LEGAL RULES

UNITED STATES CONSTITUTION

FEDERAL GOVERNMENT			**STATE CONSTITUTIONS**

STATE GOVERNMENTS

Executive Branch (headed by the president)	Legislative Branch	Judicial Branch	Executive Branch (headed by the governor)	Legislative Branch	Judicial Branch
Administrative Regulations (created by administrative agencies pursuant to statutory authority)	Statutes	Court Opinions (also called cases)	Administrative Regulations (created by administrative agencies pursuant to statutory authority)	Statutes	Court Opinions (also called cases)

Figure 1.1 shows the relationships among the branches of government and the types of legal rules they create.

An example may be useful to illustrate the relationships among the rules created by the three branches of the federal government. As you know, the U.S. Constitution, through the First Amendment, guarantees the right to free expression. Congress could pass legislation requiring television stations to provide educational programming for children. The Federal Communications Commission (FCC) is the administrative agency within the executive branch that would have responsibility for carrying out Congress's will. If the statute were not specific about what constitutes educational programming or how much educational programming must be provided, the FCC would have to create administrative regulations to execute the law. The regulations would provide the information not detailed in the statute, such as the definition of educational programming. A television station could challenge the statute and regulations by arguing to a court that prescribing the content of material that the station must broadcast violates the First Amendment. The court would then have to interpret the statute and regulations to decide whether they comport with the Constitution.

Another example illustrates the relationship between courts and legislatures in the area of common-law rules. The rules of negligence have largely been created by the courts. Therefore, liability for negligence is usually determined by common-law rules. A state supreme court could decide that a plaintiff who sues a defendant for negligence cannot recover any damages if the plaintiff herself was negligent and contributed to her own injuries. This decision would create a common-law rule governing future cases of negligence within that state. The state legislature could step in and pass a statute that changes the rule. For example, the legislature could enact a statute providing that juries are to determine the percentage of negligence attributable to each party and to apportion damages accordingly, instead of completely denying recovery to the plaintiff. Courts in that state would then be obligated to apply the rule from the statute, not the former common-law rule.

Although these examples are simplified, they demonstrate the basic roles of each of the branches of government in enunciating the legal rules governing the conduct of society. They also demonstrate that researching a legal issue may require you to research several different types of legal authority. The answer to a research question may not be found exclusively in statutes or court opinions or administrative regulations. Often, these sources must be researched together to determine all of the rules applicable to a factual scenario.

2. TYPES AND WEIGHT OF AUTHORITY

One term used to describe the rules that govern conduct in society is "legal authority." Rules, however, are only one type of legal authority, and some types of legal authority are more authoritative than others. To understand how legal authority is categorized, you must be able to differentiate "primary" authority from "secondary" authority and "mandatory" authority from "persuasive" authority. Making these distinctions will help you determine the weight, or authoritative value, a legal authority carries with respect to the issue you are researching.

a. Primary vs. Secondary Authority and Mandatory vs. Persuasive Authority

Primary authority is the term used to describe rules of law. Primary authority includes all of the types of rules discussed so far in this chapter. Constitutional provisions, statutes, court opinions, and administrative regulations contain legal rules, and as a consequence, are primary authority. Because "the law" consists of legal rules, primary authority is sometimes described as "the law."

Secondary authority, by contrast, refers to commentary on the law or analysis of the law, but not "the law" itself. An opinion from the U.S. Supreme Court is primary authority, but an article written by a private party explaining and analyzing the opinion is secondary authority. Secondary authority is often quite useful in legal research because its analysis can help you understand complex legal issues and refer you to primary authority. Nevertheless, secondary authority is not "the law" and therefore is distinguished from primary authority.

Mandatory and persuasive authority are terms courts use to categorize the different sources of law they use in making their decisions.
Mandatory authority, which can also be called binding authority, refers
to authority that the court is obligated to follow. Mandatory authority
contains rules that you must apply to determine the correct answer to the
issue you are researching. Persuasive authority, which can also be called
nonbinding authority, refers to authority that the court may follow if it is
persuaded to do so, but is not required to follow. Persuasive authority,
therefore, will not dictate the answer to an issue, although it may help
you figure out the answer. Whether an authority is mandatory or persuasive depends on several factors, as discussed in the next section.

b. Weight of Authority

The degree to which an authority controls the answer to a legal issue is
called the weight of the authority. Not all authorities have the same
weight. The weight of a legal authority depends on its status as primary
or secondary authority, and as mandatory or persuasive authority. Some
primary authorities are mandatory, and others are persuasive. Secondary
authority, by contrast, is always persuasive authority. You must be able
to distinguish among these categories of authority to determine how
much weight a particular legal authority has in the resolution of the
issue you are researching.

(1) Secondary authority: always persuasive

A legal authority's status as a primary or secondary authority is fixed. An
authority is either part of "the law," or it is not. Because secondary
authority is always persuasive authority, it is not binding. Once you
identify an authority as secondary, you can be certain that it will not
control the outcome of the issue you are researching.

Although secondary authority is not binding, some secondary
authorities are more persuasive than others. Some are so respected that
a court, while not technically bound by them, would need a good reason
to depart from or reject their statements of legal rules. Others do not
enjoy the same degree of respect, leaving a court free to ignore or reject
such authorities if it is not persuaded to follow them. Further discussion
of the persuasive value of various secondary authorities appears in Chapter 4, on secondary source research. The important thing to remember for
now is that secondary authority is always categorized as persuasive or
nonbinding authority.

(2) Primary authority: sometimes mandatory, sometimes persuasive

Sometimes primary authority is mandatory, or binding, authority, and
sometimes it is not. You must be able to evaluate the authority to determine whether it is binding on the issue you are researching. One factor
affecting whether a primary authority is mandatory is jurisdiction.

The rules contained in primary authority apply only to conduct occurring within the jurisdiction in which the authority is in force. For example, all laws in the United States must comport with the federal constitution because it is primary authority that is mandatory, or binding, in all United States jurisdictions. The New Jersey constitution is also primary authority because it contains legal rules establishing the scope of state government authority, but it is mandatory authority only in New Jersey. The New Jersey constitution's rules do not apply in Illinois or Michigan.

Determining the weight of court opinions is a little more complex. All court opinions are primary authority. Whether a particular opinion is mandatory or persuasive is a function not only of jurisdiction, but also level of court. To understand how these factors work together, it is easiest to consider level of court first and jurisdiction second.

(i) *Determining the weight of court opinions: level of court*
The judicial branches of government in all states and in the federal system have multiple levels of courts. Trial courts are at the bottom of the judicial hierarchy. In the federal system, the United States District Courts are trial-level courts, and each state has at least one federal district court. Intermediate appellate courts hear appeals of trial court cases. Most, but not all, states have intermediate appellate courts. In the federal system, the intermediate appellate courts are called United States Courts of Appeals, and they are divided into 13 separate circuits: 11 numbered circuits (First through Eleventh), the District of Columbia Circuit, and the Federal Circuit. The highest court or court of last resort is often called the supreme court. It hears appeals of cases from the intermediate appellate courts or directly from trial courts in states that do not have intermediate appellate courts. In the federal system, of course, the court of last resort is the U.S. Supreme Court.

Trial court opinions, including those from federal district courts, are not mandatory authority. These opinions bind the parties to the cases but do not bind other courts considering similar cases. They are persuasive authority.

The opinions of intermediate appellate courts bind the courts below them. In other words, intermediate appellate opinions are mandatory authority for the trial courts subordinate to them in the court structure. The weight of intermediate appellate opinions on the intermediate appellate courts themselves varies. In jurisdictions with multiple appellate divisions, the opinions of one division may or may not be binding on other divisions. In addition, in some circumstances, intermediate appellate courts can overrule their own prior opinions. Intermediate appellate opinions are persuasive authority for the court of last resort.

The court of last resort may, but is not required to, follow the opinions of the courts below it. The opinions of the court of last resort, however, are mandatory authority for both intermediate appellate courts and trial courts subordinate to it in the court structure. The court of last resort is not bound by its own prior opinions, but will be reluctant to change an earlier ruling without a compelling justification.

Figure 1.2 illustrates the structures of federal and state court systems and shows how level of court affects the weight of opinions.

FIGURE 1.2   STRUCTURE OF THE FEDERAL COURT SYSTEM AND MOST STATE COURT SYSTEMS

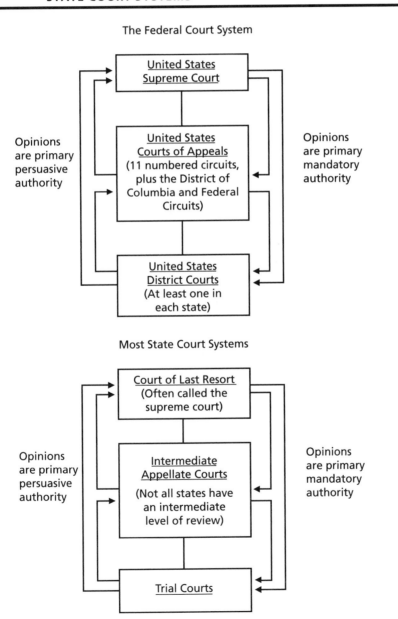

(ii) *Determining the weight of court opinions: jurisdiction*

The second factor affecting the weight of court opinions is jurisdiction. As with other forms of primary authority, rules stated in court opinions are mandatory authority only within the court's jurisdiction. An opinion from the Texas Supreme Court is mandatory only for a court applying Texas law. A California court deciding a question of California law would consider the Texas opinion persuasive authority. If the California court had to decide a new issue not previously addressed by mandatory California authority (a "question of first impression"), it might choose to follow the Texas Supreme Court's opinion if it found the opinion persuasive.

On questions of federal law, opinions of the U.S. Supreme Court are mandatory authority for all other courts because it has nationwide jurisdiction. An opinion from a circuit court of appeals is mandatory only within the circuit that issued the opinion and is persuasive everywhere else. Thus, a decision of the U.S. Court of Appeals for the Eleventh Circuit would be binding within the Eleventh Circuit, but not within the Seventh Circuit. **Figure 1.3** shows the geographic boundaries of the federal circuit courts of appeal.

In considering the weight of a court opinion, it is important to remember that the federal government and each state constitute different

FIGURE 1.3   GEOGRAPHIC BOUNDARIES OF THE FEDERAL COURTS OF APPEALS

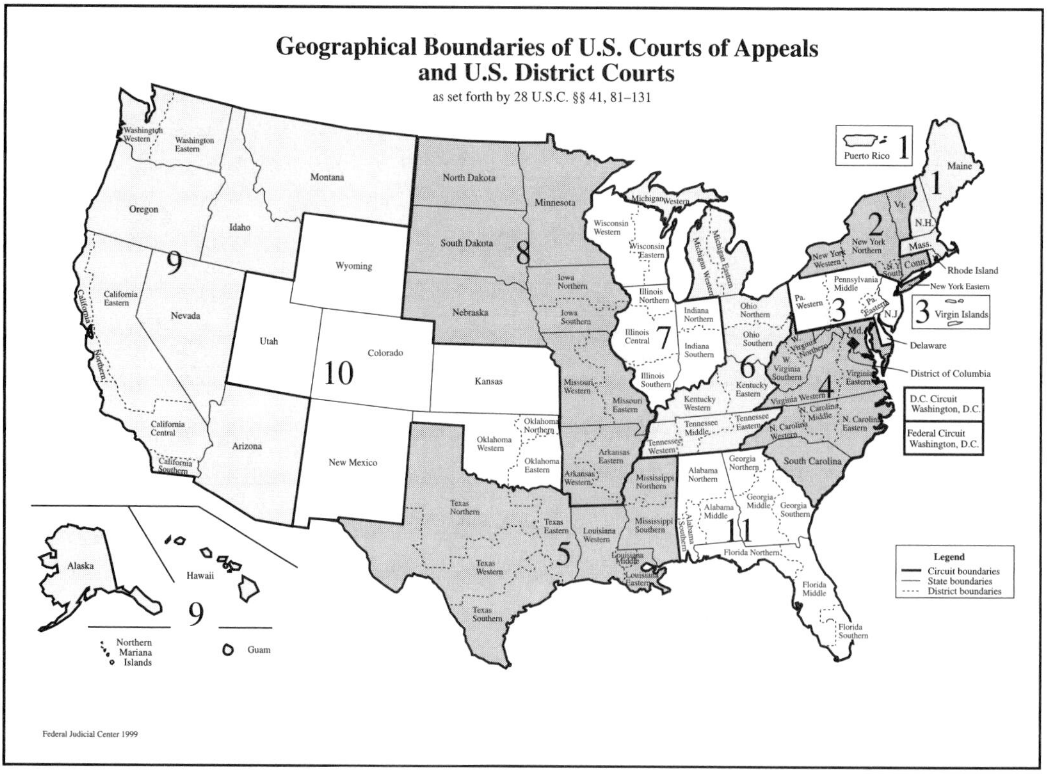

Geographical Boundaries of U.S. Courts of Appeals and U.S. District Courts
as set forth by 28 U.S.C. §§ 41, 81–131

jurisdictions. On questions of state law, each state's courts get the last word, and on questions of federal law, the federal courts get the last word. For an issue governed by state law, the opinions of the courts within the relevant state are mandatory authority. For an issue governed by federal law, the opinions of the relevant federal courts are mandatory authority.

Ordinarily, understanding how jurisdiction affects weight of authority is fairly intuitive. When a Massachusetts trial court is resolving a case arising out of conduct that took place in Massachusetts, it will treat the opinions of the Massachusetts Supreme Judicial Court as mandatory authority. Sometimes, however, a court has to resolve a case governed by the law of another jurisdiction. State courts sometimes decide cases governed by the law of another state or by federal law. Federal courts sometimes decide cases governed by state law. When that happens, the court deciding the case will treat the law of the controlling jurisdiction as mandatory authority.

For example, assume that the U.S. District Court for the Western District of Texas, a federal trial court, has to decide a case concerning breach of a contract to build a house in El Paso, Texas. Contract law is, for the most part, established by the states. To resolve this case, the federal court will apply the contract law of the state where the dispute arose, in this case, Texas. The Texas Supreme Court's opinions on contract law are mandatory authority for resolving the case. Now assume that the same court has to decide a case concerning immigration law. Immigration law is established by the federal government. To resolve the case, the court will apply federal law. The opinions of the U.S. Supreme Court and the U.S. Court of Appeals for the Fifth Circuit are mandatory authority for resolving the case.

This discussion provides an overview of some common principles governing the weight of authority. These principles are subject to exceptions and nuances not addressed here. Entire fields of study are devoted to resolving questions of jurisdiction, procedure, and conflicts regarding which legal rules apply to various types of disputes. As you begin learning about research, however, these general principles will be sufficient to help you determine the weight of the authority you locate to resolve a research issue.

Figure 1.4 illustrates the relationships among the different types of authority.

B. INTRODUCTION TO THE PROCESS OF LEGAL RESEARCH

Imagine that you are standing in the parking lot at Disney World. You have a key in your hand, but you have no idea which car it starts. The key is not much use to you unless you have some way of figuring out which car it starts. The more information you can gather about the car, the easier the car will be to find. Knowing the make, model, or color would narrow the options. Knowing the license plate number would allow you to identify the individual vehicle.

FIGURE 1.4   TYPES OF AUTHORITY

TYPE OF AUTHORITY	MANDATORY (BINDING)	PERSUASIVE (NONBINDING)
PRIMARY (legal rules)	Constitutional provisions, statutes, and regulations in force within a jurisdiction are mandatory authority for courts within the same jurisdiction. Decisions from higher courts within a jurisdiction are mandatory authority for lower courts within the same jurisdiction.	Decisions from courts within one jurisdiction are persuasive authority for courts in other jurisdictions. Decisions from lower courts within a jurisdiction are persuasive authority for higher courts within the same jurisdiction.
SECONDARY (anything that is not primary authority; usually commentary on the law)	Secondary authority is *not* mandatory authority.	Secondary authority is persuasive authority.

Understanding the mechanics of using various legal research tools is like having that key in your hand. You have to know the features of the research tools available to you to conduct research, just as you must have the key to start the car. But that is not enough to make you an effective researcher. Effective legal research combines mastery of the mechanics of research with legal problem solving skills. The research process is part of the reasoning process. It is not a rote task you complete before you begin to evaluate an issue. Rather, it is an analytical task in which you narrow the field of all legal information available to the subset of information necessary to assess an issue. As you locate and evaluate information, you will learn about the issue you are researching, and that knowledge will help you determine both whether you have located useful information and what else you should be looking for to complete your understanding of the issue.

To understand the process of research, you must first understand how legal information is organized. Most, if not all, of the authorities you will learn to research are available from a variety of sources. They may be published in print, electronically, or in both formats. Electronic research services that provide access to legal publications include commercial databases that charge a fee for access and Internet sources freely available to anyone.

Most legal information is organized by type of authority and jurisdiction. In print, this means individual types of authority from individual jurisdictions are published in separate sets of books. Court opinions from Maryland will be in one set of books (called "reporters"), and those from Massachusetts will be in another set of reporters. The same holds true for print collections of statutes and other types of legal authority.

Electronic research tools are organized similarly. Some are like print sets of books in that they provide access to one type of authority from one jurisdiction. The website for the Texas Supreme Court, for example, contains only Texas Supreme Court opinions. Others provide access to multiple types of authority from many different jurisdictions. Although these services aggregate a wide range of legal authority, they subdivide their contents much like print sources into individual databases organized by jurisdiction and type of authority. There are many commercial and government sources that provide electronic access to legal authority.

Westlaw and Lexis are the best known electronic legal research services. They are commercial databases that allow you to access all of the types of legal authority discussed in this chapter. They charge subscribers for use of their services, although your law school undoubtedly subsidizes the cost of student research while you are in school. Both Lexis and Westlaw offer two versions of their services. Lexis offers Lexis.com and Lexis Advance. Westlaw offers Westlaw.com and WestlawNext. When you see a general reference to one of these services in this text, that general reference includes both versions (e.g., a general reference to Lexis includes both Lexis.com and Lexis Advance). This text refers to the specific version of each service (e.g., Westlaw.com or WestlawNext) when describing functions unique to that version.

The organization of legal information by jurisdiction and type of authority affects the way individual legal authorities are identified. All legal authorities have citations assigned to them. The citation is the identifying information you can use to retrieve a document from a book or database. Thus, if you have the citation to an authority, you can locate it using that identifying information. To return to the key analogy, this is like knowing the license plate number of the car you are trying to locate in the parking lot.

Citations were originally formulated so that researchers could find authorities in print. Although most authorities are now available electronically, they are still primarily identified by their print citations. In print research, the citation generally includes the name of the book in which the source is published, the volume of the book containing the specific item, and the page or section number where the item begins. For example, each court opinion is identified by a citation containing the volume number of the reporter in which it is published, the name of the reporter, and the starting page of the opinion. If you had the citation for a case, you could go to the library or get online and locate it easily. Statutes, secondary sources, and other forms of authority also have citations you can use to retrieve specific documents.

Of course, with most research projects, you will not know the citations to the authorities you need to find. You will have been assigned the project to find out which legal authorities, if any, pertain to the subject of your research issue. Moreover, although occasionally you will need to locate only one specific item, such as a specific case, more often you will need to collect a range of authorities that pertain to the issue, such as a statute and cases that have interpreted the statute. Therefore, you will need to narrow the field of all legal information to that subset of information necessary to analyze your research issue.

The choices for narrowing the field are driven largely by the organization of legal information by jurisdiction and type of authority. To narrow the field, you must determine the jurisdiction whose legal rules will govern the issue you are analyzing, the type or types of legal authority you want to research (e.g., cases, statutes, or secondary sources), and the subject or topic of the information you need.

With most research tools, you must determine jurisdiction and type of authority before you begin to look for content related to your research issue because the information available is organized into separate books or databases according to jurisdiction and type of authority. In other words, you pre-filter, or narrow, the scope of your research by source first and then identify relevant content within each source. This is a source-driven approach to research. With WestlawNext and Lexis Advance you can, but do not have to, pre-filter by jurisdiction or type of authority. You have the option of searching for content related to your research issue first and then filtering the results by jurisdiction, type of authority, or both. This is a content-driven approach to research. With either approach, once you locate information, you must evaluate the results of your research to determine whether the information you have found is useful. The source-driven and content-driven approaches are illustrated in **Figure 1.5**.

One question you may have is whether it is better to use a source- or content-driven approach. The answer depends on the nature of your research project and your level of expertise about the subject matter. With a source-driven approach, you have to think carefully about a research issue to figure out which type(s) of authority are most likely to contain relevant information. Although selecting a type of authority can be challenging, choosing specific types of authority to research can make it easier to analyze the results because they are confined to the particular type of authority you selected. In addition, a savvy researcher may know exactly what type of authority governs—such as a state statute—and may not want to bother filtering through other types of authority included in the results. Conversely, if you are not sure

FIGURE 1.5   SOURCE-DRIVEN AND CONTENT-DRIVEN APPROACHES TO RESEARCH

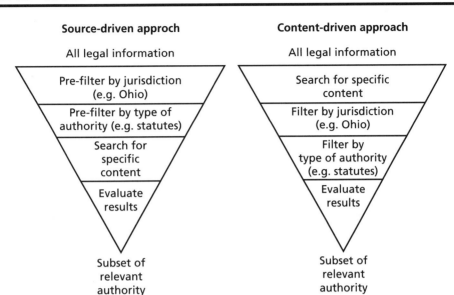

which type(s) of authority to use, you may miss some relevant material altogether if it is in a source you did not consider using.

Because the content-driven approach allows you to search without first selecting a source, it shifts much of the analytical work involved in research to filtering the search results. This can be an advantage because the search results can include sources you might not have considered using. On the other hand, this approach frequently retrieves a large amount of information that has to be sifted carefully. Retrieving hundreds or thousands of documents can feel overwhelming if you do not understand your research issue well enough to filter the results effectively. Chapter 3 explains source-driven and content-driven searching in greater detail to help you learn how to determine which approach is better for your research project.

C. INTRODUCTION TO RESEARCH PLANNING

The chapters that follow explain how to use both print and electronic research tools to locate various types of legal authority. As noted above, however, knowing the mechanics of the research tools available to you is only part of learning to be an effective researcher. To research effectively, you must incorporate your technical knowledge into a research plan so that you can find the information you need to analyze your research issue. To do this, you will want to proceed in an organized manner to make sure your research is accurate and complete. Chapter 11,

Developing a Research Plan, explores research planning in depth. This introduction to the planning process will help provide context as you learn the features of various research tools.

When you have a research task to complete, you will ordinarily proceed as follows:

■ Define the scope of your research project and the issue(s) you need to research.
■ Generate a list of search terms specific to your research issue(s).
■ Plan your research path for each issue.
■ Execute your research plan to search for relevant information.
■ Assess the information you find and update your research to ensure that all the information is current.
■ Revise your search terms and research plan as necessary and repeat the search process to complete your understanding of your research issue.

It is always a good idea to define the scope of your project before searching for information. Think about what you are being asked to do. Are you being asked to spend three weeks locating all information from every jurisdiction on a particular subject, or do you have a day to find out how courts in one state have ruled on an issue? Will you write an extensive analysis of your research, or will you summarize the results orally to the person who made the assignment? Evaluating the type of work product you are expected to produce, the amount of time you have, and the scope of the project will help you determine the best way to proceed.

You should also think carefully about the issue(s) you are being asked to research. Sometimes you will be asked to research a specific issue. Sometimes you will be presented with a research scenario and asked to determine the issue(s) it presents. It sounds almost silly to say this, but knowing what you are looking for will make it easier to find what you need.

Once you have defined your research task, you will need to generate search terms to use to search for information. Chapter 2 discusses different ways to do this. In general, however, you will need to construct a list of words or concepts to use to search for relevant content.

You will then want to plan your research path. The more you know about your research issue going in, the easier it will be to plan your research process. The less you know, the more flexible you will need to be in your approach. One of the goals of this text is to help you learn to plan your research path and assess the appropriate starting, middle, and ending points for your research.

Your ultimate goal in most research projects will be to locate primary mandatory authority, if it exists, on your research issue. Thus, regardless of whether you use a source- or content-driven approach, at some point you must consider type of authority and jurisdiction because these two factors determine whether the information you have located is primary mandatory authority. If primary mandatory authority is not available or does not directly answer your research question, persuasive authority (either primary or secondary) may help you analyze the issue. Therefore, in planning your research path, it may be helpful for you to think about three categories of authority: primary mandatory authority, primary persuasive authority, and secondary authority.

Because your goal will usually be to locate primary mandatory authority, you might think that that should be the starting point for all your research. In fact, if you know a lot about the issue you are researching, you might begin with primary mandatory authority, but that is not always the case. Secondary authorities that cite, analyze, and explain the law can provide a very efficient way to obtain background information and references to primary authority. Although secondary authorities are not controlling in your analysis, they are invaluable research tools and can be a good starting point for your project. Persuasive primary authority will rarely provide a good starting place because it provides neither the controlling rules nor analysis explaining the law. **Figure 1.6** shows the relationships among these three categories of authority.

Many research sources contain notes that refer to other sources, so once you locate one relevant source, you may be able to use the research notes to find additional useful information. Thus, there may be more than one appropriate starting point for your research. This text explains the features of a wide range of research sources so you can learn to make this assessment for different types of research projects.

Once you have planned your research path, you will execute your plan to search for information. As you locate information, you will need to evaluate its relevance to your research issue. One important aspect of assessing the information you find is making sure it is up-to-date. The law can change at any time. New cases are decided; older cases may be overruled; statutes can be enacted, amended, or repealed. Therefore, keeping your research current is essential. One way to update your research is with a specialized research tool called a citator, which is explained in Chapter 6. In addition, most sources of legal information will indicate how recently they have been updated to help you assess whether the information is current.

Most print research sources consist of hardcover books that can be difficult to update when the law changes. Some print resources are published in chronological order. For those resources, new books are published periodically as new material is compiled. Many, however, are organized by subject. For those resources, publishers cannot print new books every time the law changes. This would be prohibitively expensive, and because the law can change at any time, the new books would likely be out of date as soon as they were printed. To keep the books current, therefore, many print sources are updated with softcover pamphlets

FIGURE 1.6   WHERE TO BEGIN YOUR RESEARCH PROJECT

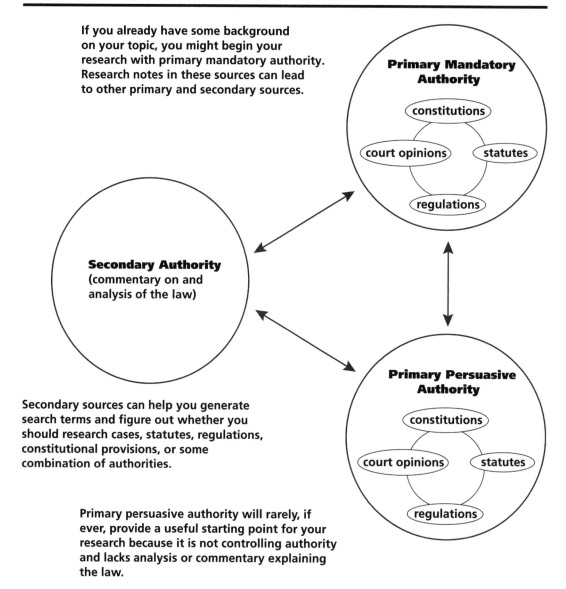

If you already have some background
on your topic, you might begin your
research with primary mandatory authority.
Research notes in these sources can lead
to other primary and secondary sources.

**Primary Mandatory
Authority**

constitutions

court opinions   statutes

regulations

Secondary Authority
(commentary on and
analysis of the law)

Secondary sources can help you generate
search terms and figure out whether you
should research cases, statutes, regulations,
constitutional provisions, or some
combination of authorities.

**Primary Persuasive
Authority**

constitutions

court opinions   statutes

regulations

Primary persuasive authority will rarely, if
ever, provide a useful starting point for your
research because it is not controlling authority
and lacks analysis or commentary explaining
the law.

containing new information that became available after the hardcover
book was published. These supplementary pamphlets are often called
"pocket parts" because many of them fit into a "pocket" in the inside
back cover of the hardcover book. Both the hardcover book and the pocket
part will indicate the period of time each covers. You will see pocket parts
mentioned throughout this text in reference to print research tools.

Electronic sources also usually contain publication or revision date
information that you can use to assess how current it is. Electronic
sources can be updated easily in the sense that new information can be

added and older information revised at any time and as frequently as necessary. Westlaw and Lexis update at least some of their content on a daily basis. Providers other than major commercial vendors may not update their content as frequently. In addition, updates for some content may only become available when the print version of the source is updated, which means the electronic version may only be as current as the latest print version. Therefore, whether you conduct research in print or electronically, you must pay careful attention to the date of the information you locate.

Because research is not a linear process, you may find that you have to revise your search terms or your research plan to complete your research. If you do not find any information, or find too much information, you may need to backtrack or rethink your approach. Even if you find relevant information from the start, what you learn when you assess that information may take you in new directions. The process of searching, reading, and assessing will continue until you have narrowed the field of all legal information to the subset of information necessary to evaluate your research issue. This text explains a variety of search strategies you can use to tailor your research process to the specific issue you are researching.

D. INTRODUCTION TO LEGAL CITATION

When you present the results of your research in written form, you will need to include citations to the legal authorities you have found. One place to find the rules for citing legal authority is *The Bluebook: A Uniform System of Citation* (19th ed. 2010). Another source for rules on citation is the *ALWD Citation Manual: A Professional System of Citation* (4th ed. 2010). The citation rules in these two sources overlap to a large degree, but they are not identical. You should use whichever citation manual your professor directs you to use.

This text provides information on citations in both *Bluebook* and *ALWD Manual* formats. This section provides a brief overview of the organization of both citation manuals and will make the most sense if you have your citation manual in front of you as you read. Later chapters contain instructions for citing individual sources of legal authority. In many cases, the citation rules in the *Bluebook* and the *ALWD Manual* will be identical. Where there are differences, this text will alert you to that fact.

1. THE *BLUEBOOK*

The *Bluebook* is available in both print and electronic form. Both versions contain the same citation rules. The electronic version offers search options unavailable in the print version. Additionally, it allows you to bookmark commonly used rules and add your own annotations to the rules, tasks you would otherwise need to do manually with a print *Bluebook*. The electronic version also requires an annual subscription fee, whereas a print *Bluebook* requires only a single purchase. Most of the discussion in this section applies equally to the print and electronic versions of the *Bluebook*, but a few variations are noted.

The first part of the *Bluebook* that you should review is the Introduction. This section explains how the *Bluebook* is organized. As you will see when you review the Introduction, the *Bluebook* contains two sets of instructions for citing authority: "basic" citation rules used in legal practice and more complex rules used for citations in law journals. The "basic" citation rules apply to the types of documents most students write in their first year of law school, such as briefs and memoranda. The remainder of the citation rules apply primarily to law journals, a type of secondary source discussed in more detail in Chapter 4, although some aspects of these rules may also apply to practice documents. You are unlikely to write documents in law journal format at the beginning of your legal studies; therefore, you will want to focus your attention on the format for citations in briefs, memoranda, and other similar legal documents.

Learning to cite authority in *Bluebook* format requires you to become familiar with five items:

- the Bluepages and corresponding Bluepages Tables;
- the text of the citation rules in the Rules section of the *Bluebook*;
- the Tables;
- the finding tools for locating individual citation rules (i.e., Table of Contents and Index; Quick Reference guides in print; search features in the electronic version);
- Blue Tips and *Bluebook* updates.

THE BLUEPAGES AND CORRESPONDING BLUEPAGES TABLES. The Bluepages section contains the rules for citing legal authority in briefs, memoranda, and legal documents other than law journals. This section contains general information applicable to any type of citation, such as the uses of citations in legal writing. It also contains specific instructions for citing cases, statutes, secondary sources, and other forms of authority, as well as examples of many types of citations. The Bluepages Table BT1 contains the abbreviations for words commonly found in the titles of court documents. In addition, because some jurisdictions have their own "local" citation rules that supplement or supersede the *Bluebook* rules, Table BT2 refers you to sources for local citation rules. In print, the Bluepages appear at the beginning of the *Bluebook*. In the electronic version, use the **Bluepages** link to review the outline of the Bluepages rules.

THE TEXT OF THE CITATION RULES. Most of the *Bluebook* is devoted to explaining the rules for citing different types of authority. In print, the Rules section appears in the white pages in the middle of the *Bluebook*. In the electronic version, you can access the Rules section from the **Rules** link. These rules can be divided into five categories:

1. Rules 1 through 9 are general rules applicable to a citation to any type of authority. For example, Rule 5 discusses the proper format for quotations.
2. Rules 10 through 17 contain rules for citing various primary and secondary authorities published in print. For example, Rule 10 explains how to cite a court opinion, and Rule 12 explains how to cite a statute.
3. Rule 18 contains rules for citing authorities published in electronic format.
4. Rule 19 contains rules for citing authorities published in services for researching law related to specific subject areas.
5. Rules 20 and 21 contain rules for citing foreign and international materials.

Some of the material contained in the Rules section also appears in the Bluepages. If the information you need for the authority you are citing is contained in the Bluepages, you may not need to consult the individual rules in the Rules section. If you face a citation question not addressed in the Bluepages, however, you should consult the individual rules for more detailed guidance. Most of the rules for citing specific types of legal authority begin with a description of the elements necessary for a full citation. The remainder of the rule will explain each component in greater detail.

Frequently, a rule will be accompanied by examples. Although this might seem like it would simplify things, in fact, sometimes it just complicates the citation. This is because the examples in the Rules section are in the typefaces (e.g., italics, large and small capital letters) required for law journals. These typefaces are not always used in other types of legal documents. Therefore, although the examples in the Rules section will be somewhat useful to you in understanding how to cite legal authority, you cannot rely on them exclusively. The instructions in Bluepages B1 explain the differences between typeface conventions for citations in law journals and other documents.

THE TABLES. In print, the Tables appear in the white pages with blue borders at the back of the *Bluebook*. In the electronic version, you can access them from the **Tables** link. The citation rules in the Bluepages and Rules sections of the *Bluebook* explain the general requirements for different types of citations. Often they require that certain words be abbreviated. The Tables contain abbreviations necessary for proper citations.[1] For example, Table T1 lists each jurisdiction in the United States, and under each jurisdiction, it shows the proper abbreviations for citations to that jurisdiction's cases and statutes. Whenever you have a citation that includes an abbreviation, you will need to check the appropriate Table to find the precise abbreviation required for a proper citation. You should note, however, that the type styles of some of the abbreviations in the Tables are in law journal format and may need to be modified according to Bluepages B1 for the work you will produce in your first year of law school.

THE FINDING TOOLS FOR LOCATING INDIVIDUAL RULES. As noted above, the Bluepages should be your starting point for determining how to construct a citation in *Bluebook* format. If you cannot find what you need in the Bluepages, you can find individual citation rules in the Rules section using the Table of Contents or the Index. In the print version of the *Bluebook*, the Index references in black type refer to the pages with relevant rules. Those in blue type refer to examples of citations. The Index in the electronic version refers only to rule numbers, not page numbers.

In the print version, you can also refer to the Quick Reference examples of different types of citations on the inside front and back covers. The examples on the inside front cover are in the format for law review and journal footnotes and will be of little or no use to you in your first year of law school. The examples on the inside back cover are in the proper format for the types of documents you are likely to draft in your first year.

The electronic version does not contain the Quick Reference examples, but it offers additional search options. The search box at the top of the screen allows you to do a basic search for rules. The advanced search options allow you to tailor your search more specifically. As noted above, you can bookmark frequently used rules and add annotations to the rules. The search functions in the electronic version allow you to search your bookmarked rules and annotations in addition to the text of the rules themselves.

BLUE TIPS AND *BLUEBOOK* UPDATES. You will find citation tips and updates to the *Bluebook* on the *Bluebook* website. This material is available without a subscription, so you will want to take advantage of these resources whether you use the *Bluebook* in print or electronic form. The

---

[1] Citations in *ALWD Manual* format also require abbreviations. The *Bluebook* and the *ALWD Manual* use identical abbreviations for many words. Some abbreviations vary, however, depending on which format you use.

Internet address for the *Bluebook*'s online resources appears in Appendix A at the end of this text.

All of the pieces of the *Bluebook* work together to help you determine the proper citation format for a legal authority:

1. Use the Bluepages to find citation instructions governing the authority you want to cite.
2. If the Bluepages do not contain all the information you need for the citation, use the Index, Table of Contents, Quick Reference guides (in print) or search functions (in the electronic version) to find the relevant rule in the Rules section.
3. Use the Tables to find abbreviations and other information necessary for a complete citation.
4. If necessary, convert the typefaces in the examples and Tables into the proper format for briefs and memoranda according to Bluepages.

As you read the remaining chapters in this text, you will find more specific information about citing individual legal authorities. In general, however, you will be able to figure out how to cite almost any type of authority in *Bluebook* format by following these four steps.

2. THE *ALWD MANUAL*

The first part of the *ALWD Manual* that you should review is Part 1, Introductory Material. This section explains what citations are and how to use them, how to use the *ALWD Manual*, how local citation rules can affect citation format, and how your word processor's settings may affect citations. It explains the *ALWD Manual*'s organization clearly, so it would be redundant to repeat all of that information here. Nevertheless, a few comments on the *ALWD Manual* may be useful as you begin learning about it.

Perhaps the biggest difference between the *ALWD Manual* and the *Bluebook* is that the *ALWD Manual* uses the same citation format for all documents. The *Bluebook*, by contrast, uses one format for citations in law journal footnotes and another for practice documents like briefs and memoranda. When you are using the *ALWD Manual*, you do not need to convert any of the citations into different formats for different documents.

As you will see when you review Part 1, learning to cite authority in *ALWD Manual* format requires you to become familiar with five items:

■ the Table of Contents and Index;
■ the text of the citation rules;
■ the Appendices;
■ the "Fast Formats" and "Snapshots";
■ the *ALWD Manual* website.

THE TABLE OF CONTENTS AND INDEX. To locate individual citation rules, you can use the Table of Contents at the beginning of the *ALWD Manual* or the Index at the end. Unless otherwise indicated, the references in the Index are to rule numbers, not page numbers or specific examples.

THE TEXT OF THE CITATION RULES. Most of the *ALWD Manual* is devoted to explaining the rules for citing different types of authority. The rules are divided into the following Parts:

1. Part 2 (Rules 1 through 11) contains general rules applicable to a citation to any type of authority. For example, Rule 3 discusses spelling and capitalization.
2. Part 3 (Rules 12 through 37) contains rules for citing various primary and secondary authorities published in print. For example, Rule 12 explains how to cite a court opinion, and Rule 14 explains how to cite a statute.
3. Part 4 (Rules 38 through 42) contains rules for citing authorities published in electronic format.
4. Part 5 (Rules 43 through 46) contains rules for incorporating citations into documents.
5. Part 6 (Rules 47 through 49) contains rules regarding quotations.

At the beginning of each citation rule in Parts 3 and 4, you will find a description of the elements necessary for a full citation, followed by an annotated example showing how all of the elements fit together to create a complete citation. You should read this part of the rule first. The remainder of the rule will explain each component in greater detail.

Within the text of each rule in the *ALWD Manual*, you will find cross-references to other citation rules and to Appendices containing additional information that you may need for a complete citation. An explanation of the Appendices appears below.

You will also find "Sidebars" in some rules. The "Sidebars" are literally asides on citation. They provide information about sources of legal authority, help you avoid common citation errors, and offer citation tips.

THE APPENDICES. The *ALWD Manual* contains eight Appendices that follow the Parts containing the citation rules. The citation rules in Parts 3 and 4 explain the general requirements for citations to different types of authority. Most of these rules require that certain words be abbreviated. Appendices 1, 3, 4, and 5 contain abbreviations necessary for proper citations. For example, Appendix 1 lists Primary Sources by Jurisdiction. It lists each jurisdiction in the United States, and under each jurisdiction, it shows the proper abbreviations for citations to that jurisdiction's cases and statutes. Whenever you have a citation that includes an abbreviation, you will need to check the appropriate Appendix to find the precise abbreviation required for a proper citation.[2]

Appendix 2 contains local court citation rules. Some courts require special citation formats for authorities cited in documents filed with those courts. The *ALWD Manual* includes these rules in Appendix 2, so you do not have to look them up in another source if you need to use them.

Appendix 6 contains an example of a memorandum with citations included. This example can help you see how citations are integrated into a document.

Appendix 7 contains information on citations to federal taxation materials, and Appendix 8 contains information on selected federal administrative publications.

THE "FAST FORMATS" AND "SNAPSHOTS." Before the text of each rule for citing an individual type of authority in Parts 3 and 4, you will find a section called "Fast Formats." The "Fast Formats" provide citation examples for each rule, in addition to the examples interwoven with the text of the rule. A "Fast Formats Locator" appears on the inside front cover of the *ALWD Manual*. You can use this alphabetical list to find "Fast Formats" pages without going to the Table of Contents or Index.

"Snapshots" also accompany the citation rules for some of the most commonly cited types of legal authority. "Snapshots" are annotated sample pages from sources of law that show you where to find the components of a full citation within the document.

THE *ALWD MANUAL* WEBSITE. Updates to the *ALWD Manual* are posted on the Internet. The Internet address for the *ALWD Manual* website is listed in Appendix A at the end of this text.

All of the pieces of the *ALWD Manual* work together to help you determine the proper citation format for a legal authority:

1. Use the Table of Contents or Index to find the rule governing the authority you want to cite.
2. Read the rule, beginning with the components of a full citation at the beginning of the rule.
3. Use the Appendices to find additional information necessary for a correct citation.

---

[2] Citations in *Bluebook* format also require abbreviations. The *Bluebook* and the *ALWD Manual* use identical abbreviations for many words. Some abbreviations differ, however, depending on which format you use.

4. Use the "Fast Formats" and "Snapshots" preceding the rule for additional examples and information.
5. If necessary, check the website for any updates.

As you read the remaining chapters in this text, you will find more specific information about citing individual legal authorities. In general, however, you will be able to figure out how to cite almost any type of authority in *ALWD Manual* format by following these five steps.

E. OVERVIEW OF THIS TEXT

Because different research projects have different starting and ending points, it is not necessary that you follow all of the chapters in this text in order. The sequence of assignments in your legal research class will determine the order in which you need to cover the material in this text.

Although you may not cover the chapters in order, a brief overview of the organization of this text may provide useful context for the material that follows. As noted earlier, Chapter 2 discusses how to generate search terms, one of the first steps in any research project, and Chapter 3 describes source- and content-driven search strategies. Chapters 4 through 9 explain how to research different types of authority. Chapter 10 discusses electronic search techniques, and Chapter 11 covers how to create a research plan.

Chapters 4 through 9 are all organized in a similar way. They all begin with an overview of the type of authority discussed. Then you will find an explanation of the print research process, followed by a description of electronic research sources. The material on print and electronic research will include excerpts from various research tools to highlight some of their key features. After the discussion of the research process, you will find information on citation format. The next item in each of these chapters is a section of sample pages. The sample pages contain step-by-step illustrations of the research process described earlier in the chapter. As you read through the text, you may find it helpful to review both the excerpts within the chapter and the sample pages section to get a sense of the research process for each type of authority. These chapters conclude with research checklists that summarize the research process and may be helpful as you conduct research.

Chapter 10 discusses general techniques for electronic research. The process of using print research sources varies according to the type of authority you are researching, which is why the preceding chapters largely focus on individual types of authority. With electronic research, however, there are certain common search techniques that can be used to research many types of authority. As a consequence, the discussion of electronic research in Chapters 4 through 9 focuses on search techniques specific to individual sources, and Chapter 10 focuses on more general electronic search techniques and strategies. If you are learning about print and electronic research simultaneously, you should read Chapter 10 early in your studies. If you are learning about print research first, save Chapter 10 until you begin instruction in electronic research. When you begin learning about electronic research, you may also want to review Appendix A at the end of the text, which lists a number of Internet research sites.

The final chapter, Chapter 11, discusses research strategy and explains how to create a research plan. You do not need to read all of the preceding chapters before reading Chapter 11, although you may find Chapter 11 easier to follow after you have some background on a few research sources. Learning about research involves more than simply learning how to locate individual types of authority. You must also be able to plan a research strategy that will lead to accurate research results, and you must be able to execute your research strategy efficiently and economically. Chapter 11 sets out a process that will help you achieve these goals in any research project, whether in your legal research class or in legal practice.

CHAPTER 2

GENERATING SEARCH TERMS

A. Generating search terms based on categories of information

B. Expanding the initial search

C. Prioritizing search terms

As Chapter 1 explains, generating search terms is part of the research planning process. Developing a list of words or concepts that are likely to lead you to useful information is a preliminary step necessary for almost any type of research. Regardless of whether you use a source-driven or content-driven approach, you must generate a list of search terms related to your research issue to find relevant information. This chapter explains techniques you can use to generate search terms for virtually any research project.

A. GENERATING SEARCH TERMS BASED ON CATEGORIES OF INFORMATION

When presented with a set of facts, you could generate a list of search terms by constructing a random list of words that seem relevant to the issue. But a more structured approach—working from a set of categories, instead of random terms that sound relevant—will help ensure that you are covering all of your bases in conducting your research.

There are a number of ways that you could categorize the information in your research issue to create a list of search terms. Some people prefer to use the six questions journalists ask when covering a story: who, what, when, where, why, and how. Another way to generate search terms is to categorize the information presented by the facts as follows.

■ **THE *PARTIES* INVOLVED IN THE PROBLEM, DESCRIBED ACCORDING TO THEIR RELATIONSHIPS TO EACH OTHER**

Here, you might be concerned not only with parties who are in direct conflict with each other, but also any other individuals, entities, or groups involved. These might include fact witnesses who can testify as to what happened, expert witnesses if appropriate to the situation, other potential plaintiffs (in civil cases), or other potential defendants (in criminal or civil cases).

In describing the parties, proper names will not ordinarily be useful search terms, although if one party is a public entity or corporation, you might be able to locate other cases in which the entity or corporation was a party. Instead, you will usually want to describe the parties in terms of their legal status or relationships to each other, such as landlords and tenants, parents and children, employers and employees, or doctors and patients.

■ THE *PLACES AND THINGS* INVOLVED IN THE PROBLEM

In thinking about place, both geographical locale and type of location can be important. For example, the conduct at issue might have taken place in Pennsylvania, which would help you determine which jurisdiction's law applies. It might also have taken place at a school or in a church, which could be important for determining which legal rules apply to the situation.

"Things" can involve tangible objects or intangible concepts. In a problem involving a car accident, tangible things could include automobiles or stop signs. In other types of situations, intangible "things," such as a vacation or someone's reputation, could be useful search terms.

■ THE *POTENTIAL CLAIMS AND DEFENSES* THAT COULD BE RAISED

As you become more familiar with the law, you may be able to identify claims or defenses that a research problem potentially raises. The facts could indicate to you that the problem potentially involves particular claims (such as breach of contract, defamation, or bribery) or particular defenses (such as consent, assumption of the risk, or self-defense).

Lawyers use their accumulated knowledge, including both specialized knowledge gained in practice and foundational legal principles that all lawyers learn in law school, to identify legal doctrines that may apply to a client's situation. Even as a beginning law student, you are being introduced to a body of information common to all lawyers that you can use to brainstorm potential legal theories. When that is the case, you can often use claims and defenses effectively as search terms to help you identify applicable rules of law.

If you are dealing with an unfamiliar area of law, however, you might not know of any claims or defenses potentially at issue. In that situation, you can generate search terms by thinking about the conduct and mental states of the parties, as well as the injury suffered by the complaining party. Claims and defenses often flow from these considerations, and as a result, these types of terms can appear in a research tool's indexing system. When considering conduct, consider what was not done, as well as what was done. The failure to do an act might also give rise to a claim or defense. For example, you could be asked to research a situation in which one person published an article falsely asserting that another person was guilty of tax evasion, knowing that the accusation was not true. You might recognize this as a potential claim for the tort of defamation, which occurs when one person publishes false information that is damaging to another person's reputation. Even if you were unfamiliar with this tort, however, you could still generate search terms relevant to the claim by considering the defendant's conduct (publication) or mental state (intentional actions), or the plaintiff's injury (to reputation). These search terms would likely lead you to authority on defamation.

■ THE *RELIEF* SOUGHT BY THE COMPLAINING PARTY

The relief a party is seeking is another way to categorize information. Damages, injunction, specific performance, restitution, attorneys' fees, and other terms relating to the relief sought can lead you to pertinent information.

As an example of how you might go about using these categories to generate search terms, assume you have been asked to research the following situation:

> Your client recently ended a long-term relationship with her partner. She and her partner never participated in a formal marriage ceremony, but they had always planned to get married "someday." They lived together for five years and referred to each other as husband and wife. Your client and her former partner orally agreed to provide support for each other, and your client's former partner repeatedly made statements like, "What's mine is yours." Your client wants to know if she is entitled to part of the value of the assets her former partner acquired during their relationship or to any support payments.

- PARTIES: husband, wife, spouse, unmarried couple, unmarried cohabitants.
- PLACES AND THINGS: property, assets, ownership, support, non-marital relationship.
- POTENTIAL CLAIMS AND DEFENSES: common-law marriage, breach of contract, detrimental reliance.
  These terms might not have occurred to you if were not already familiar with the relevant legal principles. Additional terms could be generated according to conduct ("reliance" on "promises" of support) or mental state ("misrepresentation" if the client was misled into believing the parties shared ownership of the assets).
- RELIEF: damages, division or disposition of assets, support.

This is not an exhaustive list of search terms for this problem, but it illustrates how you can use these categories of information to develop useful search terms.

B. EXPANDING THE INITIAL SEARCH

Once you have developed an initial set of search terms for your issue, the next task is to try to expand that list. The terms you originally generated may not appear in an index or database. Therefore, once you have developed your initial set of search terms, you should try to increase both the breadth and the depth of the list. You can increase the breadth of the list by identifying synonyms and terms related to the initial search terms, and you can increase the depth by expressing the concepts in your search terms both more abstractly and more concretely.

Increasing the breadth of your list with synonyms and related terms is essential to your research strategy. This is especially true for database word searches. As Chapter 3 explains in more detail, some research tools can cross-reference content related to your search terms. A literal word search, however, searches only for the specific terms you identify. Therefore, to make sure you locate all of the pertinent information on your issue, you need to have a number of synonyms for the words and concepts in your search. In the research scenario described above, there are a number of synonyms and related terms for one of the initial search terms: ownership. As **Figure 2.1** illustrates, you might also search for terms such as title or possession.

You are also more likely to find useful research material if you increase the depth of your list by varying the level of abstraction. In the research scenario described above, the client and her former partner were unmarried cohabitants. You might find relevant information if you described the relationship more abstractly as "intimate partners" or more concretely as "boyfriend" or "girlfriend." See **Figure 2.2**.

FIGURE 2.1   EXPANDING THE BREADTH OF SEARCH TERMS

Increasing breadth with synonyms and related terms:	title ↕ ownership ↕ possession

FIGURE 2.2   INCREASING THE DEPTH OF SEARCH TERMS

Increasing depth with varying levels of abstraction: intimate partners
↕
unmarried cohabitants
↕
boyfriend, girlfriend

C. PRIORITIZING SEARCH TERMS

Once you have generated and expanded a list of search terms, you must prioritize them. Recall the key analogy from Chapter 1: If you had the key to a car parked at Disney World, how would you figure out which car it starts? Three relevant criteria would be make, model, and color, and ideally you would narrow the field by all three together. If that were not possible, which criterion would you use first? When you generate an extensive list of search terms for legal research, you will often use some combination of terms together, but you usually will not use all of them simultaneously. You can only look up one term or concept at a time in a print index. You can combine terms together in a word search, but putting too many in one search may limit the search's effectiveness. Consequently, you must decide where to focus your attention first.

You may find it helpful to think about two goals when you prioritize your search terms: identifying the legal rules that apply to your client's situation, and determining how the facts of the situation fit with the requirements of the rules. Of course, this is a bit of a chicken-or-egg problem in that the facts of the situation determine which rules apply and the application of the rules depends on the facts of the situation. Nevertheless, one element of your search strategy will be deciding whether to prioritize terms describing legal doctrines or terms describing the specific facts of your client's situation. This does not mean that you will ignore or discard other terms; it simply means that you must decide which terms to emphasize initially and which to use in fine-tuning the search results.

Prioritizing terms relating to legal doctrines makes sense when you know the theory or theories most likely to apply to your client's situation. To return to the key analogy, using the make and model to narrow the field of options would make sense. Prioritizing search terms related to the legal doctrine that applies to your research issue can similarly be an effective way to narrow the field of legal information.

As you begin learning about legal research, your professor may specify the legal doctrines you are to research. In the research scenario in

Section A, above, regarding the dissolution of a long-term relationship, your professor might direct you to research whether the parties formed a common-law marriage. You would certainly prioritize "common-law marriage" as a search term based on your professor's instructions.

In real life, clients bring the facts of their problems to you, not instructions to research particular legal theories, and as you become a more experienced researcher, the less likely your professor is to identify the legal doctrines or rules that apply to your research scenario. As you gain experience in the law, you will learn to identify the legal issues a situation presents and will be able to prioritize terms related to those issues in your research.

Sometimes, however, you will not begin your research with a sense of the applicable legal doctrines and will need to prioritize the facts of your client's situation instead. You can then use the search results to determine the legal doctrines that govern situations involving those types of facts. To return to the key analogy again, prioritizing facts is like trying to find the parked car by searching by color. This will narrow the field, but the remaining choices will reflect substantial diversity of makes and models. Similarly, prioritizing terms relating to the specific facts of the client's situation can lead to diffuse search results involving many different legal rules. The search results will also be affected by the level of abstraction of your terms. Search terms that are too concrete may yield little information, or little relevant information. More abstract factual terms may better steer you toward authority that describes applicable legal doctrines.

In the example involving dissolution of a client's long-term relationship, prioritizing factual terms relating to the parties' relationship could lead to rules about common-law marriage but would also likely lead to information about a variety of other legal doctrines. This is especially true for concrete terms like "boyfriend" or "girlfriend," which can occur in virtually any legal context. Although prioritizing factual terms may not be a useful approach when you need to locate information about a particular legal doctrine (such as common-law marriage), it can be useful when you need to identify all possible avenues of recovery for a client or do not have a sense of the legal doctrines that may apply to the situation.

Neither the list nor the priority of your search terms should remain static. Reading the information you find early in your research may reveal new search terms you can use to locate better information. The terminology of applicable legal rules that you did not consider at first might appear in the documents you locate in your initial research efforts, and they can then become useful terms for additional research (unless you have been instructed to limit your research to a particular legal doctrine). Facts that did not seem important at first could turn out to be critical to your analysis. As you work through your research path, therefore, you should revise both the content and priority of your search terms.

CHAPTER 3

EVALUATING SEARCH OPTIONS

A. Introduction to search approaches

B. Source-driven search process

C. Content-driven search process

D. Evaluating search options

A. INTRODUCTION TO SEARCH APPROACHES

Recall the research scenario introduced in Chapter 2:

> Your client recently ended a long-term relationship with her partner. She and her partner never participated in a formal marriage ceremony, but they had always planned to get married "someday." They lived together for five years and referred to each other as husband and wife. Your client and her former partner orally agreed to provide support for each other, and your client's former partner repeatedly made statements like, "What's mine is yours." Your client wants to know if she is entitled to part of the value of the assets her former partner acquired during their relationship or to any support payments.

Assume that your supervisor asked you to find out whether the parties' relationship qualified as a common-law or "informal" marriage under the state's family law statutes and to submit a summary of your research by the end of the day. How would you approach the task? Assume instead that your supervisor gave you a week to research the law and submit a memorandum analyzing any legal theories that might apply to your client's situation. How would you approach that task?

Neither of these assignments requires you to explain how you conducted your research. Your supervisor and the client will be focused on the substantive results of your research, not on the process. But each of these research tasks is different in terms of the complexity of the research required, the work product to be produced, and the deadline for completion. Accordingly, you would use a different research process for each one. Knowing how to vary your research process to suit the task you need to accomplish is vital for performing complete, accurate, and efficient research.

Chapter 1 gave you a brief introduction to the source-driven and content-driven approaches to research and summarized the research planning process. This chapter will explain these search approaches in more detail so you can learn how to assess which approach is best for the specific research tasks you will be asked to do as a student and in legal practice. This assessment is important for effective research planning. As you read this chapter, consider how you might approach the research tasks described above. The last section of this chapter sets out possible approaches to these assignments. You can compare your approaches with those outlined in Section D.

As a starting point, Sections B and C, below, contrast source- and content-driven research strategies and are organized around two questions:

- What source(s) will be included in my search?
- What content will my search strategy identify?

B. SOURCE-DRIVEN SEARCH PROCESS

The source-driven approach can be used with virtually any source of information: print, Lexis.com, Lexis Advance, Westlaw.com, WestlawNext, Bloomberg Law, and other providers of legal information. When you use the source-driven approach, you will select a source to search, search for content within the source, and read and evaluate the information you find.

1. WHAT SOURCE(S) WILL BE INCLUDED IN MY SEARCH?

With the source-driven approach, only the publication(s) you select will be included in the search. In print, each publication is a separate book or set of books, and, as explained in Chapter 1, the publication will often be organized by jurisdiction and type of authority. For example, each set of statutes for each jurisdiction is in a separate set of books. The California state code is in one set of books, and the Illinois state code is in another. Therefore, the source you would select to research California statutes is the California state code.

Electronic services typically divide individual sources of information into separate databases organized by jurisdiction and type of authority, although some databases will combine related information. For example, in Westlaw.com and Lexis.com, you would research California statutes by selecting the California code database and Illinois statutes by selecting the Illinois code database, but a database containing all state codes is also available in both of those services.

To research effectively with the source-driven approach, you need to know two things: the range of publications or databases available to you and the type of source you want to research. You have to know that a publication or database exists to select it as a source. You also have to have at least a general idea about the type of information you need so you can select a source that contains that information. If you do not realize that an issue is likely one of federal law instead of state law or statutory law instead of common law, you may have trouble finding relevant information because you will not be looking in the right source or sources. Conversely, however, when you know the source of the information you need, researching only that source is efficient because all the information you find will be from the appropriate source.

2. What Content Will My Search Strategy Identify?

Once you have selected a source, you are ready to search for information within that source. In print or electronically, you can search by subject. Electronic providers also allow you to execute word searches. Both of these methods of searching are discussed below.

a. Subject Searching

In print, you can search by subject using the table of contents or index to a publication to find information within that publication. The index will usually contain more detail than the table of contents, and because it is organized by subject, will contain cross-references to related material. Some electronic providers provide access to the tables of contents or indices of selected publications, and you can use those the same way you would in print. Electronic providers also often offer specialized subject-searching tools that provide a directory of subject area topics.

One advantage to subject searching is that if the concept you are searching is described with commonly used words, an index or other subject compilation will reference only significant discussions of the concept, not every occurrence of commonly used words. For example, virtually every civil law suit is initiated by the filing of a document called a complaint. "Complaint," however, is both a technical legal term and a common, everyday word. If you wanted to research "complaints," you would want references to the document used to initiate a civil suit, not to the everyday use of the term. Subject-searching tools like an index prioritize the information within a source to help direct you to the most important information even when the topic you are researching is described with commonly used words.

Another advantage of subject searching is that index cross-references will point you in the right direction if you look up terms that are close to, but perhaps not exactly on point with, the topic you are researching. For example, a concept in contract law called the "mailbox" rule is also known as the "deposit acceptance" rule and the "postal acceptance" rule. If you knew one of those terms but not the others, index cross-references would likely direct you to an alternative entry containing relevant information under a different heading.

On the other hand, if you want to search for terms or topics that the publisher did not include in the index or subject compilation, you have no way to find the information you need. And if the publisher has compiled the material using topic names that are completely unfamiliar to you, you may not be able to find index or subject entries that are helpful.

b. Word Searching

Word searching is a search option when you use electronic services. A word search allows you to search for documents that contain terms you specify. You have probably executed thousands of word searches in search engines like Google. Most electronic services offer two options for word searching: terms and connectors searching, and natural language searching. WestlawNext uses a variation on natural language searching that this text calls descriptive term searching. Terms and connectors, natural language, and descriptive term search techniques are discussed in Chapter 10.

Because word searches look for specific terms, you can establish your own search criteria without regard for whether the publisher included those words in the index. This can be helpful for fact-specific research, such as when you are searching for cases with specific facts similar to the facts of your research issue, or when the applicable legal concepts are expressed with relatively unique phrasing, such as "negligence per se," a well-known tort doctrine.

But because a word search is a literal search for the terms you identify, it can retrieve irrelevant documents or miss important documents. For example, executing a word search for a commonly used term such as "complaint" can retrieve many documents that use the term in an everyday sense instead of as a term of art. Although all concepts must ultimately be expressed in words, a literal search for the individual terms that express a general concept may not be focused enough to be as effective as a subject search. Conversely, a word search for the "mailbox" rule in a source that uses the alternative label "deposit acceptance" rule to characterize the concept may miss important documents because the search term "mailbox" will not appear in that source.

C. CONTENT-DRIVEN SEARCH PROCESS

As this text goes to press, the content-driven process is available only through Lexis Advance and WestlawNext. Other search providers may change their search capabilities over time. The capabilities of Lexis Advance and WestlawNext are continuing to evolve as these products become more established. The discussion here focuses on research techniques that are, at this point in time, unique to these two services.

The content-driven approach uses the same steps as the source-driven approach, but it modifies the order of the steps. With content-driven research, you can search for content before you select a source.

1. WHAT SOURCE(S) WILL BE INCLUDED IN MY SEARCH?

With Lexis Advance and WestlawNext you can do a true general search for information from all jurisdictions and all types of authority, much as you search for content without regard to source in Google. Although this sort of broad search is possible, it is not likely to be a strategy you will use often. What you are more likely to do with Lexis Advance or WestlawNext is pre-filter or narrow the scope of your research before you execute a search for specific content. For example, if you pre-filter by selecting a specific jurisdiction, the search results will be limited to sources from that jurisdiction but will include many types of information, including cases, statutes, secondary sources, court filings, and the like.

When you search this way, you may retrieve hundreds or thousands of documents. Your task then becomes one of narrowing the results to target the information you need. You can narrow or filter the results by type of authority, level of court, or other more specific criteria. You can also search for terms within the results.

The advantage of this approach is that it may prompt you to review sources you would not otherwise have considered. For example, if you thought an issue was governed by common law, but in fact, a statute applied to the issue, the general search may retrieve the relevant statute. The disadvantage is that a search that retrieves a large number of documents may be overwhelming, especially if you do not know enough about the issue to filter the results effectively. Another caution is the need to pay close attention to differences among sources of information. Regulations issued by agencies may look very similar to statutes. Briefs and other court filings may look very similar to a court's opinion, but only the opinion constitutes legal authority. When all sources of information are combined in a single search result, it is easy to lose track of the authoritative value of an individual document.

2. WHAT CONTENT WILL MY SEARCH STRATEGY IDENTIFY?

The default option for searching in Lexis Advance is natural language searching. The Lexis Advance search engine uses a more complex natural language algorithm than the Lexis.com search engine. This means you may get different results from the same natural language search executed in both services.

WestlawNext uses a form of natural language searching that this text calls descriptive term searching. It not only looks for your search terms within the text of documents, but also searches background information (meta-data) and evaluates prior search results to identify documents that appear to be relevant to your research issue even if they do not contain your precise search terms.

Both Lexis Advance and WestlawNext offer menu options and search commands that will allow you to execute a terms and connectors search without first selecting a source or database. In addition, terms and connectors searching is very important in filtering your search results. One filtering option in both services allows you to execute a word search within your search results. This search within the search results will be a terms and connectors search. Therefore, even when you execute a natural language search in Lexis Advance or WestlawNext, you must be familiar with terms and connectors searches to filter your search results effectively.

Natural language, descriptive term, and terms and connectors search techniques are discussed in Chapter 10.

D. EVALUATING SEARCH OPTIONS

Now that you have read about the source-driven and content-driven approaches to research, consider how you might approach the research tasks described at the beginning of this chapter. Compare your approach with the potential research strategies outlined below.

The scenario involved disposition of assets upon dissolution of a non-marital relationship:

> Your client recently ended a long-term relationship with her partner. She and her partner never participated in a formal marriage ceremony, but they had always planned to get married "someday." They lived together for five years and referred to each other as husband and wife. Your client and her former partner orally agreed to provide support for each other, and your client's former partner repeatedly made statements like, "What's mine is yours." Your client wants to know if she is entitled to part of the value of the assets her former partner acquired during their relationship or to any support payments.

The first task was to determine whether the parties' relationship qualified as a common-law or "informal" marriage and summarize your research by the end of the day. For this task, your supervisor has given you some direction about the type of authority you need to locate: family law statutes. The statutes will likely set out the requirements for establishing a common-law marriage. The statutory language alone, however, may not fully answer the question. For example, if the statutory language does not say how long people must hold themselves out as married to establish a common-law marriage, cases interpreting the statute may provide some guidance.

After you generate your search terms, using a source-driven approach would be a good way to accomplish your research task. You know the jurisdiction and type of authority you need, so you can limit your search to the state code. This will reduce the number of documents you locate and make it easier to evaluate what you have found. Your search terms would relate to the legal theory you have been instructed to research. Looking up index entries or executing word searches for terms such as "common-law marriage" or "informal marriage" would likely lead you in the right direction.

Once you locate the relevant provision(s) of the code, you can read the language to determine the requirements for this type of marriage. Research notes accompanying the statute will likely summarize cases interpreting the statute, making it easy for you to locate and read pertinent cases. Given the short deadline for reporting the results of your research, this would be a good approach for making a preliminary assessment of the law so that you and your supervisor can decide whether further research is appropriate.

Now consider the second task: to research any legal theories that might apply to your client's situation. This is a more complex research task because you have not been instructed to research any specific legal theory or type of authority. Your job is to identify the theories that potentially provide a remedy. Unless you are already familiar with applicable legal rules, you will need to begin in a more general way by learning about potential theories of recovery and then evaluating the potential success of those theories under your state's law. This work could be accomplished with either a source-driven or content-driven approach.

Again, you would begin by generating search terms. Terms relating to property rights of unmarried cohabitants or boyfriend and girlfriend living together would likely be relevant. From there, you could use a source-driven approach for your research. You know that your state is the controlling jurisdiction, but you may not know which type(s) of primary mandatory authority will apply to your client's situation. Recall from Chapter 1, however, that secondary authorities can be a good starting point for research when you need background information because they cite, analyze, and explain the law. You could begin your research by selecting a secondary source. Chapter 4, on secondary source research, describes a range of secondary sources you could use to obtain background information. One that might be useful is *American Jurisprudence*, Second Edition, a legal encyclopedia with general information about a wide range of legal issues. You could use *American Jurisprudence* in print or online to search for content related to property rights of unmarried cohabitants. The results of your search would reveal that legal rules relating to detrimental reliance on a promise, common-law marriage, and breach of contract (among other theories) may apply to your client's situation. You could then use this information to search for relevant cases and statutes to determine whether your client might be able to prevail under these or other theories.

Another option would be to use a content-driven approach in Lexis Advance or WestlawNext. You would likely pre-filter the search by selecting your state as the jurisdiction. By searching for content related to property rights of unmarried cohabitants, you could retrieve secondary sources, cases, statutes, and other material that may be germane to your client's situation. After executing a search, you could filter this information according to any number of criteria and read what you found to identify rules that might apply to your client's situation. For example, you might retrieve secondary sources (like *American Jurisprudence*) describing detrimental reliance on a promise, a statute regarding the status of common-law marriage in your state, and a case analyzing a breach of contract claim by an unmarried person against a former partner. The search might also retrieve documents relating to domestic violence, wills and estates, same-sex marriage, or any number of other legal matters that could arise between unmarried partners but that do not apply to your client's situation. With no limitation on the type of authority, the search would likely retrieve several hundred to several thousand documents, making the post-search filtering process critical to identifying relevant information.

The differences between the source- and content-driven approaches can seem abstract when you read a textual description of the research process. When you start doing research, the differences will become readily apparent. You might try searching for information about the property rights of unmarried cohabitants in your state using the source- and content-driven approaches to see how the results differ and which you think is most effective. More detailed information on research planning appears in Chapter 11.

As you begin conducting research independently, you may find yourself gravitating toward the content-driven process that is presently only available through WestlawNext and Lexis Advance. It will likely feel familiar because it strives to replicate the types of Internet searching everyone does on a regular basis, and it has appealing features that make it a good choice for many types of research. It is worthwhile for you to learn effective content-driven searching.

Nevertheless, it is important for you to gain facility with source-driven searching as well. Source-driven searching is often the most effective way to conduct research, which is why it remains an option with Lexis Advance and WestlawNext. Additionally, many employers continue to rely on providers of legal information that offer only source-driven searching. Lexis Advance and WestlawNext can cost more than Westlaw.com, Lexis.com, and other services. Employers may proceed cautiously before subscribing to premium products that are unfamiliar to them. Some employers have invested thousands of dollars in print collections and see more benefit in having their attorneys use those resources than in investing in new electronic services.

Incentives such as reward points that can be redeemed for products may also provide inducements unrelated to your research goals to use particular research services. There is nothing wrong with these incentives as long as you understand that they are marketing efforts by commercial entities directed toward you as a consumer of information products. You do not rely exclusively on sellers' marketing messages when making purchases in your daily life. You should not do so when you select research services, either. As a consumer, you should make your own assessment of the resources available to you so that you can employ search processes most in line with your professional goals and needs.

Secondary Source Research

A. INTRODUCTION TO SECONDARY SOURCES

As you read in Chapter 1, primary authority refers to sources of legal rules, such as cases, statutes, and administrative regulations. Secondary sources, by contrast, provide commentary on the law. Although they are not binding on courts and are not cited as frequently as primary sources, secondary sources are excellent research tools. Because they often summarize or collect authorities from a variety of jurisdictions, they can help you find mandatory or persuasive primary authority on a subject. They also often provide narrative explanations of complex concepts that would be difficult for a beginning researcher to grasp thoroughly simply from reading primary sources. Equipped with a solid understanding of the background of an area of law, you will be better able to locate and evaluate primary authority on your research issue.

1. WHEN SECONDARY SOURCES WILL BE MOST USEFUL

Secondary sources will be most useful to you in the following situations:

(1) WHEN YOU ARE RESEARCHING AN AREA OF LAW WITH WHICH YOU ARE UNFAMILIAR. Secondary sources can give you the necessary background to generate search terms. They can also lead you directly to primary authorities.

(2) WHEN YOU ARE LOOKING FOR PRIMARY PERSUASIVE AUTHORITY BUT DO NOT KNOW HOW TO NARROW THE JURISDICTIONS THAT ARE LIKELY TO HAVE USEFUL INFORMATION. If you need to find primary persuasive authority on a subject, conducting a nationwide survey of the law on the topic is not likely to be an efficient research strategy. Secondary sources can help you locate persuasive authority relevant to your research issue.

(3) WHEN YOU ARE RESEARCHING AN UNDEVELOPED AREA OF THE LAW. When you are researching a question of first impression, commentators may have analyzed how courts should rule on the issue.

(4) WHEN AN INITIAL SEARCH OF PRIMARY SOURCES YIELDS EITHER NO AUTHORITY OR TOO MUCH AUTHORITY. If you are unable to find any authority at all on a topic, you may not be looking in the right places. Secondary sources can educate you on the subject in a way that may allow you to expand or refocus your research efforts. When your search yields an unmanageable amount of information, secondary sources can do two things. First, their citations to primary authority can help you identify the most important authorities pertaining to the research issue. Second, they can provide you with information that may help you narrow your search or weed out irrelevant sources.

2. LIMITS ON THE APPROPRIATE USE OF SECONDARY SOURCES

Knowing when *not* to use secondary sources is also important. As noted above, secondary sources are not binding on courts. Therefore, you will not ordinarily cite them in briefs or memoranda. This is especially true if you use secondary sources to lead you to primary authority. It is important never to rely exclusively on a discussion of a primary authority that appears in a secondary source. If you are discussing a primary authority in a legal analysis, you must read that authority yourself and update your research to make sure it is current.

This is true for two reasons. First, a summary of a primary authority might not include all of the information necessary to your analysis. It is important to read the primary authority for yourself to make sure you represent it correctly and thoroughly in your analysis.

Second, the information in the secondary source might not be completely current. Although most secondary sources are updated on a regular basis, the law can change at any time. The source may contain incomplete information simply because of the inevitable time lag between changes to the law and the publication of a supplement. One mistake some beginning researchers make is citing a secondary source for the text of a case or statute without checking to make sure that the case has not been overturned or that the statute has not been changed.

Another potential error is citing a secondary source for a proposition about the state of the law generally, such as, "Forty-two states now recognize a cause of action for invasion of privacy based on disclosure of private facts." While statements of that nature were probably true when the secondary source was written, other states may have acted, or some of those noted may have changed their law, in the intervening time period. Accordingly, secondary sources should only be used as a starting point for locating primary authority, not an ending point.

3. COMMONLY USED SECONDARY SOURCES

This section describes the following commonly used secondary sources: legal encyclopedias, treatises, legal periodicals, *American Law Reports*, Restatements of the law, and uniform laws and model acts.

a. Legal Encyclopedias

Legal encyclopedias are just like the general subject encyclopedias you have used in the past, except they are limited in scope to legal subjects. Legal encyclopedias provide a general overview of the law on a variety of topics. They do not provide analysis or suggest solutions to conflicts in the law. Instead, they simply report on the general state of the law. Because encyclopedias cover the law in such a general way, you will usually use them to get background information on your research topic and, to a lesser extent, to locate citations to primary authority. You will rarely, if ever, cite a legal encyclopedia.

There are two general legal encyclopedias, *American Jurisprudence*, Second Edition (Am. Jur. 2d) and *Corpus Juris Secundum* (C.J.S.). In addition, encyclopedias are published for many individual states (e.g., *California Jurisprudence*, *Maryland Law Encyclopedia*, and *Michigan Law and Practice*). When you are researching a question of state law, state encyclopedias are often more helpful than general encyclopedias for two reasons. First, the summary of the law will be tailored to the law of that state, and therefore is likely to be more helpful. Second, the citations to primary authority will be from the controlling jurisdiction. Consequently, state encyclopedias can be more useful for leading you to primary sources.

b. Treatises

Treatises have a narrower focus than legal encyclopedias. Where legal encyclopedias provide a general overview of a broad range of topics, treatises generally provide in-depth treatment of a single subject, such as torts or constitutional law. The goal of a treatise is to address in a systematic fashion all of the major topics within a subject area. Treatises often trace the history of the development of an area of law and explain the relationship of the treatise's subject to other areas of the law. To provide a comprehensive treatment of the subject's major topics, a treatise will explain the legal rules in the subject area, analyze major cases and statutes, and address policy issues underlying the rules. In addition to providing textual explanations, treatises also usually contain citations to many primary and secondary authorities.

Some treatises are widely respected and considered definitive sources in their subject areas. These treatises have often existed for a number of years and may be identified by the names of their original authors, even though other scholars now update and revise them. These well-known treatises may address broad areas of the law (Prosser on torts, Corbin on contracts, Wright & Miller on federal civil procedure) or more specialized subjects (Nimmer on copyright, White & Summers on the Uniform Commercial Code, Sutherland on statutory interpretation). These are not, however, the only treatises. Any book that provides comprehensive treatment of a single subject in a systematic fashion is a treatise, and many treatises exist on both broad areas of the law and narrower subjects. If you use a definitive treatise in your research, you might cite it in a brief or memorandum. Ordinarily, however, you will use treatises for research purposes and will not cite them in your written analysis.

c. Legal Periodicals

Articles in legal periodicals can be very useful research tools. You may hear periodical articles referred to as "law review" or "journal" articles. Many law schools publish periodicals known as law reviews or journals that collect articles on a wide range of topics. Many other types of legal periodicals also exist, however, including commercially published journals, legal newspapers, and magazines.

The commercial legal press includes magazines such as the *ABA Journal* and local bar journals and newspapers such as *The National Law Journal*. These publications are good for keeping abreast of newsworthy developments in the law. Because they are news sources, their articles are generally short and focused more on describing legal developments than on analysis. These types of articles can provide limited background information, but they usually do not focus on the kinds of issues first-year law students research.

Articles published in law reviews or journals, by contrast, are thorough, thoughtful treatments of legal issues by law professors, judges, practitioners, and even students. The articles are usually focused fairly narrowly on specific issues, although they often include background or introductory sections that provide a general overview of the topic. They are generally well researched and contain citations to many primary and secondary authorities. In addition, they often address undeveloped areas in the law and propose solutions for resolving problems in the law. As a result, periodical articles can be useful for obtaining an overview of an area of law, finding references to primary and secondary authority, and developing ideas for analyzing a question of first impression or resolving a conflict in the law.

Law review or journal articles fall into the following general categories:

■ ARTICLES WRITTEN BY LEGAL SCHOLARS

These are articles written by law professors and other scholars. They frequently address problems or conflicts in the law. They may propose solutions to legal problems, advocate for changes to the law, identify new legal theories, or explore the relationship between the law and some other discipline. Articles by leading or established scholars may be helpful in your research, especially if they explain doctrines or developments in a useful way. The weight of an individual article will depend on a number of factors, including the author's expertise, the reputation of the journal in which it is published, the article's age, and the depth of the article's research and analysis.

■ ARTICLES WRITTEN BY JUDGES AND PRACTITIONERS

These are articles written by people who work with the law on a daily basis in very practical ways. Judges often write about their judicial philosophies or to offer advice or insights to practitioners. Practitioners may write about areas of law in which they practice. These articles may help you understand a legal issue and provide an overview of important authorities, but practitioner articles in particular may not have the depth of other types of articles.

■ STUDENT NOTES OR COMMENTS

These are articles written by law students. Often, they describe a significant new case or statute. They may analyze a problem in the law and propose a solution. Because these articles are written by students, they carry less weight than other periodical articles and are useful primarily for background information and citations to primary authorities.

These are, of course, generalizations that may not hold true in every instance. For the most part, however, law review and journal articles will be useful to you as research tools, rather than as support for written analysis. You will not ordinarily cite an article if you can support your analysis with primary authority. If you cannot find primary support, however, you might cite a persuasive article. Additionally, if you incorporate an argument or analysis from an article in your written work, it is important to cite the source to avoid plagiarism.

Periodical articles are unique among legal authorities in that there is no way to update an individual article, short of locating later articles that add to or criticize an earlier article. As a consequence, it is important to note the date of any periodical article you use. If the article is more than a few years old, you may want to supplement your research with more current material. In addition, if you use the article to lead you to primary authority, you will need to update your research using the updating tools available for those primary sources to make sure your research is completely current.

d. American Law Reports

American Law Reports, or A.L.R., contains articles called "Annotations." Annotations collect summaries of cases from a variety of jurisdictions to provide an overview of the law on a topic. A.L.R. combines the breadth of topic coverage found in an encyclopedia with the depth of discussion in a treatise or legal periodical. Nevertheless, A.L.R. is different from these other secondary sources in significant ways. Because A.L.R. Annotations provide summaries of individual cases, they are more detailed than encyclopedias. Unlike treatises or legal periodicals, however, they mostly report the results of the cases without much analysis or commentary. A.L.R. Annotations are especially helpful at the beginning of your research to give you an overview of a topic. Because Annotations collect summaries of cases from many jurisdictions, they can also be helpful in directing you toward mandatory or persuasive primary authority. More recent Annotations also contain references to other research sources, such as other secondary sources and tools for conducting additional case research. Although A.L.R. is a useful research tool, you will rarely, if ever, cite an A.L.R. Annotation.

There are eight series of A.L.R. that address United States law: A.L.R., A.L.R.2d, A.L.R.3d, A.L.R.4th, A.L.R.5th, A.L.R.6th, A.L.R. Fed., and A.L.R. Fed. 2d.[1] Each series contains multiple volumes organized by volume number. A.L.R. Fed. and Fed. 2d cover issues of federal law. The remaining series usually cover issues of state law, although they do bring in federal law as appropriate to the topic.

e. Restatements

The American Law Institute publishes what are called Restatements of the law in a variety of fields. You may already be familiar with the Restatements for contracts or torts from your other classes. Restatements

---

[1] A new A.L.R. series—A.L.R. International—was introduced in 2010 and addresses international law issues. As this text goes to press, it is unclear how many law libraries are adding this series to their print collections. It is not a publication that is typically available with student Lexis and Westlaw passwords.

essentially "restate" the common-law rules on a subject. Restatements have been published in the following fields:

- Agency
- Conflicts of Laws
- Contracts
- Foreign Relations Law of the United States
- Judgments
- Property
- Restitution
- Security
- Suretyship and Guaranty
- The Law Governing Lawyers
- Torts
- Trusts
- Unfair Competition.

In determining what the common-law rules are, the Restatements often look to the rules in the majority of United States jurisdictions. Sometimes, however, the Restatements will also state emerging rules where the rules seem to be changing or proposed rules in areas where the authors believe a change in the law would be appropriate. Although the Restatements are limited to common-law doctrines, the rules in the Restatements are set out almost like statutes, breaking different doctrines down into their component parts. In addition to setting out the common-law rules for a subject, the Restatements also provide commentary on the proper interpretations of the rules, illustrations demonstrating how the rules should apply in certain situations, and summaries of cases applying and interpreting the Restatement.

Although a Restatement is a secondary source, it is one with substantial weight. Courts can adopt a Restatement's view of an issue, which then makes the comments and illustrations especially persuasive in that jurisdiction. If you are researching the law of a jurisdiction that has adopted a Restatement, you can use the Restatement effectively to locate persuasive authority from other Restatement jurisdictions. As a result, a Restatement is an especially valuable secondary source.

f. Uniform Laws and Model Acts

Uniform laws and model acts are proposed statutes that can be adopted by legislatures. Two examples with which you may already be familiar are the Uniform Commercial Code (U.C.C.) and the Model Penal Code. Uniform laws and model acts are similar to Restatements in that they set out proposed rules, followed by commentary, research notes, and summaries of cases interpreting the rules. Unlike Restatements, which are limited to common-law doctrines, uniform laws and model acts exist in areas governed by statutory law.

Although uniform laws and model acts look like statutes, they are secondary sources. Their provisions do not take on the force of law unless they are adopted by a legislature. When that happens, however, the commentary, research references, and case summaries become very useful research tools. They can help you interpret the law and direct you to persuasive authority from other jurisdictions that have adopted the law.

You are most likely to research uniform laws and model acts when your project involves research into state statutes. If you decide to use this resource, you may also want to review Chapter 7, which discusses statutory research.

4. METHODS OF LOCATING SECONDARY SOURCES

You can locate secondary sources using either a source-driven or content-driven approach. If you use a source-driven approach, the first step will be deciding which type(s) of source(s) to use.

Once you know which types of secondary sources are likely to meet your research needs, you will need to locate relevant information within each source. Three common search techniques are retrieving a document from its citation, searching by subject, and executing a word search. Some secondary sources are only published in print. Few of the ones published electronically are available on the Internet. Therefore, you will use these search techniques most often either in print or in a commercial database such as Westlaw or Lexis.

If you are just beginning your research, searching by subject is often a good strategy. Most secondary sources, other than legal periodicals, have subject indices (in print) and tables of contents (in print and online). To locate legal periodicals, you can use a separate periodical index that organizes periodical citations by subject. Word searching is another search option for locating secondary sources in a full-text database and may be an option in a periodical index as well.

If you choose content-driven searching in Lexis Advance or WestlawNext, your search results will include secondary sources. In Lexis Advance, secondary sources appear under the **Secondary Materials** tab. In WestlawNext, a few secondary sources will appear on an **Overview** page summarizing your search results. You will see more results if you choose the **Secondary Sources** link from the **View** menu; this link typically appears below the links for primary authorities and court filings. When you view the secondary sources your search retrieved, you can filter the results according to a number of criteria to focus on specific publications or types of content.

Many secondary sources cross reference other secondary sources. Therefore, once you have located one secondary source on your research issue, it may refer you to other secondary sources that you can locate by citation.

Sections B and C, below, explain how to research secondary sources in print and electronically. Not all law libraries maintain print collections of all of the secondary sources discussed in this chapter. Even if you will be accessing these sources primarily (or exclusively) electronically, you may want to read the section on print research because the citation rules for these sources flow from their print formats and may make more sense to you if you understand how secondary sources are organized in print.

B. RESEARCHING SECONDARY SOURCES IN PRINT

This section discusses how to research the following secondary sources in print: legal encyclopedias, treatises, legal periodicals, *American Law Reports*, Restatements of the law, and uniform laws and model acts. It first sets out the typical print research process and then provides specifics for researching the individual types of secondary sources.

The print research process generally involves three steps: (1) using an index or table of contents to find references to material on the topic you are researching; (2) locating the material in the main text of the source; and (3) updating your research.

The first step is using an index or table of contents to find out where information on a topic is located within the secondary source. As with the index or table of contents in any other book, those in a secondary source will refer you to volumes, chapters, pages, or sections where you will find text explaining the topic you are researching. Some secondary sources consist only of a single volume. In those situations, you need simply to look up the table of contents or index references within the text. Often, however, the information in a secondary source is too comprehensive to fit within a single volume. In those cases, the source will consist of a multivolume set of books, which may be organized alphabetically by topic or numerically by volume number. The references in the index or table of contents will contain sufficient information for you to identify the appropriate book within the set, as well as the page or section number specifically relating to the topic you are researching. Locating material in the main text of the source is the second step in the process.

The final step in your research is updating the information you have located. Most secondary sources are updated with pocket parts, as described in Chapter 1. The pocket part will be organized the same way as the main volume of the source. Thus, to update your research, you need to look up the same provisions in the pocket part that you read in the main text to find any additional information on the topic. If you do not find any reference to your topic in the pocket part, there is no new information to supplement the main text.

As you will see below, there are some variations on this technique that apply to some secondary sources. For the most part, however, you will be able to use this three-step process to research a variety of secondary sources.

1. Legal Encyclopedias

Legal encyclopedias are multivolume sets organized alphabetically by topic that you can research using the three-step process described above. The indices for *American Jurisprudence*, Second Edition (Am. Jur. 2d) and *Corpus Juris Secundum* (C.J.S.) are contained in separate softcover volumes that are usually shelved at the end of the set. The index volumes are published annually, so be sure to use the most current set. You can also find information by scanning the table of contents at the beginning of each topic. State-specific encyclopedias also typically have separate index volumes and can be researched using the same process you would use with Am. Jur. 2d or C.J.S.

The example in **Figure 4.1** is from Am. Jur. 2d.

2. Treatises

Using a treatise, once you have located it, ordinarily is not difficult. With most treatises, you can use the three-step process (index, main volume, pocket part) described at the beginning of this section. The more difficult aspect of using treatises is finding one on your research topic. Your library may keep important treatises on reserve. You can also find treatises by using the online catalog for your library. Treatises will be listed in the catalog by call number with all other library holdings. Because treatises do not usually have titles identifying them as treatises, sometimes it can be difficult figuring out which listings refer to treatises. The reference librarians in your library are a great asset in this area; they should be able to recommend treatises on your subject.

Figure 4.2 is an example from a treatise on torts.

3. Legal Periodicals

Researching legal periodicals is somewhat different from researching the other secondary sources discussed in this chapter. Thousands of articles in hundreds of periodicals are published each year. Because each periodical is an independent publication, trying to find articles through the indices or tables of contents within individual publications would be impossible. Instead, you need to use an indexing service that collects references to a wide range of legal periodicals. Two print indices, the *Index to Legal Periodicals and Books* and the *Current Law Index*, will lead you to periodical articles, but they are cumbersome to use, and some libraries no longer carry them. Electronic indexing services are a better research option. The electronic version of the *Index to Legal Periodicals* (ILP) and LegalTrac, another popular indexing service, are available through most law libraries.

ILP is available as an indexing-only service, but many law libraries subscribe to ILP in a format that provides full text of some articles. ILP is

FIGURE 4.1 AM. JUR. 2d MAIN VOLUME ENTRY UNDER FALSE IMPRISONMENT

§ 1   AMERICAN JURISPRUDENCE 2D

interference with that person's personal liberty.[6]

§ 2 False arrest

Research References

West's Key Number Digest, False Imprisonment ⚮2
Am. Jur. Pleading and Practice Forms, Instructions to jury defining false
  imprisonment, False Imprisonment § 7

False arrest, a name sometimes given to the tort more generally
known as false imprisonment,[1] has been defined as the unlawful restraint by one person of the physical liberty of another by acting to
cause a false arrest, that is, an arrest made without legal authority,[2]
or without sufficient legal authority,[3] resulting in an injury.[4] The
claim usually arises from being unlawfully imprisoned through some
extrajudicial act that does not amount to legal process, such as an
unlawful detention by the police.[5] However, the tort of false arrest
does not require a formal arrest, but a manifest intent to take someone into custody and subject that person to the defendant's control.[6]
For false arrest to give rise to a cause of action, there is no requirement that the arrest be formal, that the detention be for the purpose
of arraignment, or that the detention continue until [...]
judicial officer.[7]

> References to primary authority from multiple jurisdictions

§ 3 Distinction between false imprisonment a[...]

Research References

West's Key Number Digest, False Imprisonment ⚮2

> Sections on false imprisonment

[...]me courts have stated that false arrest and false imprisonment
[...]distinguishable only in terminology.[1] The two have been called

---

[6]Phillips v. District of Columbia, 458 A.2d 722 (D.C. 1983).

[Section 2]

[1]Headrick v. Wal-Mart Stores, Inc., 293 Ark. 433, 738 S.W.2d 418 (1987); Highfill v. Hale, 186 S.W.3d 277 (Mo. 2006).

[2]Stern v. Thompson & Coates, Ltd., 185 Wis. 2d 220, 517 N.W.2d 658 (1994).

[3]Limited Stores, Inc. v. Wilson-Robinson, 317 Ark. 80, 876 S.W.2d 248 (1994).

[4]Landry v. Duncan, 902 So. 2d 1098 (La. Ct. App. 5th Cir. 2005).

[5]Snodderly v. R.U.F.F. Drug Enforcement Task Force, 239 F.3d 892

(7th Cir. 2001); Dumas v. City of New Orleans, 803 So. 2d 1001, 161 Ed. Law Rep. 713 (La. Ct. App. 4th Cir. 2001), writ denied, 811 So. 2d 912 (La. 2002).

[6]Cooper v. Dyke, 814 F.2d 941 (4th Cir. 1987).

[7]Day v. Wells Fargo Guard Service Co., 711 S.W.2d 503 (Mo. 1986).

[Section 3]

[1]Johnson v. Weiner, 155 Fla. 169, 19 So. 2d 699 (1944); Fox v. McCurnin, 205 Iowa 752, 218 N.W. 499 (1928); Holland v. Lutz, 194 Kan. 712, 401 P.2d 1015 (1965).

46

FIGURE 4.2   TREATISE MAIN VOLUME ENTRY FOR FALSE IMPRISONMENT

Topic E.   False Imprisonment

§ 36.   Simple False Imprisonment

Elements of the tort. Courts protect personal freedom of movement by imposing liability for false imprisonment. False imprisonment in its simple form[1] is established by proof that the defendant intentionally confined[2] or instigated[3] the confinement of the plaintiff. Confinement implies that the plaintiff is constrained against her will.[4] A third element, according to the Restatement and some authority, is that the plaintiff must have been aware of the confinement at the time.[5]

"False arrest." False arrest is a term that describes the setting for false imprisonment when it is committed by an officer or by one who claims the power to make an arrest. Although false arrest is not essentially different from false imprisonment,[6] detention by an officer or one acting under color of law may also amount to a civil rights violation.[7]

Burden of proof. When intent, confinement, and awareness are established, the plaintiff is entitled to recover unless the defendant can establish an affirmative defense. Many false imprisonment cases actually

> **Textual explanation of false imprisonment**

ing reasonable fear by the plaintiff for her-self or an immediate family member. In ___nt must either make a ___olate a restraining or-

§ 36

1. As to false imprisonment secondary to some other tort, see § 40.

2. Restatement § 35. Confinement, detention, restraint are all terms used; they appear to refer to the same underlying idea.

3. Deadman v. Valley Nat. Bank of Arizona, 154 Ariz. 452, 743 P.2d 961 (Ct. App. 1987); Desai v. SSM Health Care, 865 S.W.2d 833 (Mo.App.1993); Restatement § 45A. This rule explains why a physician who testifies that he examined the plaintiff and found her mentally ill when in fact he never examined her at all may be held for the plaintiff's false imprisonment when she is later confined as a mentally ill person. See Crouch v. Cameron, 414 S.W.2d 408, 30 A.L.R.3d 520 (Ky. 1967). The rule is presumably the basis for imposing liability upon one who makes a false report of crime to police in the expectation that police will arrest the plaintiff. Washington v. Farlice, 1 Cal.App.4th 766, 2 Cal.Rptr.2d 607 (1991) (defendant reported her car stolen, knowing it was rightfully in possession of plaintiff's family; plaintiff was subjected to a humiliating arrest for which defendant was liable). When the defendant instigates an inappropriate *warrant* for prosecution, however, the action must be for malicious prosecu-

> **Reference to another secondary source**

tion. See Montgomery Ward v. Wilson, 339 Md. 701, 664 A.2d 916 (1995) . Nor does a mere report of facts to ___ instigation of the arre___ Watson Company, 1___ S.E.2d 630 (1991).

4. A plaintiff who ___ apparent confinement is not confined if she can leave at any time. See Pounders v. Trinity Court Nursing Home, 265 Ark. 1, 576 S.W.2d 934, 4 A.L.R.4th 442 (1979). In other cases the plaintiff consents in advance to a confinement from which she cannot escape, in which case the confinement is real but the consent is a defense until it is properly revoked. See Day v. Providence Hospital, 622 So.2d 1273 (Ala.1993) (consent to stay overnight in locked psychiatric ward).

5. Douthit v. Jones, 619 F.2d 527 (5th Cir.1980); Parvi v. City of Kingston, 41 N.Y.2d 553, 362 N.E.2d 960, 394 N.Y.S.2d 161 (1977); Restatement §§ 35, 42; but cf. Scofield v. Critical Air Medicine, Inc., 45 Cal.App.4th 990, 52 Cal.Rptr.2d 915 (1996) (seemingly, liability without actual knowledge or actual harm). Consciousness of confinement is required only for the purely dignitary tort; the plaintiff can recover for actual harm without consciousness of confinement.

6. See, e.g., Asgari v. City of Los Angeles, 15 Cal.4th 744, 937 P.2d 273, 63 Cal. Rptr.2d 842 (1997).

7. §§ 44–48.

> **References to primary authority from multiple jurisdictions**

Reprinted with permission from Thomson Reuters/West. Dan B. Dobbs, *The Law of Torts* (2001), p. 67. © 2000 Thomson/Reuters/West.

divided into two separate databases: *Index to Legal Periodicals Retrospective*, which indexes articles from 1908 to 1980, and *Index to Legal Periodicals Full Text*, which covers articles from 1980 to the present and includes the full text of selected articles. LegalTrac indexes articles from

1980 to present and also provides access to the full text of some articles. Both services allow you to search for legal periodicals in a variety of ways, including by author, subject, or keyword. When you execute the search, you will retrieve a list of citations to articles that fit the specifications of your search. If the document is available in full text, you can access it from the appropriate link. If the search results include articles that are not available electronically, you can print a list of citations and locate the articles in print.

Figure 4.3 shows partial results of a subject search for articles on false imprisonment in LegalTrac.

The citations in ILP and LegalTrac will typically appear as follows:

Publication Name volume.issue (date) page range.

Thus, a reference to *SMU Law Review* 64.4 (Fall 2011) p1405-1431 tells you to locate the *SMU Law Review*; locate volume 64, issue number 4; and turn to page 1405. You can locate the periodical on the shelves by checking the online catalog for the call number of the publication.

FIGURE 4.3   LEGALTRAC CITATION LIST

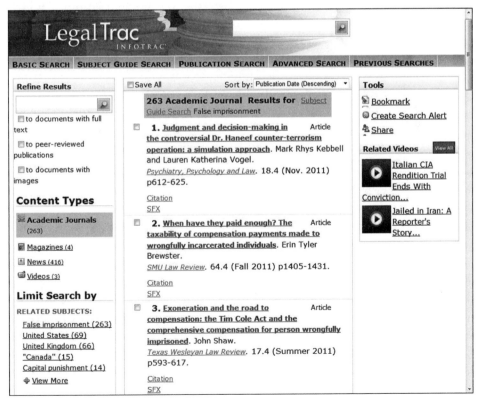

4. AMERICAN LAW REPORTS

A.L.R. Annotations can be researched using the three-step process described earlier in this chapter. Annotations can be located using the A.L.R. Index.[2] The A.L.R. Index is a separate set of index volumes usually shelved near the A.L.R. sets. It contains references to Annotations in A.L.R.2d, 3d, 4th, 5th, 6th, Fed., and Fed. 2d. The A.L.R. Index and the individual volumes in A.L.R.3d, 4th, 5th, 6th, Fed. and Fed. 2d are updated with pocket parts.

Note that A.L.R. and A.L.R.2d are, for the most part, out of date. They are also updated using special tools not applicable to any of the other A.L.R. series. Therefore, if you are researching in print, you will usually find A.L.R.3d, 4th, 5th, 6th, Fed., and Fed. 2d to be the most useful.

Figures 4.4 and **4.5** illustrate some of the features of an A.L.R. Annotation.

5. RESTATEMENTS

As noted above, the American Law Institute publishes Restatements in a number of areas of law. **Figures 4.6** and **4.7** show parts of one Restatement, the *Restatement (Second) of Torts*. There are two components to the *Restatement (Second) of Torts*: the Restatement volumes, which contain the Restatement rules, comments, and illustrations; and the Appendix volumes, which contain case summaries. To research the *Restatement (Second) of Torts*, you must follow two steps: (1) find relevant sections of the Restatement in the Restatement volumes; and (2) find case summaries interpreting the Restatement in the Appendix volumes.

In the first step, the subject index or table of contents in the Restatement volumes will direct you to individual rules within the Restatement. After the formal statement of the rule, the comments and illustrations will follow. **Figure 4.6** shows the text of § 35 of the *Restatement (Second) of Torts* on false imprisonment.

In the second step, you need to go to the separate Appendix volumes. The Appendix volumes are organized numerically by Restatement section number. By looking up the appropriate section number, you will find cases from a variety of jurisdictions interpreting that section. The Appendix volumes are not cumulative: Each volume covers only a specific period of time. Therefore, to find all of the cases interpreting a section, you would need to look it up in each Appendix volume. The latest Appendix volume will have a pocket part with the most recent references. **Figure 4.7** shows summaries of cases interpreting § 35 of the *Restatement (Second) of Torts* from the Appendix volume.

---

[2] A.L.R. also publishes "digests," which are separate finding tools from the A.L.R. Index. You do not need to use the A.L.R. digests to locate Annotations. Annotations can be located directly from the A.L.R. Index.

FIGURE 4.4   INTRODUCTORY PAGE OF AN A.L.R. ANNOTATION

Outline of the Annotation

KIDNAPPING—TAKING OF OWN CHILD   20 ALR4th
20 ALR4th 823

Kidnapping or related offense by taking or removing of child by or under authority of parent or one in loco parentis

I. PRELIMINARY MATTERS

§ 1. Introduction:
    [a] Scope
    [b] Related matters
§ 2. Summary and comment:
    [a] Generally
    [b] Practice pointers

Note that cases coming to different conclusions are summarized in the Annotation.

II. EFFECT ON CRIMINAL LIABILITY OF COURT ORDER AWARDING CUSTODY

§ 3. Absence of decree awarding custody—liability of parent or person in loco parentis
§ 4. —Liability of agent:
    [a] View that agent may be held liable
    [b] View that agent may not be held liable
    [c] View that liability of agent depends on circumstances
§ 5. Presence of decree—generally:
    [a] Parent or agent held liable or subject to liability
    [b] Parent or agent held not liable or subject to liability
§ 6. —Where parent or agent lacked actual knowledge of custody decree

III. ASSERTED DEFENSES

§ 7. Consent of custodian
§ 8. Consent of child
§ 9. Unconstitutional vagueness of criminal statute

After the outline, each Annotation has its own subject index to help you locate information within the Annotation.

INDEX

824

Reprinted with permission from Thomson Reuters/West, *American Law Reports*, 4th Ser., Vol. 20 (1983), p. 823. © 1983 Thomson Reuters/West.

FIGURE 4.5   LATER PAGE OF AN A.L.R. ANNOTATION

20 ALR4th   KIDNAPPING—TAKING OF OWN CHILD   § 4
                                        20 ALR4th 823

Citations to cases from multiple jurisdictions

Discussion of the law with a more detailed case summary

of a parent would be greater where the child passes into the hands of one having no parental obligations towards it.

For Kansas cases, see § 4[b].

In State v Brandenburg (1911) 232 Mo 531, 134 SW 529, the court, sustaining the conviction of one acting as agent of the mother, said that, under the applicable statute, the right of one parent to invade the possession of another parent, to take or decoy away their mutual offspring, if such a right exists, cannot be delegated to an agent. Under a different construction of the statute, the court reasoned, before a person could be arrested for taking a child from a parent, the parent would be required to first ascertain whether the person who took the child acted as an agent for the other parent, or was a mere kidnapper. In this case the child's mother had left the father, taking the child with her, and apparently obtained a foreign divorce. Thereafter she married the defendant. After experiencing some financial difficulties, she returned the child to the father, allegedly in return for a promise that the child would be returned to her when her situation improved. But the father instituted his own action for divorce and sought sole custody of the child. Then the defendant decoyed the child away, at a time when the father was not home, by telling the child that he was going to take it to its mother. Instead of going directly to the mother, he took the child to San Francisco where, he claimed, the mother had agreed to meet him later.

[b] View that agent may not be held liable

In the following cases the courts held or recognized that one who acts as an agent of a parent or assists a parent in taking exclusive possession of a child is not criminally liable for kidnapping or a similar crime, where there has been no court order establishing custody of the child.

Idaho—State v Beslin (1911) 19 Idaho 185, 112 P 1053.

Iowa—State v Dewey (1912) 155 Iowa 469, 136 NW 533.

Kan—State v Angel (1889) 42 Kan 216, 21 P 1075.

La—State v Elliott (1930) 171 La 306, 131 So 28.

Mich—People v Nelson (1948) 322 Mich 262, 33 NW2d 786.

NC—State v Walker (1978) 35 NC App 182, 241 SE2d 89.

NY—People v Workman (1916) 94 Misc 374, 157 NYS 594.

Or—State v Edmiston (1979) 43 Or App 13, 602 P2d 282.

Pa—Burns v Commonwealth (18) 129 Pa 138, 18 A 756; Commonwealth v Myers (1892) 146 Pa 24, 23 A 164.

In State v Angel (1889) 42 **Kan** 216, 21 P 1075, the court reversed the conviction of a man who had merely assisted a woman in leaving her husband and, in doing so, had assisted her in taking her child. The woman had wanted to leave her husband, and the man assisted by going to her house at her request and falsely saying that she was needed to help a sick child at a nearby home. The woman bundled her child and the man drove them away. After leaving, the mother had lawful charge of the child all of the time. Since there had been no judicial decree as to custody of the child, the court stated that the mother had an equal right with her husband to the actual care and control of the child; and she could not be punished under applicable kidnapping statutes. The court

831

FIGURE 4.6   SECTION 35 OF THE *RESTATEMENT (SECOND) OF TORTS*

Rule from the Restatement

Comment

§ 35   TORTS, SECOND   Ch. 2

TOPIC 4.   THE INTEREST IN FREEDOM FROM
CONFINEMENT

§ 35. False Imprisonment

(1) An actor is subject to liability to another for false imprisonment if

(a) he acts intending to confine the other or a third person within boundaries fixed by the actor, and

(b) his act directly or indirectly results in such a confinement of the other, and

(c) the other is conscious of the confinement or is harmed by it.

(2) An act which is not done with the intention stated in Subsection (1, a) does not make the actor liable to the other for a merely transitory or otherwise harmless confinement, although the act involves an unreasonable risk of imposing it and therefore would be negligent or reckless if the risk threatened bodily harm.

See Reporter's Notes.

Caveat:

The Institute expresses no opinion as to whether the actor may not be subject to liability for conduct which involves an unreasonable risk of causing a confinement of such duration or character as to make the other's loss of freedom a matter of material value.

Comment on Subsection (1):

a.   Common-law action of trespass for false imprisonment. At common law, the appropriate form of action for imposing a confinement was trespass for false imprisonment except where the confinement was by arrest under a valid process issued by a court having jurisdiction, in which case the damages for the confinement were recoverable, if at all, as part of the damages in an action of trespass on the case for malicious prosecution or abuse of process. Therefore, an act which makes the actor liable under this Section for a confinement otherwise than by arrest under a valid process is customarily called a false imprisonment.

b.   As to the meaning of the words "subject to liability," see § 5.

See Appendix for Reporter's Notes, Court Citations, and Cross References

52

FIGURE 4.7   APPENDIX VOLUME, *RESTATEMENT (SECOND) OF TORTS*

Ch. 2   CITATIONS TO RESTATEMENT SECOND   § 35

TOPIC 4. THE INTEREST IN FREEDOM FROM CONFINEMENT

C.A.1, 1995. §§ 35–45A, constituting all of Ch. 2, Topic 4, cit. in sup. and adopted. Puerto Rican resident was arrested by federal agents who mistakenly believed that she was the subject of a 1975 arrest warrant; following the dismissal of all proceedings against her, she sued the United States for false arrest. Affirming the district court's grant of summary judgment for the United States, this court held that the United States was not liable for the false arrest of plaintiff, since the name in the warrant, together with information contained in the arrest packet, provided ample basis for the arresting agents to form an objectively reasonable belief that plaintiff was the person named in the warrant. The court also held that the conduct of the federal agent responsible for instigating the errant arrest was conditionally privileged, since the arrestee was sufficiently named in the warrant and the agent reasonably believed that plaintiff was the subject of the warrant. Rodriguez v. U.S., 54 F.3d 41, 45.

> Cases interpreting § 35

§ 35. False Imprisonment

C.A.1, 1995. Cit. in ftn. Two men who were arrested and acquitted of selling cocaine sued police officers of Puerto Rico and their confidential informants for constitutional violations, alleging that defendants falsely identified them as sellers. District court held that the false-arrest claims were barred by the one-year statute of limitations and that the malicious-prosecution claims were not actionable under 42 U.S.C. § 1983. This court vacated and remanded, holding that, for purposes of determining the appropriate accrual rule, both the Fourth and Fourteenth Amendment claims more closely resembled the common law tort of malicious prosecution. Consequently, plaintiffs' § 1983 claims did not accrue until their respective criminal prosecutions ended in acquittals. Calero-Colon v. Betancourt-Lebron, 68 F.3d 1, 3.

C.A.1, 2000. Cit. in headnote, quot. in disc. After being detained by store employees who accused them of shoplifting on a prior occasion, two children and their mother sued the store for false imprisonment. District court entered judgment on jury verdict awarding plaintiffs damages. This court affirmed, holding, inter alia, that plaintiffs stated a viable false-imprisonment claim, because a reasonable jury could conclude that the store's employees intended to confine plaintiffs within boundaries fixed by the store, that the store's acts resulted in such confinement, and that plaintiffs were conscious of the confinement. Employees' direction to plaintiffs, their reference to the police, and their continued presence were enough to induce reasonable people to either believe that they would be restrained physically if they sought to leave, or that the store was claiming lawful authority to confine them until the police arrived, or both. McCann v. Wal–Mart Stores, Inc., 210 F.3d 51, 51, 53.

C.A.7, 2003. Quot. in sup. African–American store employee who was fired for allegedly stealing from a coemployee sued store for federal civil-rights violations and false imprisonment under Indiana law, alleging that store representatives locked her in her manager's office for several minutes while they investigated the theft charges. District court granted store summary judgment. This court affirmed, holding, inter alia, that plaintiff did not establish a claim of false imprisonment under Indiana law, because her several-minute confinement was accidental, and store established justification for the brief detention. No one told plaintiff that she could not leave, and store provided a reasonable explanation for having left her alone in the office: so that she could draft her written statement without distraction. Adams v. Wal–Mart Stores, Inc., 324 F.3d 935, 941.

C.A.9, 2003. Com. (a) quot. in sup. California resident who had been director of Australian corporation was extradited to Australia for criminal trial. After Australian government dropped fraud charges and jury acquitted extraditee on other charge, he sued two instrumentalities and two employees of Australian government for malicious prosecution, abuse of process, and false imprisonment. District court granted motion to dismiss for employees, but denied motion as to instrumentalities. This court reversed in part, holding that plaintiff's claims of malicious prosecution and abuse of process were barred by Foreign Sovereign Immunities Act, since plaintiff could not overcome sovereign immu-

Cit.–cited; fol.–followed; quot.–quoted; sup.–support.
A complete list of abbreviations precedes page 1.

119

6. UNIFORM LAWS AND MODEL ACTS

One of the best ways to locate uniform laws and model acts in print is through a publication entitled *Uniform Laws Annotated, Master Edition* (ULA). This is a multivolume set of books containing the text of a number of uniform laws and model acts. You can locate it through the online catalog in your library.

Once you have located the ULA set, you have several research options. To determine the best research option for your project, you should review the *Directory of Uniform Acts and Codes: Tables and Index*. This softcover booklet is published annually and explains the finding tools available in this resource. You can research uniform laws and model acts by subject, by the name of the law, or by adopting jurisdiction. Once you have located relevant information in the main volumes of the ULA set, use the pocket part to update your research.

Figure 4.8 shows a uniform law as it appears in the ULA set.

C. RESEARCHING SECONDARY SOURCES ELECTRONICALLY

1. LEXIS AND WESTLAW

Lexis and Westlaw can be useful in locating secondary sources, especially if you are looking for material that is not available in print in your law library. As this text goes to press, Lexis Advance contains relatively few secondary sources. The content is expected to increase over time. Depending on how quickly Lexis Advance expands its coverage, however, it is possible that some of the sources described in this section will only be available in Lexis.com.

Am. Jur. 2d is available in both Lexis and Westlaw, and C.J.S. is available in Westlaw. Westlaw provides the most comprehensive coverage of A.L.R. Annotations. All of the print series of A.L.R. are available in Westlaw. Westlaw also contains electronic A.L.R. Annotations ("e-annos") that are not available in print. E-annos are identified by year and number, e.g., 2005 A.L.R.6th 1. Many, but not all, are published later in bound A.L.R. volumes, at which point they also become available in print. Lexis provides access to most A.L.R. Annotations; only the first series of A.L.R. and e-annos are excluded from its coverage. Restatements of the law and a number of uniform laws and model acts are available in both services. Lexis and Westlaw provide access to many legal periodicals, but not all of them, and their periodical databases go back only until the early to mid-1980s. In addition, only a limited number of treatises can be accessed through these services. Thus, while Lexis and Westlaw are very good sources of secondary material, they are not exhaustive. You may find that these services do not provide all of the secondary material you need and must be supplemented with print research.

FIGURE 4.8   ULA ENTRY FOR THE UNIFORM SINGLE PUBLICATION ACT

UNIFORM SINGLE PUBLICATION ACT

1952 ACT

Section
1. [Limitation of Tort Actions Based on Single Publication or Utterance; Damages Recoverable].
2. [Judgment as Res Judicata].
3. [Uniformity of Interpretation].
4. [Short Title].
5. [Retroactive Effect].
6. [Time of Taking Effect].

Outline of the uniform law

Westlaw Computer Assisted Legal Research

Westlaw supplements your legal research in many ways. Westlaw allows you to
- update your research with the most current information
- expand your library with additional resources
- retrieve current, comprehensive history and citing references to a case with KeyCite

For more information on using Westlaw to supplement your research, see the Westlaw Electronic Research Guide, which follows the Preface.

Text of the law that could be adopted by a legislature

§ 1.   [Limitation of Tort Actions Based on Single Publication or Utterance; Damages Recoverable].

No person shall have more than one cause of action for damages for libel or slander or invasion of privacy or any other tort founded upon any single publication or exhibition or utterance, such as any one edition of a newspaper or book or magazine or any one presentation to an audience or any one broadcast over radio or television or any one exhibition of a motion picture. Recovery in any action shall include all damages for any such tort suffered by the plaintiff in all jurisdictions.

References to law review articles

Action in Adopting Jurisdictions

Variations from Official Text:

CALIFORNIA

In the first sentence substitutes "issue" for "edition".

NORTH DAKOTA

In the first sentence substitutes "claim for relief" for "cause of action".

Explanation of any changes to the law in adopting jurisdictions

Law Review and Journal Commentaries

the general-damage award Stan.L.Rev. 504 (1968). form Single Publication Act. 44 Cal.L.Rev. 146 (1956).

Extraterritorial jurisdiction.   57 Ill.B.J. 672 (1969).

471

FIGURE 4.8   ULA ENTRY FOR THE UNIFORM SINGLE PUBLICATION ACT *(Continued)*

§ 1   **SINGLE PUBLICATION**

Additional research references

Celebrity v. Scandal Magazine—the ce-
~~right~~ to privacy. Irivin O. Spiegel. 30
~~S~~~~.Cal.L.~~Rev. 280 (1957).

Purpose of the Uniform Single Publication
Act. 30 Cal.St.B.J. 305 (1955).

Library References

Action ⊕38(4).
Libel and Slander ⊕23 to 27.

Westlaw Topic Nos. 13, 237.
C.J.S. Actions §§ 135, 137, 195 to 196.

Westlaw Electronic Research

See Westlaw Electronic Research Guide following the Preface.

Notes of Decisions

Generally 2
Construction and application 1
Definitions 4
Knowledge statement untrue 6
Parties 9
Pleadings 10
Publication 5
Purpose of law 3
Self-publication 8
Single publication within section 7
Statute of limitations 11
Sufficiency of evidence 12

---

1. Construction and application

Summary of a case interpreting the uniform law

[Appella]t Court of Appeal may take judicial [notice of] assembly final history and senate jour-
[nal c]ontents of each to determine legislative
[intent o]f this Act. Belli v. Roberts Bros. Furs,
[Ca]l[.]App[.] 1 Dist.1966, 49 Cal.Rptr. 625, 240 Cal.
App.2d 284. Evidence ⊕ 33

2. Generally

In light of the significant First Amendment
issues implicated by claims of libel or slander or
invasion of privacy or any other tort founded
upon any single publication or exhibition or
utterance, and in recognition of the vast multiplicity of suits which could arise from mass
publications which transcend a variety of medi-
as and state lines, and the attendant problems of
choice of law, indefinite liability, and endless
tolling of the statute of limitations, courts have
interpreted the Uniform Single Publication Act
(USPA) expansively. Long v. Walt Disney Co.,
Cal.App. 2 Dist.2004, 10 Cal.Rptr.3d 836, 116
Cal.App.4th 868, 71 U.S.P.Q.2d 1523. Constitutional Law ⊕ 90.1(1); Constitutional Law ⊕
90.1(5); Libel And Slander ⊕ 26.1; Limitation
Of Actions ⊕ 5(1); Torts ⊕ 350

Illinois courts adopted single publication rule
before enactment of this Act in Illinois. Wheel-
er v. Dell Pub. Co., C.A.7 (Ill.) 1962, 300 F.2d
372. Libel And Slander ⊕ 23.1

Compelled self-defamation is not a valid
cause of action. Harrel v. Dillards Dept.

Stores, Inc., Ill.App. 5 Dist.1994, 644 N.E.2d
448, 205 Ill.Dec. 892, 268 Ill.App.3d 537, rehearing denied, appeal denied 652 N.E.2d 341,
209 Ill.Dec. 801, 162 Ill.2d 567. Libel And
Slander ⊕ 23.1

Publication is essential element of defamation
claim and requires communication of allegedly
defamatory statement to someone other than
the plaintiff. Girsberger v. Kresz, Ill.App. 1
Dist.1993, 633 N.E.2d 781, 198 Ill.Dec. 940,
261 Ill.App.3d 398, appeal denied 642 N.E.2d
1278, 205 Ill.Dec. 161, 157 Ill.2d 499. Libel
And Slander ⊕ 23.1

Rationale for Uniform Single Publication Act
is that cause of action for libel is complete at
time of first publication, and any subsequent
appearances or distributions of copies of original publication are of no consequence to cre-
ation or existence of cause of action, but are
only relevant in computing damages; thus, subsequent distribution of existing copies of original publication neither creates fresh cause of
action nor tolls applicable statute of limitations.
Founding Church of Scientology of Washington,
D. C. v. American Medical Ass'n, Ill.App. 1
Dist.1978, 377 N.E.2d 158, 18 Ill.Dec. 5, 60
Ill.App.3d 586. Action ⊕ 38(4); Limitation Of
Actions ⊕ 55(6)

3. Purpose of law

"Single publication rule" was intended to
protect communication industry from undue
harassment and unjust punishment by prevent-
ing plaintiff from filing multitude of lawsuits
based on one tortious act, and by restricting
time for commencing lawsuits, but rule permitted recovery for damages suffered by plaintiff in
all communities in which defamatory statement
had been communicated. Graham v. Today's
Spirit, Pa.1983, 468 A.2d 454, 503 Pa. 52. Action ⊕ 38(4); Libel And Slander ⊕ 113

To alleviate problem of multiplicity of causes
of action for defamation under common law,
legislature passed predecessor of "Uniform Single Publication Act"; this legislation was
adopted to eliminate successive, oppressive

472

If you have the citation to a secondary source, you can retrieve it from the citation in Westlaw or Lexis. Additional options for researching secondary sources in these services are described below. More information on researching in Lexis and Westlaw appears in Chapter 10. Examples of sources available in Lexis and Westlaw appear in the sample pages in Section E, below.

a. Westlaw.com and WestlawNext

Both Westlaw.com and WestlawNext offer source-driven search options for secondary sources. In general, if you know which type of secondary authority you want to research, you will begin a source-driven search by selecting the database for that publication.

Once you select the database, you have several search options. One option is executing a word search. Another option is searching by subject by browsing the table of contents for a secondary source. This will allow you to retrieve sections of the publication by selecting them from the table of contents without having to execute a word search. Table of contents searching is available for legal encyclopedias, treatises, Restatement rules, and many uniform laws but not for A.L.R. Annotations or legal periodicals. WestlawNext also provides access to the indices to selected secondary sources, including A.L.R.

In Westlaw.com, you can see the secondary sources available to you under the **Law School** tab or your customized tabs. You can view the table of contents for a secondary source by selecting the **Table of Contents** link next to the name of the publication. Clicking on the link to a publication will bring up a search screen, and a link to the table of contents will appear in the top right corner of the search screen. You can also use the **Site Map**. Under the list of Westlaw search features, select the **Table of Contents** option to view a list of publications for which tables of contents are available.

In WestlawNext, browse the menu options on the home page until you locate the page for the publication you want to research. You can choose **Secondary Sources** under the **All Content** tab to select a publication. You can also drill down through the **State Materials** tab to state-specific secondary sources or through the **Topics** tab for subject-specific secondary sources. On the page for an individual publication you will see the table of contents, and if the index is available, a link to the index will appear under **Tools & Resources** on the right side of the screen. To research uniform laws in *Uniform Laws Annotated* (ULA), you must select the database for that publication.

To research Restatements, remember that each Restatement consists of rules, comments, and illustrations, as well as annotations summarizing cases interpreting the rules. Westlaw combines all of the components for individual Restatements together. When you view a Restatement section, the case annotations will follow the comments and illustrations in a single document. This means that any word search you execute in a Restatement database will search for the terms in both the rules and the case annotations (unless you specifically limit the search).

When you research a Restatement in Westlaw.com, be aware that the **Restatements of the Law** database under the **Law School** tab is a combined database containing all of the Restatements. If you want to research an individual restatement, such as the *Restatement (Second) of Torts*, you must drill down through the **Directory** of databases or search for a database by name.

In WestlawNext, you do not have to select a secondary source before executing a word search. If you use a content-driven search approach, the **Secondary Sources** section of the search results will include secondary sources such as legal encyclopedias, A.L.R. Annotations, treatises, and Restatements, but will not include uniform laws. You can filter the results as you would other search results by publication type, words in the documents, and other criteria. If you pre-filter your search by jurisdiction, WestlawNext will include secondary sources from that jurisdiction in the search results, as well as resources that are not jurisdiction-specific such as Am. Jur. 2d and A.L.R.

b. Lexis.com and Lexis Advance

Both Lexis.com and Lexis Advance offer source-driven search options for secondary sources, although your options for pre-filtering by source are limited in Lexis Advance.

In Lexis.com, you will begin a source-driven search by selecting a publication as the source you want to search. Once you select the database, you have several search options. One option is executing a word search. You can also search by subject by browsing the table of contents for some secondary sources. This will allow you to retrieve sections of the publication by selecting them from the table of contents without having to execute a word search. Table of contents searching is available for legal encyclopedias, treatises, Restatement rules, and many uniform laws but not for A.L.R. Annotations or legal periodicals. In Lexis.com, if you select a source for which the table of contents is available, the table of contents will be displayed with the search screen. Index searching is not available in Lexis.com.

To research Restatements, remember that each Restatement consists of rules, comments, and illustrations, as well as annotations summarizing cases interpreting the rules. In Lexis.com, the Restatement rules and the case citations are in separate databases. You can execute word searches or browse the table of contents in the rules databases, but word searching is the only option in the databases with case annotations. You have the option to execute a word search in both rules and case annotation databases simultaneously, with search results divided between those from the rules database and those from the case annotation database.

As this text goes to press, Lexis Advance will not allow you to select a specific secondary source to research. Using the drop-down menu, you can pre-filter your results by selecting **Secondary Materials**, which will search a range of secondary sources. If you choose a content-driven search for multiple forms of authority, the search results will include secondary sources such as law review articles and treatises under the **Analytical Materials** tab.

2. Subscription Services for Legal Periodicals

As noted earlier in this chapter, two electronic periodical indices, the *Index to Legal Periodicals* (ILP) and LegalTrac, provide access to some legal periodicals. These services index a wide range of periodicals, but their full text access is more limited. Articles in either of these services may be available in html format, .pdf format, or both, depending on the publication. For information about the search options available in ILP and LegalTrac, you may want to refer back to the discussion of these services in Section B, above.

HeinOnline is another service that provides electronic access to legal periodicals, among other types of authority. Many law libraries subscribe to this service; users generally access it through the library portal. HeinOnline's holdings go back further in time than those of ILP, LegalTrac, Lexis, or Westlaw, often dating back to the inception of the periodicals in its database. You can search for legal periodical articles in HeinOnline in several ways. You can retrieve an article from its citation, search by title or author, or conduct word searches in the full text of the articles in HeinOnline's database. You can also browse the table of contents of individual publications. HeinOnline displays articles in .pdf format.

Figure 4.9 shows the HeinOnline display of a legal periodical article.

3. Internet Sources

You use publicly accessible Internet sites on a daily basis for news, entertainment, shopping, and many other purposes. It is natural, therefore, to think of using the Internet for legal research as well. You may decide to use general Internet sources as one component of your research strategy, but you would not want that to be your sole approach for locating secondary material on an issue.

FIGURE 4.9   HEINONLINE DISPLAY OF A LEGAL PERIODICAL ARTICLE

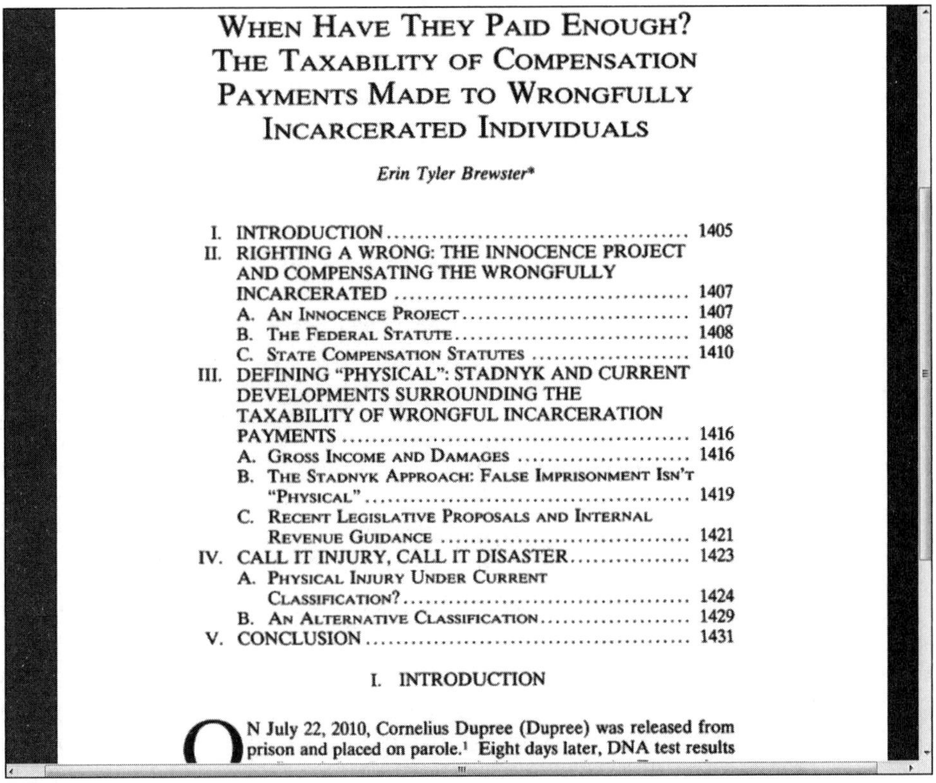

From HeinOnline. © 2012 HeinOnline. Reproduced with permission.

Legal encyclopedias, treatises, and A.L.R. Annotations are not available via publicly accessible Internet sites. You may be able to find some uniform laws or model acts and selected sections of Restatements on the Internet, but you will not generally find complete compilations of these sources, nor will you find the comments, illustrations, or annotations.

A significant amount of recent legal scholarship in law reviews and journals is available on the Internet through the Social Science Research Network (SSRN). SSRN provides free access to scholarly articles in a number of fields, including law. Authors make their published work and ongoing research available by posting it on SSRN. Because SSRN relies on authors to post their own work, its coverage is somewhat idiosyncratic, but a large number of legal academics have posted their entire publishing histories. You can research articles on SSRN in a number of ways, including by keyword or author. The Internet address for SSRN appears in Appendix A.

General legal research websites may also contain links to legal periodicals. Google Scholar, a specialty version of Google's search engine described in more detail in Chapter 5, allows you to search for law journal articles. Often, however, access to the full text requires a subscription to the service (such as HeinOnline) that hosts the article. A few law schools publish special online versions of their law journals. Many make at least their current volume, and often prior volumes, available on their websites. If you have the citation or title of an article that is available on the Internet, this can be a quick and economical way to obtain it. Searching individually by publication, especially for material that is more than a couple of years old, is not likely to be an effective strategy.

The secondary sources discussed so far in this chapter are the traditional sources used for legal research, but many non-traditional secondary sources are now available on the Internet. Sources such as Wikipedia contain information about the law. Free legal research sites like FindLaw often include articles written by lawyers or legal commentators. Using a search engine such as Google could retrieve a pathfinder or bibliography compiled by a law librarian that lists sources on an area of law. These non-traditional Internet sources are secondary sources, and all of the caveats regarding appropriate uses of traditional legal secondary sources apply to them with equal force. Lawyers do not consider these sources authoritative, and it is difficult to imagine circumstances under which you would cite one.

Using publicly available Internet sites can be both easier and harder than using more traditional legal research tools. It can be easier in the sense that Internet sources are cost-effective to use and can provide easy access to information relevant to your research. It can be harder in the sense that you cannot assume that a non-traditional secondary source is reliable. It is important to remember that any person with a message and the appropriate equipment can publish material on the Internet. Because electronic sources can be updated at any time, they may be perceived as providing current information even if they have not been updated for a long period of time. Therefore, you must take special care to evaluate any secondary information you find on the Internet. Chapter 10, on electronic legal research, discusses publicly available websites, blogs, and other Internet-based research sources. You may want to review that chapter before using the Internet to locate non-traditional secondary sources. In addition, Appendix A lists Internet sites that may be useful for secondary source research.

D. CITING SECONDARY SOURCES

The chart in **Figure 4.10** lists the rules in the *ALWD Manual* (4th ed.) and the *Bluebook* (19th ed.) governing citations to secondary sources. Citations to each of these sources are discussed in turn.

FIGURE 4.10   RULES FOR CITING SECONDARY SOURCES

SECONDARY SOURCE	ALWD MANUAL (4th ed.)	BLUEBOOK (19th ed.)
Legal encyclopedias	Rule 26	Bluepages B8
Treatises	Rule 22	Bluepages B8
Legal periodicals	Rule 23	Bluepages B9
A.L.R. Annotations	Rule 24	Rule 16.7.6
Restatements	Rule 27	Bluepages B5.1.3
Uniform laws & Model acts	Rule 27	Uniform laws—Bluepages B5.1.3; see also Rule 12.9.4 Model acts—Rule 12.9.5

1. LEGAL ENCYCLOPEDIAS

Citations to legal encyclopedias are covered in *ALWD Manual* Rule 26 and *Bluebook* Bluepages B8 and are the same using either format. The citation consists of five elements: (1) the volume number; (2) the abbreviated name of the encyclopedia; (3) the name of the topic, underlined or italicized; (4) the section cited (with a space between the section symbol (§) and the section number); and (5) a parenthetical containing the date of the book, including, if appropriate, the date of the pocket part or supplement. Here is an example:

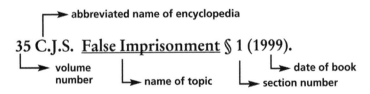

Sometimes determining which date or dates to include in the parenthetical can be confusing. The answer is always a function of where a reader would have to look to find all of the text and footnote information on the section you are citing. If all of the information appears in the main volume of the encyclopedia, the date in the parenthetical should refer only to the main volume. If the section is a new section that appears only in the pocket part, the date should refer only to the pocket part. If the reader must refer both to the main volume and to the pocket part, the parenthetical should list both dates. Here are several examples:

35 C.J.S. <u>False Imprisonment</u> § 1 (1999).

In this example, the reference is only to the main volume.

35 C.J.S. <u>False Imprisonment</u> § 1 (1999 & Supp. 2012).

In this example, the reference is both to the main volume and to the pocket part.

32 Am. Jur. 2d <u>False Imprisonment</u> § 1 (Supp. 2012).

In this example, the reference is only to the pocket part.

2. TREATISES

Citations to treatises contain roughly the same elements in both *ALWD Manual* and *Bluebook* formats. There are a few differences between them, however, and the order of the elements varies in minor respects.

In the *ALWD Manual*, citations to treatises are covered in Rule 22 and consist of four elements: (1) the author's full name (if the treatise has more than two authors, you may list the first, followed by et al.); (2) the title of the treatise, underlined or italicized; (3) a pinpoint reference containing the volume of the treatise (in a multivolume treatise), the section cited (with a space between the section symbol (§) and the section number), and the specific page or pages cited; and (4) a parenthetical containing the edition (if more than one edition has been published), the publisher, and the date, including, if appropriate, the date of the pocket part. Here is an example in *ALWD Manual* format:

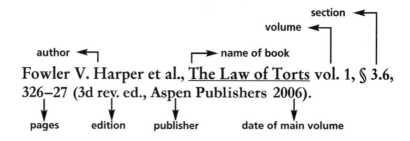

In the *Bluebook*, citations to treatises are covered in Bluepages B8 and consist of five elements: (1) the volume number of the treatise (in a multivolume set); (2) the author's full name (if the treatise has more than two authors, list the first, followed by et al.); (3) the title of the treatise, underlined or italicized; (4) the section cited (with a space between the section symbol (§) and the section number); and (5) a parenthetical containing the edition (if more than one edition has been published) and the date, including, if appropriate, the date of the pocket part. Here is an example in *Bluebook* format:

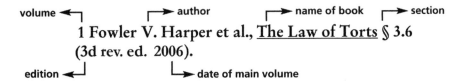

1 Fowler V. Harper et al., <u>The Law of Torts</u> § 3.6 (3d rev. ed. 2006).

Note that in both citation formats, a comma separates the part of the citation identifying the author or authors from the title of the treatise. No other commas appear in a *Bluebook* citation. In an *ALWD Manual* citation, commas also separate the components of the pinpoint reference, as well as the edition and publisher's name in the parenthetical.

Both the *ALWD Manual* and the *Bluebook* have additional requirements for books with editors or translators.

3. LEGAL PERIODICALS

Legal periodicals are published in two formats. Some publications begin the first issue within each volume with page one and continue numbering the pages of subsequent issues within that volume consecutively. These are called consecutively paginated publications. Most law reviews and journals are consecutively paginated. Other publications, such as monthly magazines, begin each new issue with page one, regardless of where the issue falls within the volume. These are called nonconsecutively paginated publications.

There are some differences in the citations to articles published in consecutively and nonconsecutively paginated periodicals. The explanation in this section focuses on citations to articles published in consecutively paginated law reviews, which are covered in *ALWD Manual* Rule 23 and *Bluebook* Bluepages B9.

A citation to a law review article in both *ALWD Manual* and *Bluebook* formats consists of seven elements: (1) the author's full name; (2) the title of the article, underlined or italicized; (3) the volume number of the publication; (4) the abbreviated name of the publication; (5) the starting page of the article; (6) the pinpoint citation to the specific page or pages cited; and (7) a parenthetical containing the date of the publication. Here is an example:

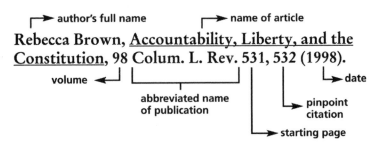

Rebecca Brown, <u>Accountability, Liberty, and the Constitution</u>, 98 Colum. L. Rev. 531, 532 (1998).

Note that the author's name, the name of the article, and the starting page of the article are followed by commas. The comma following the name of the article is not underlined or italicized.

Publication abbreviations can be found in *ALWD Manual* Appendix 5 and *Bluebook* Table T13. Notice that the periodical abbreviations in *Bluebook* Table T13 appear in large and small capital letters. According to Bluepages B1, however, you should not use large and small capitals when citing authority in a brief or memorandum. Use ordinary roman type for the publication's name. Both the *ALWD Manual* and the *Bluebook* have additional rules for citing articles appearing in nonconsecutively paginated publications, articles written by students, and articles with more than one author.

4. A.L.R. ANNOTATIONS

Citations to A.L.R. Annotations are covered in *ALWD Manual* Rule 24 and *Bluebook* Rule 16.7.6. They are almost identical in both formats, with only one minor difference between them. A citation to an A.L.R. Annotation consists of seven elements: (1) the author's full name (in a *Bluebook* citation, the author's name is followed by the notation "Annotation"); (2) the title of the Annotation, underlined or italicized; (3) the volume number; (4) the A.L.R. series; (5) the starting page of the Annotation; (6) the pinpoint citation to the specific page or pages cited; and (7) a parenthetical containing the date, including, if appropriate, the date of the pocket part. Here is an example in *ALWD Manual* format:

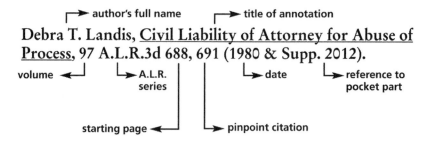

Here is an example in *Bluebook* format:

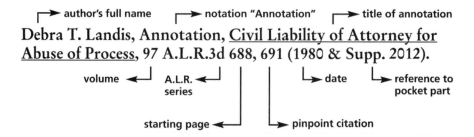

Although the example in *Bluebook* Rule 16.7.6 shows A.L.R. Fed. in large and small capital letters, use ordinary roman type pursuant to Bluepages B1 for a citation in a memorandum or brief.

5. RESTATEMENTS

Citations to Restatements are covered in *ALWD Manual* Rule 27 and *Bluebook* Bluepages B5.1.3. They contain three elements using either format: (1) the name of the Restatement; (2) the section cited (with a space between the section symbol (§) and the section number); and (3) a parenthetical containing the date. The only difference is that the name of the Restatement is underlined or italicized in *ALWD Manual* format, but not in *Bluebook* format. Here is an example in *ALWD Manual* format:

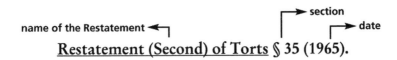

<u>Restatement (Second) of Torts</u> § 35 (1965).

Here is an example in *Bluebook* format:

name of the Restatement ◄┐　　　　　　　┌► section
　　　　　　　　　　　　　　　　┌► date

Restatement (Second) of Torts § 35 (1965).

6. UNIFORM LAWS AND MODEL ACTS

The citation format for a uniform law depends on whether the law has been adopted by a jurisdiction. If a jurisdiction adopts a uniform law, the law will be published with all of the other statutes for that jurisdiction. In that situation, cite directly to the jurisdiction's statute. The requirements for statutory citations are explained in Chapter 7.

Citations to uniform laws published in the ULA set are governed by *ALWD Manual* Rule 27. In the *Bluebook*, Bluepages B5.1.3 gives an example of a citation to a uniform law; additional information on citing laws published in the ULA set appears in Rule 12.9.4. The citation is the same using either format and consists of six elements: (1) the abbreviated title of the act; (2) the section cited (with a space between the section symbol (§) and section number); (3) the ULA volume number; (4) the abbreviation "U.L.A."; (5) the page of the ULA on which the section appears; and (6) a parenthetical containing the date of the ULA volume, including, if appropriate, the date of the pocket part. Here is an example:

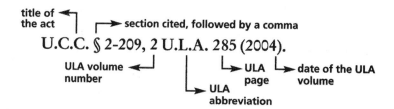

Citations to model acts are covered in *ALWD Manual* Rule 27 and *Bluebook* Rule 12.9.5. Model act citations are almost identical in both formats, with only one minor difference between them. The citation consists of three elements: (1) the name of the act; (2) the section cited (with a space between the section symbol (§) and the section number); and (3) a parenthetical.

In *ALWD Manual* citations, the parenthetical contains the name of the organization that issued the act, abbreviated according to Appendix 3, and the date. Here is an example in *ALWD Manual* format:

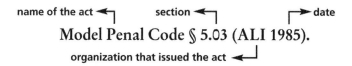

The *Bluebook* requires that the parenthetical include the name of the organization that issued the act for some model acts, but not others. In all model act citations, however, the *Bluebook* requires the date in the parenthetical. Here is an example in *Bluebook* format:

name of the act ◄┐   section ◄┐
Model Penal Code § 5.03 (1985).
date ◄┘

The examples of citations to uniform laws and model acts in Rules 12.9.4 and 12.9.5 show the names of the laws in large and small capital letters. According to Bluepages B1, however, you should use ordinary roman type to cite these authorities in a memorandum or brief.

E. SAMPLE PAGES FOR SECONDARY SOURCE RESEARCH

Beginning on the next page, **Figures 4.11** through **4.16** are sample pages from Am. Jur. 2d and A.L.R showing what you would see in the books if you had researched false imprisonment. **Figures 4.17** through **4.20** show documents and search options in Lexis and Westlaw.

To locate information with Am. Jur. 2d, begin by looking up your subject in the latest index volume. The index entries will refer you to the subject name and section number(s) with relevant information.

FIGURE 4.11   INDEX TO AM. JUR. 2d

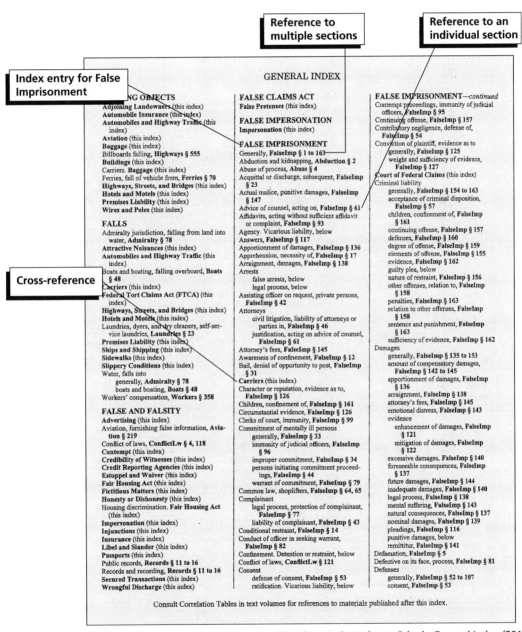

Reference to multiple sections

Reference to an individual section

Index entry for False Imprisonment

Cross-reference

GENERAL INDEX

...NG OBJECTS
Adjoining Landowners (this index)
Automobile Insurance (this index)
Automobiles and Highway Traffic (this index)
Aviation (this index)
Baggage (this index)
Billboards falling, **Highways § 555**
Buildings (this index)
Carriers. **Baggage** (this index)
Ferries, fall of vehicle from, **Ferries § 70**
Highways, Streets, and Bridges (this index)
Hotels and Motels (this index)
Premises Liability (this index)
Wires and Poles (this index)

FALLS
Admiralty jurisdiction, falling from land into water, **Admiralty § 78**
Attractive Nuisances (this index)
Automobiles and Highway Traffic (this index)
Boats and boating, falling overboard, **Boats § 48**
Carriers (this index)
Federal Tort Claims Act (FTCA) (this index)
Highways, Streets, and Bridges (this index)
Hotels and Motels (this index)
Laundries, dyers, and dry cleaners, self-service laundries, **Laundries § 23**
Premises Liability (this index)
Ships and Shipping (this index)
Sidewalks (this index)
Slippery Conditions (this index)
Water, falls into
    generally, **Admiralty § 78**
    boats and boating, **Boats § 48**
Workers' compensation, **Workers § 358**

FALSE AND FALSITY
Advertising (this index)
Aviation, furnishing false information, **Aviation § 219**
Conflict of laws, **ConflictLw § 4, 118**
Contempt (this index)
Credibility of Witnesses (this index)
Credit Reporting Agencies (this index)
Estoppel and Waiver (this index)
Fair Housing Act (this index)
Fictitious Matters (this index)
Honesty or Dishonesty (this index)
Housing discrimination. **Fair Housing Act** (this index)
Impersonation (this index)
Injunctions (this index)
Insurance (this index)
Libel and Slander (this index)
Passports (this index)
Public records, **Records § 11 to 16**
Records and recording, **Records § 11 to 16**
Secured Transactions (this index)
Wrongful Discharge (this index)

FALSE CLAIMS ACT
False Pretenses (this index)

FALSE IMPERSONATION
Impersonation (this index)

FALSE IMPRISONMENT
Generally, **FalseImp § 1 to 163**
Abduction and kidnapping, **Abduction § 2**
Abuse of process, **Abuse § 4**
Acquittal or discharge, subsequent, **FalseImp § 23**
Actual malice, punitive damages, **FalseImp § 147**
Advice of counsel, acting on, **FalseImp § 61**
Affidavits, acting without sufficient affidavit or complaint, **FalseImp § 93**
Agency. Vicarious liability, below
Answers, **FalseImp § 117**
Apportionment of damages, **FalseImp § 136**
Apprehension, necessity of, **FalseImp § 17**
Arraignment, damages, **FalseImp § 138**
Arrests
    false arrests, below
    legal process, below
Assisting officer on request, private persons, **FalseImp § 42**
Attorneys
    civil litigation, liability of attorneys or parties in, **FalseImp § 46**
    justification, acting on advice of counsel, **FalseImp § 61**
Attorney's fees, **FalseImp § 145**
Awareness of confinement, **FalseImp § 12**
Bail, denial of opportunity to post, **FalseImp § 31**
Carriers (this index)
Character or reputation, evidence as to, **FalseImp § 126**
Children, confinement of, **FalseImp § 161**
Circumstantial evidence, **FalseImp § 126**
Clerks of court, immunity, **FalseImp § 99**
Commitment of mentally ill persons
    generally, **FalseImp § 33**
    immunity of judicial officers, **FalseImp § 96**
    improper commitment, **FalseImp § 34**
    persons initiating commitment proceedings, **FalseImp § 44**
    warrant of commitment, **FalseImp § 79**
Common law, shoplifters, **FalseImp § 64, 65**
Complainant
    legal process, protection of complainant, **FalseImp § 77**
    liability of complainant, **FalseImp § 43**
Conditional restraint, **FalseImp § 14**
Conduct of officer in seeking warrant, **FalseImp § 82**
Confinement. Detention or restraint, below
Conflict of laws, **ConflictLw § 121**
Consent
    defense of consent, **FalseImp § 53**
    ratification. Vicarious liability, below

FALSE IMPRISONMENT—*continued*
Contempt proceedings, immunity of judicial officers, **FalseImp § 95**
Continuing offense, **FalseImp § 157**
Contributory negligence, defense of, **FalseImp § 54**
Conviction of plaintiff, evidence as to
    generally, **FalseImp § 125**
    weight and sufficiency of evidence, **FalseImp § 127**
Court of Federal Claims (this index)
Criminal liability
    generally, **FalseImp § 154 to 163**
    acceptance of criminal disposition, **FalseImp § 57**
    children, confinement of, **FalseImp § 161**
    continuing offense, **FalseImp § 157**
    defenses, **FalseImp § 160**
    degree of offense, **FalseImp § 159**
    elements of offense, **FalseImp § 155**
    evidence, **FalseImp § 162**
    guilty plea, below
    nature of restraint, **FalseImp § 156**
    other offenses, relation to, **FalseImp § 158**
    penalties, **FalseImp § 163**
    relation to other offenses, **FalseImp § 158**
    sentence and punishment, **FalseImp § 163**
    sufficiency of evidence, **FalseImp § 162**
Damages
    generally, **FalseImp § 135 to 153**
    amount of compensatory damages, **FalseImp § 142 to 145**
    apportionment of damages, **FalseImp § 136**
    arraignment, **FalseImp § 138**
    attorney's fees, **FalseImp § 145**
    emotional distress, **FalseImp § 143**
    evidence
        enhancement of damages, **FalseImp § 121**
        mitigation of damages, **FalseImp § 122**
    excessive damages, **FalseImp § 140**
    foreseeable consequences, **FalseImp § 137**
    future damages, **FalseImp § 144**
    inadequate damages, **FalseImp § 140**
    legal process, **FalseImp § 138**
    mental suffering, **FalseImp § 143**
    natural consequences, **FalseImp § 137**
    nominal damages, **FalseImp § 139**
    pleadings, **FalseImp § 116**
    punitive damages, below
    remittitur, **FalseImp § 141**
Defamation, **FalseImp § 5**
Defective on its face, process, **FalseImp § 81**
Defenses
    generally, **FalseImp § 52 to 107**
    consent, **FalseImp § 53**

Consult Correlation Tables in text volumes for references to materials published after this index.

Once you have references from the index, locate the relevant subject volume, and turn to the section(s) you want to read. The text will explain general principles applicable to your topic, and the footnotes will provide references to primary and secondary authority.

FIGURE 4.12   AM. JUR. 2d MAIN VOLUME ENTRY UNDER FALSE IMPRISONMENT

---

§ 1   AMERICAN JURISPRUDENCE 2D

interference with that person's personal liberty.[6]

§ 2   False arrest

Research References
West's Key Number Digest, False Imprisonment ⟜2
Am. Jur. Pleading and Practice Forms, Instructions to jury defining false imprisonment, False Imprisonment § 7

False arrest, a name sometimes given to the tort more generally known as false imprisonment,[1] has been defined as the unlawful restraint by one person of the physical liberty of another by acting to cause a false arrest, that is, an arrest made without legal authority,[2] or without sufficient legal authority,[3] resulting in an injury.[4] The claim usually arises from being unlawfully imprisoned through some extrajudicial act that does not amount to legal process, such as an unlawful detention by the police.[5] However, the tort of false arrest does not require a formal arrest, but a manifest intent to take someone into custody and subject that person to the defendant's control.[6] For false arrest to give rise to a cause of action, there is no requirement that the arrest be formal, that the detention be for the purpose of arraignment, or that the detention continue until judicial officer.[7]

§ 3   Distinction between false imprisonment a[n]

Research References
West's Key Number Digest, False Imprisonment ⟜2

[So]me courts have stated that false arrest and false imprisonment [are] distinguishable only in terminology.[1] The two have been called

> **References to primary authority from multiple jurisdictions**

> **Sections on false imprisonment**

---

[6]Phillips v. District of Columbia, 458 A.2d 722 (D.C. 1983).

[Section 2]

[1]Headrick v. Wal-Mart Stores, Inc., 293 Ark. 433, 738 S.W.2d 418 (1987); Highfill v. Hale, 186 S.W.3d 277 (Mo. 2006).

[2]Stern v. Thompson & Coates, Ltd., 185 Wis. 2d 220, 517 N.W.2d 658 (1994).

[3]Limited Stores, Inc. v. Wilson-Robinson, 317 Ark. 80, 876 S.W.2d 248 (1994).

[4]Landry v. Duncan, 902 So. 2d 1098 (La. Ct. App. 5th Cir. 2005).

[5]Snodderly v. R.U.F.F. Drug Enforcement Task Force, 239 F.3d 892

(7th Cir. 2001); Dumas v. City of New Orleans, 803 So. 2d 1001, 161 Ed. Law Rep. 713 (La. Ct. App. 4th Cir. 2001), writ denied, 811 So. 2d 912 (La. 2002).

[6]Cooper v. Dyke, 814 F.2d 941 (4th Cir. 1987).

[7]Day v. Wells Fargo Guard Service Co., 711 S.W.2d 503 (Mo. 1986).

[Section 3]

[1]Johnson v. Weiner, 155 Fla. 169, 19 So. 2d 699 (1944); Fox v. McCurnin, 205 Iowa 752, 218 N.W. 499 (1928); Holland v. Lutz, 194 Kan. 712, 401 P.2d 1015 (1965).

46

Reprinted with permission from Thomson Reuters/West, *American Jurisprudence*, 2d ed., Vol. 32 (2007), p. 46.
© 2007 Thomson Reuters/West.

To update, check the pocket part. The pocket part is organized by topic name and section number.

FIGURE 4.13   AM. JUR. 2d POCKET PART ENTRY FOR FALSE IMPRISONMENT

No new reseach references are listed for § 2.

FALSE IMPRISONMENT

KeyCite®: Cases and other legal materials listed in KeyCite Scope can be researched through the KeyCite service on Westlaw®. Use KeyCite to check citations for form, parallel references, prior and later history, and comprehensive citator information, including citations to other decisions and secondary materials.

I. CIVIL ACTIONS

B. ELEMENTS

2. Detention or Restraint

§ 15 Period of confinement

Cases
Even if existence of exigent circumstances could have required release of airline passengers during nine hour tarmac delay, passenger presented insufficient facts to show that airline acted without legal authority as required under Texas law to support false imprisonment claim arising from delay; passenger presented no statute or regulation that placed limit on number of hours airline was permitted to keep passengers aboard airplane, and while airplane became "stuffy" and "smelly" during delay, passengers received only limited refreshments, and one of airplane's lavatories stopped working, passenger did not complain of any of this to any member of the flight crew, and moreover, passenger turned down two opportunities to deplane. Ray v. American Airlines, Inc., 609 F.3d 917 (8th Cir. 2010).

3. Unlawfulness of Detention or Restraint

b. Conduct Making Arrest Unlawful

(1) In Making Arrest

§ 28 Use of excessive force

Cases
Bureau of Alcohol, Tobacco, Firearms, and Explosives (ATF) agent who fired two shots at passenger in fleeing motor vehicle was entitled to qualified immunity from liability, in passenger's Fourth Amendment excessive force claim; agent's conduct did not violate clearly established law, as vehicle posed immediate threat of death to agent, as it was moving towards him in confined area. U.S.C.A. Const.Amend. 4. Thomas v. Durastanti, 607 F.3d 655 (10th Cir. 2010).
Degree of force used to arrest individual for violating leash law and assaulting a police officer was not so excessive that no reasonable officer could have believed in the lawfulness of his actions; arrestee's refusal to obey officer's order prior to his arrest suggested that he might try to resist or escape, and arrestee suffered no bruise or injury. Wasserman v. Rodacker, 557 F.3d 635 (D.C. Cir. 2009).
Court, in addressing overlapping excessive force and unlawful arrest claims, must engage in a two-part inquiry addressing whether was there an unlawful arrest, and, if there was an unlawful arrest, whether the amount of force used was greater than what would have been necessary to affect a lawful arrest. U.S.C.A. Const.Amend. 4. Sisneros v. Fisher, 685 F. Supp. 2d 1188 (D.N.M. 2010).

C. LIABILITY OF PARTICULAR PERSONS

2. Persons Procuring or Participating in Arrest

§ 40 Private persons instigating arrest by officer

Cases
Neither store nor store supervisor was liable for instigating arrestee's subsequent imprisonment or for procuring criminal theft proceedings against him, and thus, neither store nor supervisor was liable for false imprisonment or malicious prosecution; there was no indication that store or supervisor knowingly provided false information to the police, at no time did store or supervisor do much more than report a crime and mistakenly identify the wrong person, and neither store nor supervisor pressured officer to refer the case to the district attorney's office, and choice to detain and arrest arrestee was made by the police department. Dangerfield v. Ormsby, 264 S.W.3d 904 (Tex. App. Fort Worth 2008).

§ 41 Private persons instigating arrest by officer—What constitutes direction or instigation

Cases
A civilian complainant, by merely seeking police assistance or furnishing information to law enforcement authorities who are then free to exercise their own judgment as to whether an arrest should be made and criminal charges filed, will not be held liable for false arrest or malicious prosecution under New York law. Kraft v. City of New York, 696 F. Supp. 2d 403 (S.D. N.Y. 2010).

To locate an A.L.R. Annotation, begin by looking up your subject in the A.L.R. Index. The A.L.R. Index will refer you to Annotations. The reference will tell you the volume number, series, and starting page of the Annotation. This example refers you to an Annotation that contains information about whether a parent who takes a child without permission commits false imprisonment.

FIGURE 4.14   A.L.R. INDEX

ALR INDEX

FALLS AND FALLING OBJECTS —Cont'd
Workers' compensation—Cont'd
postaccident conduct by employer, employer's insurer, or employer's employees in relation to workers' compensation claim as waiving, or estopping employer from asserting, exclusivity otherwise afforded by workers' compensation statute, **120 ALR5th 513**
presumption or inference that accidental death of employee engaged in occupation of manufacturing or processing arose out of and in course of employment, **47 ALR5th 801**
receipts, injuries incurred while traveling to or from work with employer's receipts, **63 ALR4th 253**
travel, right to worker's compensation for injury suffered by worker en route to or from worker's home where home is claimed as "work situs," **15 ALR6th 633**

FALSE ALARMS
Alarm systems, liability of person furnishing, installing, or servicing burglary or fire alarm system for burglary or fire loss, **37 ALR4th 47**
Penalties, validity and construction of statutes or ordinances imposing civil or criminal penalties on alarm system users, installers, or servicers for false alarms, **17 ALR5th 825**

FALSE ARREST
False Imprisonment and Arrest (this index)

FALSE CLAIMS ACT
Attorney-client privilege, privilege of communication to attorney by client in attempt to establish false claim, **9 ALR 1081**
Corporation's vicarious liability for fraud of its agent under False Claims Act (31 U.S.C.A. § 3729-3733), **107 ALR Fed 665**

FALSE CLAIMS ACT—Cont'd
Damages, measure and elements of damages under False Claims Act (31 U.S.C.A. § 231 et seq.), **35 ALR Fed 805**
Jurisdictional bars, construction and application of "public disclosure" and "original source" jurisdictional bars under 31 U.S.C.A. § 3730(e)(4) (civil actions for false claims), **117 ALR Fed 263**
Measure and elements of damages under False Claims Act (31 U.S.C.A. § 231 et seq.), **35 ALR Fed 805**
Reverse false claim provision, construction and application of "reverse false claim provision" of False Claims Act (31 U.S.C.A. § 3729(a)(7)), **162 ALR Fed 147**
Specific intent to defraud government as necessary to impose liability under provisions of False Claims Act (31 U.S.C.A. § 231) pertaining to false or fictitious claims or statements, **26 ALR Fed 307**
When is claim upon or against the United States so as to sustain civil liability under False Claims Act (31 U.S.C.A. § 231), **59 ALR Fed 886**

FALSE IMPRISONMENT AND ARREST
Abduction and kidnapping
authority of parent or one in loco parentis, taking under, **20 ALR4th 823**
foreign country, district court jurisdiction over criminal suspect who was abducted in foreign country and returned to United States for trial or sentencing, **64 ALR Fed 292**
included offense within charge of kidnapping, **68 ALR3d 828**
prison official, seizure by inmates as kidnapping, **59 ALR3d 1306**
separate offense, seizure or detention for purpose of committing rape, robbery, or other offense as constituting separate crime of kidnapping, **39 ALR5th 283**

Index entry for false imprisonment

Reference to an Annotation

Consult POCKET PART for Later Annotations

The Annotation will begin with a list of research references, an outline of the Annotation, and an alphabetical index of topics within the Annotation.

FIGURE 4.15   A.L.R. ANNOTATION

ANNOTATION

KIDNAPPING OR RELATED OFFENSE BY TAKING OR REMOVING OF CHILD BY OR UNDER AUTHORITY OF PARENT OR ONE IN LOCO PARENTIS

by

William B. Johnson, J.D.

References to other research sources, including Am. Jur. 2d

TOTAL CLIENT-SERVICE LIBRARY® REFERENCES

1 Am Jur 2d, Abduction and Kidnapping § 19; 24 Am Jur 2d, Divorce and Separation §§ 801–804, 811 59 Am Jur 2d, Parent and Child §§ 108–110

Annotations: See the related matters listed in the annotation, infra.

19 Am Jur Pl & Pr Forms (Rev), Parent and Child, Forms 62–65

13 Am Jur Legal Forms 2d, Parent and Child § 191:53

15 Am Jur Proof of Facts 1, Child Custody; 1 Am Jur Proof of Facts 2d, 41 Change in Circumstances Justifying Modification of Child Support Order; 2 Am Jur Proof of Facts 2d 791, Denial of Child Visitation Rights

2 Am Jur Trials 171, Investigating Particular Crimes; 22 Am Jur Trials 347, Child Custody Litigation

18 USCS § 1201

US L Ed Digest, Abduction and Kidnapping § 1

L Ed Index to Annos, Abduction; Children and Minors; False Imprisonment; Kidnapping

ALR Quick Index, Abduction and Kidnapping; Children; Custody and Support of Children; False Imprisonment or Arrest; Uniform Child Custody Jurisdiction Act

Federal Quick Index, Abduction and Kidnapping; Children and Minors; Custody of Children; Divorce and Separation; False Imprisonment and Arrest

Consult POCKET PART in this volume for later cases

FIGURE 4.15   A.L.R. ANNOTATION (Continued)

Outline of the
Annotation

Note that cases coming to
different conclusions are
summarized in the Annotation.

KIDNAPPING—TAKING OF OWN CHILD   20 ALR4th
20 ALR4th 823

**Kidnapping or related offense by taking or removing of child by or
under authority of parent or one in loco parentis**

I. PRELIMINARY MATTERS

§ 1. Introduction:
   [a] Scope
   [b] Related matters
§ 2. Summary and comment:
   [a] Generally
   [b] Practice pointers

II. EFFECT ON CRIMINAL LIABILITY OF COURT ORDER AWARDING CUS-
   TODY

§ 3. Absence of decree awarding custody—liability of parent or person in loco
   parentis
§ 4. —Liability of agent:
   [a] View that agent may be held liable
   [b] View that agent may not be held liable
   [c] View that liability of agent depends on circumstances
§ 5. Presence of decree—generally:
   [a] Parent or agent held liable or subject to liability
   [b] Parent or agent held not liable or subject to liability
§ 6. —Where parent or agent lacked actual knowledge of custody decree

III. ASSERTED DEFENSES

§ 7. Consent of custodian
§ 8. Consent of child
§ 9. Unconstitutional vagueness of criminal statute

After the outline, each
Annotation has its own
subject index to help you
locate information within
the Annotation.

INDEX

Absence of decree awarding custody, §§ 3, 4
Actual knowledge of custody decree, parent or agent lacking, § 6
Adoptive parents, taking child from, §§ 5[b], 8
Agent, liability of, generally, §§ 4-6
Annulment proceedings pending, taking child while, § 4[a]
Assault by stepfather, § 7
Asserted defenses, §§ 7-9
Breaking and entering with intent to kidnap, § 4[c]
Circumstances, liability of agent depending on, § 4[c]
Comment, § 2
Consent of child, § 8

Consent of custodian, § 7
Conspiracy to kidnap, §§ 4[c], 5[a]
Court officer, impersonation of, § 3
Court order awarding custody, effect on criminal liability of, §§ 3-6
Custodian, consent of, § 7
Defenses asserted, §§ 7-9
False pretense, taking child under, §§ 3, 4[b], 5[a], 8
Father, agent of, §§ 3-5[a], 6, 7
Firearms, §§ 4[b], 5[a]
Foreign divorce, § 4[a]
Grandparents, taking child from, §§ 4[c], 5[a]
Grandparents, taking child by, §§ 5[b], 7, 8
Gun, use of, §§ 4[b], 5[a]

Following the index, you will see a list of the jurisdictions from which authority is cited within the Annotation. The first part of the Annotation will set out the scope of coverage, list Annotations on related subjects, and summarize the law on the topic.

FIGURE 4.15 A.L.R. ANNOTATION *(Continued)*

---

20 ALR4th   KIDNAPPING—TAKING OF OWN CHILD   § 1[a]
20 ALR4th 823

Impersonating court officer, § 3
Interlocutory decree, § 5[a]
Introduction, § 1
Joint custody arrangement, § 5[a]
Knowledge of custody decree, parent or agent lacking, § 6
Mother, agent of, §§ 4, 5, 8
Neglected children, § 3
Oral order divesting father of parental rights, § 3
Out of state, taking child, §§ 3, 4[c], 5-9
"Person having lawful charge of such child" as vague, § 9
Pistol or gun, use of, §§ 4[b], 5[a]
Practice pointers, § 2[b]
Preliminary matters, §§ 1, 2
Presence of decree awarding custody, §§ 5, 6
Private investigator as agent, § 4[c]
Probate court, temporary wards of, § 3
"Protracted period" as vague, § 9
Related matters, § 1[b]
Schoolbus, taking of child from, § 7
School, removing child from, §§ 5[a], 8

Scope of annotation, § 1[a]
Security guard service operator as agent, § 5[a]
Show cause order, § 3
Social worker, taking children from custody of, § 3
State human service agency, taking child from, § 3
Stepfather, assault by, § 7
Stepmother, taking child from, § 5[a]
Summary, § 2
Temporary custody, §§ 3, 7
Uncle as agent, § 4[b, c]
Unconstitutional vagueness of criminal statute, § 9
Unfitness of custodial parent, § 5[a]
Vagueness of statute, § 9
Visitation privilege, use of in taking children, §§ 5[a], 7
Weapons, use of, §§ 4[b], 5[a]
Witness, taking of child to prevent appearance as, § 7
Writ of prohibition, § 4[a]
Written judgment, taking child two days before, § 3

[Jurisdictions from which authority is cited]

TABLE OF JURISDICTIONS REPRESENTED
Consult POCKET PART in this volume for later cases

US: §§ 3
Ariz: §§ 2[b], 5[a]
Cal: §§ 2[b], 3, 4[a], 5[a]
Colo: §§ 5[a]
DC: §§ 3
Ga: §§ 3
Idaho: §§ 3, 4[b]
Ill: §§ 2[b], 5[a]
Ind: §§ 5[a], 9
Iowa: §§ 3, 4[b]
Kan: §§ 3, 4[a, b], 5[a], 6
La: §§ 3, 4[b]
Me: §§ 5[b]
Mass: §§ 5[a, b], 6, 8
Mich: §§ 3, 4[b, c], 5[b], 8

Minn: §§ 5[b]
Miss: §§ 3
Mo: §§ 3, 4[a]
NH: §§ 5[a], 7, 8
NJ: §§ 3, 4[c]
NM: §§ 3
NY: §§ 3, 4[b], 5[a, b], 6, 9
NC: §§ 3, 4[b], 7
Ohio: §§ 2[b], 5[a, b]
Or: §§ 3, 4[b]
Pa: §§ 3, 4[b]
Tenn: §§ 5[a], 6, 9
Wash: §§ 5[a], 8
Wyo: §§ 3, 7, 8

I. Preliminary matters

§ 1. Introduction

[a] Scope

This annotation[1] collects and ana-

lyzes the state and federal criminal cases in which the courts have discussed or decided whether, or under what circumstances, a parent or or

---

1. This annotation supersedes the annotation at 77 ALR 317.

[Introduction to the Annotation]

After the introductory material, the Annotation will explain the law on the topic in greater detail, summarize key cases, and provide citations to additional cases on the topic.

FIGURE 4.15   A.L.R. ANNOTATION (Continued)

20 ALR4th   KIDNAPPING—TAKING OF OWN CHILD
                              20 ALR4th 823

of a parent would be greater where the child passes into the hands of one having no parental obligations towards it.

For Kansas cases, see § 4[b].

In State v Brandenburg (1911) 232 **Mo** 531, 134 SW 529, the court, sustaining the conviction of one acting as agent of the mother, said that, under the applicable statute, the right of one parent to invade the possession of another parent, to take or decoy away their mutual offspring, if such a right exists, cannot be delegated to an agent. Under a different construction of the statute, the court reasoned, before a person could be arrested for taking a child from a parent, the parent would be required to first ascertain whether the person who took the child acted as an agent for the other parent, or was a mere kidnapper. In this case the child's mother had left the father, taking the child with her, and apparently obtained a foreign divorce. Thereafter she married the defendant. After experiencing some financial difficulties, she returned the child to the father, allegedly in return for a promise that the child would be returned to her when her situation improved. But the father instituted his own action for divorce and sought sole custody of the child. Then the defendant decoyed the child away, at a time when the father was not home, by telling the child that he was going to take it to its mother. Instead of going directly to the mother, he took the child to San Francisco where, he claimed, the mother had agreed to meet him later.

[b] View that agent may not be held liable

In the following cases the courts held or recognized that one who acts as an agent of a parent or assists a

parent in taking exclusive possession of a child is not criminally liable for kidnapping or a similar crime, where there has been no court order establishing custody of the child.

Idaho—State v Beslin (1911) 19 Idaho 185, 112 P 1053.

Iowa—State v Dewey (1912) 155 Iowa 469, 136 NW 533.

Kan—State v Angel (1889) 42 Kan 216, 21 P 1075.

La—State v Elliott (1930) 171 La 306, 131 So 28.

Mich—People v Nelson (1948) 322 Mich 262, 33 NW2d 786.

NC—State v Walker (1978) 35 NC App 182, 241 SE2d 89.

NY—People v Workman (1916) 94 Misc 374, 157 NYS 594.

Or—State v Edmiston (1979) 43 Or App 13, 602 P2d 282.

Pa—Burns v Commonwealth (1889) 129 Pa 138, 18 A 756; Commonwealth v Myers (1892) 146 Pa 24, 23 A 164.

In State v Angel (1889) 42 **Kan** 216, 21 P 1075, the court reversed the conviction of a man who had merely assisted a woman in leaving her husband and, in doing so, had assisted her in taking her child. The woman had wanted to leave her husband, and the man assisted by going to her house at her request and falsely saying that she was needed to help a sick child at a nearby home. The woman bundled her child and the man drove them away. After leaving, the mother had lawful charge of the child all of the time. Since there had been no judicial decree as to custody of the child, the court stated that the mother had an equal right with her husband to the actual care and control of the child; and she could not be punished under applicable kidnapping statutes. The court

831

> **Citations to cases from multiple jurisdictions**

> **Discussion of the law with a more detailed case summary**

To update, check the pocket part. The pocket part is organized by the page numbers of the Annotations.

FIGURE 4.16   POCKET PART ACCOMPANYING AN A.L.R. VOLUME

The pocket part is organized by page number

.L.R.4th 773   ALR4th

f shoplifting and detaining shopper did not constitute tort of outrage with respect to shopper's four–year–old daughter, even though employees allegedly grabbed shopper's arm and purse, acted in a "very rude" manner, told shopper to "shut up" and to "keep [her] kid quite," and refused to permit shopper to telephone her husband for purpose of having him pick up shopper's daughter. Johnson v. Hills Dept. Stores, Inc., 200 **W. Va.** 196, 488 S.E.2d 471 (1997).

20 A.L.R.4th 823

Kidnapping or related offense by taking or removing of child by or under authority of parent or one in loco parentis

Table of New and Retitled Sections

§ 7.5   **Consent of custodian invalid as defense**

§ 10   **Other defenses**

Related A.L.R. Annotations

Research References
West's Key Number Digest

Constitutional Law ☞258(2), 258(3); Criminal Law ☞13.1(8), 371(9); False Imprisonment ☞43, 44; Indictment and Information ☞110(42), 110(48), 125(21); Kidnapping ☞1-6; Parent and Child ☞18

A.L.R. Library

Construction and Application of Uniform Child Custody Jurisdiction and Enforcement Act's Exclusive, Continuing Jurisdiction Provision—Other Than No Significant Connection/ Substantial Evidence, 60 A.L.R.6th 193

Construction and Application of Uniform Child Custody Jurisdiction and Enforcement Act's Home State Jurisdiction Provision, 57 A.L.R.6th 163

Construction and Application of Uniform Child Custody Jurisdiction and Enforcement Act's Significant Connection Jurisdiction Provision, 52 A.L.R.6th 433

Construction and Operation of Uniform Child Custody Jurisdiction and Enforcement Act, 100 A.L.R.5th 1

Significant connection jurisdiction of court to modify foreign child custody decree under §§ 3(a)(2) and 14(b) of the Uniform Child Custody Jurisdiction Act (UCCJA) and the Parental Kidnapping Prevention Act (PKPA), 28 U.S.C.A. §§ 1738A(c)(2)(b) and 1738A(f)(1), 67 A.L.R.5th 1

Validity, construction, and application of "hold to service" provision of kidnapping statute, 28 A.L.R.5th 754

94

Inconvenience of forum as ground for declining jurisdiction under § 7 of the Uniform Child Custody Jurisdiction Act (UCCJA), 21 A.L.R.5th 396

Pending proceeding in another state as ground for declining jurisdiction under § 6(a) of the Uniform Child Custody Jurisdiction Act (UCCJA) or the Parental Kidnapping Prevention Act (PKPA), 28 U.S.C.A. § 1738A(g), 20 A.L.R.5th 700

Parties' misconduct as ground for declining jurisdiction under § 8 of the Uniform Child Custody Jurisdiction Act (UCCJA), 16 A.L.R.5th 650

Default jurisdiction of court under § 3(a)(4) of the Uniform Child Custody Jurisdiction Act (UCCJA) or the Parental Kidnapping Prevention Act (PKPA), 28 U.S.C.A. § 1738A(c)(2)(D), 6 A.L.R.5th 69

Home state jurisdiction of court under § 3(a)(1) of the Uniform Child Custody Jurisdiction Act (UCCJA) or the Parental Kidnapping Prevention Act (PKPA), 28 U.S.C.A. § 1738A(c)(2)(A), 6 A.L.R.5th 1

Abandonment and emergency jurisdiction of court under § 3(a)(3) of the Uniform Child Custody Jurisdiction Act (UCCJA) and the Parental Kidnapping Prevention Act (PKPA), 28 U.S.C.A. § 1738A(c)(2)(c), 5 A.L.R.5th 788

Significant connection jurisdiction of court under § 3(a)(2) of the Uniform Child Custody Jurisdiction Act (UCCJA) and the Parental Kidnapping Prevention Act (PKPA), 28 U.S.C.A. § 1738A(c)(2)(B), 5 A.L.R.5th 550

Child custody: when does state that issued previous custody determination have continuing jurisdiction under Uniform Child Custody Jurisdiction Act (UCCJA) or Parental Kidnapping Prevention Act (PKPA), 28 U.S.C.A. § 1738A, 83 A.L.R.4th 742

Applicability of Uniform Child Custody Jurisdiction Act (UCCJA) to temporary custody orders, 81 A.L.R.4th 1101

What types of proceedings or determinations are governed by the Uniform Child Custody Jurisdiction Act (UCCJA) or the Parental Kidnapping Prevention Act (PKPA), 78 A.L.R.4th 1028

Liability of legal or natural parent, or one who aids and abets, for damages resulting from abduction of own child, 49 A.L.R.4th 7

Validity of guardianship proceeding based on brainwashing of subject by religious, political, or social organization, 44 A.L.R.4th 1207

Liability of religious association for damages for intentionally tortious conduct in recruitment, indoctrination, or related activity, 40 A.L.R.4th 1062

Construction and application of Interna-

For latest cases, call the toll free number appearing on the cover of this supplement.

FIGURE 4.16   POCKET PART ACCOMPANYING AN A.L.R. VOLUME (Continued)

SUPPLEMENT   20 A.L.R.4th 823

> Newer cases are summarized

tional Child Abduction Remedies Act (42 U.S.C.A. §§ 11601 et seq.), 125 A.L.R. Fed. 217
   Requirement, under Federal Kidnapping Act (18 U.S.C.A. § 1201(a)), that person be held "for ransom or reward or otherwise", 71 A.L.R. Fed. 687

I. PRELIMINARY MATTERS

§ 1[b] Introduction—Related matters
   Supplemental related annotations, if any, are now located under the Research Reference heading of this annotation.

II. EFFECT ON CRIMINAL LIABILITY OF COURT ORDER AWARDING CUSTODY

§ 3 Absence of decree awarding custody— Liability of parent or person in loco parentis
   Also recognizing that, in absence of legally effective court order awarding custody of child to another, parent, or person in loco parentis, does not commit crime of kidnaping or similar crime by taking exclusive possession of child:
   US—U.S. v. Amer, 110 F.3d 873 (2d Cir. 1997), cert. denied, 118 S. Ct. 258 (U.S. 1997) (construing International Parental Kidnapping Crime Act); U.S. v. Floyd, 81 F.3d 1517 (10th Cir. 1996) (stepparent who relinquished custody of child to state following death of child's biological mother).
   Colo—Anderson v Cramlet (1986, CA10 Colo) 789 F2d 840, 12 Media L R 2121 (applying Colo law).
   Tex—Lugo v State (1995, Tex App Houston (1st Dist)) 923 SW2d 598.
   Va—Taylor v. Com., 28 Va. App. 498, 507 S.E.2d 89 (1998), reh'g en banc granted, mandate stayed, 28 Va. App. 723, 508 S.E.2d 888 (1999).
   Pending custody proceedings were not a prerequisite to a prosecution for custodial interference, and thus, father who took parties' son to another state without mother's knowledge or consent could be charged with custodial interference, though mother had not yet filed her petition for dissolution of marriage and for temporary custody of parties' son prior to father taking son out of state; custodial interference statute applied when one parent, having no legal right to do so, denied the other parent access to the child, and thus legislature must have intended for it to be a crime to interfere with custody of a child, even when there were no ongoing custody proceedings. A.R.S. § 13–1302. State v. Wood, 8 P.3d 1189 (**Ariz. Ct. App. Div. 1** 2000).
   As reconciliation by husband and wife canceled child custody order granted as part of interlocutory decree of dissolution, father of child

could not be convicted of child stealing under state statute. People v Howard (1984) 36 **Cal 3d** 852, 206 Cal Rptr 124, 686 P2d 644.
   Evidence that husband denied paternity for first year of child's life, that he moved to another state, that he sent no support payments to wife, and that he visited child approximately three times in first four years of child's life supported finding that husband, as presumed father, refused to take custody of the child, so that he lacked a right of custody, as element of child abduction. West's Ann.Cal.Fam.Code § 3010; West's Ann.Cal.Penal Code §§ 278, 279(f)(2) (1995). People v. Ryan, 76 **Cal. App. 4th** 1304, 91 Cal. Rptr. 2d 160 (1st Dist. 1999).
   In prosecution of father for molestation of minor daughter, court did not err in allowing jury to find kidnapping enhancement, despite general rule that parent entitled to custody cannot be liable for kidnapping his or her own child, where such parent is liable for kidnapping if he or she exercises custodial rights for illegal purpose, and where father therefore became liable for kidnapping own daughter by taking her to motel in order to molest her. People v Senior (1992, 6th Dist) 3 **Cal App 4th** 765, 5 Cal Rptr 2d 14, 92 CDOS 1444, later proceeding (Cal App 6th Dist) 92 Daily Journal DAR 2303.
   Under Parental Kidnapping Prevention Act (28 U.S.C.A. § 1738A), a colorable claim to right to custody, such as will qualify the one asserting that claim as "a person acting as a parent" for jurisdictional purposes, can arise in many ways. It may arise by virtue of a natural relationship with the child, such as parental relationship or other close familial relationships that give rise to a right to custody pursuant to law. It may arise where, pursuant to law, a parent has relinquished right to custody to claimant. In absence of such circumstances, right to claim custody can only arise through state intervention. Rogers v Platt (1988, 3rd Dist) 199 **Cal App 3d** 1204, 245 Cal Rptr 532.
   Father was properly convicted of malicious concealment of child without good cause from one having right of custody, even assuming statute was unconstitutionally vague by its failure to define "good cause," since his conduct manifested malice and thus clearly fell within its proscription. He concealed his child from the mother, who also had right of custody, he arranged to speak with the mother only at designated pay phones while accompanied by his own mother, and he demanded that she meet certain demands if she ever wanted to see the child again. He also warned her not to contact police, and threatened to kill her family if she attempted to retrieve the child. In contrast, his self-serving testimony toward

95

For latest cases, call the toll free number appearing on the cover of this supplement.

Am. Jur. 2d is available in Lexis.com and Westlaw. The text of an individual section is followed by footnotes. In Lexis.com, use Book Browse to browse preceding or subsequent sections. Change the view or use the TOC link to view the table of contents of the entry on False Imprisonment.

FIGURE 4.17   SECTION OF AM. JUR. 2d IN LEXIS.COM

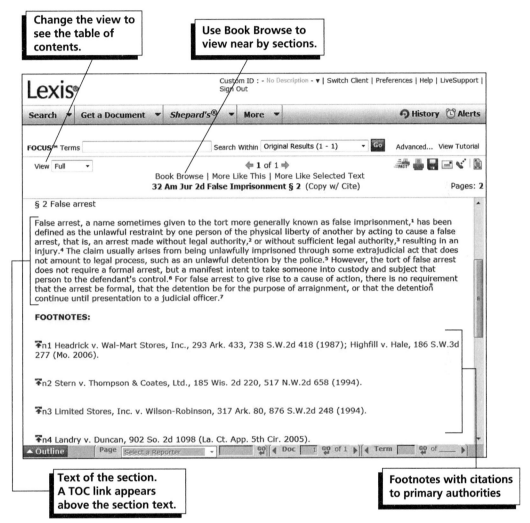

Section of Am. Jur. 2d in Lexis.com. Copyright 2012 LexisNexis, a division of Reed Elsevier Inc. All Rights Reserved. LexisNexis and the Knowledge Burst logo are registered trademarks of Reed Elsevier Properties Inc. and are used with the permission of LexisNexis.

In Lexis Advance, you must execute a search to retrieve information. A search for Secondary Materials from Michigan retrieves the results below, including references to a state legal encyclopedia. Notice the options for filtering the search results.

FIGURE 4.18 ANALYTICAL MATERIALS SEARCH RESULTS

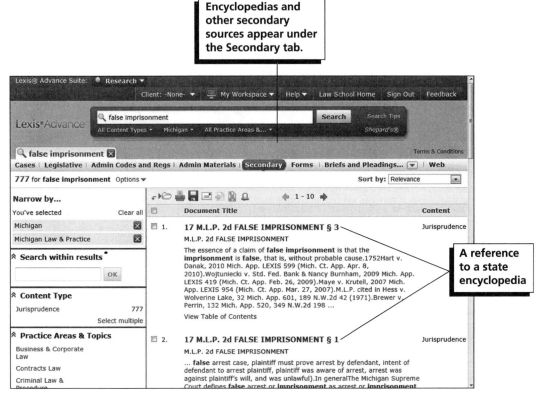

Lexis Advance Search Results. Copyright 2012 LexisNexis, a division of Reed Elsevier Inc. All Rights Reserved. LexisNexis and the Knowledge Burst logo are registered trademarks of Reed Elsevier Properties Inc. and are used with the permission of LexisNexis.

To research secondary sources in WestlawNext, you can search All Content. You can also drill down through menu options to search either a specific publication or secondary sources from a specific jurisdiction. In Westlaw.com, you must select a publication to search.

FIGURE 4.19   SELECTED SEARCH OPTIONS IN WESTLAWNEXT

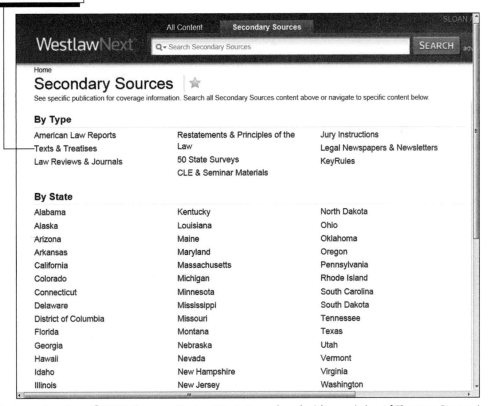

WestlawNext search options © 2012 Thomson Reuters/West. Reproduced with permission of Thomson Reuters/West.

Figure 4.20 shows part of an A.L.R. Annotation in WestlawNext. When you view an A.L.R. Annotation in WestlawNext or Westlaw.com, the updated material from the pocket part follows the text of the main volume.

FIGURE 4.20   PORTION OF AN A.L.R. ANNOTATION IN WESTLAWNEXT

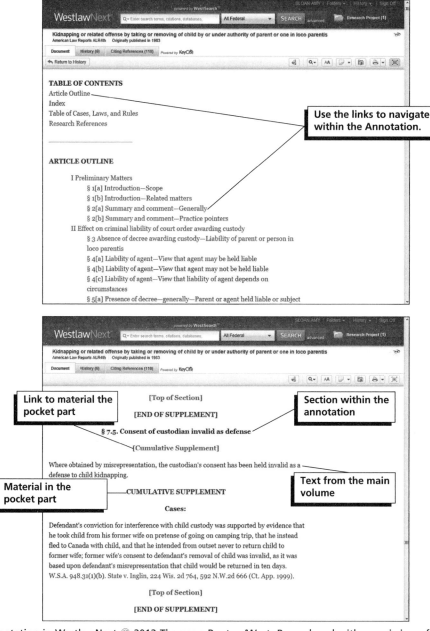

A.L.R. Annotation in WestlawNext © 2012 Thomson Reuters/West. Reproduced with permission of Thomson Reuters/West.

F. CHECKLIST FOR SECONDARY SOURCE RESEARCH

1. LEGAL ENCYCLOPEDIAS

- ❏ Use legal encyclopedias for very general background information and limited citations to primary authority, but not for in-depth analysis of a topic.
- ❏ Use Am. Jur. 2d or C.J.S. for a general overview; look for a state encyclopedia for an overview of the law in an individual state.
- ❏ Locate material in a print encyclopedia by (1) using the subject index or table of contents; (2) locating relevant sections in the main subject volumes; and (3) updating with the pocket part.
- ❏ Locate material in legal encyclopedias in Lexis.com, Westlaw.com, and WestlawNext by executing word searches in the databases for individual publications or by viewing the table of contents.
- ❏ Locate material in legal encyclopedias in WestlawNext and Lexis Advance by executing a content-driven search, reviewing results for secondary sources, and filtering the content by source or other appropriate criteria.

2. TREATISES

- ❏ Use treatises for an in-depth discussion and some analysis of an area of law and for citations to primary authority.
- ❏ Locate treatises in print through the online catalog or by asking a reference librarian for a recommendation; locate material within a treatise by (1) using the subject index or table of contents; (2) locating relevant sections within the main text; and (3) updating with the pocket part.
- ❏ Locate material in treatises in Lexis.com, Westlaw.com, and WestlawNext by executing word searches in the databases for individual publications. View the table of contents for individual publications, if available.
- ❏ Locate material in treatises in WestlawNext and Lexis Advance by executing a content-driven search, reviewing results for secondary sources, and filtering the content by source or other appropriate criteria.

3. LEGAL PERIODICALS

- ❏ Use legal periodicals for background information, citations to primary authority, in-depth analysis of a narrow topic, or information on a conflict in the law or an undeveloped area of the law.
- ❏ Locate citations to periodical articles with the *Index to Legal Periodicals* (ILP) or LegalTrac periodical indices; execute a search to obtain a list of citations. Full text of some articles is available through these services.

❑ Locate legal periodicals in Lexis.com, Westlaw.com, and Westlaw-Next by searching in the databases for multiple or individual publications.

❑ Locate legal periodicals in WestlawNext and Lexis Advance by executing a content-driven search, reviewing results for secondary sources, and filtering the content by appropriate criteria.

❑ Locate legal periodicals in .pdf format using HeinOnline or SSRN.

❑ Locate selected legal periodicals using a law-related website or general Internet search engine.

4. *AMERICAN LAW REPORTS*

❑ Use A.L.R. Annotations for an overview of an area of law and citations to primary authority (especially to locate persuasive authority from other jurisdictions), but not for in-depth analysis of a topic.

❑ Locate material within A.L.R. in print by (1) using the A.L.R. Index; (2) locating relevant Annotations in the main volumes; and (3) updating with the pocket part.

❑ Locate A.L.R. Annotations in Lexis.com, Westlaw.com, and WestlawNext by executing word searches in the *American Law Reports* (ALR) database.

❑ Locate A.L.R. Annotations in WestlawNext by executing a content-driven search, reviewing results for secondary sources, and filtering the content by source or other appropriate criteria. The same process should apply to Lexis Advance when its coverage includes A.L.R. Annotations.

5. RESTATEMENTS

❑ Use Restatements for research into common-law subjects and to locate mandatory and persuasive authority from jurisdictions that have adopted a Restatement.

❑ Locate Restatements in print through the online catalog.

❑ Locate information within a print Restatement by (1) using the subject index or table of contents to identify relevant sections within the Restatement volumes; (2) using the noncumulative Appendix volumes to find pertinent case summaries; and (3) using the pocket part in the latest Appendix volume to locate the most recent cases.

❑ Locate Restatements in Lexis.com, Westlaw.com, and Westlaw-Next by executing word searches or viewing the table of contents.

■ In Lexis.com, Restatement rules and case annotations are in separate databases.

■ In Westlaw, Restatement rules and case annotations are combined; case annotations will follow individual Restatement rules.

❐ Locate Restatements in WestlawNext by executing a content-driven search, reviewing results for secondary sources, and filtering the content by source or other appropriate criteria. The same process should apply to Lexis Advance when its coverage includes Restatements.

6. UNIFORM LAWS AND MODEL ACTS

❐ Use uniform laws and model acts to interpret a law adopted by a legislature and to locate persuasive authority from other jurisdictions that have adopted the law.

❐ Locate uniform laws and model acts in print using *Uniform Laws Annotated, Master Edition* (ULA).

❐ Locate information in the ULA set by (1) using the *Directory of Uniform Acts and Codes: Tables and Index* to search by subject, by the name of the law, or by adopting jurisdiction; (2) locating relevant provisions in the main volumes; and (3) updating with the pocket part.

❐ Locate selected uniform laws and model acts in Lexis.com, Westlaw.com, and WestlawNext by executing word searches in the appropriate database or viewing the table of contents. Lexis Advance may include uniform laws and model acts as its coverage increases.

CASE RESEARCH

A. INTRODUCTION TO CASES

1. THE STRUCTURE OF THE COURT SYSTEM

The United States has more than 50 separate court systems, including the federal system, the 50 state systems, and the District of Columbia system. You may recall from Chapter 1 that there are three levels of courts in the federal system: the United States District Courts (the trial courts), the United States Courts of Appeals (the intermediate appellate courts), and the United States Supreme Court (the court of last resort). Most state court systems are structured the same way as the federal court system.

Judges from any of these courts can issue written decisions, and their decisions are one source of legal rules. This chapter focuses on where these decisions are published and how they are indexed.

2. CASE REPORTERS

Court opinions, or cases, are published in books called reporters. Reporters are sets of books collecting cases in chronological order. Many sets of reporters are limited to opinions from a single jurisdiction or level of court. Thus, for example, federal reporters contain opinions from federal courts, and state reporters contain opinions from state courts. In addition, each set of reporters may be subdivided into different series covering different time periods.

A reporter published under government authority is known as an official reporter.[1] Reporters published by commercial publishers are called unofficial reporters. Because these two types of reporters exist, the same opinion may be published in more than one reporter. The text of the opinion should be exactly the same in an official and an unofficial reporter; the only difference is that the former is published by the government, and the latter is not. When a case appears in more than one reporter, it is described as having parallel citations. This is because each set of reporters will have its own citation for the case.

The only federal court opinions published by the government are those of the U.S. Supreme Court; these are published in a reporter called *United States Reports*. State governments usually publish the decisions of their highest courts, and most also publish decisions from some of their lower courts.

Perhaps the largest commercial publisher of cases is Thomson Reuters/West, formerly West Publishing Company. West has created a network of unofficial reporters called the *National Reporter System*, which comprises reporters with decisions from almost every U.S. jurisdiction.

West publishes U.S. Supreme Court decisions in the *Supreme Court Reporter*. Decisions from the U.S. Courts of Appeals are published in the *Federal Reporter*, and those from U.S. District Courts are published in the *Federal Supplement*. West also publishes some specialized reporters that contain decisions from the federal courts. For example, *Federal Rules Decisions* (F.R.D.) contains federal district court decisions interpreting the Federal Rules of Civil and Criminal Procedure, and the *Federal Appendix* (Fed. Appx. or F. App'x) contains non-precedential decisions from the federal courts of appeals. (Non-precedential decisions are discussed in more detail below.)

West publishes state court decisions in what are called regional reporters. West has divided the country into seven regions. The reporter for each region collects state court decisions from all of the states within that region.

Because West publishes reporters for almost every jurisdiction in a common format with common indexing features, this chapter focuses on research using West publications. The chart in **Figure 5.1** shows where cases from the various state and federal courts can be found.

Decisions for most states can be found in the state's official reporter, as well as in the reporters listed in **Figure 5.1**.[2]

---

[1] The government may publish the reporter itself, or it may arrange for the reporter to be published by a commercial publisher. As long as the government arranges for the publication, the reporter is official, even if it is physically produced by a commercial publisher.

[2] West also publishes separate unofficial state reporters for New York, California, and Illinois. Thus, New York, California, and Illinois cases may appear in three places: (1) an official state reporter; (2) a West regional reporter; and (3) a West unofficial state reporter. Some lower court opinions published in West's New York and California reporters are not published in the regional reporters covering those states. By contrast, all of the cases in *West's Illinois Decisions* are included in the regional reporter covering Illinois.

FIGURE 5.1   REPORTERS

COURT or JURISDICTION	REPORTER (followed by reporter abbreviation; multiple abbreviations denote multiple series)
United States Supreme Court	*United States Reports* (U.S.)* *Supreme Court Reporter* (S. Ct.) *United States Supreme Court Reports, Lawyer's Edition* (L. Ed., L. Ed. 2d)
United States Courts of Appeals	*Federal Reporter* (F., F.2d, F.3d) *Federal Appendix* (Fed. Appx. or F. App'x)
United States District Courts	*Federal Supplement* (F. Supp., F. Supp. 2d) *Federal Rules Decisions* (F.R.D.)
Atlantic Region states (Connecticut, Delaware, District of Columbia, Maine, Maryland, New Hampshire, New Jersey, Pennsylvania, Rhode Island, Vermont)	*Atlantic Reporter* (A., A.2d, A.3d)
North Eastern Region states (Illinois, Indiana, Massachusetts, New York, Ohio)	*North Eastern Reporter* (N.E., N.E.2d) New York: *New York Supplement* (N.Y.S., N.Y.S.2d) Illinois: *Illinois Decisions* (Ill. Dec.)
South Eastern Region states (Georgia, North Carolina, South Carolina, Virginia, West Virginia)	*South Eastern Reporter* (S.E., S.E.2d)
Southern Region states (Alabama, Florida, Louisiana, Mississippi)	*Southern Reporter* (So., So. 2d, So. 3d)
South Western Region States (Arkansas, Kentucky, Missouri, Tennessee, Texas)	*South Western Reporter* (S.W., S.W.2d, S.W.3d)
North Western Region states (Iowa, Michigan, Minnesota, Nebraska, North Dakota, South Dakota, Wisconsin)	*North Western Reporter* (N.W., N.W.2d)
Pacific Region states (Alaska, Arizona, California, Colorado, Hawaii, Idaho, Kansas, Montana, Nevada, New Mexico, Oklahoma, Oregon, Utah, Washington, Wyoming)	*Pacific Reporter* (P., P.2d, P.3d) California: *California Reporter* (Cal. Rptr., Cal. Rptr. 2d, Cal. Rptr. 3d)

*Official reporter published by the federal government.

3. The Anatomy of a Published Case

A case published in a West reporter has five components:

1. The heading containing the parallel citation (if any) to an official reporter, the case name, the court that rendered the decision, and the date of the decision.
2. A synopsis of the decision written by case editors, not by the court.
3. One or more paragraphs summarizing the key points within the decision. These summary paragraphs are called headnotes, and they are written by case editors, not by the court.
4. The names of the attorneys who represented the parties and the judge or judges who decided the case.
5. The opinion of the court. If the decision has any concurring or dissenting opinions, these will follow immediately after the majority or plurality opinion.

Only the fifth item on this list, the opinion of the court, constitutes legal authority. All of the remaining items are editorial enhancements. These editorial enhancements are very useful for locating cases, but they are not part of the court's opinion. Therefore, you should never rely on any part of a case other than the text of the opinion itself.[3]

Figure 5.2 shows an excerpt from a case published in a West reporter.

4. Unpublished, or Non-Precedential, Opinions

Not all court decisions are published; only those designated by the courts for publication appear in print reporters. The decisions not designated for publication are called unpublished decisions. In the past, the only ways to obtain copies of unpublished decisions were from the parties to the case or from the clerk's office at the courthouse. This is still true today for some unpublished decisions, especially those issued by state courts. Many unpublished decisions, however, are available through electronic research services and on the Internet. The federal courts of appeals make many of their unpublished decisions available on their websites. In addition, unpublished decisions issued by the federal courts of appeals since 2001 are now available in print in the *Federal Appendix*, a West reporter.

Because these decisions are increasingly available electronically and in print, the term "unpublished" opinion has become a misnomer.

---

[3] There are limited exceptions to this rule. For example, in Ohio, the text of the opinion is preceded by a "syllabus," or summary of the opinion, which is written by the court and which contains the holding of the decision. Ordinarily, however, everything other than the opinion itself is an editorial enhancement. Unless you see a notation indicating otherwise, you should assume that only the text of the opinion is authoritative.

FIGURE 5.2 EXCERPT FROM *POPKIN v. NEW YORK STATE*

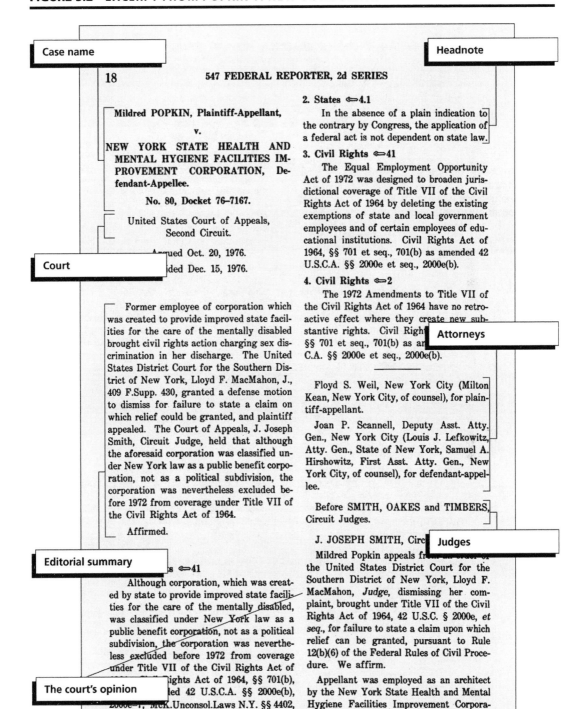

Case name

Headnote

18   547 FEDERAL REPORTER, 2d SERIES

Mildred POPKIN, Plaintiff-Appellant,

v.

NEW YORK STATE HEALTH AND MENTAL HYGIENE FACILITIES IMPROVEMENT CORPORATION, Defendant-Appellee.

No. 80, Docket 76–7167.

United States Court of Appeals, Second Circuit.

Court

Argued Oct. 20, 1976.
Decided Dec. 15, 1976.

Former employee of corporation which was created to provide improved state facilities for the care of the mentally disabled brought civil rights action charging sex discrimination in her discharge. The United States District Court for the Southern District of New York, Lloyd F. MacMahon, J., 409 F.Supp. 430, granted a defense motion to dismiss for failure to state a claim on which relief could be granted, and plaintiff appealed. The Court of Appeals, J. Joseph Smith, Circuit Judge, held that although the aforesaid corporation was classified under New York law as a public benefit corporation, not as a political subdivision, the corporation was nevertheless excluded before 1972 from coverage under Title VII of the Civil Rights Act of 1964.

Affirmed.

Editorial summary

s ⟸41

Although corporation, which was created by state to provide improved state facilities for the care of the mentally disabled, was classified under New York law as a public benefit corporation, not as a political subdivision, the corporation was nevertheless excluded before 1972 from coverage under Title VII of the Civil Rights Act of

The court's opinion

ights Act of 1964, §§ 701(b), led 42 U.S.C.A. §§ 2000e(b), 2000e-1, McK.Unconsol.Laws N.Y. §§ 4402, 4404.

2. States ⟸4.1

In the absence of a plain indication to the contrary by Congress, the application of a federal act is not dependent on state law.

3. Civil Rights ⟸41

The Equal Employment Opportunity Act of 1972 was designed to broaden jurisdictional coverage of Title VII of the Civil Rights Act of 1964 by deleting the existing exemptions of state and local government employees and of certain employees of educational institutions. Civil Rights Act of 1964, §§ 701 et seq., 701(b) as amended 42 U.S.C.A. §§ 2000e et seq., 2000e(b).

4. Civil Rights ⟸2

The 1972 Amendments to Title VII of the Civil Rights Act of 1964 have no retroactive effect where they create new substantive rights. Civil Right **Attorneys** §§ 701 et seq., 701(b) as a C.A. §§ 2000e et seq., 2000e(b).

Floyd S. Weil, New York City (Milton Kean, New York City, of counsel), for plaintiff-appellant.

Joan P. Scannell, Deputy Asst. Atty. Gen., New York City (Louis J. Lefkowitz, Atty. Gen., State of New York, Samuel A. Hirshowitz, First Asst. Atty. Gen., New York City, of counsel), for defendant-appellee.

Before SMITH, OAKES and TIMBERS, Circuit Judges.

J. JOSEPH SMITH, Circ **Judges**

Mildred Popkin appeals from an order of the United States District Court for the Southern District of New York, Lloyd F. MacMahon, *Judge*, dismissing her complaint, brought under Title VII of the Civil Rights Act of 1964, 42 U.S.C. § 2000e, *et seq.*, for failure to state a claim upon which relief can be granted, pursuant to Rule 12(b)(6) of the Federal Rules of Civil Procedure. We affirm.

Appellant was employed as an architect by the New York State Health and Mental Hygiene Facilities Improvement Corporation ("the Corporation"). In November,

FIGURE 5.2   EXCERPT FROM *POPKIN v. NEW YORK STATE (Continued)*

POPKIN v. N. Y. ST. HEALTH & MENTAL HYGIENE, ETC.   **19**

Cite as 547 F.2d 18 (1976)

1970 she was notified that her employment would be terminated as of January 15, 1971. Appellant instituted this action under Title VII alleging that the termination was an act of discrimination based on her sex. Jurisdiction was based on 42 U.S.C. § 2000e *et seq.* and 28 U.S.C. § 1332. The district court dismissed the complaint on the [Corporation was a "politi-] [New York State and was] [d from coverage of 42] [*t seq.* prior to March 24,] [amendments to Title VII,] [ge of the Act to political] [held by the district court] not to have retroactive effect.

[1, 2] The Corporation was created by the Health and Mental Hygiene Facilities Improvement Act as a "corporate governmental agency constituting a public benefit corporation." McKinney's Unconsol.Laws §§ 4402, 4404. Appellant contends that because under New York law her employer is classified as a public benefit corporation and not as a political subdivision, the Corporation was not excluded from Title VII coverage before 1972 under 42 U.S.C. § 2000e(b). We disagree. Title VII does not provide that the terms of the federal statute are to be construed according to state law. Title 42 U.S.C. § 2000e–7 merely provides that state laws prohibiting employment discrimination will remain in effect. In the absence of a plain indication to the contrary by Congress, the application of a federal statute is not dependent on state law. *Jerome v. United States,* 318 U.S. 101, 104,

> Bracketed numbers indicate the place in the opinion where material summarized in the headnotes appears.

63 S.Ct. 483, 87 L.Ed. 640 (1943). Congressional intent concerning coverage of Title VII and the actual nature of appellee's relationship to the state determine whether or not the Corporation was covered by Title VII before 1972.

[3] The Equal Employment Opportunity Act of 1972 was designed to broaden jurisdictional coverage of Title VII by deleting the existing exemptions of state and local government employees and of certain employees of educational institutions. The bill amended the Civil Rights Act of 1964 to include state and local governments, governmental agencies, and political subdivisions within the definition of "employer" in 42 U.S.C. § 2000e(b). H.R.Rep.No.92–238, 92nd Cong., 2d Sess., *reprinted in* 1972 U.S. Code Cong. & Ad.News 2137, 2152. The conference report of the Senate Amendment to H.R. 1746, which was adopted by the conference, stated explicitly that the Senate Amendment "expanded coverage to include: (1) State and local governments, governmental agencies, political subdivisions . . . ." *Id.* at 2180. The 1964 House Report on the Civil Rights Act of 1964, on the other hand, refers to the exclusion from the term "employer" of "all Federal, State, and local government agencies. . . . ." 1964 U.S.Code Cong. & Ad. News 2402. Until 1972, state agencies as well as political subdivisions were exempt from Title VII. Under the terms of the Mental Hygiene Facilities Development Corporation Act, "state agencies" include public benefit corporations.[2]

1. Section 701(b) of Title VII, the Civil Rights Act of 1964, P.L. 88–352 as enacted provided in relevant part:

(b) The term "employer" means a person engaged in an industry affecting commerce who has twenty-five or more employees for each working day in each of twenty or more calendar weeks in the current or preceding calendar year, and any agent of such a person, but such term does not include (1) the United States, a corporation wholly owned by the Government of the United States, an Indian tribe, or a State or political subdivision thereof. . . .

In 1972 § 701(b), 42 U.S.C. § 2000e(b) was amended as follows:

(b) The term "employer" means a person engaged in an industry affecting commerce who has fifteen or more employees for each working day in each of twenty or more calendar weeks in the current or preceding calendar year, and any agent of such a person, but such term does not include (1) the United States, a corporation wholly owned by the Government of the United States, an Indian tribe, or any department or agency of the District of Columbia subject by statute to procedures of the competitive service (as defined in section 2102 of Title 5). . . .

2. McKinney's Unconsol.Laws § 4403(17) contains the following definition:

"State agency" means any officer, department, board, commission, bureau division,

A more accurate term is "non-precedential" opinion. Non-precedential decisions are often subject to special court rules. For example, unlike decisions published in the *Federal Reporter*, those appearing in the *Federal Appendix* are not treated as binding precedent by the courts, which is why they are described as "non-precedential" decisions. In the past, the federal courts of appeals often limited the circumstances under which non-precedential decisions could be cited in documents filed with the court, although all non-precedential opinions issued on or after January 1, 2007, may now be cited without restriction. Because of restrictions on citations to earlier non-precedential opinions, many decisions in the *Federal Appendix* contain notations indicating that they are not binding precedent and cautioning readers to check court rules before citing the opinions. Non-precedential decisions by other courts may also be subject to special rules.

Although courts have issued non-precedential opinions for many years, the practice is not without controversy. The authoritative value of non-precedential decisions is a subject of ongoing debate in the legal community. Regardless of the controversy, non-precedential decisions can be valuable research tools. Therefore, you should not disregard them when you are conducting case research.

5. Methods of Locating Cases

You can locate cases in many ways. If you have the citation to a case that you have obtained from another source, such as a secondary source, you can easily locate the case in a print reporter or electronic database.

When you do not have a citation, you can locate cases using either a source-driven or content-driven approach. If you use a source-driven approach, the first step will be deciding which jurisdiction's cases you want to research. Once you select a jurisdiction, you can search for cases by subject, by words in the document, or by party name.

Researching by subject is often a useful way to locate cases. Reviewing summaries of cases arranged by subject can help you identify those that address the topic of your research. You can search by subject in print using a research tool called a digest. You can also sort cases by subject categories in Lexis, Westlaw, and other electronic services. Word searching is another way to locate cases electronically. This option is available in free and fee-based commercial services as well as on some court websites.

One additional search option is locating a case by party name. In print, you can use a directory of cases organized by party name. In an electronic service, you can use a party name as a term in a word search; many services also have search templates that allow you to enter party names.

If you choose content-driven searching in Lexis Advance or WestlawNext, your search results will include cases. You will ordinarily pre-filter your search by jurisdiction unless you are researching the law of all U.S. jurisdictions. Once you execute the search, the results will include a section with cases. In Lexis Advance, cases appear under the **Cases** tab. In WestlawNext, the **Overview** page will include summaries of a few cases. You can see the complete case results by following the link to **Cases** from the **View** menu. When you review the cases your search has retrieved, you can filter the results according to a number of criteria, such as cases from a particular level of court.

Sections B and C, below, explain how to research cases in print and electronically.

B. RESEARCHING CASES IN PRINT

1. LOCATING CASES BY SUBJECT USING A DIGEST

a. What Is a Digest?

Reporters are published in chronological order; they are not organized by subject. Trying to research cases in chronological order would be impossible. The research tool that organizes cases by subject is called a digest, and that is the finding tool you will ordinarily use to locate cases by topic.

The term "digest" literally means to arrange and summarize, and that is exactly what a digest does. In a digest, the law is arranged into different subject categories, such as torts, contracts, or criminal law. Then, within each category, the digest provides summaries of cases that discuss the law on that subject. You can use the summaries to decide which cases you should read to find the answer to your research question.

The digest system created by West is the most commonly used digest in legal research. West has divided the law into more than 400 subject categories, called topics. Under each topic, West provides summaries of cases relevant to the subject. Each topic is listed alphabetically in the digest. Because there are so many topics, a digest actually consists of a multivolume set of books. This is similar to a set of encyclopedias with multiple volumes covering topics in alphabetical order.

The West topics are quite broad. Subject areas such as torts or contracts generate thousands of cases. Therefore, the topics have been further subdivided into smaller categories. Each subdivision within a topic is assigned a number that West calls a key number. Thus, the case summaries within a West digest will appear under the relevant key number. Instead of requiring you to read summaries of all the cases on a very broad topic, the key number subdivisions allow you to focus more specifically on the precise issue you are researching.

The topic, key number, and case summary that you find in a West digest will correspond exactly to one of the headnotes at the beginning of an opinion published in a West reporter.

The following examples illustrate some of the features of a West digest. **Figure 5.3** shows the beginning of the West topic for "Abandoned and Lost Property," including the outline of subtopics covered in each key number. **Figure 5.4** shows a summary of a case under key number 2.

Digests, like many other research tools, are updated with pocket parts, which are explained in Chapter 1. If the pocket part gets too big to fit in the back of the book, you may find a separate softcover pamphlet on the shelf next to the hardcover volume. Whenever you use any hardcover book in digest research, it is especially important to check the pocket part for new information because hardcover digest volumes are not reprinted frequently.

b. The Digest Research Process

The digest research process consists of four steps:

1. locating the correct digest set for the type of research you are doing;
2. locating relevant topics and key numbers within the digest;
3. reading the case summaries under the topics and key numbers;
4. updating your research to make sure you find summaries of the most recent cases.

(1) Locating the correct digest set

Reporters and digests are similar in several ways. Just as there are different reporters containing cases from different jurisdictions, there are also different sets of digests for finding cases from these various jurisdictions. And just as a case may be published in more than one reporter, so also a case may be summarized in more than one digest. Thus, the first step in finding cases that will help you answer a research question is choosing the correct digest set.

Digest sets are organized by jurisdiction and by date. The four jurisdictional categories for digests are federal, state, regional, and combined. A federal digest, as you might imagine, summarizes federal cases. A state digest contains summaries of decisions from that state as well as opinions from the federal courts located in that state. A regional digest summarizes state court decisions from the states within the region, but it does not contain summaries of any federal cases. West publishes regional digests for some, but not all, of its regional reporters. A combined digest summarizes cases from all state and federal jurisdictions.

Within each category, the digest set may be divided into different series covering different time periods. For example, *West's Federal Practice Digest*, one of the federal digests, is currently in its Fourth Series. The Fourth Series contains cases from the early 1980s to the present. Earlier cases, from 1975 through the early 1980s, can be found in the

FIGURE 5.3   BEGINNING OF THE WEST TOPIC FOR "ABANDONED AND LOST PROPERTY"

Topic

ABANDONED AND LOST PROPERTY

SUBJECTS INCLUDED

General nature of relinquishment of property or other rights of any kind by abandonment, as distinguished from dedication, surrender, waiver, etc.

Effect of abandonment by way of extinguishment of the title or right

Finding and taking of possession of lost goods of another, whereby the finder may acquire title thereto

Nature, requisites and incidents of such finding and possession

Rights, duties and liabilities of finders of lost goods as to the owners or losers and as to others in general

SUBJECTS EXCLUDED AND COVERED BY OTHER TOPICS

Estrays, see ANIMALS

Lost instruments in writing, establishment of and action on, see LOST INSTRUMENTS

Negotiable paper, rights of finders, see BILLS AND NOTES

Particular persons or personal relations, abandonment of, see specific topics

Particular species of property, rights, remedies, or proceedings, abandonment of, see specific topics

Reversion of property to the state, see ESCHEAT

Rewards for recovery of lost goods, etc., see REWARDS

Sales of lost goods, see SALES

Wrecks and vessels and goods derelict at sea, see SHIPPING

For detailed references to other topics, see Descriptive-Word Index

Summary of the topic

Key number

Analysis

I. ABANDONMENT, ☞1–9.

II. FINDING LOST GOODS, ☞10–13.

I. ABANDONMENT.

    ☞1. Nature and elements.

    1.1. —— In general.

    2. —— Intent.

    3. —— Acts and omissions.

    4. Evidence and questions for jury.

    5. Operation and effect.

Outline of subtopics covered

II. FINDING LOST GOODS.

    ☞10. In general; loss of property.

    11. Rights and liabilities of finder as to owner.

FIGURE 5.4   CASE SUMMARY UNDER THE "ABANDONED AND LOST PROPERTY" TOPIC, KEY NUMBER 2

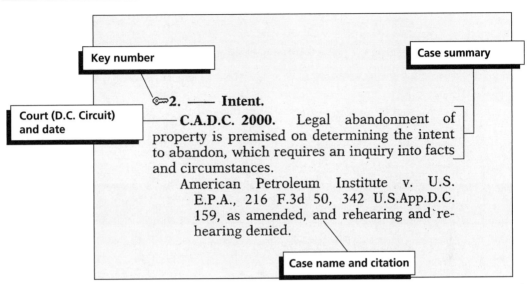

Reprinted with permission from Thomson Reuters/West, *West's Federal Practice Digest*, 4th Ser., Vol. (2006), p. 6. © 2006 Thomson Reuters/West.

Third Series of the digest. Ordinarily, you will want to begin your research in the most current series. If you are unable to find information in the most current series, however, you could locate older cases by looking in the earlier series.

Figures 5.5 through **5.7** summarize some of the characteristics of West digests.

To decide which digest is the best choice for your research, you will need to consider the nature and scope of the project. Usually, you will want to choose the narrowest digest that still has enough information for you to find relevant legal authority. Sometimes you will need to use more than one digest to find all of the cases you need.

West's Federal Practice Digest is the best place to start looking for federal cases. If you are researching case law from an individual state, the digest from that state is usually the best starting place. If you do not have access to the state digest, the regional digest is another good place to look. It is also a good place to find persuasive authority from surrounding jurisdictions. Remember, however, that regional digests summarize only state court decisions, not federal decisions. Therefore, if you also want to find cases from the federal courts located within an individual state, you will need to supplement your regional digest research by using *West's Federal Practice Digest*.

The combined digests have the most comprehensive coverage, but they are also the most difficult to use. You would probably begin with

FIGURE 5.5   FEDERAL DIGESTS

DESCRIPTION	WEST'S FEDERAL PRACTICE DIGEST, FOURTH SERIES	WEST'S UNITED STATES SUPREME COURT DIGEST
What is included	Summaries of cases from all federal courts	Summaries of United States Supreme Court cases
What is excluded	Summaries of state cases	Summaries of cases from lower federal courts and all state courts
Coverage	Summaries of cases from the early 1980s-present. Older cases are summarized in prior series of this set (e.g., *West's Federal Practice Digest*, Third Series).	Summaries of all United States Supreme Court cases

FIGURE 5.6   STATE AND REGIONAL DIGESTS

DESCRIPTION	STATE DIGESTS	REGIONAL DIGESTS
What is included	Summaries of cases from the state's courts and the federal courts within the state	Summaries of cases from the state courts within the region
What is excluded	Summaries of state and federal cases from courts outside the state	Summaries of state cases from states outside the region and all federal cases
Coverage	West publishes state digests for all states except Delaware, Nevada, and Utah. The *Virginia Digest* summarizes cases from both Virginia and West Virginia. The *Dakota Digest* summarizes cases from both North and South Dakota. Some state digests have multiple series.	West publishes Atlantic, North Western, Pacific, and South Eastern Digests. West *does not* publish North Eastern, Southern, or South Western Digests. All of the regional digests have multiple series.

FIGURE 5.7 COMBINED DIGESTS

DESCRIPTION	COMBINED DIGESTS
What is included	Summaries of state and federal cases from all jurisdictions across the United States
What is excluded	Nothing
Coverage	The combined digests are divided into the *General, Decennial,* and *Century Digests,* covering the following dates:

General Digest, Thirteenth Series (each volume in the *General Digest* set is noncumulative)	2010-2013 (expected coverage)
Twelfth Decennial Digest, Part 2	2010-2013 (publication expected in 2013)
Twelfth Decennial Digest, Part 1	2008-2010
Eleventh Decennial Digest, Part 3	2004-2007
Eleventh Decennial Digest, Part 2	2001-2004
Eleventh Decennial Digest, Part 1	1996-2001
Tenth Decennial Digest, Part 2	1991-1996
Tenth Decennial Digest, Part 1	1986-1991
Ninth Decennial Digest, Part 2	1981-1986
Ninth Decennial Digest, Part 1	1976-1981
Eighth Decennial Digest	1966-1976
Seventh Decennial Digest	1956-1966
Sixth Decennial Digest	1946-1956
Fifth Decennial Digest	1936-1946
Fourth Decennial Digest	1926-1936
Third Decennial Digest	1916-1926
Second Decennial Digest	1907-1916
First Decennial Digest	1897-1906
Century Digest	1658-1896

the most recent series of *West's General Digest.* The coverage of the Thirteenth Series begins with cases decided in late 2010 and is expected to continue through 2013. Then the Fourteenth Series will begin. The *General Digest* volumes are noncumulative. Thus, you would need to research each volume of the most recent series. For earlier cases, you would also need to use the *Twelfth Decennial Digest* and as many previous series as necessary to locate cases on your topic. Because this is a cumbersome process, the combined digests are usually only useful when you know the approximate time period you want to research or when you are conducting nationwide research.

Figure 5.8 summarizes when you might want to consider using each of these types of digests.

FIGURE 5.8   WHEN TO USE DIFFERENT DIGESTS

FEDERAL DIGESTS	STATE DIGESTS	REGIONAL DIGESTS	COMBINED DIGESTS
To research federal cases	To research state and federal cases from an individual state	To research state cases from an individual state within a region (may require additional research with the federal digest)	To research federal cases or cases from an individual state if you know the approximate time period you wish to research
To supplement regional digest research by locating federal cases within an individual state		To locate persuasive authority from surrounding jurisdictions	To research the law of all jurisdictions within the United States

(2) Locating topics and key numbers

Once you have decided which set or sets of the digest to use, the next step is locating topics and key numbers relevant to your research issue. You can do this in three ways:

i.   Using the headnotes in a case on point;
ii. Using the Descriptive-Word Index;
iii. Going directly to topics relevant to your research.

(i) Using the headnotes in a case on point

The easiest way to find relevant topics and key numbers is to use the headnotes in a case that you have already determined is relevant to your research. If you have read other chapters in this book, you already know that the digest is not the only way to locate cases. Many other research sources, including secondary sources (covered in Chapter 4) and statutes (covered in Chapter 7), can lead you to relevant cases. Therefore, when another source has led you to a relevant case that is published in a West reporter, you can use the headnotes to direct you to digest topics and key numbers.

(ii) Using the Descriptive-Word Index

If you do not already have a case on point, you will need to use the index to find topics and key numbers in the digest. The index in a West digest is called the Descriptive-Word Index (DWI). The DWI actually consists of several volumes that may be located either at the beginning or at the end of the digest set, and it lists subjects in alphabetical order.

To use the DWI, all you need to do is look up the subjects you want to research. The subjects will be followed by abbreviations indicating the topics and key numbers relevant to each subject. A list of abbreviations appears at the beginning of the volume. You may also see cross-references to other index entries with additional information on the subject. An excerpt from a page in the DWI appears in **Figure 5.9**.

The DWI volumes, like all other hardcover volumes within the digest set, are updated with pocket parts. The next step in using the index is checking the pocket part. Because the hardcover DWI volumes are not reprinted frequently, many of the newer entries may be in the pocket part. Moreover, West sometimes uses information from specific cases to generate index entries. Therefore, it is important to check the pocket part for new material that may be relevant to your research. If you do not find anything listed in the pocket part, no new index entries on that subject are available.

Once you have identified relevant topics and key numbers, the next step is looking them up within the digest volumes. Remember that digest volumes are organized alphabetically. Therefore, you will need to look on the spines of the books until you locate the volume covering your

FIGURE 5.9 EXCERPT FROM THE DESCRIPTIVE-WORD INDEX

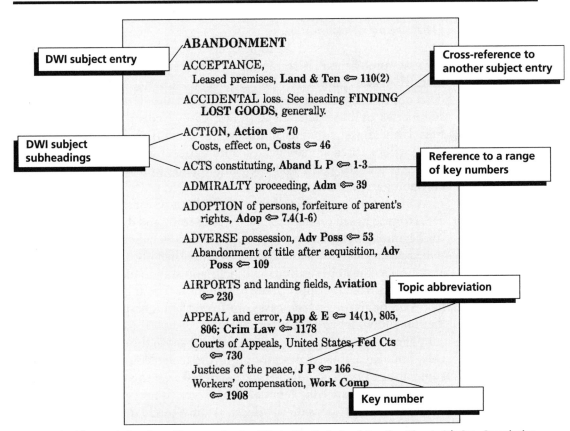

Reprinted with permission from Thomson Reuters/West, *West's Federal Practice Digest*, 4th Ser., Descriptive-Word Index, Vol. 97 (2002), p. 1. © 2002 Thomson Reuters/West.

topic. When you look up the topic, you will see that the key numbers follow in numerical order.

(iii) Going directly to relevant topics

Because digest topics are arranged alphabetically, you can bypass the DWI and go directly to the topic you are interested in researching. At the beginning of each topic, West provides an overview section that lists the subjects included and excluded, as well as an outline of all the key numbers under the topic. Case summaries, of course, follow the overview in key number order.

This can be a difficult way to start your research unless you are already familiar with an area of law and know which topics are likely to be relevant. For example, cases involving some types of real estate transactions are listed under the topic "Vendor and Purchaser," which might not be a topic you would have considered using. Although you might not want to start your research by going directly to a digest topic, once you have identified useful topics through other means, you may want to review the overview section. The list of subjects included and excluded and the outline of key numbers can provide additional helpful research leads.

(3) Reading case summaries

Once you have reviewed the topic overview, you are ready to begin reading case summaries. There is some inconsistency in the way West organizes its digest summaries, but in general, summaries are organized in descending order from highest to lowest court. If the digest contains summaries of both federal and state cases, federal cases will appear first. If the digest contains summaries of cases from multiple states, the states will be listed alphabetically. Summaries of multiple decisions from the same level of court and the same jurisdiction are listed in reverse chronological order.

One of the most difficult aspects of digest research is deciding which cases to read based on the summaries. The court and date abbreviations at the beginning of each entry will help you decide which cases to review. If you are using a digest with cases from more than one jurisdiction, paying attention to the abbreviations will help you stay focused on the summaries of cases from the appropriate jurisdiction. The abbreviations will also help you figure out which cases are from the highest court in the jurisdiction and which are the most recent decisions. In addition, many case summaries include not only a synopsis of the rule the court applied in the case, but also a concise description of the facts. You can use the factual summaries to narrow down the cases applicable to your issue.

Even a fact-specific summary, however, does not provide the full context of the case. Using the digest is only the first step in researching cases; all the digest can do is point you toward cases that may help answer your research question. Digest summaries, like headnotes, are editorial enhancements designed to assist you with your research. They are not authoritative, and you should never rely on one as a statement of the law. Always read the case in full before relying on it to answer a research question.

(4) Updating digest research

The final step in digest research is updating. The updating process involves three steps:

i.   checking the pocket part for the subject volume covering your topic;
ii. checking a separate set of interim pamphlets at the end of the digest set;
iii. updating beyond the digest set for cases published after the supplements were printed.

It is very important to update your research for new cases. Newer cases may reflect a change in the law, or cases more factually relevant to your problem may have been decided since the hardcover books were published. Obviously, in legal practice you must find these cases for your research to be complete. In law school, professors love to assign research problems for which the best material is in the updating sources. Therefore, you should get in the habit now of updating your research thoroughly.

(i) Pocket parts

Each subject volume should have either a pocket part or a separate supplement on the shelf next to the hardcover book. This is the first place to look to update your research.

The pocket part is organized the same way as the main volume. The topics are arranged alphabetically, and the key numbers are arranged in numerical order within each topic. There are two pieces of information you will find in the pocket part. First, if any cases under the key number were decided after the main volume was published, you will find summaries of those cases in the pocket part. These case summaries will be organized in the same order as those in the main volume. If no reference to your topic and key number appears in the pocket part, no new decisions have been issued during the time period covered by the pocket part. Second, you may find that West has created new key numbers or divided the key numbers from the main volume into a series of subsections. If that is the case, you will find a short outline of the new subsections at the beginning of the original key number, along with summaries of any cases categorized under the new subsections.

(ii) Interim pamphlets

The pocket part is not the only supplement you should check. Pocket parts are generally published only once a year. For some digest sets, West also publishes interim pamphlets to update for cases decided since the pocket part was published. These pamphlets are ordinarily softcover booklets, although occasionally you will see hardcover supplements. They are usually shelved at the end of the digest set. The pamphlets contain summaries of new decisions under all of the topics and key numbers within the digest set. Just as with pocket parts, the topics in the interim pamphlets are arranged alphabetically. And, as with pocket parts, if no entry appears under your topic and key number, no new cases have been decided during the time period covered by the interim pamphlet.

Some interim pamphlets are cumulative, meaning you only need to look in the one book to update your research. Others, however, are noncumulative. If the pamphlets you are using are noncumulative, each one covers a specific time period, and you must check each one to update your research completely. To determine the dates covered by an interim pamphlet, check the dates on the spine or cover of the book.

(iii) Closing tables

Once you have checked the interim pamphlets accompanying the digest, you have updated your research as far as the digest will take you. The final step in the process is checking for cases decided after the last interim pamphlet was published.

To do this, you will need to refer to the chart on the inside front cover of the latest interim pamphlet. This chart is called a closing table. **Figure 5.10** contains an example of a closing table. If the digest set you are using does not have interim pamphlets, you should check the closing table on the inside front cover of the pocket part for the subject volume.

The closing table lists the names of all of the reporters whose decisions are summarized within the digest set. For each of those reporters, the table lists the last volume with decisions summarized in the interim

FIGURE 5.10   INTERIM PAMPHLET CLOSING TABLE

Closing with Cases Reported in	
Supreme Court Reporter	131 S.Ct.
Federal Reporter, Third Series	648 F.3d 840
Federal Appendix	425 Fed.Appx.
Federal Supplement, Second Series	777 F.Supp.2d
Federal Rules Decisions	274 F.R.D.
Bankruptcy Reporter	453 B.R. 781
Federal Claims Reporter	99 Fed.Cl. 27
Military Justice Reporter — U.S.Armed Forces	70 M.J. 247
Military Justice Reporter — A.F.Ct.Crim.App.	70 M.J. 513
Veterans Appeals Reporter	24 Vet.App.

Reprinted with permission from Thomson Reuters/West, *West's Federal Practice Digest*, 4th Ser., October 2011 Pamphlet, inside cover. © 2011 Thomson Reuters/West.

pamphlet. For example, the closing table in **Figure 5.10** lists the *Federal Supplement*, Second Series, closing with volume 777. That means that decisions through volume 777 of F. Supp. 2d are summarized within the interim pamphlet. Any cases reported in volume 778 and beyond came out too late to be included in the interim pamphlet.

To find out if any relevant cases are reported after volume 777, therefore, you will need to check the reporters on the shelves. Within each reporter, you will find a mini-digest in the back of the book. The mini-digest summarizes all of the decisions within that volume. You need to look up your topic and key number in each of the reporter volumes after volume 777 through the end of the set to make sure no new relevant decisions were issued after the interim pamphlet was published. Again, if nothing is listed under the topic and key number, no new decisions were issued, and your updating is complete.

Students often ask whether this last updating step is truly necessary. The answer largely depends on the progress of your research. If you have not been able to locate a sufficient amount of authority, you might want to use the closing table and mini-digests to expand your research results. This is especially true if the digest set does not have interim pamphlets and a number of months have passed since the pocket part was printed. If you are satisfied that you have located the pertinent cases on your issue and only need to verify that they still state the law accurately, the closing table and mini-digests are not the best tools for you to use. Chapter 6 discusses resources you can use to verify case research. These resources will allow you to check your research more efficiently than the closing table and mini-digests. As Chapter 6 explains, they can also be used to expand your research results, although you may still find the case summaries in the mini-digests helpful.

2. ADDITIONAL FEATURES OF DIGESTS

In addition to collecting case summaries under subject matter topics, digests have two other features you can use to locate cases: the Table of Cases and the Words and Phrases feature. All West digest sets have a Table of Cases, but not all have the Words and Phrases feature.

a. Table of Cases

The Table of Cases lists cases alphabetically by the name of both the plaintiff and the defendant.[4] Thus, if you know either party's name,

---

[4] West used to divide the Table of Cases into two tables: the Table of Cases, which listed cases by the plaintiff's name, and the Defendant-Plaintiff Table, which listed cases by the defendant's name. West now consolidates these two tables into one, called the Table of Cases. In some older digest sets, however, you may still find a separate Defendant-Plaintiff Table.

you can find the case in the Table of Cases. In the Table of Cases, you will find the following items of information:

1. the full name of the case;
2. the court that decided the case;
3. the complete citation to the case, including the parallel citation (if any) to an official reporter;
4. a list of the topics and key numbers appearing in the headnotes to the case.

The Table of Cases usually appears at the end of the digest set. Often, it is contained in a separate volume or set of volumes, but in smaller digest sets it may be included in a volume containing other material.

The Table of Cases is updated the same way as the subject volumes. The volumes containing the Table of Cases should have pocket parts. Some older digest sets also have hardcover supplements. If the digest set has interim pamphlets, one of those pamphlets will also contain a Table of Cases listing cases decided during the time period covered by the pamphlet.

b. Words and Phrases

The Words and Phrases feature provides citations to cases that have defined legal terms or phrases. Because dictionary definitions are not legally binding on courts, Words and Phrases can help you find legally binding definitions from cases that have interpreted or construed a term. In a sense, Words and Phrases is the closest print equivalent to electronic word searching because it collects case summaries based on specific words in the opinion. Words and Phrases is organized much like a dictionary. To determine whether the courts have defined a term, you simply look up the term alphabetically. If the term is listed, you will find citations to cases construing it. Newer volumes also contain brief summaries of the cases.

Words and Phrases is usually located near the Table of Cases within the digest set and is updated the same way as that table.

C. RESEARCHING CASES ELECTRONICALLY

1. WESTLAW

a. The Format of a Case in Westlaw

The format of a case in Westlaw is the same as the format of a case in a West reporter, although the case will look different in electronic form. At the beginning of the document, you will see a caption with the name of the case and other identifying information. The caption will be followed by an editorial summary of the decision. In more recent cases, the summary is divided into two sections: background and holding. The summary will be followed by one or more numbered headnotes and then the full text of the opinion. Just as in the print version of a case, the editorial summary and headnotes, if any, are not part of the decision and are not authoritative.

In the body of the opinion, the pagination from the print version of the case will be indicated by starred numbers. For example, if a case begins on page 231 of the print reporter, the transition to the next page will be indicated by *232.

Figures 5.11 and **5.12** show what a case looks like in Westlaw.com and WestlawNext.

b. Search Options in Westlaw

You can retrieve a case in Westlaw from its citation or by party name if you do not have the citation. Westlaw also allows source-driven searching by subject or words in the document, and WestlawNext offers content-driven word searching.

To retrieve a case from its citation, use the **Find** function in Westlaw .com. The **Find** screen contains a link to a template you can use to locate a case by party name if you do not have the citation. In WestlawNext, enter the citation or party name in the search box.

You can also search by subject. Recall from Section B, above, that print digests organize case summaries by topic so that you can locate cases on specific subjects. You can access the West digest case summaries in Westlaw.com and WestlawNext in two ways. One way is from a case on point. The headnotes at the beginning of each case summarize the content of the case and assign a topic name and key number subdivision to each headnote. By following the links in the headnotes, you can retrieve a list of summaries of cases that have been assigned the same topic and key number. In Westlaw.com, following the link brings up a **Custom Digest** search template you can use to specify the kinds of case summaries you want to retrieve. In WestlawNext, following the link automatically retrieves case summaries from the same jurisdiction as the case you were viewing. You can filter the results or change the jurisdiction as appropriate.

The second way to access the West digest is to search through the digest topic headings. In Westlaw.com, you can access the **West Key Number Digest Outline** by choosing the **Key Numbers** option at the top of the Westlaw screen or from the **Site Map**. You can execute a search to locate relevant topics and key numbers, which you can then use to generate a list of case summaries organized by topics. You can also drill down through the topic headings to view individual key numbers, and select the topic(s) and key number(s) you want to search. In WestlawNext, the **Tools** tab leads to the **West Key Number System**

FIGURE 5.11   EXAMPLE OF A CASE IN WESTLAW.COM

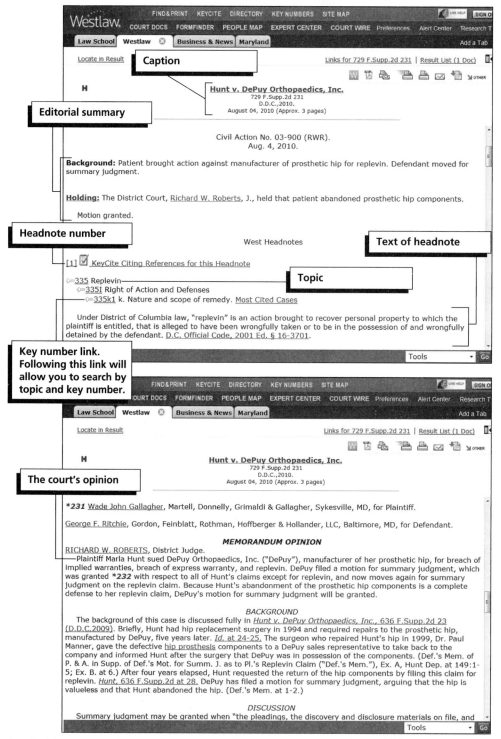

FIGURE 5.12   EXAMPLE OF A CASE IN WESTLAWNEXT

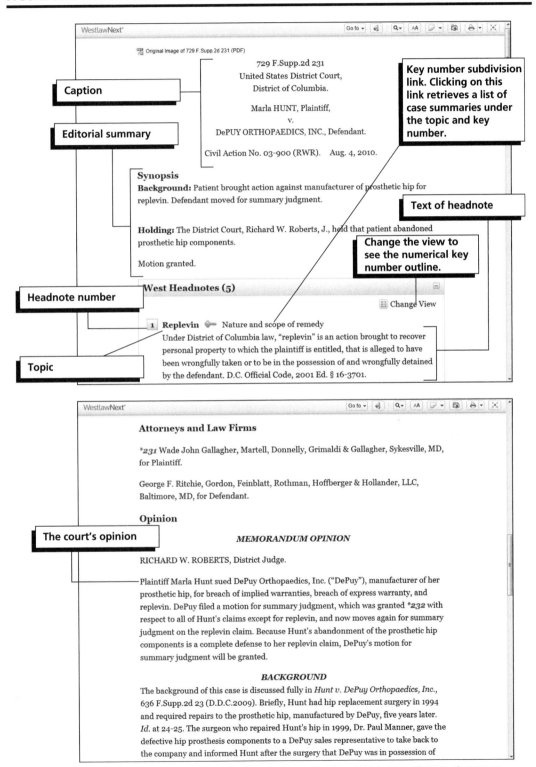

Reprinted with permission from Thomson Reuters/West, from Westlaw, 729 F. Supp. 2d 231. © 2012 Thomson Reuters/West.

link. From the list of headings, you can drill down through the digest topics. You can also execute a search within the Key Number System as a whole, without first selecting a specific topic, to generate a list of case summaries organized by subject. You can also search by subject from the **Topics** tab, although this option offers only a limited number of broad subject categories without any subtopics.

You can also locate cases in Westlaw using word searches. To execute a word search, Westlaw.com requires you to select a database as your first step. Selecting a database is similar to selecting a print digest. You should use the narrowest one that still has enough information to answer your research question. Westlaw has databases with cases from federal courts or individual states, as well as combined databases with both federal and state decisions. In addition, Westlaw has subject-matter databases containing federal and state cases in specific subject areas such as products liability or family law. Once you have selected a database, you are ready to construct and execute a word search.

WestlawNext will allow you to execute source-driven or content-driven searches for cases. To execute a source-driven search for cases, pre-filter the search by following the appropriate links under the tabs on the home page. To execute a content-driven word search, you will usually want to pre-filter by jurisdiction(s) using the jurisdiction selection box next to the search box. A content-driven search will retrieve many types of authority, including cases, which you can view in the **Cases** section. After you execute a word search, you will have a variety of options for filtering the search results.

The organization of the results in Westlaw.com and WestlawNext may be by date or relevance depending on the type of searching you do. You have some ability to modify the default sort options, again depending on the type of search. It is important to pay close attention to the date and level of court as you review the search results so you can assess whether each case is mandatory or persuasive authority.

Chapter 10 contains more information on the process of word searching.

2. LEXIS

a. The Format of a Case in Lexis

The format of a case in Lexis is similar to the format of a case in Westlaw. At the beginning of the document, you will see a caption with the name of the case and other identifying information. The caption will be followed by an editorial summary of the decision. The summary is divided into three components: procedural posture, overview, and outcome. No key number headnotes appear in the Lexis version of a case because the key number system is an editorial feature unique to West. Lexis has a similar editorial feature, however, called LexisNexis Headnotes. These head-notes are summary paragraphs organized by subject that quote passages from the case. Even though the LexisNexis Headnotes usually quote the opinion verbatim, they are not part of the decision and are not authoritative.

In the body of the opinion, the pagination from the print version of the case will be indicated by numbers in brackets. For example, if a case begins on page 23 of the print reporter, the transition to the next page will be indicated by [*24] in Lexis.com and [24] in Lexis Advance. For cases with parallel citations (that is, those published in multiple reporters), Lexis.com includes the pagination for all reporters within the same document. In Lexis Advance, the **Reporter** link near the top of the document allows you to select a reporter, and the bracketed numbers will reflect the pagination in the reporter you select.

Figures 5.13 and **5.14** show what a case looks like in Lexis.com and Lexis Advance.

b. Search Options in Lexis

You can retrieve a case in Lexis from its citation or by party name if you do not have the citation. Lexis also allows source-driven searching by subject or words in the document, and Lexis Advance offers content-driven searching. Because of the differences between the two versions of Lexis, each is addressed separately below. Like Westlaw, Lexis organizes search results in various ways, depending on the type of searching you do. You have some ability to modify the default sort options, again depending on the type of search. It is important to pay close attention to the date and level of court as you review the search results so you can assess whether each case is mandatory or persuasive authority.

(1) Lexis.com

To retrieve a case from its citation in Lexis.com, use the **Get a Document** function. Under the **Get a Document** tab, you will find a link to a template you can use to locate a case by party name if you do not have the citation.

Although the West topic and key number system is not available in Lexis, Lexis has its own subject searching capabilities. In Lexis.com, you can choose the option to search by topic or headnote. This option appears under the **Search** tab. Choosing this option brings up an alphabetical list of search topics. Each topic contains multiple subtopics, and most subtopics are further subdivided into even narrower categories. You can find a subject to search in three ways: You can select a subject you have searched before by browsing the recently searched topics; you can search for a subject using the search box; or you can explore a general subject by expanding the list and browsing the subtopics.

FIGURE 5.13   EXAMPLE OF A CASE IN LEXIS.COM

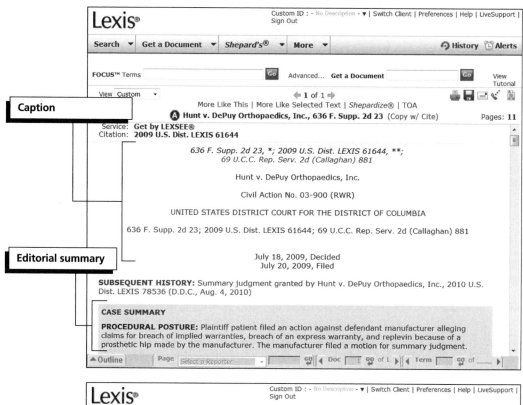

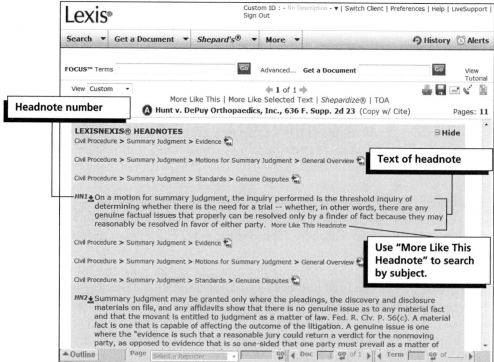

FIGURE 5.13   EXAMPLE OF A CASE IN LEXIS.COM *(Continued)*

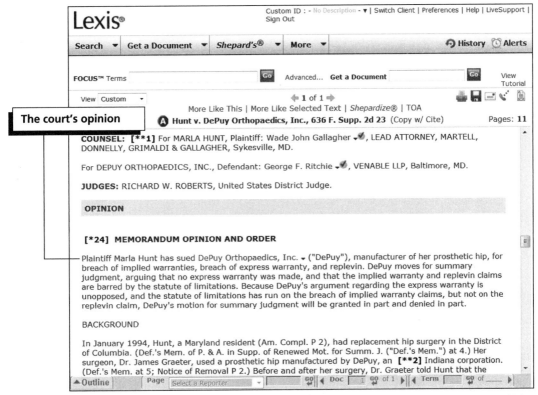

Copyright 2012 LexisNexis, a division of Reed Elsevier Inc. All Rights Reserved. LexisNexis and the Knowledge Burst logo are registered trademarks of Reed Elsevier Properties Inc. and are used with the permission of LexisNexis. 636 F. Supp. 2d 23.

After you select a search topic, Lexis.com displays a search screen. You can search in two ways. One option is to search across sources. With this option, you can choose to search for multiple types of authority (e.g., cases and statutes) simultaneously in the subject area you selected, or you can limit your search to a particular source. A second option is to search by headnote. A headnote search will retrieve cases containing the headnote topic you selected. You can select the jurisdiction to search, but the results will be limited to cases.

If you locate a relevant case, you can also search by headnote by selecting the More Like This Headnote option. This brings up a slightly different search screen that will also allow you to search for cases with material relevant to the headnote you selected. Although the option to search across sources allows you to add search terms to the search, the search by headnotes and More Like This Headnote options do not.

You can also locate cases in Lexis.com using word searches. To execute a word search, you must first select a database from the source directory. You should use the narrowest source that still has enough

FIGURE 5.14   EXAMPLE OF A CASE IN LEXIS ADVANCE

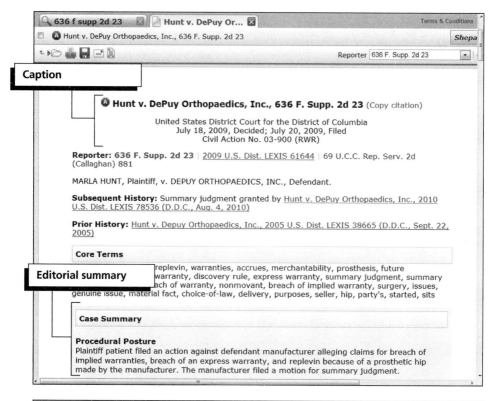

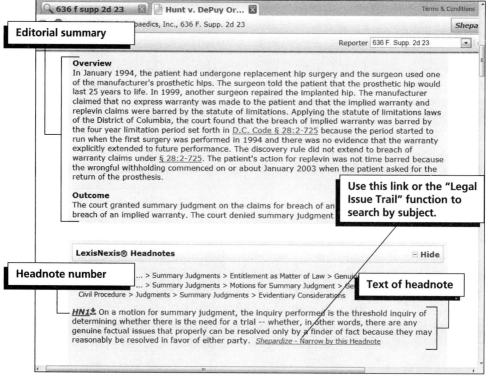

FIGURE 5.14   **EXAMPLE OF A CASE IN LEXIS ADVANCE** *(Continued)*

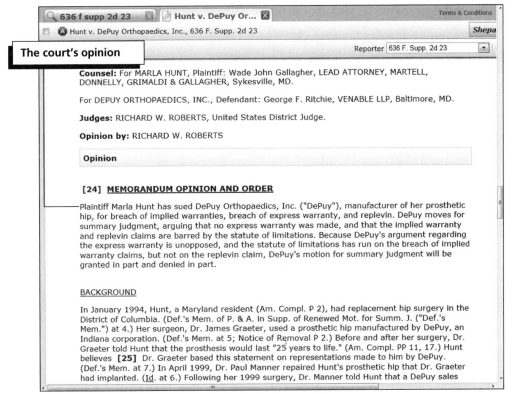

Copyright 2012 LexisNexis, a division of Reed Elsevier Inc. All Rights Reserved. LexisNexis and the Knowledge Burst logo are registered trademarks of Reed Elsevier Properties Inc. and are used with the permission of LexisNexis. Lexis Advance, 636 F. Supp. 2d 23.

information to answer your research question. Lexis.com has sources with cases from federal courts or individual states, as well as combined databases with both federal and state decisions. In addition, Lexis.com has sources devoted to specific subject areas that contain federal and state cases on topics such as products liability or family law.

Once you have selected a source, you are ready to construct and execute a word search. Chapter 10 contains more information on the process of word searching.

(2) Lexis Advance

To retrieve a case in Lexis Advance, enter the citation in the search box or use a party name as a search term. If you have located a case on point, you can use that to search by subject. Lexis Advance does not allow you to search by LexisNexis Headnote the way you can in Lexis.com. You can Shepardize by headnote. Shepardizing is a way of updating case research that is discussed in Chapter 6. You can also use the **Legal Issue Trail** function. This function allows you to mark passages within a case to generate a list of cases that cite the case you are viewing on the topic of the marked text, as well as cases cited within the case you are viewing.

To conduct a source-driven word search for cases only or a content-driven search for multiple forms of authority, you will execute a search in the search box, but you will vary the selections from the drop-down menus. For a source-driven search, select **Cases** as the content type. For a content-driven search, choose **All Content** as the content type. With either search you will usually want to pre-filter the search by jurisdiction. You may want to pre-filter by topic as well, but you do not have to. As this text goes to press, Lexis Advance offers only the broad topic categories listed in the drop-down menu; you cannot drill down to subtopics. After you execute a word search, you will have a variety of options for filtering the search results.

3. GOOGLE SCHOLAR

In addition to offering a general Internet search engine, Google also offers a specialized search vehicle called Google Scholar, which allows you to search for cases. The Internet address for Google Scholar appears in Appendix A. You can also access it from the main Google search engine page by using the **More** drop-down menu.

As this text goes to press, Google Scholar coverage includes published appellate opinions from all 50 states and the District of Columbia since 1950, opinions from the lower federal courts since 1923, and U.S. Supreme Court cases since 1791. Google Scholar does not include trial court opinions or non-precedential or unpublished opinions.

On the Google Scholar search page you can choose to search legal opinions and journals. Executing a search from this screen searches all jurisdictions and includes both cases and articles. To pre-filter the results by jurisdiction and exclude articles from the search, choose the **Advanced Scholar Search** option next to the search box. This will open a search screen from which you can select specific jurisdictions and enter your search terms in a search template.

The search results are ranked by relevance. It is important to pay close attention to the date and level of court as you review the search results so you can assess whether each case is mandatory or persuasive authority. In addition, the Google Scholar search engine not only looks for your search terms within the text of documents, but it also searches background information (meta-data). Therefore, the search engine is similar to the WestlawNext search engine described in Chapter 3. More information about how the type of search engine can affect search results, as well as more information on word searching generally, appears in Chapter 10.

When you view a case, you will see the text of the opinion, but not any of the editorial enhancements that Lexis and Westlaw provide. You can, however, view information under the **How Cited** tab to locate citations to other authorities that have referenced the case you are viewing.

4. OTHER INTERNET SOURCES

Internet sources other than Google Scholar can also lead you to relevant cases, although using a general search engine is not likely to be an efficient strategy for comprehensive case research. Two other approaches are likely to be more effective. The first is to review the website for the court whose decisions you are trying to locate. The second is to go to general legal research websites. Many of these websites either include links to websites with court opinions or index their own databases of cases. Appendix A lists the Internet addresses for a number of legal research websites that may be useful for case research.

Once you have located a source containing cases, several searching options may be available. You may be able to search by date, docket number, case name, or key word, depending on how the website is organized.

Internet searching has some limitations. Because comprehensive digesting tools are not yet available on the Internet, it is difficult to search for cases by subject, and the full-text search options available on many websites are limited. In addition, a number of databases only contain decisions going back a few years, so comprehensive research over time may not be possible. Once you have located a case, you will usually only see the text of the court's opinion. Internet sources generally lack the editorial enhancements available with commercial research services, which may hinder your research efforts.

Despite these limitations, the Internet can be useful for targeted case research. If you know which jurisdiction's cases you want to research and the relevant court's website offers full-text searching, searching court websites is one way of gathering some citations to get started with your research. Internet sources are also useful for locating the most recent opinions and opinions from tribunals whose decisions are not published in print reporters or commercial databases. For example, U.S. Supreme Court decisions are available on the Internet almost immediately after issuance. Opinions of municipal courts or local agencies may only be available on the Internet. Unpublished opinions that are not included in a Google Scholar search may be accessible on a court website. In addition, the Internet is a more cost-effective way to access cases otherwise available in Lexis, Westlaw, or other commercial services.

D. CITING CASES

As Chapter 1 explains, any time you report the results of your research in written form, you must cite your sources properly. This is especially important for cases because the information in the citation can help the reader assess the weight of the authority you are citing.

A case citation has three basic components:

1. the case name;
2. information on the reporter in which the case is published;
3. a parenthetical containing the jurisdiction, the level of court that decided the case, and the year of decision.

You can find rules for each component in the *ALWD Manual* and the *Bluebook*. Using the *ALWD Manual* (4th ed.), you should read Rule 12 and use Appendices 1, 3, and 4 for any necessary abbreviations. Using the *Bluebook* (19th ed.), you should begin with Bluepages B4 and use Tables T1, T6, and T10 to find any necessary abbreviations. **Figure 5.15** directs you to the citation rules for cases.

The remainder of this section uses an example citation to illustrate each of these components. The example citation is to a fictional 1983 decision of the Delaware Court of Chancery in the case of Patricia Ellis and Sam Anson versus Acme Manufacturing Company, published in volume 327 of the *Atlantic Reporter*, Second Series, beginning on page 457.

1. THE CASE NAME

The name of the case appears first and must be underlined or *italicized*. The case name consists of the name of the first party on either side of the "v." In other words, if more than one plaintiff or defendant is listed in the

FIGURE 5.15 *ALWD MANUAL* AND *BLUEBOOK* RULES GOVERNING CASE CITATIONS

CITATION COMPONENT	*ALWD MANUAL* (4th ed.), RULE 12	*BLUEBOOK* (19th ed.), BLUEPAGES B4
Case name	Rule 12.2 & Appendix 3	Bluepages B4.1.1 & Tables T6 & T10
Reporter information	Rules 12.3-12.5 & Appendix 1	Bluepages B4.1.2, B4.1.3, & Table T1
Parenthetical	Rules 12.6-12.7 & Appendices 1 & 4	Bluepages B4.1.3 & Table T1

full case name, give only the name of the first named plaintiff or first named defendant. In the example citation, Sam Anson would not be listed. Do not include "et al." when a case has multiple parties; simply refer to the first named party on both sides. If a person is named as a party, use only the person's last name, but if a company or other entity is listed, use the entity's full name.

Often, the case name will be abbreviated. The abbreviation rules vary slightly in the *ALWD Manual* and the *Bluebook*. You will need to read the rules and refer to the appropriate appendix or table to determine when words should be abbreviated and what the proper abbreviations are. The case name should be followed by a comma, which is not underlined or italicized.

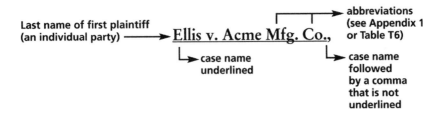

2. THE REPORTER

After the case name, the citation should list information on the reporter in which the case is published. If the case is published in more than one reporter, you will need to determine which reporter or reporters to cite, as explained in *ALWD Manual* Rule 12.4 and *Bluebook* Bluepages B4.1.3. In the citation, the name of the reporter will be abbreviated, so you must also determine the proper abbreviation. In the *ALWD Manual*, you can find this information in Appendix 1, which lists each jurisdiction in the United States alphabetically. For each jurisdiction, Appendix 1 lists reporter names and abbreviations. In the *Bluebook*, this same information appears in Table T1.

Ordinarily, you will list the volume of the reporter, the reporter abbreviation, and the starting page of the case. If you are citing a specific page within the case, you will also usually cite to that page as well, using what is called a pinpoint citation. A comma should appear between the starting page and the pinpoint citation, but the pinpoint citation should not be followed by a comma.

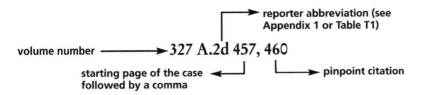

3. THE PARENTHETICAL

Following the information on the reporter, the case citation should include a parenthetical containing the abbreviated name of the jurisdiction, the abbreviated name of the level of court that decided the case, and the year the court issued its decision. This information is important because it can help the reader assess the weight of the authority you are citing.

The place to find the proper abbreviation for the jurisdiction and level of court is Appendix 1 in the *ALWD Manual* or Table T1 in the *Bluebook*. Appendix 1 and Table T1 list the levels of courts under each jurisdiction. Next to the name of each court, an abbreviation will appear in parentheses. This is the abbreviation for both the jurisdiction and the level of court, and this is what should appear in your parenthetical. You will notice that for the highest court in each state, the jurisdiction abbreviation is all that is necessary. This alerts the reader that the decision came from the highest court in the state; no additional court name abbreviation is necessary. Neither Appendix 1 nor Table T1 lists the abbreviations for all courts. If you do not find the abbreviations you need in Appendix 1 in the *ALWD Manual*, consult Appendix 4, which contains court abbreviations. In the *Bluebook*, Table T7 contains court names.

The last item to appear in the parenthetical is the year of the decision. The date when the court heard the case is not necessary in the citation; only the year of decision is required. No comma should appear before the year. After the year, the parenthetical should be closed.

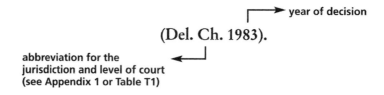

When all of the pieces are put together, the citation should look like this:

Ellis v. Acme Mfg. Co., 327 A.2d 457, 460 (Del. Ch. 1983).

E. SAMPLE PAGES FOR CASE RESEARCH

On the following pages, you will find sample pages illustrating the process of case research. For purposes of this illustration, assume that your client left personal property with someone else who now refuses to return it on the ground that your client abandoned the property. You want to research an action to recover personal property (known as replevin) and the rules regarding when property is considered abandoned under District of Columbia law. If you were researching this issue, you might want to look for relevant federal cases as persuasive authority applying District of Columbia law. **Figures 5.16** through **5.20** show what you would see in *West's Federal Practice Digest*, Fourth Series. **Figures 5.21** and **5.22** show search results in Westlaw and Lexis. **Figure 5.23** is a case published in West's *Federal Supplement*, Second Series.

The first step in print digest research is using the Descriptive-Word Index to lead you to relevant topics and key numbers. One search term you might have used is *Abandonment*. Under this heading, the entry for "Accidental loss" cross-references "Finding Lost Goods," which is another index entry that could contain useful references. The entry for "Acts constituting" refers to relevant topics and key numbers. The abbreviation "Aband L P" refers to the "Abandoned and Lost Property" topic, and the numbers refer to a range of key numbers under that topic.

After checking the main index volume, you should check the pocket part for any updated index entries.

FIGURE 5.16   DESCRIPTIVE-WORD INDEX

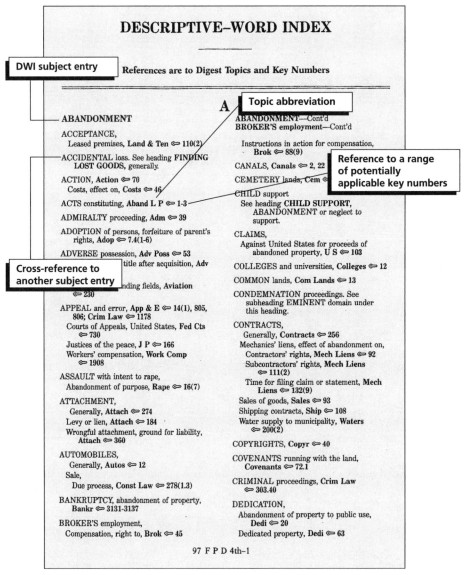

Reprinted with permission from Thomson Reuters/West, *West's Federal Practice Digest*, 4th Ser., Vol. 97 (2002), p. 1. © 2002 Thomson Reuters/West.

The next step is looking up the topic "Abandoned and Lost Property" in the subject volumes. The outline at the beginning of the topic identifies a range of key numbers that may be relevant.

FIGURE 5.17   KEY NUMBER OUTLINE, "ABANDONED AND LOST PROPERTY" TOPIC

ABANDONED AND LOST PROPERTY

SUBJECTS INCLUDED

General nature of relinquishment of property or other rights of any kind by abandonment, as distinguished from dedication, surrender, waiver, etc.

Effect of abandonment by way of extinguishment of the title or right

Finding and taking of possession of lost goods of another, whereby the finder may acquire title thereto

Nature, requisites and incidents of such finding and possession

Rights, duties and liabilities of finders of lost goods as to the owners or losers and as to others in general

SUBJECTS EXCLUDED AND COVERED BY OTHER TOPICS

Estrays, see ANIMALS

Lost instruments in writing, establishment of and action on, see LOST INSTRUMENTS

Negotiable paper, rights of finders, see BILLS AND NOTES

Particular persons or personal relations, abandonment of, see specific topics

Particular species of property, rights, remedies, or proceedings, abandonment of, see specific topics

Reversion of property to the state, see ESCHEAT

Rewards for recovery of lost goods, etc., see REWARDS

Sales of lost goods, see SALES

Wrecks and vessels and goods derelict at sea, see SHIPPING

For detailed references to other topics, see Descriptive-Word Index

---

Analysis

I. ABANDONMENT, ⚷1–9.

II. FINDING LOST GOODS, ⚷10–13.

> Relevant key numbers

I. ABANDONMENT.
   ⚷1. Nature and elements.
     1.1. —— In general.
     2. —— Intent.
     3. —— Acts and omissions.
     4. Evidence and questions for jury.
     5. Operation and effect.

II. FINDING LOST GOODS.
   ⚷10. In general; loss of property.
     11. Rights and liabilities of finder as to owner.

FIGURE 5.17   KEY NUMBER OUTLINE, "ABANDONED AND LOST PROPERTY" TOPIC *(Continued)*

ABANDONED & LOST PROPERTY   1 F P D 4th—2

II. FINDING LOST GOODS.—Continued.
    12. Title and rights of finder as to third persons.
    13. Title and rights of finders inter se.

For detailed references to other topics, see Descriptive-Word Index

---

Reprinted with permission from Thomson Reuters/West, *West's Federal Practice Digest*, 4th Ser., Vol. 1 (2006), pp. 1-2. © 2006 Thomson Reuters/West.

The case summaries under key number 2 include a potentially relevant case from the U.S. Court of Appeals for the District of Columbia Circuit.

FIGURE 5.18   CASE SUMMARIES UNDER "ABANDONED AND LOST PROPERTY" TOPIC

☞1.1   **ABANDONED & LOST PROPERTY**   1 F P D 4th—6

For later cases, see same Topic and Key Number in Pocket Part

purchasers who bought forfeited vehicle acquired ownership of currency in gas tank, where drug traffickers intentionally placed currency in gas tank as part of drug trafficking scheme and chose not to reclaim currency or challenge forfeiture of vehicle and its contents for fear of prosecution for drug conspiracy.

In re Seizure of $82,000 More or Less, 119 F.Supp.2d 1013.

Abandonment consists of two elements: (1) intent to abandon, and (2) external act by which intention is carried into effect.

In re Seizure of $82,000 More or Less, 119 F.Supp.2d 1013.

D.Nev. 1998.   Abandonment is the voluntary relinquishment of a known right.

U.S. v. Alpine Land and Reservoir Co., 27 F.Supp.2d 1230.

E.D.Va. 1990.   In determining whether property has been lost or abandoned, court must first determine whether location of property is known, and then, even if its location was known, whether it has been abandoned.

Columbus-America Discovery Group, Inc. v. Unidentified, Wrecked and Abandoned Sailing Vessel, 742 F.Supp. 1327, reversed Columbus-America Discovery Group v. Atlantic Mut. Ins. Co., 974 F.2d 450, certiorari denied 113 S.Ct. 1625, 507 U.S. 1000, 123 L.Ed.2d 183, on remand 1993 WL 580900, rescinded 56 F.3d 556, certiorari denied 116 S.Ct. 352, 516 U.S. 938, 133 L.Ed.2d 248, certiorari denied Grimm v. Columbus-America Discovery Group, Inc., 116 S.Ct. 521, 516 U.S. 990, 133 L.Ed.2d 429.

Whether there is abandonment is to be determined from consideration of nature of property and conduct of parties in relation to it.

Columbus-America Discovery Group, Inc. v. Unidentified, Wrecked and Abandoned Sailing Vessel, 742 F.Supp. 1327, reversed Columbus-America Discovery Group v. Atlantic Mut. Ins. Co., 974 F.2d 450, certiorari denied 113 S.Ct. 1625, 507 U.S. 1000, 123 L.Ed.2d 183, on remand 1993 WL 580900, rescinded 56 F.3d 556, certiorari denied 116 S.Ct. 352, 516 U.S. 938, 133 L.Ed.2d 248, certiorari denied Grimm v. Columbus-America Discovery Group, Inc., 116 S.Ct. 521, 516 U.S. 990, 133 L.Ed.2d 429.

In determining whether property has been abandoned, consideration must be given to property, time, place and circumstances, actions and conduct of parties, opportunity or expectancy of recovery and all other facts and circumstances.

Columbus-America Discovery Group, Inc. v. Unidentified, Wrecked and Abandoned Sailing Vessel, 742 F.Supp. 1327, reversed Columbus-America Discovery Group v. Atlantic Mut. Ins. Co., 974 F.2d 450, certiorari denied 113 S.Ct. 1625, 507 U.S. 1000, 123 L.Ed.2d 183, on remand 1993 WL 580900, rescinded 56 F.3d 556, certiorari denied 116 S.Ct. 352, 516 U.S. 938, 133 L.Ed.2d 248, certiorari denied Grimm v. Columbus-America Discovery Group, Inc., 116 S.Ct. 521, 516 U.S. 990, 133 L.Ed.2d 429.

Bkrtcy.W.D.Mo. 1993.   Under Missouri law, "abandonment" is voluntary relinquishment of ownership of property so that property ceases to be property of any person and becomes subject of appropriation by first taker.

In re Usery, 158 B.R. 470.

Under Missouri law, abandonment is complete at moment intention to abandon and relinquishment of possession of property unite.

In re Usery, 158 B.R. 470.

Bkrtcy.D.S.C. 2005.   Under South Carolina law, the primary elements of abandonment of property are intent to abandon and the external act by which the intention is carried into effect, with intent to abandon being the paramount inquiry.

In re Willcox, 329 B.R. 554.

Under South Carolina law, "abandonment" is the relinquishment of property with intent to never resume ownership or possession.

In re Willcox, 329 B.R. 554.

Under South Carolina law, time generally is of no importance to the issue of abandonment of property, except possibly to be considered as indicative of intention.

In re Willcox, 329 B.R. 554.

☞2.   —— **Intent.**

C.A.D.C. 2000.   Legal abandonment of property is premised on determining the intent to abandon, which requires an inquiry into facts and circumstances.

American Petroleum Institute v. U.S. E.P.A., 216 F.3d 50, 342 U.S.App.D.C. 159, as amended, and rehearing and rehearing denied.

C.A.5 (La.) 1988.   Whether property has been abandoned is question of intent, which may be inferred from all relevant facts and circumstances. U.S.C.A. Const.Amend. 4.

U.S. v. Sylvester, 848 F.2d 520, rehearing denied.

C.A.2 (N.Y.) 1991.   To prove abandonment, both owner's intent to abandon property

Key number 2

Summaries of federal circuit court cases are listed first.

† This Case was not selected for publication in the National Reporter System. For cited U.S.C.A. sections and legislative history, see United States Code Anno[...]

FIGURE 5.18   CASE SUMMARIES UNDER "ABANDONED AND LOST PROPERTY" TOPIC *(Continued)*

---

1 F P D 4th—7   **ABANDONED & LOST PROPERTY**   ⚷3

For references to other topics, see Descriptive-Word Index

and some affirmative act or omission demonstrating that intention must be shown.

Hoelzer v. City of Stamford, Conn., 933 F.2d 1131.

N.D.Cal. 1995. To show that property has been "abandoned," party must prove intent by original owner to abandon property and physical acts carrying that intent into effect.

Deep Sea Research, Inc. v. Brother Jonathan, 883 F.Supp. 1343, affirmed 102 F.3d 379, certiorari granted California v. Deep Sea Research, Inc., 117 S.Ct. 2430, 520 U.S. 1263, 138 L.Ed.2d 192, stay denied 117 S.Ct. 2537, 521 U.S. 1131, 138 L.Ed.2d 1036, affirmed in part, vacated in part 118 S.Ct. 1464, 523 U.S. 491, 140 L.Ed.2d 626, on remand 143 F.3d 1299, vacated in part 143 F.3d 1299, affirmed 89 F.3d 680, opinion amended and superseded on denial of rehearing 102 F.3d 379, certiorari granted 117 S.Ct. 2430, 520 U.S. 1263, 138 L.Ed.2d 192, stay denied 117 S.Ct. 2537, 521 U.S. 1131, 138 L.Ed.2d 1036, affirmed in part, vacated in part 118 S.Ct. 1464, 523 U.S. 491, 140 L.Ed.2d 626, on remand 143 F.3d 1299, vacated in part 143 F.3d 1299.

N.D.Ill. 1990. To show "abandonment," a party must prove intent to abandon and physical acts carrying that intent into effect.

Zych v. Unidentified, Wrecked and Abandoned Vessel, Believed to be SB Lady Elgin, 755 F.Supp. 213.

E.D.Va. 1995. Key to ownership of sunken property under the law of finds is whether owner has abandoned the property, and abandonment can be express or implied, and lapse of time and nonuse by owner may give rise to inference of intent to abandon.

Bemis v. RMS Lusitania, 884 F.Supp. 1042, affirmed 99 F.3d 1129, certiorari denied 118 S.Ct. 1558, 523 U.S. 1093, 140 L.Ed.2d 791.

E.D.Va. 1990. Abandonment may be accomplished by either express or implied act of leaving or deserting the property without hope of recovering it and without intention of returning to it.

Columbus-America Discovery Group, Inc. v. Unidentified, Wrecked and Abandoned Sailing Vessel, 742 F.Supp. 1327, reversed Columbus-America Discovery Group v. Atlantic Mut. Ins. Co., 974 F.2d 450, certiorari denied 113 S.Ct. 1625, 507 U.S. 1000, 123 L.Ed.2d 183, on remand 1993 WL 580900, rescinded 56 F.3d 556, certiorari denied 116 S.Ct. 352, 516 U.S. 938, 133 L.Ed.2d 248, certiorari denied Grimm v. Columbus-America Discovery Group, Inc., 116 S.Ct. 521, 516 U.S. 990, 133 L.Ed.2d 429.

Whether property has been abandoned is question of intent, which may be inferred from all relevant facts and circumstances.

Columbus-America Discovery Group, Inc. v. Unidentified, Wrecked and Abandoned Sailing Vessel, 742 F.Supp. 1327, reversed Columbus-America Discovery Group v. Atlantic Mut. Ins. Co., 974 F.2d 450, certiorari denied 113 S.Ct. 1625, 507 U.S. 1000, 123 L.Ed.2d 183, on remand 1993 WL 580900, rescinded 56 F.3d 556, certiorari denied 116 S.Ct. 352, 516 U.S. 938, 133 L.Ed.2d 248, certiorari denied Grimm v. Columbus-America Discovery Group, Inc., 116 S.Ct. 521, 516 U.S. 990, 133 L.Ed.2d 429.

Bkrtcy.W.D.Mo. 1993. Under Missouri law, abandonment of property requires intent plus act.

In re Usery, 158 B.R. 470.

Bkrtcy.D.S.C. 2005. Under South Carolina law, to conclude that an abandonment of property has occurred, there must be some clear and unmistakable affirmative act or series of acts indicating a purpose to repudiate ownership.

In re Willcox, 329 B.R. 554.

Under South Carolina law, intent to abandon property is to be considered from all the surrounding facts and circumstances.

In re Willcox, 329 B.R. 554.

⚷3.   —— **Acts and omissions.**

C.A.2 (N.Y.) 1991. To prove abandonment, both owner's intent to abandon property and some affirmative act or omission demonstrating that intention must be shown.

Hoelzer v. City of Stamford, Conn., 933 F.2d 1131.

N.D.Cal. 1995. There is no "abandonment" when one discovers some sunken property and then, even after extensive efforts, is unable to locate its owner.

Deep Sea Research, Inc. v. Brother Jonathan, 883 F.Supp. 1343, affirmed 102 F.3d 379, certiorari granted California v. Deep Sea Research, Inc., 117 S.Ct. 2430, 520 U.S. 1263, 138 L.Ed.2d 192, stay denied 117 S.Ct. 2537, 521 U.S. 1131, 138 L.Ed.2d 1036, affirmed in part, vacated in part 118 S.Ct. 1464, 523 U.S. 491, 140 L.Ed.2d 626, on remand 143 F.3d 1299, vacated in part 143 F.3d 1299, affirmed 89 F.3d 680, opinion amended and superseded on denial of rehearing 102 F.3d 379, certiorari granted 117 S.Ct. 2430, 520 U.S. 1263, 138 L.Ed.2d 192, stay denied 117 S.Ct. 2537, 521 U.S.

> **Summaries of federal district court cases follow summaries of circuit court cases.**

† This Case was not selected for publication in the National Reporter System
For cited U.S.C.A. sections and legislative history, see United States Code Annotated

---

The next step is checking the pocket part for this volume. The entry under key number 2 in the pocket part lists one case from the U.S. District Court for the District of Columbia.

FIGURE 5.19 DIGEST VOLUME, POCKET PART

1 F P D 4th—1   ABANDONED & LOST PROPERTY ⚷3

ABANDONED AND LOST PROPERTY

I. ABANDONMENT.

Library references
C.J.S. Abandonment § 2 et seq.

⚷1. **Nature and elements.**
See ⚷1.1.

⚷1.1. —— **In general.**
C.A.7 (Ill.) 2011. Under Illinois law, abandonment of property is a deliberate act.—Enbridge Pipelines (Illinois) L.L.C. v. Moore, 633 F.3d 602.
C.A.8 (Mo.) 2008. Under Missouri law, abandonment is the voluntary relinquishment of ownership so that the property ceases to be the property of any person and becomes the subject of appropriation by the first taker.—Jackson v. U.S., 526 F.3d 394, on remand 2009 WL 2757040.
C.D.Cal. 2008. Under California law, intent to abandon, as required to establish abandonment, is determined based on consideration of all the circumstances of the case, including all acts of ownership and dominion, or a want of such acts. —UMG Recordings, Inc. v. Augusto, 558 F.Supp.2d 1055, affirmed 628 F.3d 1175.
Under California law, there is no such thing as an abandonment to particular persons; the owner must leave the property free to the occupation of the next comer, whoever he may be.—Id.
E.D.Ky. 2009. Kentucky statute which shortened the presumptive period of abandonment of uncashed traveler's checks from 15 years to seven years was arbitrary and capricious and, thus, violated the Due Process Clause; state's objective was to raise revenue rather than to reunite citizens with lost property, and, even if revenue raising were a legitimate state purpose, shortening presumptive abandonment period was not rationally related to raising revenue. U.S.C.A. Const.Amend. 14; KRS 393.060(2).—American Exp. Travel Related Services, Inc. v. Hollenbach, 630 F.Supp.2d 757, reconsideration denied 2009 WL 2382407, vacated and remanded 641 F.3d 685.
E.D.Va. 2009. Active-duty servicemembers did not abandon vehicles under state law as would permit storage lienholders to sell vehicles at auction to enforce liens without court order without violating Servicemembers Civil Relief Act (SCRA), where lienholders did not pursue statutory abandonment procedure by initiating search with motor vehicle department and sending notice to vehicles' owners, and vehicles were thus still servicemembers' property protected by SCRA. Servicemembers Civil Relief Act, § 307(a)(1), 50 App.U.S.C.A. § 537(a)(1).—U.S. v. B.C. Enterprises, Inc., 667 F.Supp.2d 650.
E.D.Va. 1990. Columbus-America Discovery Group, Inc. v. Unidentified, Wrecked and Abandoned Sailing Vessel, 742 F.Supp. 1327, reversed Columbus-America Discovery Group v. Atlantic Mut. Ins. Co., 974 F.2d 450, certiorari denied 113 S.Ct. 1625, 507 U.S. 1000, 123 L.Ed.2d 183, on remand 1993 WL 580900, rescinded 56 F.3d 556, certiorari denied 116 S.Ct. 352, 516 U.S. 938, 133 L.Ed.2d 248, certiorari denied Grimm v. Columbus-America Discovery Group, Inc., 116 S.Ct. 521, 516 U.S. 990, 133 L.Ed.2d 429.
Bkrtcy.S.D.Ohio 2006. Under Ohio law, "abandoned property" is property over which the owner has relinquished all right, title, claim, and possession with the intention of not reclaiming it or resuming its ownership, possession, or enjoyment.—In re Panel Town of Dayton, Inc., 338 B.R. 764.
Under Ohio law, aba[ndonment re]quires affirmative pro[cess to show] coupled with acts or om[ission of] intent.—Id.
Bkrtcy.D.S.C. 2006. Under South Carolina law, "abandonment" is the relinquishment a property right.—In re T 2 Green, LLC, 363 B.R. 753.

⚷2. —— **Intent.**
C.A.9 (Cal.) 2010. Under California law, abandonment is a question of intent to be determined upon all the facts and circumstances.— CRS Recovery, Inc. v. Laxton, 600 F.3d 1138.
C.A.8 (Mo.) 2008. Under Missouri law, abandonment of property requires intent plus an act. —Jackson v. U.S., 526 F.3d 394, on remand 2009 WL 2757040.
C.D.Cal. 2008. Under California law, one has intent to abandon, as required to establish abandonment, when one relinquishes possession without any present intention to repossess.—UMG Recordings, Inc. v. Augusto, 558 F.Supp.2d 1055, affirmed 628 F.3d 1175.
Under California law, abandonment requires something more than passivity; there must be some clear and unmistakable affirmative act or series of acts indicating an intention to relinquish ownership.—Id.
D.D.C. 2010. To prove abandonment of property under District of Columbia law, a party must demonstrate both an intent to abandon and an act or omission that effectuates the intention.— Hunt v. DePuy Orthopaedics, Inc., 729 F.Supp.2d 231.
E.D.Va. 1990. Columbus-America Discovery Group, Inc. v. Unidentified, Wrecked and Abandoned Sailing Vessel, 742 F.Supp. 1327, reversed Columbus-America Discovery Group v. Atlantic Mut. Ins. Co., 974 F.2d 450, certiorari denied 113 S.Ct. 1625, 507 U.S. 1000, 123 L.Ed.2d 183, on remand 1993 WL 580900, resc[inded 56 F.3d 556,] certiorari denied 116 S.Ct. [352, 516 U.S. 938,] 133 L.Ed.2d 248, certiorari [denied Grimm v.] Columbus-America Discove[ry Group, Inc., 116] S.Ct. 521, 516 U.S. 990, 133 [L.Ed.2d 429.]
Bkrtcy.S.D.Ohio 2006. U[nder Ohio law,] intent to abandon property must be shown by unequivocal and decisive acts indicative of abandonment.—In re Panel Town of Dayton, Inc., 338 B.R. 764.
Under Ohio law, a debtor's delay in attempting to retrieve already converted property does not show intent to abandon that property.—Id.

⚷3. —— **Acts and omissions.**
C.A.8 (Mo.) 2008. Under Missouri law, abandonment of property requires intent plus an act. —Jackson v. U.S., 526 F.3d 394, on remand 2009 WL 2757040.
C.D.Cal. 2008. Under California law, intent to abandon, as required to establish abandonment, is determined based on consideration of all the circumstances of the case, including all acts of ownership and dominion, or a want of such acts. —UMG Recordings, Inc. v. Augusto, 558 F.Supp.2d 1055, affirmed 628 F.3d 1175.
Under California law, abandonment may arise from a single act or a series of acts.—Id.
Under California law, abandonment requires something more than mere passivity; there must be some clear and unmistakable affirmative act

† This Case was not selected for publication in the National Reporter System

[Pocket part entry for key number 2]

[Summary of a potentially relevant case]

At the end of *West's Federal Practice Digest*, Fourth Series, are a series of noncumulative interim pamphlets with cases decided after the pocket part was published. Under the topic "Abandoned and Lost Property" in this example, one new case is summarized under key number 2.

On the inside front cover of the interim pamphlet is the closing table indicating the last volumes of the reporters with cases summarized in this pamphlet. To find cases decided after the interim pamphlet closed, the next step would be to check the mini-digest in the back of each individual volume of F.3d and F. Supp. 2d after the volumes listed in the closing table.

FIGURE 5.20   NONCUMULATIVE INTERIM PAMPHLET

West's
FEDERAL PRACTICE
DIGEST 4th

For Later Cases, See Same Topic and Key Number
in Any Advance Sheet or Bound Volume of the
NATIONAL REPORTER SYSTEM® or WESTLAW®

> **Interim pamphlet entry for Abandoned and Lost Property**

ABANDONED AND LOST PROPERTY

I. ABANDONMENT.

☞1. Nature and elements.
See ☞1.1.
☞1.1. —— In general.
   E.D.Va. 2011. Abandonment requires an intentional relinquishment of rights in private property with no intention to return to that property at a later time; further, the amount of time that has passed between the relinquishment and the subsequent discovery of the property by a third party is informative on the topic of abandonment, but not dispositive.—Tait v. U.S., 763 F.Supp.2d 786.

☞2. —— Intent.
   E.D.Va. 2011. Abandonment requires an intentional relinquishment of rights in private property with no intention to return to that property at a later time; further, the amount of time that has passed between the relinquishment and the subsequent discovery of the property by a third party is informative on the topic of abandonment, but not dispositive.—Tait v. U.S., 763 F.Supp.2d 786.

☞4. Evidence and questions for jury.

> **One new case summarized under key number 2**

... raditional rational basis test, ... rational basis scrutiny, ap- ... due process challenge to ... the period after which state ... mption of abandonment on ... eby accelerating the date at which the issuer of an unclaimed traveler's check must remit the outstanding funds to the state; thus, revenue raising was a legitimate legislative purpose for purposes of such analysis. U.S.C.A. Const. Amend. 14; KRS 393.060.—American Exp. Travel Related Services Co., Inc. v. Kentucky, 641 F.3d 685.
   Amendment shortening the period after which state law imposed a presumption of abandonment on traveler's checks, thereby accelerating the date at which the issuer of an unclaimed traveler's check must remit the outstanding funds to the state, was rationally related to legitimate legislative purpose of revenue raising, and therefore did not violate substantive due process. U.S.C.A. Const. Amend. 14; KRS 393.060.—Id.

ABATEMENT AND REVIVAL

III. DEFECTS AND OBJECTIONS AS TO PARTIES AND PROCEEDINGS.

☞19. Nonperformance of condition precedent.
   E.D.Tex. 2011. Abatement, not dismissal, is the proper remedy for failure to satisfy the pre-suit notice requirements under the Texas Deceptive Trade Practices Act (DTPA) and Texas Insurance Code. V.T.C.A., Bus. & C. § 17.505; V.T.C.A., Insurance Code § 541.154(a).—Encompass Office Solutions, Inc. v. Ingenix, Inc., 775 F.Supp.2d 938.
   Abatement of medical equipment and services provider's action against insurers was unwarranted despite provider's failure to provide insurers with 60-day pre-suit notice of action pursuant to Texas Deceptive Trade Practices Act (DTPA) and Texas Insurance Code and insurers' timely filing of plea in abatement, where more than sixty days had passed since provider represented to court that it had filed its belated pre-filing notice. V.T.C.A., Bus. & C. § 17.505; V.T.C.A., Insurance Code § 541.154(a).—Id.

ABORTION AND BIRTH CONTROL

☞110. Clinics, facilities, and practitioners.
   D.Md. 2011. City ordinance, requiring any provider of pregnancy-related services that did not also provide or refer its clients for abortions or certain birth-control services to post a conspicuous sign in its waiting room to that effect, regulated speech, implicating the First Amendment; the requirement of a disclaimer sign in the waiting room was form of compelled speech, and the ordinance mandated the timing and content of the organization's introduction of the subjects of abortion and birth-control. U.S.C.A. Const.Amend. 1.—O'Brien v. Mayor and City Council of Baltimore, 768 F.Supp.2d 804.
   Strict scrutiny applied to pregnancy-related services provider's First Amendment challenge to city ordinance, requiring any provider of pregnancy-related services that did not also provide or refer its clients for abortions or certain birth-control services to post a conspicuous sign in its waiting room to that effect; ordinance regulated non-com-

1

In WestlawNext, you can conduct a content-driven search that will retrieve cases and other authorities. You can also access the West Key Number System under the Tools tab. Executing a word search within the West Key Number System retrieves a list of case summaries organized by topic. The search can also be pre-filtered by jurisdiction. Figure 5.21 shows a portion of the results of a search for summaries of District of Columbia and related federal cases that relate to *abandoned property*.

FIGURE 5.21 RESULTS OF WORD SEARCH WITHIN WEST KEY NUMBER SYSTEM

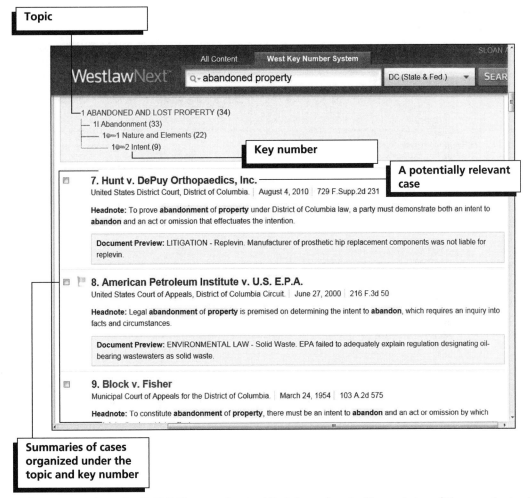

WestlawNext search results. © 2012 Thomson Reuters/West. Reproduced with permission of Thomson Reuters/ West.

In Lexis Advance, you can execute a content-driven search and use a variety of filters to narrow the search results. In Figure 5.22, the initial search for *replevin* in federal and District of Columbia cases retrieves over 5,000 cases, but filtering the results by circuit and court reduces the number significantly.

FIGURE 5.22   RESULTS OF A WORD SEARCH IN LEXIS ADVANCE

The search retrieves many cases.

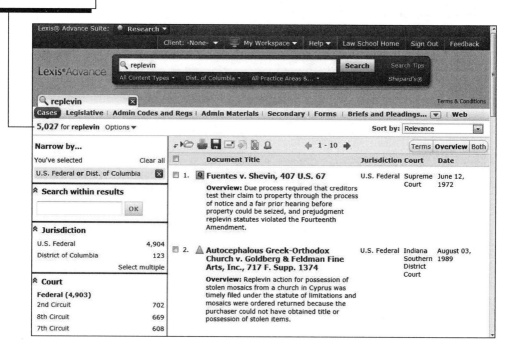

FIGURE 5.22   RESULTS OF A WORD SEARCH IN LEXIS ADVANCE *(Continued)*

Filtering by circuit and
court reduces the
number of cases.

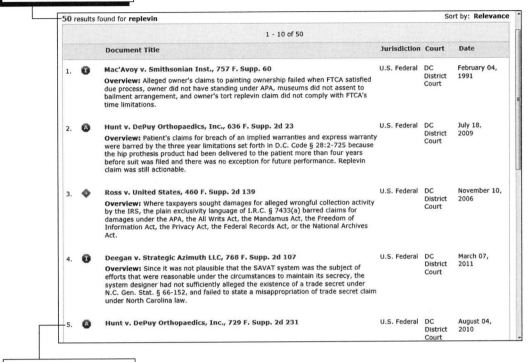

50 results found for **replevin**   Sort by: **Relevance**

1 - 10 of 50

	Document Title	Jurisdiction	Court	Date
1.	**Mac'Avoy v. Smithsonian Inst., 757 F. Supp. 60** **Overview:** Alleged owner's claims to painting ownership failed when FTCA satisfied due process, owner did not have standing under APA, museums did not assent to bailment arrangement, and owner's tort replevin claim did not comply with FTCA's time limitations.	U.S. Federal	DC District Court	February 04, 1991
2.	**Hunt v. DePuy Orthopaedics, Inc., 636 F. Supp. 2d 23** **Overview:** Patient's claims for breach of an implied warranties and express warranty were barred by the three year limitations set forth in D.C. Code § 28:2-725 because the hip prothesis product had been delivered to the patient more than four years before suit was filed and there was no exception for future performance. Replevin claim was still actionable.	U.S. Federal	DC District Court	July 18, 2009
3.	**Ross v. United States, 460 F. Supp. 2d 139** **Overview:** Where taxpayers sought damages for alleged wrongful collection activity by the IRS, the plain exclusivity language of I.R.C. § 7433(a) barred claims for damages under the APA, the All Writs Act, the Mandamus Act, the Freedom of Information Act, the Privacy Act, the Federal Records Act, or the National Archives Act.	U.S. Federal	DC District Court	November 10, 2006
4.	**Deegan v. Strategic Azimuth LLC, 768 F. Supp. 2d 107** **Overview:** Since it was not plausible that the SAVAT system was the subject of efforts that were reasonable under the circumstances to maintain its secrecy, the system designer had not sufficiently alleged the existence of a trade secret under N.C. Gen. Stat. § 66-152, and failed to state a misappropriation of trade secret claim under North Carolina law.	U.S. Federal	DC District Court	March 07, 2011
5.	**Hunt v. DePuy Orthopaedics, Inc., 729 F. Supp. 2d 231**	U.S. Federal	DC District Court	August 04, 2010

A potentially relevant
case

Lexis Advance search results. Copyright 2012 LexisNexis, a division of Reed Elsevier Inc. All Rights Reserved. LexisNexis and the Knowledge Burst logo are registered trademarks of Reed Elsevier Properties Inc. and are used with the permission of LexisNexis.

This is the opinion in *Hunt v. DePuy Orthopaedics, Inc.*, a case that is summarized in the pocket part of the digest and within the subject and word search results in Westlaw and Lexis. You would want to review this case, as well as others, in conducting your research.

FIGURE 5.23   *HUNT v. DEPUY ORTHOPAEDICS, INC.*, 729 F. SUPP. 2d 231
          (D.D.C. 2010)

HUNT v. DEPUY ORTHOPAEDICS, INC.   **231**
Cite as 729 F.Supp.2d 231 (D.D.C. 2010)

Sank and Prof. Penley as expert witnesses in this case.

Marla HUNT, Plaintiff,

v.

**DePUY ORTHOPAEDICS,
INC., Defendant.**

Civil Action No. 03–900 (RWR).

United States District Court,
District of Columbia.

Aug. 4, 2010.

Background: Patient brought action against manufacturer of prosthetic hip for replevin. Defendant moved for summary judgment.

Holding: The District Court, Richard W. Roberts, J., held that patient abandoned prosthetic hip components.

Motion granted.

1. Replevin ⇐1

 Under District of Columbia law, "replevin" is an action brought to recover personal property to which the plaintiff is entitled, that is alleged to have been wrongfully taken or to be in the possession of and wrongfully detained by the defendant. D.C. Official Code, 2001 Ed. § 16–3701.

> See publication Words and Phrases for other judicial constructions and definitions.

2. Replevin ⇐9
 Trover and Conversion ⇐1

 The essence of both a replevin action and a conversion action is the wrongful withholding of the property in question.

3. Replevin ⇐12(1)

 As predicted by federal district court, abandonment serves as a complete defense to a replevin action under District of Co-

lumbia law, since a defendant cannot wrongfully withhold property that a plaintiff has abandoned.

4. Abandoned and Lost Property ⇐2, 3

 To prove abandonment of property under District of Columbia law, a party must demonstrate both an intent to abandon and an act or omission that effectuates the intention.

5. Abandoned and Lost Property ⇐3
 Replevin ⇐12(1)

 Under District of Columbia law, manufacturer of prosthetic hip components, whose sales representative had been given defective hip piece from patient's surgeon after he removed it from her body, was not liable to patient for replevin, since patient had abandoned the appliance; patient understood that manufacturer had taken possession of the component but she never voiced objections, asked for return of the property, or sought assurance of property's safekeeping over a four year period. D.C. Official Code, 2001 Ed. § 16–3701.

 Wade John Gallagher, Martell, Donnelly, Grimaldi & Gallagher, Sykesville, MD, for Plaintiff.

 George F. Ritchie, Gordon, Feinblatt, Rothman, Hoffberger & Hollander, LLC, Baltimore, MD, for Defendant.

MEMORANDUM OPINION

 RICHARD W. ROBERTS, District Judge.

 Plaintiff Marla Hunt sued DePuy Orthopaedics, Inc. ("DePuy"), manufacturer of her prosthetic hip, for breach of implied warranties, breach of express warranty, and replevin. DePuy filed a motion for summary judgment, which was granted

FIGURE 5.23   *HUNT v. DEPUY ORTHOPAEDICS, INC.*, 729 F. SUPP. 2d 231
(D.D.C. 2010) *(Continued)*

---

232   729 FEDERAL SUPPLEMENT, 2d SERIES

with respect to all of Hunt's claims except for replevin, and now moves again for summary judgment on the replevin claim. Because Hunt's abandonment of the prosthetic hip components is a complete defense to her replevin claim, DePuy's motion for summary judgment will be granted.

BACKGROUND

The background of this case is discussed fully in *Hunt v. DePuy Orthopaedics, Inc.*, 636 F.Supp.2d 23 (D.D.C.2009). Briefly, Hunt had hip replacement surgery in 1994 and required repairs to the prosthetic hip, manufactured by DePuy, five years later. *Id.* at 24–25. The surgeon who repaired Hunt's hip in 1999, Dr. Paul Manner, gave the defective hip prosthesis components to a DePuy sales representative to take back to the company and informed Hunt after the surgery that DePuy was in possession of the components. (Def.'s Mem. of P. & A. in Supp. of Def.'s Mot. for Summ. J. as to Pl.'s Replevin Claim ("Def.'s Mem."), Ex. A, Hunt Dep. at 149:1–5; Ex. B. at 6.) After four years elapsed, Hunt requested the return of the hip components by filing this claim for replevin. *Hunt*, 636 F.Supp.2d at 28. DePuy has filed a motion for summary judgment, arguing that the hip is valueless and that Hunt abandoned the hip. (Def.'s Mem. at 1–2.)

DISCUSSION

Summary judgment may be granted when "the pleadings, the discovery and disclosure materials on file, and any affidavits show that there is no genuine issue as to any material fact and that the movant is entitled to judgment as a matter of law." Fed. R. Civ. P. 56(c); *see also Moore v. Hartman*, 571 F.3d 62, 66 (D.C.Cir.2009). A court considering a motion for summary judgment must draw all "justifiable inferences" from the evidence in favor of the nonmovant. *Anderson v. Liberty Lobby, Inc.*, 477 U.S. 242, 255, 106 S.Ct. 2505, 91 L.Ed.2d 202 (1986). The nonmoving party, however, must do more than simply "show that there is some metaphysical doubt as to the material facts." *Matsushita Elec. Indus. Co., Ltd. v. Zenith Radio Corp.*, 475 U.S. 574, 586, 106 S.Ct. 1348, 89 L.Ed.2d 538 (1986). Rather, the nonmovant must "come forward with specific facts showing that there is a genuine issue for trial." *Id.* at 587, 106 S.Ct. 1348 (internal quotation marks and emphasis omitted). In the end, "the plain language of Rule 56(c) mandates the entry of summary judgment ... against a party who fails to make a showing sufficient to establish the existence of an element essential to that party's case, and on which that party will bear the burden of proof at trial." *Celotex Corp. v. Catrett*, 477 U.S. 317, 322, 106 S.Ct. 2548, 91 L.Ed.2d 265 (1986).

[1–3] Replevin is an action "brought to recover personal property to which the plaintiff is entitled, that is alleged to have been wrongfully taken or to be in the possession of and wrongfully detained by the defendant[.]" D.C. Code § 16–3701. While the D.C. Court of Appeals has never held explicitly that abandonment of personal property is a defense to a replevin action, it has held that "[a]bandonment of personal property is a complete defense to an action for conversion." *Block v. Fisher*, 103 A.2d 575, 576 (D.C.1954). The "essence" of both a replevin action and a conversion action is the "wrongful withholding of the property in question." *Mac'Avoy v. Smithsonian Inst.*, 757 F.Supp. 60, 67 (D.D.C.1991). Because a defendant cannot wrongfully withhold property that the plaintiff has abandoned, abandonment must also serve as a complete defense to a replevin action. *Accord Graff v. Triple B Dev. Corp.*, 622 S.W.2d 755, 756 (Mo.Ct.App.1981) ("Abandonment, if proved, is a complete defense to an action for replevin and precludes recovery.").

FIGURE 5.23   *HUNT v. DEPUY ORTHOPAEDICS, INC.*, 729 F. SUPP. 2d 231
(D.D.C. 2010) *(Continued)*

APPLEWHAITE v. SHINTON   **233**
Cite as 729 F.Supp.2d 233 (D.D.C. 2010)

[4] To prove abandonment, a party must demonstrate both an intent to abandon and an act or omission that effectuates the intention. *Block*, 103 A.2d at 576. Determining the intent to abandon is a fact-intensive inquiry. *Am. Petroleum Inst. v. EPA*, 216 F.3d 50, 57 (D.C.Cir. 2000) (per curiam).

[5] Here, Dr. Manner turned over the defective prosthetic hip components to a DePuy sales representative after Hunt's surgery. Hunt argues in her brief that "[a]s a practical matter the defendant would have seemed to have been a safe repository for the appliance and plaintiff had no reason to request its return until such time as she sought redress from the defendant for its promotion and sale of the defective component[.]" (Pl.'s Opp'n at 5.) However, she presents no discovery materials, affidavits, or declarations reflecting specific facts showing her intent that DePuy hold the components for safekeeping until she requested their return in 2003. The facts in the record show the opposite. Hunt knew right after her surgery that DePuy had taken possession of the components. She neither voiced any objection nor asked for the return of the components nor asked that DePuy's possession be temporary. During the four years that went by after DePuy took possession of the components, Hunt never asked for them back, and there is no evidence that she sought assurance of their safekeeping. The facts support only the inference that Hunt abandoned the property. *See Block*, 103 A.2d at 576 (finding that appellant abandoned property he left in appellees' yard for eight months). DePuy is therefore entitled to summary judgment on the replevin claim.

CONCLUSION

The undisputed material facts demonstrate that Hunt abandoned the components. That provides a complete defense against her replevin claim, and entitles

DePuy to judgment as a matter of law. Accordingly, DePuy's motion [58] for summary judgment will be granted. An appropriate Order accompanies this Memorandum Opinion.

Andrew **APPLEWHAITE**, Plaintiff,

v.

Matthew **SHINTON** et al., Defendants.

Civil Action No.: 09–2195 (RMU).

United States District Court,
District of Columbia.

Aug. 5, 2010.

Background: Pro se plaintiff, an individual convicted of misdemeanor in District of Columbia court, brought action alleging misconduct on part of investigators, prosecutors and witnesses allegedly responsible for his arrest and conviction. Defendants argued that United States should be substituted in their place, pursuant to Westfall Act, and also moved to dismiss.

Holdings: The District Court, Ricardo M. Urbina, J., held that:

(1) United States would be substituted, pursuant to Westfall Act, for individual federal defendants, and

(2) plaintiff failed to exhaust his administrative remedies, as was required by Federal Tort Claims Act (FTCA), prior to bringing action.

Motion granted.

1. United States ⟜50.5(1)

Westfall Act confers immunity on federal employees by making a Federal Tort

---

F. CHECKLIST FOR CASE RESEARCH

1. SELECT A PRINT DIGEST

❐ Use *West's Federal Practice Digest* to locate all federal cases.

❐ Use a state digest to locate state and federal cases from an individual state.

❐ Use a regional digest to locate state cases only within the region.

❐ Use a combined digest to locate state and federal cases from all U.S. jurisdictions.

2. LOCATE TOPICS AND KEY NUMBERS IN A PRINT DIGEST

❐ From a case on point, use the headnotes at the beginning of the decision to identify relevant topics and key numbers.

❐ From the Descriptive-Word Index, look up relevant subjects, check the pocket part for new index headings, and look up the topics and key numbers in the subject volumes.

❐ From a topic entry, review subjects included and excluded and the outline of key numbers.

3. READ THE CASE SUMMARIES IN THE PRINT DIGEST

❐ Use the court and date abbreviations to target appropriate cases.

4. UPDATE PRINT DIGEST RESEARCH

❐ Check the pocket part for the subject volume.

❐ Check any cumulative or noncumulative interim pamphlets at the end of the digest set.

❐ Check the closing table on the inside front cover of the most recent interim pamphlet (if there is no interim pamphlet, check the closing table on the inside front cover of the pocket part).

❐ If necessary, check the mini-digests in the back of each reporter volume published after the latest volume listed in the closing table.

5. ELECTRONIC CASE RESEARCH—SEARCHING BY SUBJECT

❐ In Westlaw, search for cases by subject.

■ Use the **West Key Number** (Custom Digest) function to find summaries of cases organized by topic and key number.

■ From a case on point, search for cases under a particular topic and key number by following the link to the key number in a relevant headnote.

❐ In Lexis.com, search for cases by subject.

■ Use the **Topic or Headnote** search function to find citations to cases organized by topic and headnote subject.

- From a case on point, use the **More Like This Headnote** option to search for cases under the same headnote subject.

6. ELECTRONIC CASE RESEARCH—WORD SEARCHING

❑ In Westlaw and Lexis, execute word searches.

- In Westlaw.com, WestlawNext, and Lexis.com, select a database to search for cases from a specific jurisdiction.
- In WestlawNext, pre-filter by jurisdiction and execute a content-driven search; filter the results to target appropriate cases.
- In Lexis Advance, pre-filter by content type (cases), jurisdiction, and/or topic and execute a search; filter the results to target appropriate cases.

❑ In Google Scholar, search for published legal opinions; choose **Advanced Scholar Search** to pre-filter by jurisdiction.

❑ Use websites for courts or other tribunals to locate very recent opinions, unpublished (non-precedential) opinions, or opinions unavailable from other sources.

CHAPTER 6

RESEARCH WITH CITATORS

A. Introduction to citators

B. Using Shepard's in Lexis for case research

C. Using KeyCite in Westlaw for case research

D. Choosing among citators

E. Sample pages for case research with Shepard's and KeyCite

F. Checklist for case research with citators

A. INTRODUCTION TO CITATORS

1. THE PURPOSE OF A CITATOR

Virtually all cases contain citations to legal authorities, including other cases, secondary sources, statutes, and regulations. These decisions can affect the continued validity of the authorities they cite. For example, earlier cases can be reversed or overruled, or statutes can be held unconstitutional. Even if an authority remains valid, the discussion of the authority in later cases can be helpful in your research. As a consequence, when you find an authority that helps you answer a research question, you will often want to know whether the authority has been cited elsewhere, and if so, what has been said about it.

The tool that helps you do this is called a citator. Citators catalog cases, secondary sources, and other authorities, analyzing what they say about the sources they cite. Some citators also track the status of statutes and regulations, indicating, for example, whether a statute has been amended or repealed. Citators will help you determine whether an authority is still "good law," meaning it has not been changed or invalidated since it was published. They will also help you locate additional authorities that pertain to your research question.

The most well-known print citator is Shepard's Citations. Because Shepard's was, for many years, the only citator most lawyers ever used, checking citations came to be known as "Shepardizing." Generations of law students learned how to interpret print Shepard's entries, which are filled with symbols and abbreviations. Today, however, few legal researchers use Shepard's in print. Many libraries no longer carry the print version of Shepard's. Instead, virtually all legal researchers use electronic citators. Shepard's is still a well-respected citator, and it is available in Lexis. Westlaw also has its own citator—called KeyCite—and other electronic service providers offer their own citators.

Because print citators are largely unavailable, this chapter focuses on electronic citators. Sections B and C explain how to use Shepard's in Lexis and KeyCite in Westlaw for case research. Section D discusses how to choose which citator(s) to use. Citators can be used in researching many types of authority, including cases, statutes, regulations, and some secondary sources. The process of using a citator, however, is the same for almost any type of authority. Accordingly, for purposes of introducing you to this process, this chapter focuses on the use of citators in case research. Later chapters in this book discuss the use of Shepard's and KeyCite in researching other types of authority.

2. WHEN TO USE A CITATOR IN CASE RESEARCH

You must check every case on which you rely to answer a legal question to make sure it is still good law. In general, you will want to use Shepard's or KeyCite early in your research, after you have identified what appear to be a few key cases, to make sure you do not build your analysis on authority that is no longer valid. Using a citator at this stage will help direct you to other relevant authorities as well. You should also check every case you cite before handing in your work to make sure each one continues to be authoritative. Citing bad authority is every attorney's nightmare, and failing to check your citations can constitute professional malpractice. As a consequence, now is the time to get in the habit of updating your case research carefully.

3. TERMS AND PROCEDURAL CONCEPTS USED IN CITATOR RESEARCH

Before you begin learning how to use citators, it is important to understand the terminology and procedural concepts used in the process. A case citator contains entries for decided cases that list the later authorities (cases, secondary sources, and other forms of authority) that have cited the case. This chapter uses the term "original case" to describe the case that is the subject of the citator entry. The terms "citing case" and "citing source" refer to the later authorities that cite the original case. Thus, for example, if you located the case of *Uddin v. Embassy Suites Hotel*, 165 Ohio App. 3d 699 (2005), and wanted to use a citator to verify its continued validity, *Uddin* would be referred to as the original case.

The later authorities that cite *Uddin* would be referred to as citing cases (for cases) or citing sources (for all other types of authority).

Two procedural concepts you need to understand are direct and indirect case history. Direct history refers to all of the opinions issued in conjunction with a single piece of litigation. One piece of litigation may generate multiple opinions. A case may be appealed to a higher court, resulting in opinions from both an intermediate appellate court and the court of last resort. A higher court may remand a case—that is, send a case back to a lower court—for reconsideration, again resulting in opinions issued by both courts. Or a court might issue separate opinions to resolve individual matters arising in a case. All of these opinions, whether issued before or after the original case, constitute direct history. Opinions issued before the original case may be called prior history; those issued after the original case may be called subsequent history or subsequent appellate history, as appropriate. Indirect history refers to an opinion generated from a different piece of litigation than the original case. Every unrelated case that cites the original case is part of the indirect history of the original case.

Both direct and indirect case history can be positive, negative, or neutral. Thus, if the original case is affirmed by a higher court, it has positive direct history, but if the original case is reversed, it has negative direct history. A related opinion in the same litigation on a different issue could be neutral; the opinion resolving the second issue could have no effect on the continued validity of the opinion resolving the first issue. Similarly, if the original case is relied upon by a court deciding a later, unrelated case, the original case has positive indirect history, but if the original case is overruled, it has negative indirect history. A citing case could discuss the original case in a way that does not include any positive or negative analysis. In that situation, the indirect history would be considered neutral.

B. USING SHEPARD'S IN LEXIS FOR CASE RESEARCH

Shepard's entries in Lexis.com and Lexis Advance contain the same information, although the appearance and options for filtering the content vary. To use Shepard's in either version of Lexis effectively, you need to know how to access the service, interpret the entries, and limit the display to target the information you want. You can also create a Shepard's Alert to continue updating your research over time.

1. ACCESSING SHEPARD'S

One way to Shepardize a case is by accessing the Shepard's function and entering the citation you want to Shepardize. To access Shepard's in Lexis .com, use the **Shepard's** tab at the top of the screen. When you do this, you will see two options for retrieving entries: **Shepard's for Research** or **Shepard's for Validation**. The research entry will be the most complete; it will list all citing cases and sources for the original case. The validation entry is more limited. If you are not sure which option you need, choose **Shepard's for Research**. If it contains more information than you need, you can limit the display after you retrieve the entry. To access Shepard's in Lexis Advance, use the **Sheparadize** link in the red search box or type *shep:* followed by the citation.

Another way to access Shepard's is from a case. If you are viewing a case in Lexis.com or Lexis Advance, you can choose the **Sheparadize** option at the top of the display to Sheparadize the case without having to enter the citation.

2. INTERPRETING SHEPARD'S ENTRIES

Once you have retrieved the entry for the original case, you must evaluate the information you find. A Shepard's entry is divided into three sections: history, citing decisions, and other authorities.

In Lexis.com, the Shepard's entry is a single document that begins with a summary of the entry and includes headings dividing the history, citing decisions, and individual types of other authority contained within the entry, such as law review articles and treatises. You can use the links in the summary section to navigate within the entry. **Figure 6.1** shows part of a Shepard's entry in Lexis.com. In Lexis Advance, the three sections of the entry appear under separate sub-tabs: **History**; **Citing Decisions**; and **Citing Law Reviews, Treatises, and Other Authorities**. **Figure 6.2** shows part of a Shepard's entry in Lexis Advance.

When you view a Shepard's entry, one of the first things you will notice is a symbol such as a red stop sign or a yellow triangle. These symbols are called "Shepard's Signals," and they indicate the type of treatment the original case has received from the citing cases. If you retrieve the full text of a case before Sheparadizing it, you will also see a Shepard's Signal at the beginning of the case. A list of Shepard's Signals and Lexis's definition for each signal appear in **Figure 6.3**.

It is often difficult to reduce the status of a case to a single notation. Determining the continued validity of an original case often requires study of the citing cases. For example, an original case with a negative Shepard's Signal such as a red stop sign may no longer be good law for one of its points, but it may continue to be authoritative on other points. If you were to rely on the red stop sign without further inquiry, you might miss a case that is important for the issue you are researching. As a consequence, although Shepard's Signals can be helpful research tools, you should not rely on them in deciding whether the original case is valid. Always research the Shepard's entry and review the citing cases carefully to satisfy yourself about the status of the original case. You can view any document in the entry from the links provided.

FIGURE 6.1   SHEPARD'S® ENTRY EXCERPT FOR 165 OHIO APP. 3d 699 IN LEXIS.COM

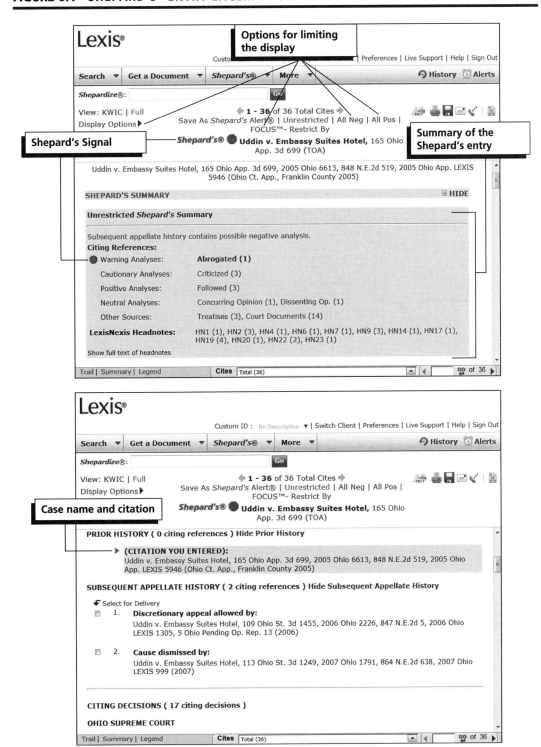

**FIGURE 6.1   SHEPARD'S® ENTRY EXCERPT FOR 165 OHIO APP. 3d 699
IN LEXIS.COM (Continued)**

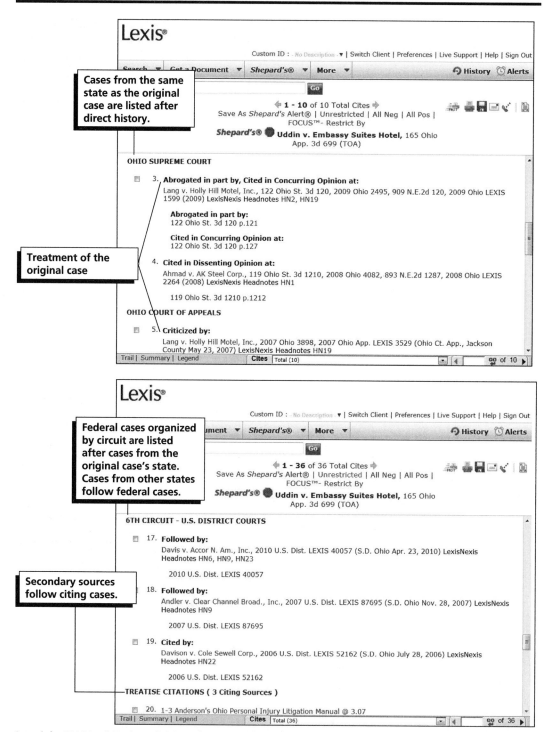

FIGURE 6.2   SHEPARD'S® ENTRY EXCERPT FOR 165 OHIO APP. 3d 699 IN LEXIS ADVANCE

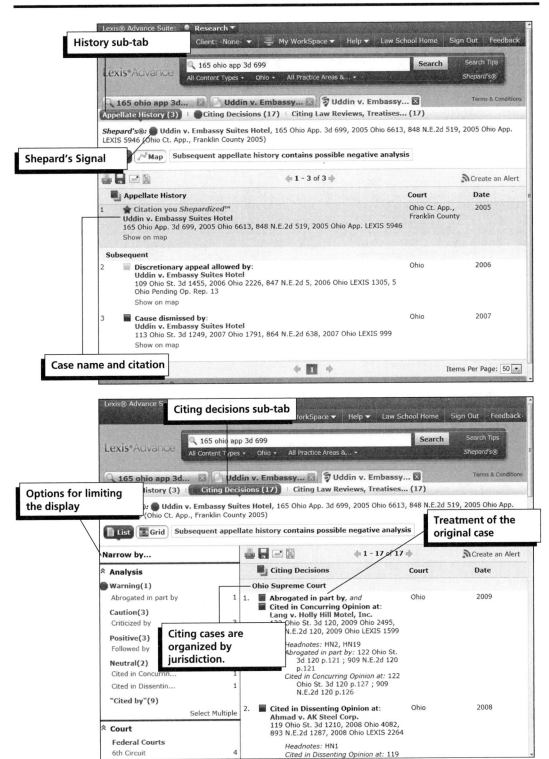

FIGURE 6.2   SHEPARD'S® ENTRY EXCERPT FOR 165 OHIO APP. 3d 699 IN LEXIS ADVANCE *(Continued)*

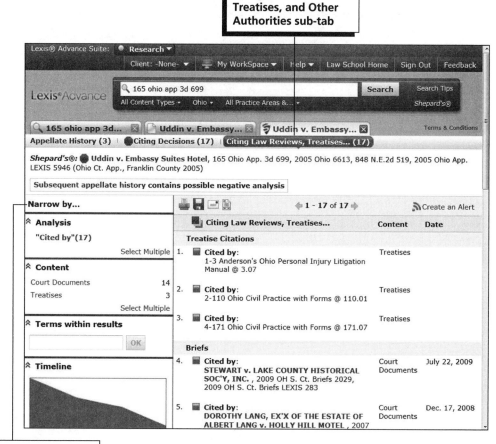

Copyright 2012 LexisNexis, a division of Reed Elsevier Inc. All Rights Reserved. LexisNexis and the Knowledge Burst logo are registered trademarks of Reed Elsevier Properties Inc. and are used with the permission of LexisNexis. SHEPARD'S® entry for 165 Ohio App. 3d 699.

The history section of a Shepard's entry lists the direct history of the case, meaning prior and subsequent opinions arising from the same litigation. The information in this section will help you determine whether the case is still good law. If a later opinion in the direct line of appeal affects the continued validity of the original case (e.g., reversing or affirming the original case), that information will be noted in the history section. The citation for the original case will be highlighted so you can identify it easily within the history. To retrieve any citing case in the direct history, use the link to the case name. Lexis Advance will also give you a visual snapshot of the original case's history with the **Map** view. This can be useful if a case has an extensive or complex history.

FIGURE 6.3 SHEPARD'S® SIGNALS

SIGNAL	MEANS
Red stop sign	*Warning: Negative treatment is indicated.* This signal indicates that citing references in the Shepard's® Citations Service contain strong negative history or treatment of your case (e.g., overruled by or reversed).
Orange square surrounding the letter Q	*Questioned: Validity questioned by citing references.* This signal indicates that citing references in the Shepard's® Citations Service contain treatment that questions the continuing validity or precedential value of your case because of intervening circumstances, including judicial or legislative overruling.
Yellow triangle	*Caution: Possible negative treatment.* This signal indicates that citing references in the Shepard's® Citations Service contain history or treatment that may have a significant negative impact on your case (e.g., limited or criticized by).
Green diamond surrounding a plus sign	*Positive treatment is indicated.* This signal indicates that citing references in the Shepard's® Citations Service contain history or treatment that has a positive impact on your case (e.g., affirmed or followed by).
Blue circle surrounding the letter A	*Citing references with neutral analysis available.* This signal indicates that citing references in the Shepard's® Citations Service contain treatment of your case that is neither positive nor negative (e.g., explained).
Blue circle surrounding the letter I	*Citation information available.* This signal indicates that citing references are available in the Shepard's® Citations Service for your case, but the references do not have history or treatment analysis (e.g., the references are law review citations).

The citing decisions section lists indirect history, meaning later cases that have cited the original case. The information in this section will help you determine whether the case is still good law. It will also help you identify additional cases that are relevant to your research issue.

When you Shepardize a federal case, the list of citing decisions will begin with federal cases divided according to circuit. For each circuit, appellate cases will appear first, followed by federal district court cases. After all of the federal cases, state cases will be listed alphabetically by state, again with cases from higher courts first, followed by those from subordinate courts. When you Shepardize a state case, the list of citing decisions will begin with cases from the same state as the original case. Then you will see federal cases by circuit and cases from other states.

Along with the full name and citation to the citing case, the entry will note the treatment the citing case has given the original case. Often, the citing case will simply have "cited" the original case without significant analysis. If, however, the citing case has given the original case treatment that could affect its continued validity (e.g., following, explaining, criticizing, or distinguishing it), Shepard's will note that.

Lexis Advance has two additional features to show the treatment of the original case. It uses colored blocks next to citing cases to indicate the degree of positive or negative treatment given to the original case. Roll your cursor over the block to see its definition. Lexis Advance also allows you to view a color-coded grid that provides a snapshot of the way all of the citing cases have treated the original case. Click on a box in the grid to show the list view of the cases included in the category you selected. **Figure 6.4** shows the grid view.

Another feature in the citing decisions section is the headnote references. You may recall from Chapter 5, on case research, that headnotes are summary paragraphs added by case editors identifying the key points in the case. If a citing case cites the original case for a point that is summarized in a headnote at the beginning of the original case, the headnote will be referenced in the Shepard's entry. In the example citation, *Uddin* discusses a point of law that is summarized in headnote 9. A citing case, *Davis v. Accor North America, Inc.*, has cited *Uddin* for the same proposition of law summarized in headnote 9. Thus, the Shepard's entry includes the reference to headnote 9. The illustrations in **Figures 6.5** through **6.7** trace a headnote from an original case to a Shepard's entry and then to a citing case. You may again recall from Chapter 5 that West publishes many state and federal reporters and adds headnotes to those cases. LexisNexis

FIGURE 6.4   CITING DECISIONS GRID VIEW IN LEXIS ADVANCE

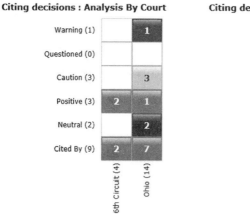
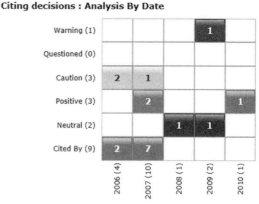

FIGURE 6.5   HEADNOTE 9 FROM THE ORIGINAL CASE, *UDDIN v. EMBASSY SUITES HOTEL*

Headnote 9 of *Uddin*

HN9 ↓ An owner or occupier of business premises owes business invitees a duty of ordinary care in maintaining the premises in a reasonably safe condition and has the duty to warn invitees of latent or hidden dangers. However, the owner or occupier of a business premise is not an insurer of a business invitee's safety. More Like This Headnote | *Shepardize:* Restrict By Headnote

FIGURE 6.6   SHEPARD'S® ENTRY EXCERPT FOR *UDDIN v. EMBASSY SUITES HOTEL*

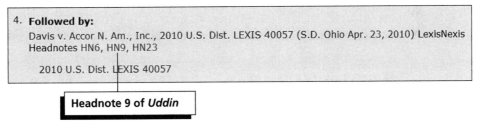

4. **Followed by:**
   Davis v. Accor N. Am., Inc., 2010 U.S. Dist. LEXIS 40057 (S.D. Ohio Apr. 23, 2010) LexisNexis Headnotes HN6, HN9, HN23

   2010 U.S. Dist. LEXIS 40057

Headnote 9 of *Uddin*

FIGURE 6.7   *DAVIS v. ACCOR NORTH AMERICA, INC.,* CITING *UDDIN v. EMBASSY SUITES HOTEL*

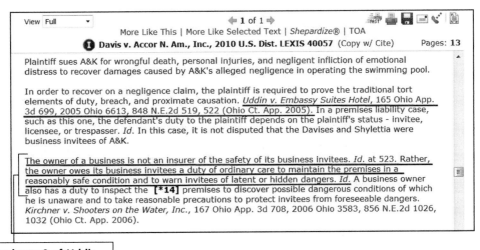

View Full ▼   ⇐ 1 of 1 ⇒
          More Like This | More Like Selected Text | *Shepardize*® | TOA
     ① **Davis v. Accor N. Am., Inc., 2010 U.S. Dist. LEXIS 40057** (Copy w/ Cite)   Pages: 13

Plaintiff sues A&K for wrongful death, personal injuries, and negligent infliction of emotional distress to recover damages caused by A&K's alleged negligence in operating the swimming pool.

In order to recover on a negligence claim, the plaintiff is required to prove the traditional tort elements of duty, breach, and proximate causation. *Uddin v. Embassy Suites Hotel*, 165 Ohio App. 3d 699, 2005 Ohio 6613, 848 N.E.2d 519, 522 (Ohio Ct. App. 2005). In a premises liability case, such as this one, the defendant's duty to the plaintiff depends on the plaintiff's status - invitee, licensee, or trespasser. *Id.* In this case, it is not disputed that the Davises and Shylettia were business invitees of A&K.

The owner of a business is not an insurer of the safety of its business invitees. *Id.* at 523. Rather, the owner owes its business invitees a duty of ordinary care to maintain the premises in a reasonably safe condition and to warn invitees of latent or hidden dangers. *Id.* A business owner also has a duty to inspect the **[*14]** premises to discover possible dangerous conditions of which he is unaware and to take reasonable precautions to protect invitees from foreseeable dangers. *Kirchner v. Shooters on the Water, Inc.*, 167 Ohio App. 3d 708, 2006 Ohio 3583, 856 N.E.2d 1026, 1032 (Ohio Ct. App. 2006).

Headnote 9 of *Uddin*

Headnotes are different from West headnotes, and the two sets of head-notes do not correspond to each other. The LexisNexis Headnotes are the ones that are displayed in the Shepard's entry.

The third section of the entry is other citing sources. This section lists sources other than cases that have cited the original case. It will help you locate additional information on your research issue. Not all of the types of other authorities described here will appear in each entry. The authorities included will depend on where the original case has been cited.

If any statutory annotations include a summary of the original case, that information will appear first. Statutory annotations are research references in an annotated code. (Annotated codes are discussed in Chapter 7, on statutory research.) Secondary sources follow, divided by type of authority (law review articles, treatises, etc.). Shepard's entries do not include references to A.L.R. Annotations (a type of secondary source described in Chapter 4). Because A.L.R. is published by West, references to that publication appear only in KeyCite. The last item in the entry is court documents. These are filings submitted by parties in other cases that have cited the original case, not documents issued by courts.

3. LIMITING THE DISPLAY

Although the full Shepard's entry provides the most complete information about the original case, you may want to view a more limited entry depending on your research task. Shepard's offers several options for filtering the display to focus on the information most relevant to you.

In Lexis.com, you can choose **Shepard's for Validation (KWIC)** when you enter the citation to view a restricted Shepard's entry limited to citing cases that have given the original case significant treatment. You can switch between the validation (**KWIC**) and research (**FULL**) views using the links in the top left corner of the screen. From the full Shepard's entry, you also have several options for customizing the display. Using the links in the center at the top of the screen and the **Display Options** function at the top left, you can limit the display as indicated (e.g., all positive cases; all negative cases).

Lexis.com's **FOCUS™-Restrict By** option contains a menu of filtering options. From this screen, you can filter by type of analysis, jurisdiction of citing cases and sources, headnote, date, or terms you specify. In the headnote restrictions, you may have the option to choose whether to filter by LexisNexis, West, or official reporter headnotes, although that will not be true for all cases. You can combine the choices to filter the entry according to multiple criteria, as shown in **Figure 6.8**.

In Lexis Advance, the narrowing options appear in the left margin under the sub-tabs containing citing decisions and law reviews and other authorities. You can filter the results according to a number of criteria, including treatment, jurisdiction, and LexisNexis Headnote.

FIGURE 6.8   SHEPARD'S® FOCUS™-RESTRICT BY OPTIONS

Analysis available in FULL: Select All Clear All		**FOCUS Terms:**
Negative: Select All Clear All		Return a list of citations to cases that contain your terms.
☐ Abrogated (1)	☐ Criticized (3)	
Positive:		
☐ Followed (3)		
Other: Select All Clear All		**FOCUS HINT:** The FOCUS search will only identify citing references that have corresponding documents available in the LexisNexis® service. The FOCUS feature is not available if your current results contain more than 2000 documents.
☐ Concurring Opinion (1)	☐ Dissenting Op. (1)	

Jurisdictions available in FULL: Select All   Clear All

Federal:
☐ 6th Circuit (4)

State:
☐ Ohio (13)

Other: Select All   Clear All
☐ Treatises (3)   ☐ Court Documents (14)

Headnotes available in FULL:

LexisNexis [Show full text of headnotes]   Select All   Clear All

| ☐ HN1 (1) | ☐ HN4 (1) | ☐ HN7 (1) | ☐ HN14 (1) | ☐ HN19 (4) | ☐ HN22 (2) |
| ☐ HN2 (3) | ☐ HN6 (1) | ☐ HN9 (3) | ☐ HN17 (1) | ☐ HN20 (1) | ☐ HN23 (1) |

Dates:

◉ No additional date restrictions: ▾   [   ]   (4-digit years)

◯ From: [   ]   To: [   ]   (4-digit years)

4. USING SHEPARD'S ALERT®

One additional feature you can use is Shepard's Alert®. If you find a case that is especially important in your research, you may want to monitor it over time to make sure it remains valid and to review any new citing cases or sources added to the Shepard's entry. This will be especially useful when you are working on a project over a long period of time. Shepard's Alert® automatically Shepardizes the authorities you select and delivers periodic reports to you. To set up a Shepard's Alert®, choose the **Save as Shepard's Alert®** option in Lexis.com or the **Create an Alert** option in Lexis Advance and follow the instructions to specify the content, delivery format, and frequency of the report.

C. USING KEYCITE IN WESTLAW FOR CASE RESEARCH

Westlaw provides a citator called KeyCite. Like Shepard's, KeyCite is available for cases, statutes, and administrative materials. KeyCite is similar to Shepard's in the information it provides, and the process of using KeyCite is very similar to the process of Shepardizing. To use KeyCite effectively, you need to know how to access the service, interpret the entries, and filter the results to target the information you want. You can also create a KeyCite Alert to continue updating your research over time.

1. ACCESSING KEYCITE, INTERPRETING THE ENTRIES, AND FILTERING THE RESULTS

To access KeyCite in Westlaw.com, you can select the **KeyCite** link at the top of the Westlaw screen and enter the citation you want to check. Another way to access KeyCite is from a case. When you view a case, a **KeyCite** box appears under the **Links for** tab at the left margin. You can access KeyCite by choosing one of the options in the **KeyCite** box. In WestlawNext, you can access KeyCite by typing *kc:* followed by the citation in the search box or by retrieving a case. The tabs accompanying the document contain the information from the KeyCite entry. The organization of the entries in the two versions of Westlaw is described below.

In both versions of Westlaw, KeyCite is linked with cases with a notation system similar to Shepard's Signals in Lexis. A symbol called a status flag will appear at the beginning of both the case and the KeyCite entry to give you some indication of the case's treatment in KeyCite. Westlaw's definitions of the status flags are explained in **Figure 6.9**. Like Shepard's Signals, KeyCite status flags are useful research tools, but they cannot substitute for your own assessment of the continued validity of a case. You should always research the KeyCite entry and review the citing sources carefully to satisfy yourself about the status of a case.

Once you have retrieved the entry for the original case, you must evaluate the information you find. KeyCite entries for cases include

FIGURE 6.9   WESTLAW STATUS FLAGS INDICATING KEYCITE HISTORY

NOTATION	MEANS
Red flag	The case is no longer good law for at least one of the points it contains.
Yellow flag	The case has some negative history but has not been reversed or overruled.
Blue H	The case has direct history.
Green C	The case has citing references but no direct history or negative citing references.

the following information: the direct history of the case in list and graphical formats, the indirect negative history, court filings in the original case, and citing references. The organization of this information is different in Westlaw.com and WestlawNext.

a. Westlaw.com

A KeyCite entry in Westlaw.com is divided into three sections: full history, direct history (graphical view), and citing references. **Figure 6.**10 shows the full history of a case in KeyCite. The full history includes the direct history of the original case, any negative indirect

FIGURE 6.10   KEYCITE FULL HISTORY ENTRY FOR 165 OHIO APP. 3d 699

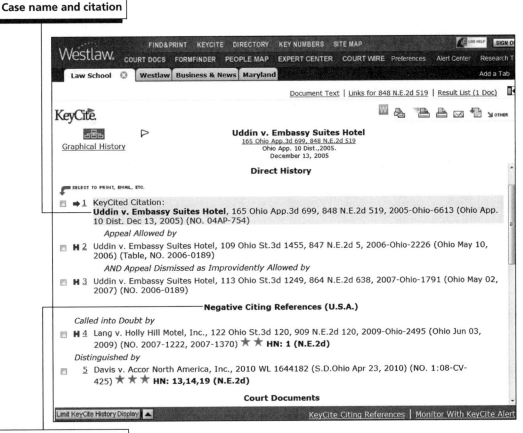

Reprinted with permission from Thomson Reuters/West, from Westlaw, KeyCite entry for 165 Ohio App. 3d. © 2012 Thomson Reuters/West.

history that could affect the validity of the original case, and court filings in the original case. Procedural phrases (e.g., affirmed, reversed) and other notations (e.g., distinguished, disagreed with, overruled) will indicate the effects of the history cases on the validity of the original case. The citation for the original case will be highlighted so you can identify it easily within the history. If the direct history of the original case includes any separate but related cases, those will be listed after any negative indirect history. You can retrieve any case listed in the entry by using the link to the number next to the citation.

The direct history option shows the history of the case in chart form; it is sometimes called **Graphical KeyCite**. Like the Shepard's **Map** view of a case's direct history, Graphical KeyCite will give you a visual snapshot of the original case's history, which can be useful if a case has an extensive or complex history.

The citing references portion of the entry shows the complete indirect history of the original case along with other citing sources. **Figure 6.11** shows a citing references entry. KeyCite in Westlaw.com organizes citing cases by type and depth of treatment, not by jurisdiction the way Shepard's does. The KeyCite entry is divided into sections for negative cases, positive cases, secondary sources (including A.L.R.

FIGURE 6.11   KEYCITE CITING REFERENCES FOR 165 OHIO APP. 3d 699

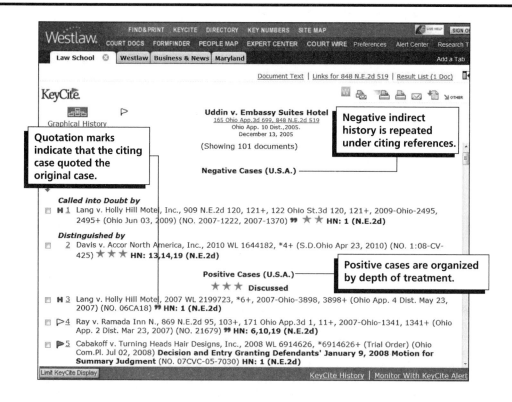

FIGURE 6.11   KEYCITE CITING REFERENCES FOR 165 OHIO APP. 3d 699 *(Continued)*

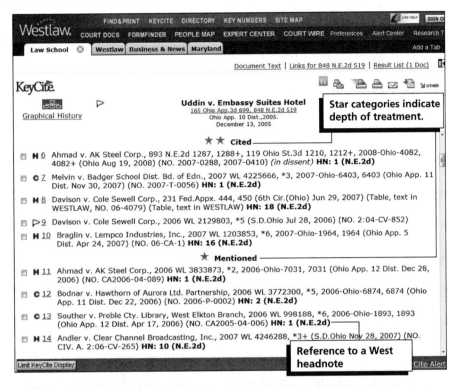

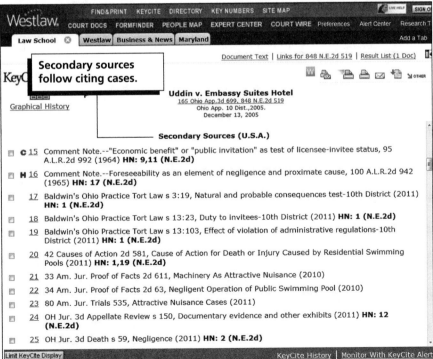

Reprinted with permission from Thomson Reuters/West, from Westlaw, KeyCite entry for 165 Ohio App. 3d 699.
© 2012 Thomson Reuters/West.

Annotations), and court documents. The negative cases section lists any negative indirect history; the list here will include notations to tell you what negative treatment the original case received (e.g., distinguished, overruled, etc.). It then lists citing cases that give the original case positive treatment. The positive citing cases are organized by depth of treatment and then by jurisdiction within the depth of treatment category.

KeyCite uses a system of star categories to indicate depth of treatment. The star categories indicate how much discussion of the original case you will find in the citing case. There are four star categories: (a) examined (four stars); (b) discussed (three stars); (c) cited (two stars); and (d) mentioned (one star). **Figure 6.12** delineates how West defines these terms. If a citing case quotes the original case, quotation marks will appear after the citation to the citing case in the KeyCite entry.

Headnote references also follow the citations to citing cases and sources. The headnote references in KeyCite work the same way as those in Shepard's. If a citing case cites the original case for a proposition of law summarized in a headnote at the beginning of the original case, the headnote reference will appear in the KeyCite entry. The headnote references in KeyCite correspond only to West headnotes, not to LexisNexis Headnotes or headnotes in an official reporter.

Although the full KeyCite entry provides the most complete information about the original case, you may want to view a more limited entry depending on your research task. KeyCite offers several options for limiting the display to focus on the information most relevant to you.

To limit the display, select the **Limit KeyCite Display** option at the bottom of the screen. From the full history of the case, choosing this

FIGURE 6.12   DEFINITIONS OF KEYCITE DEPTH OF TREATMENT CATEGORIES

NUMBER OF STARS	MEANING	DEFINED
Four stars	Examined	Contains an extended discussion of the original case, usually more than a printed page of text.
Three stars	Discussed	Contains a substantial discussion of the original case, usually more than a paragraph but less than a printed page.
Two stars	Cited	Contains some discussion of the original case, usually less than a paragraph.
One star	Mentioned	Contains a brief reference to the original case, usually in a string citation.

option will allow you to show negative treatment only. From the list of citing references, you will have a menu of options, as shown in **Figure 6.13**. You can limit the display by document type, headnote, terms you specify (using the Locate option), jurisdiction, date, or depth of treatment. Although each option appears on a different screen, you can combine options to limit the entry according to multiple criteria.

b. WestlawNext

When you retrieve a case in WestlawNext, the tabs accompanying the document contain the KeyCite information. You will see four tabs:

- **Filings**—This tab lists the court filings in the case you retrieved.
- **Negative Treatment**—This tab lists both direct and indirect negative history of the case, as illustrated in **Figure 6.14**.

FIGURE 6.13 KEYCITE LIMITED DISPLAY OPTIONS

Reprinted with permission from Thomson Reuters/West, from Westlaw, Limit KeyCite Display options. © 2012 Thomson Reuters/West.

FIGURE 6.14   KEYCITE "NEGATIVE TREATMENT" TAB

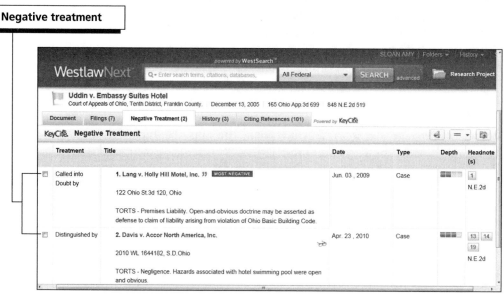

Reprinted with permission from Thomson Reuters/West, from Westlaw, KeyCite entry for 165 Ohio App. 3d 699. © 2012 Thomson Reuters/West.

- **History**—This tab shows the direct history of the case in both list and graphical form, as illustrated in **Figure 6.15**.
- **Citing References**—This tab shows the complete indirect history of the case, including citing cases and other citing sources, as illustrated in **Figure 6.16**.

If the case has received negative treatment, the citation to what West editors consider the most negative treatment will appear at the top of the document view to give you a sense of the status of the case. This may not include all the negative history of the case. You need to view the **Negative Treatment** and **History** tabs to get complete information about the original case.

The **Citing References** tab shows the complete indirect history of the original case along with other citing sources. The default organization of citing sources in WestlawNext is by depth of treatment, without regard for type of document or jurisdiction. WestlawNext uses green blocks, not stars, to indicate depth of treatment. See **Figure 6.12** for the depth of treatment categories. You can change the default search option to organize by date. The filtering options in the left margin will allow you to limit the results according to a number of criteria, including type of document, treatment, jurisdiction, and headnote. **Figure 6.17** shows the filtering options for cases.

FIGURE 6.15 KEYCITE "HISTORY" TAB

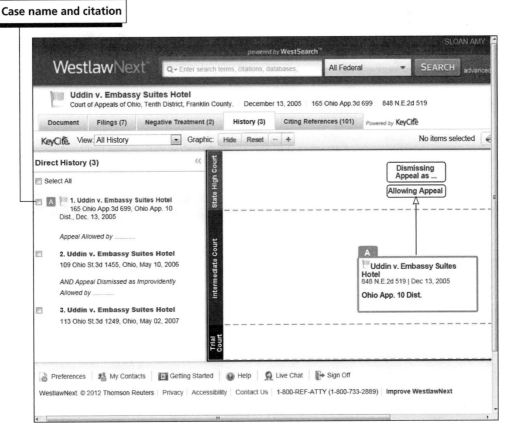

Reprinted with permission from Thomson Reuters/West, from Westlaw, KeyCite entry for 165 Ohio App. 3d 699.
© 2012 Thomson Reuters/West.

Headnote references also follow the citations to citing cases and sources. Headnote references in KeyCite work the same way as those in Shepard's. If a citing case cites the original case for a proposition of law summarized in a headnote at the beginning of the original case, the headnote reference will appear in the KeyCite entry. Headnote references in KeyCite correspond only to West headnotes, not to LexisNexis Headnotes or headnotes in an official reporter. You can see the text of a headnote by rolling your cursor over the headnote number. If a citing case quotes the original case, quotation marks will appear after the citation to the citing case in the KeyCite entry.

2. USING KEYCITE ALERT

Like Shepard's Alert®, KeyCite Alert automatically checks the authorities you select and delivers periodic reports to you. To set up a KeyCite

FIGURE 6.16 KEYCITE "CITING REFERENCES" TAB

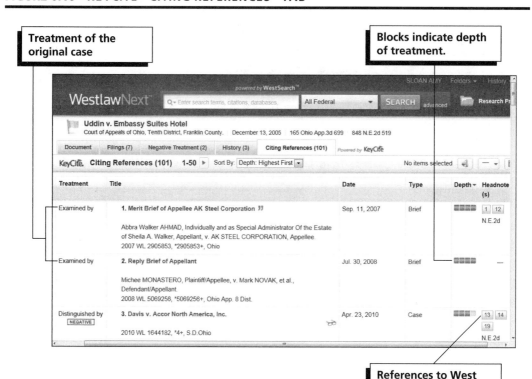

Reprinted with permission from Thomson Reuters/West, from Westlaw, KeyCite entry for 165 Ohio App. 3d 699.
© 2012 Thomson Reuters/West.

Alert in Westlaw.com, choose the option to **Monitor with KeyCite Alert** and follow the instructions to specify the content, delivery format, and frequency of the report. As this text goes to press, WestlawNext does not allow you to set up a KeyCite Alert directly from the case you are viewing. Instead, from the home page, access the **Alert Center** under the **Tools** tab and follow the instructions to create a KeyCite Alert.

D. CHOOSING AMONG CITATORS

Because Shepard's and KeyCite are the most widely used citators, they are the focus of this chapter, but they are not the only citators. Other electronic service providers have their own citators. For example, Bloomberg Law has **BCite**, LoislawConnect has **GlobalCite**, and VersusLaw has **V.Cite**. Google Scholar also includes a **How Cited** tab with its search results. This is not a citator in the traditional sense, but it is a tool that can refer you to later cases that have cited the original case. (The Internet addresses for all of these services appear in Appendix A.) Further,

FIGURE 6.17   KEYCITE FILTERING OPTIONS

Reprinted with permission from Thomson Reuters/West, from Westlaw, KeyCite entry for 165 Ohio App. 3d 699.
© 2012 Thomson Reuters/West.

although Shepard's and KeyCite provide largely the same information, they are not identical. As a result, you must decide which citator(s) to use for your research.

The decision will depend on several factors. Shepard's and KeyCite are the most accepted citators in legal research, and you should use them whenever you have access to them. Certainly, while you are in law school, you should use both services enough to become comfortable with them. When you are out of school, you may continue to have access to one or both services. As of this writing, Shepard's and KeyCite are fairly economical to use, costing subscribers only a few dollars per citation, and many law libraries that have discontinued subscriptions to Shepard's in print provide free public access to these services. If you do not have access to Shepard's or KeyCite but do have access to another citator, you should use it, understanding that the coverage of the citator may be limited to holdings within that service's database.

Using either Shepard's or KeyCite should be sufficient to verify the continued validity of a case as long as you carefully interpret the information they provide. Characterizing the treatment of a case requires the exercise of editorial judgment. From time to time, Shepard's and KeyCite will characterize the status of a case differently. And while both Shepard's and KeyCite are generally reliable, both occasionally contain errors. Therefore, if a case is especially important to your analysis, you would do well to check it in more than one citator.

If you are looking for research references, you may also want to use more than one citator. Any citator should provide references to later cases that you can use for research, but not all include references to secondary sources. Shepard's and KeyCite include references to secondary sources, but they do not index all the same secondary sources. Thus, you may get slightly different research results in each service. Of course, there is more than one way to find almost any source, so a single citator—even one that does not include references to secondary sources—may be sufficient for your research when used in combination with other research tools. If you are having trouble finding relevant information, however, consider using a different citator to see if it identifies additional research references.

E. SAMPLE PAGES FOR CASE RESEARCH WITH SHEPARD'S AND KEYCITE

Beginning below, **Figures 6.18** and **6.19** contain portions of the Shepard's and KeyCite entries for *Uddin v. Embassy Suites Hotel*, 165 Ohio App. 3d 699. The entries here show differences in how Shepard's and KeyCite analyzed the citing sources and provide an example of differences in editorial judgment regarding the citing cases' analysis of the original case.

Uddin v. Embassy Suites Hotel involves a negligence claim for injuries to a child at a hotel swimming pool. *Davis v. Accor North America, Inc.* involves a negligence claim by an adult against the operator of a swimming pool. The *Davis* opinion discusses *Uddin*. Reproduced below is a passage from *Davis*. Read this passage and review the Shepard's and KeyCite entries for *Uddin*. Consider whether you agree with how the citators have characterized the treatment that *Davis* gave to *Uddin*. (The references to all cases except *Uddin v. Embassy Suites Hotel* have been omitted.)

Excerpt from **Davis v. Accor North America, Inc.,** *discussing*
Uddin v. Embassy Suites Hotel:

In order to recover on a negligence claim, the plaintiff is required to prove the traditional tort elements of duty, breach, and proximate causation. [Citing *Uddin.*] In a premises liability case, such as this one, the defendant's duty to the plaintiff depends on the plaintiff's status—invitee, licensee, or trespasser. [Citing *Uddin.*] In this case, it is not disputed that the [plaintiffs] were business invitees of [the defendant].

The owner of a business is not an insurer of the safety of its business invitees. [Citing *Uddin.*] Rather, the owner owes its business invitees a duty of ordinary care to maintain the premises in a reasonably safe condition and to warn invitees of latent or hidden dangers. [Citing *Uddin.*] A business owner also has a duty to inspect the premises to discover possible dangerous conditions of which he is unaware and to take reasonable precautions to protect invitees from foreseeable dangers.

Where, however, the hazard on the premises is open and obvious, a business owner owes no duty of care to invitees.... Where the open and obvious doctrine applies, it operates as a complete bar to negligence claims....

In Ohio, "a swimming pool presents an open and obvious condition that should be appreciated by both minors and adults."[4]

---

4. In *Uddin*, the court held that a swimming pool is not an open and obvious danger to children of tender years, i.e., ten years old or less. This aspect of the *Uddin* decision is inapposite, however, because the [plaintiff's] children were not at risk of drowning and [another family member in the pool] was age 17 at the time.

Figure 6.18 shows the Shepard's entry for *Uddin v. Embassy Suites Hotel* in Lexis Advance. The entry in Lexis.com has a different display but contains the same information. The display in Figure 6.18 is limited to citing cases that have given the original case significant treatment, both positive and negative. *Davis v. Accor North America, Inc.* is listed as having "followed" the original case.

FIGURE 6.18 SHEPARD'S DISPLAY

Citing Decisions	Court	Date
Ohio Supreme Court		
1. **Abrogated in part by**,and **Cited in Concurring Opinion at:** Lang v. Holly Hill Motel, Inc. 122 Ohio St. 3d 120, 2009 Ohio 2495, 909 N.E.2d 120, 2009 Ohio LEXIS 1599	Ohio	2009
Headnotes: HN2, HN19 *Abrogated in part by:* 122 Ohio St. 3d 120 p.121; 909 N.E.2d 120 p.121 *Cited in Concurring Opinion at:* 122 Ohio St. 3d 120 p.127; 909 N.E.2d 120 p.126		
Ohio Court of Appeals		
2. **Criticized by:** Lang v. Holly Hill Motel, Inc. 2007 Ohio 3898, 2007 Ohio App. LEXIS 3529	Ohio Ct. App., Jackson County	May 23, 2007
Headnotes: HN19		
3. **Followed by:** Ray v. Ramada Inn North 171 Ohio App. 3d 1, 2007 Ohio 1341, 869 N.E.2d 95, 2007 Ohio App. LEXIS 1220	Ohio Ct. App., Montgomery County	2007
Headnotes: HN7, HN9 *Followed by:* 171 Ohio App. 3d 1 p.11; 869 N.E.2d 95 p.103		
4. **Criticized by:** Ahmad v. Ak Steel Corp. 2006 Ohio 7031, 2006 Ohio App. LEXIS 7029	Ohio Ct. App., Butler County	Dec. 28, 2006
Headnotes: HN2		
5. **Criticized by:** Souther v. Preble County Dist. Library 2006 Ohio 1893, 2006 Ohio App. LEXIS 1745	Ohio Ct. App., Preble County	Apr. 17, 2006
Headnotes: HN2		
6th Circuit - U.S. District Courts		
6. **Followed by:** Davis v. Accor N. Am., Inc. 2010 U.S. Dist. LEXIS 40057	S.D. Ohio	Apr. 23, 2010
Headnotes: HN6, HN9, HN23		
7. **Followed by:** Andler v. Clear Channel Broad., Inc. 2007 U.S. Dist. LEXIS 87695	S.D. Ohio	Nov. 28, 2007
Headnotes: HN9		

Figure 6.19 shows the KeyCite entry for *Uddin v. Embassy Suites Hotel* in WestlawNext. The entry in Westlaw.com has a different display but contains the same information. The display in Figure 6.19 is limited to citing cases that have given the original case negative treatment. Notice the difference between the analysis of the citing cases in KeyCite and Shepard's. KeyCite does not characterize *Davis* as following the original case, but rather, as distinguishing it.

FIGURE 6.19   KEYCITE DISPLAY

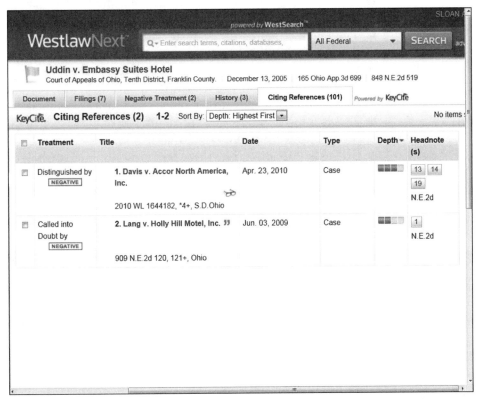

Reprinted with permission from Thomson Reuters/West, from Westlaw, KeyCite entry for 165 Ohio App. 3d 699. © 2012 Thomson Reuters/West.

F. CHECKLIST FOR CASE RESEARCH WITH CITATORS

1. USE SHEPARD'S IN LEXIS

❐ Access Shepard's and enter a citation or use the **Shepardize** link from a relevant case.

❐ Interpret the entry.

■ Use the Shepard's Signal as a qualified indicator of case status, not a definitive determination.

■ The entry contains direct history, citing decisions (divided by jurisdiction) and other citing sources.

■ Use the descriptions of the history (e.g., affirmed, reversed) and treatment (e.g., followed, distinguished, overruled) to identify citing cases that may affect the validity of the original case.

■ Use headnote references to identify citing cases that discuss propositions most relevant to your research.

■ In Lexis Advance, use the **Map** view for a snapshot of case history in chart form and the **Grid** view for a snapshot of treatment by later citing cases in chart form.

❐ Filter the display in Lexis.com.

■ Use **Shepard's for Validation** to retrieve an abbreviated entry.

■ Use the display options and **All Neg** or **All Pos** restrictions to limit the display.

■ Use FOCUS™-**Restrict By** to limit the display by type of analysis, jurisdiction, headnote, date, or terms you specify.

❐ Filter the display in Lexis Advance with the narrowing options in the left margin.

❐ Create a Shepard's Alert® for automatic updates to the Shepard's entry for the original case.

2. USE KEYCITE IN WESTLAW

❐ Access KeyCite from a relevant case (or the **KeyCite** link in Westlaw.com).

❐ Interpret the entry.

■ Use the KeyCite status flag as a qualified indicator of case status, not a definitive determination.

■ In Westlaw.com:

■ View the **Full History** of the original case to see direct history and negative indirect history.

■ View the **Direct History (Graphical View)** to see the history of the original case in chart form.

- View the **Citing References** to see indirect history and citing sources; negative cases appear first, followed by positive cases (divided by depth of treatment and then by jurisdiction) and citing sources.

■ In WestlawNext:

- View direct and indirect negative history under the **Negative Treatment** tab.
- View the direct history in list and chart form under the **History** tab.
- View citing references under the **Citing References** tab.

■ Use the descriptions of the history (e.g., affirmed, reversed) and treatment (e.g., distinguished, disagreed with, overruled) to identify citing cases that may affect the validity of the original case.

■ Use headnote references to identify citing cases that discuss propositions most relevant to your research.

■ Use quotation marks to identify citing cases that quote the original case.

❏ Filter the results.

■ In Westlaw.com, use the **Limit KeyCite Display** option to show negative treatment only and to limit the display by headnote, specific terms using Locate, jurisdiction, date, document type, or depth of treatment.

■ In WestlawNext, use the narrowing options in the left margin to limit the display by document type, treatment, jurisdiction, and other criteria.

❏ Create a KeyCite Alert for automatic updates to the KeyCite entry for the original case.

CHAPTER 7

STATUTORY RESEARCH

A. Introduction to statutory law

B. Researching statutes in print

C. Researching statutes electronically

D. Citing statutes

E. Sample pages for statutory research

F. Checklist for statutory research

A. INTRODUCTION TO STATUTORY LAW

1. THE PUBLICATION OF STATUTORY LAW

Statutes enacted by a legislature are organized by subject matter into what is called a "code." Codes are published by jurisdiction; each jurisdiction that enacts statutes collects them in its own code. Thus, the federal government publishes the federal code, which contains all federal statutes. Statutes for each state are published in individual state codes. Most codes contain too many statutes to be included in a single volume. Instead, a code usually consists of a multivolume set of books containing all of the statutes passed within a jurisdiction. The federal code also includes the text of the U.S. Constitution. Most state codes contain the text of the state constitution, and many include the text of the U.S. Constitution as well.

When a federal law is enacted, it is published in three steps: (1) it is published as a separate document; (2) it is included in a chronological listing of all statutes passed within a session of Congress; and (3) it is reorganized by subject matter and placed within the code. In the first step of the process, every law passed by Congress is assigned a public law number. The public law number indicates the session of Congress in which the law was passed and the order in which it was passed. Thus, Public Law 103-416 was the 416th law passed during the 103d session of Congress. Each public law is published in a separate booklet or pamphlet containing the full text of the law as it was passed by Congress. This booklet is known as a slip law and is identified by its public law number.

In the second step of the process, slip laws for a session of Congress are compiled together in chronological order. Laws organized within this chronological compilation are called session laws because they are organized according to the session of Congress during which they were enacted. Session laws are compiled in a publication called *United States Statutes at Large*. A citation to *Statutes at Large* will tell you the volume of *Statutes at Large* containing the law and the page number on which the text of the law begins. Thus, a citation to 108 Stat. 4305 tells you that this law can be located in volume 108 of *Statutes at Large*, beginning on page 4305. Both the slip law and session law versions of a statute should be identical. The only difference is the form of publication.

The third step in the process is the codification of the law. When Congress enacts a law, it enacts a block of legislation that may cover a wide range of topics. A single bill can contain provisions applicable to many different parts of the government. For example, a drug abuse prevention law could contain provisions applicable to subject areas such as food and drugs, crimes, and public health. If federal laws remained organized chronologically by the date of passage, it would be virtually impossible to research the law by subject. Laws relating to individual subjects could have been passed at so many different times that it would be extremely difficult to find all of the relevant provisions.

In the third step of the process, therefore, the pieces of the bill are reorganized according to the different subjects they cover, and they are placed by subject, or codified, within the federal code. Once legislation is codified, it is much easier to locate because it can be indexed by subject much the way cases are indexed by subject in a digest.

Figure 7.1 illustrates the publication process.

Figure 7.2 contains an example of a statute that has been codified within the federal code.

2. TITLE AND SUBJECT-MATTER ORGANIZATION OF CODES

Although all codes are organized by subject, not all codes are numbered the same way. The federal code is organized into Titles. For many years, the federal code had 50 Titles. In 2010, however, Congress enacted Title 51, so now the federal code has 51 Titles. Additional Titles may be enacted in the future. Each Title covers a different subject area. Title 18, for instance, contains the laws pertaining to federal crimes, and Title 35 contains the laws pertaining to patents. Each Title is subdivided into chapters, and each chapter is further subdivided into sections. To locate a provision of the federal code from its citation, you would

FIGURE 7.1 PUBLICATION PROCESS FOR A FEDERAL STATUTE

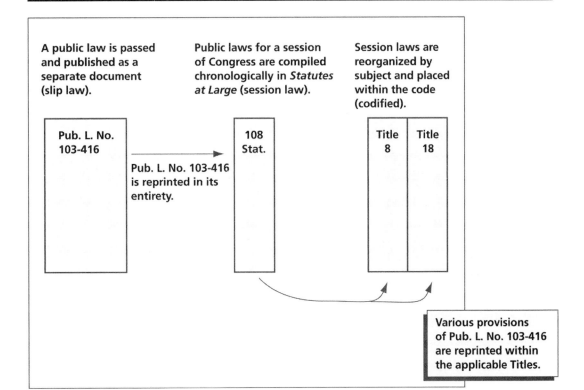

need to know the Title and the section number assigned to it. For example, the provision of the federal code prohibiting bank robbery is located in Title 18, section 2113.

Not all codes are organized this way. Some states organize their codes by subject name, rather than Title number. Within each subject name, the code is then usually subdivided into chapters and sections. To find a provision of the code from its citation, you would need to know the subject area and the section number assigned to that provision. For example, the provision of New York law that prohibits issuing a bad check is located in the subject volume of the New York code containing the Penal Law, section 190.05.

3. OFFICIAL VS. UNOFFICIAL CODES AND ANNOTATED VS. UNANNOTATED CODES

Although there is only one "code" for each jurisdiction, in the sense that each jurisdiction has only one set of statutes in force, the text of the laws may be published in more than one set of books or electronic databases. Sometimes a government arranges for the publication of its laws; this is

FIGURE 7.2   18 U.S.C.A. § 2725

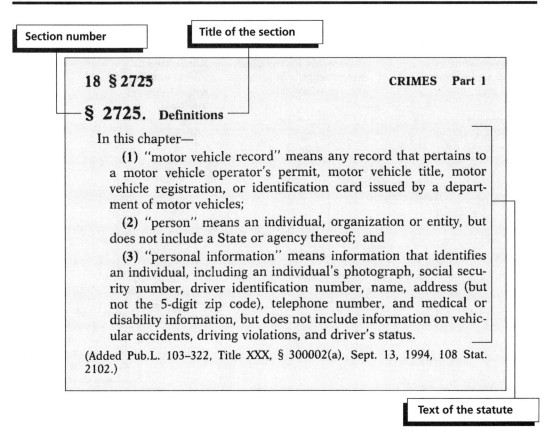

Reprinted with permission from Thomson Reuters/West, *United States Code Annotated*, Title 18 (2000), p. 340.
© 2000 Thomson Reuters/West.

known as an "official" code.[1] Sometimes a commercial publisher will publish the laws for a jurisdiction without government authorization; this is known as an "unofficial" code. Some jurisdictions have both official and unofficial codes. If both official and unofficial codes are published for a jurisdiction, they will usually be organized and numbered identically (e.g., all sets will be organized by subject or by Title). For federal laws, the government publishes an official code, *United States Code* or U.S.C. Two other sets of the federal code are also available through commercial publishers, *United States Code Annotated* (U.S.C.A.) and *United States Code Service* (U.S.C.S.).

---

[1] The government may publish the code itself, or it may arrange for a commercial publisher to publish the code. As long as the government arranges for the publication, the code is an official code, even if it is physically produced by a commercial publisher.

FIGURE 7.3 CHARACTERISTICS OF OFFICIAL AND UNOFFICIAL CODES

OFFICIAL CODES	UNOFFICIAL CODES
Published under government authority (e.g., U.S.C.).	Published by a commercial publisher without government authorization (e.g., U.S.C.A. and U.S.C.S.).
May or may not contain research references (annotations). U.S.C. is not an annotated code.	Usually contain research references (annotations). Both U.S.C.A. and U.S.C.S. are annotated codes.

In addition, a published code can come in one of two formats: annotated or unannotated. An annotated code contains the text of the law, as well as different types of research references. The research references may include summaries of cases or citations to secondary sources discussing a statute. An unannotated code contains only the text of the law. It may have a few references to the statutes' original public law numbers, but other than that, it will not contain research references. Most unofficial codes are annotated codes. Official codes may or may not be annotated. As you might imagine, an annotated code is much more useful as a research tool than an unannotated code.

In the federal code, U.S.C. (the official code) is an unannotated code. The two unofficial codes, U.S.C.A. and U.S.C.S., are annotated codes. See **Figure 7.3** for a summary of the characteristics of official and unofficial codes.

4. METHODS OF LOCATING STATUTES

You can locate statutes in many ways. If you have the citation to a statute that you have obtained from another source, such as a secondary source, you can easily locate the statute in a print code or retrieve it from an electronic database.

When you do not have a citation, you can locate statutes using either a source-driven or content-driven approach. If you use a source-driven approach, the first step will be deciding which jurisdiction's statutes you want to research. Once you select a jurisdiction, you can search for statutes by subject, by words in the document, or by the name of an act.

Researching by subject is often a useful way to locate statutes. The index to a code will be organized by subject, and using an index is one of the most common subject searching techniques for statutory research. All print codes have subject indices. If you are searching electronically, you may or may not have access to the index. Every code also has a table of contents, which you can view in print or electronically. Reviewing the table of contents can be a difficult way to begin your research unless you know the subject area of the statute you are trying to find. Once you find a relevant provision of the code, however, viewing the table of contents can help you find related code sections, as described more fully below.

Word searching is another way to locate statutes electronically. Because legislatures often use technical terms in statutes, however, word searching can be more difficult than subject searching if you are not already familiar with the statutory terminology.

An additional search option is locating a statute by name. Many statutes are known by their popular names, such as the Americans with Disabilities Act. In print, you can use a directory listing statutes according to their popular names. In an electronic service, you can use a statute's name as a word search; many services also have popular name search options.

If you choose content-driven searching in Lexis Advance or Westlaw-Next, your search results will include statutes. You will ordinarily pre-filter your search by jurisdiction unless you are researching the law of all U.S. jurisdictions. Once you execute the search, the results will include a section with statutes. In WestlawNext, statutes appear under the **Statutes** link from the **View** menu. In Lexis Advance, statutes appear under the **Legislative** tab. When you view the statutes your search retrieved, you can filter the results according to a number of criteria.

Regardless of the search method you use initially to locate a relevant section of a code, you should plan to expand your search to consider the entire statutory scheme. Rarely will an individual code section viewed in isolation resolve your research question. More often you will need to research interrelated code provisions. For example, assume you retrieved a code provision applicable to your research issue but failed to retrieve a nearby section containing definitions of terms used in the applicable provision. If you relied only on the one section your initial search revealed, your research would not be accurate. Because electronic sources often retrieve individual code sections as separate documents, it is especially easy to lose sight of the need to research multiple sections when you are working online. Whether you use print or electronic sources for statutory research, however, be sure to research the entire statutory scheme to ensure that you consider all potentially applicable code sections.

Once you have located a relevant code section, the easiest way to research a statutory scheme is to use the statutory outline or table of contents to identify related code provisions. In print, you will often find a chapter or subchapter outline of sections. **Figure 7.4** shows the outline for a chapter within Title 18 of the federal code. And of course, all you have to do is turn the pages to see preceding and subsequent code sections. Electronic sources often either display or provide links to statutory outlines or tables of contents, and many have functions that allow you to browse preceding and subsequent code sections.

Sections B and C, below, explain how to research statutes in print and electronically.

FIGURE 7.4 CHAPTER OUTLINE IN TITLE 18

CHAPTER 123—PROHIBITION ON RELEASE AND USE OF CERTAIN PERSONAL INFORMATION FROM STATE MOTOR VEHICLE RECORDS

Outline of Chapter 123 in Title 18

Sec.
2721. Prohibition on release and use of certain personal information from State motor vehicle records.
2722. Additional unlawful acts.
2723. Penalties.
2724. Civil action.
2725. Definitions.

HISTORICAL AND STATUTORY NOTES

Amendments
1996 Amendments. Pub.L. 104–294, Title VI, § 604(a)(3), Oct. 11, 1996, 110 Stat. 3506, added items 2721 to 2725, which had previously been editorially supplied. Therefore, no further change was required.

WESTLAW COMPUTER ASSISTED LEGAL RESEARCH

WESTLAW supplements your legal research in many ways. WESTLAW allows you to

• update your research with the most current information

• expand your library with additional resources

• retrieve current, comprehensive history citing references to a case with KeyCite

For more information on using WESTLAW to supplement your research, see the WESTLAW Electronic Research Guide, which follows the Explanation.

§ 2721. Prohibition on release and use of certain personal information from State motor vehicle records

(a) **In general.**—Except as provided in subsection (b), a State department of motor vehicles, and any officer, employee, or contractor, thereof, shall not knowingly disclose or otherwise make available to any person or entity personal information about any individual obtained by the department in connection with a motor vehicle record.

(b) **Permissible uses.**—Personal information referred to in subsection (a) shall be disclosed for use in connection with matters of motor vehicle or driver safety and theft, motor vehicle emissions, motor vehicle product alterations, recalls, or advisories, performance monitoring of motor vehicles and dealers by motor vehicle manufacturers, and removal of non-owner records from the original owner records

331

Reprinted with permission from Thomson Reuters/West, *United States Code Annotated*, Title 18 (2000), p. 331. © 2000 Thomson Reuters/West.

B. RESEARCHING STATUTES IN PRINT

The process of researching statutes is fairly uniform for state and federal codes. This section illustrates the process of researching federal statutes in detail using U.S.C.A. You should be able to adapt this process to almost any kind of statutory research. After the detailed discussion of U.S.C.A., this section discusses two additional sources for federal statutory research, U.S.C. and U.S.C.S., as well as state statutes, rules of procedure, and uniform codes and model acts. This section concludes with a discussion of statutory citators.

1. RESEARCHING FEDERAL STATUTES

a. Researching Federal Statutes in *United States Code Annotated*

You can research federal statutes in U.S.C.A. in several ways. The most common way to locate statutes is to search by subject using the General Index. You can also use tables accompanying the code to search by the popular name of the law or public law number.

(1) Researching in U.S.C.A. by subject

Researching federal statutes by subject in U.S.C.A. is a four-step process:

 i. Look up the topics you want to research in the General Index.
 ii. Locate the relevant code section(s) in the main volumes of U.S.C.A. and evaluate the material in the accompanying annotations.
 iii. Update your research using the pocket part.
 iv. Update your research using the supplementary pamphlets at the end of the code.

Because U.S.C.A. contains the U.S. Constitution, you can locate federal constitutional provisions by subject the same way you would locate any federal statute.

(i) Using the general index

The General Index to U.S.C.A. is an ordinary subject index that consists of a series of softcover books. It is published annually, so be sure to check the most recent set of index books.

Using the General Index is just like using any other subject index. Topics are listed alphabetically. Next to each topic are references to the Title and section number(s) of the statutory provisions relevant to that topic. The abbreviation "et seq." means that the index is referring to a series of sections beginning with the section listed; often, this will be a reference to an entire chapter within the Title. The index also contains cross-references to other subjects relevant to the topic. An example of an index page appears in **Figure 7.5**.

FIGURE 7.5 EXCERPT FROM THE U.S.C.A. GENERAL INDEX

Index entry

MOTOR

MOTOR VEHICLES—Cont'd
Parts—Cont'd
  Exports and imports, fair trade, 15 § 4705 et seq.
  Fair trade, 15 § 4705 et seq.
  Major parts, standards, 49 § 33110 nt
  Origin, small parts, 49 § 32304
  Small parts, origin, 49 § 32304
  Standards, major parts, 49 § 33110 nt
Passenger motor vehicle equipment, definitions, 49 § 32101
Passenger motor vehicles,
  Automotive fuel economy, ante
  Definitions, 49 § 32101
  Safety, generally, post
  Standards, generally, post
Passenger restraints. Seat Belts, generally, this index
Passive alcohol sensors, driving while intoxicated or under the influence, 23 § 410
Peace Corps, 22 § 2514
Penalties. Fines, penalties and forfeitures, generally, ante
Permits. Licenses and permits, generally, ante
Personal information, States, records and recordation, release, 18 § 2725
Personal injuries,
  Airbags, 49 § 30127 nt
  Database, nontraffic, noncrash incident situations, 49 § 30111 nt
  Insurance, consumer information, 49 § 32303
Peru, free trade, 19 § 3805 nt
Petroleum Administration for Defense District, 42 § 7545
Plans and specifications,
  Heritage area, 16 § 461 nt
  Research, 23 § 501 et seq.
Plug In Electric Drive Vehicles, generally, this index
Political subdivisions,
  Fuel economy, preemption, 49 §§ 32918, 32919
  Social Security account numbers, 42 § 405
Power of attorney, odometers, disclosure, 49 § 32705
Power windows, safety, 49 § 30111 nt
Preemption,
  Automotive fuel economy, ante
  Bumper standards, 49 § 32511
  Country of origin, 49 § 32304
  Larceny, 49 § 33118
  Leases, liability, 49 § 30106
President-elect and Vice-President-elect, 3 § 102 nt
President of the United States, this index
Privileges and immunities,
  National motor vehicle title information system, 49 § 30502
  National Stolen Passenger Motor Vehicle Information System, 49 § 33109
Proceedings. Actions and proceedings, generally, ante
Production of books and papers, commercial vehicle safety regulations, 49 § 31133
Proration, excise tax, 26 § 4481

MOTOR VEHICLES—Cont'd
Public Buildings and Works, this index
Public Lands, this index
Public policy, automotive fuel economy, 42 § 6201
Public transit vehicles, maximum axle weight, 23 § 127 nt
Purchasers and purchasing,
  Federal agencies, fuel cell vehicles, 42 § 16121 et seq.
  Maximum prices, 31 § 1343 nt
  Prices, maximum prices, 3
  States, fuel cell vehicles,
Qualified clean fuel vehicle tax, deduction, 26 § 17
Races. Motor Sports, gene
Rear seatbelts, 49 §§ 30101
Rearward visibility, safety, 49 § 30111 nt
Recall, defects, 49 §§ 30111 nt, 30120
Rechargeable batteries, 42 § 14301 et seq.
Records and recordation,
  Bumper standards, 49 §§ 32505, 32506
  Commercial vehicle safety regulations, 49 § 31133
  Consumer Assistance to Recycle and Save Program, 49 § 32901 nt
  Crimes and offenses, privacy, 18 § 2721 et seq.
  Investigations, 49 § 32307
  Larceny, ante
  Odometers, 49 § 32706
  State, personal information, privacy, 18 § 2721 et seq.
  Trade-in, Consumer Assistance to Recycle and Save Program, 49 § 32901 nt
Recreation and Recreational Facilities, this index
Recycling and resource recovery, Consumer Assistance to Recycle and Save Program, 49 § 32901 nt
Red Cliffs National Conservation Area, 16 § 460www
Red Rock Canyon National Conservation Area, 16 § 460ccc–2
Refusal, tests, driving under influence of drugs or alcohol, 18 § 3118
Registration,
  Inauguration ceremonies, 36 § 502
  International Registration Plan and International Fuel Tax Agreement, generally, ante
  Social security, account numbers, 42 § 405
  States, post
Registry, National Driver Register, 49 § 30301 et seq.
Release, trunk lids, 49 § 30
Renewable fuel program, 42
Rental vehicles, insurance, § 6781
Repairs, 15 § 2301 et seq.
  Asian markets, fair trade, 15 § 4705 et seq.
  Disabling maintenance or support personnel, 18 § 33
  Insurance, consumer information, 49 § 32303
  Odometers, 49 § 32704

Reference to Title 18, § 2721 and beyond; indicates multiple sections may apply.

Reference to an individual code section

Reprinted with permission from Thomson Reuters/West, *United States Code Annotated*, 2011 General Index J-R p. 453. © 2011 Thomson Reuters/West.

(ii) Locating statutes and reading the annotations

Once you have located relevant Title and section numbers in the General Index, the next step is finding the statute within the books. The books are organized numerically by Title, although some Titles span more than one volume. Using the Title number, you should be able to locate the correct volume. The sections within the Title will be listed in numerical order within the volume.[2] As noted earlier, an outline of the statute will appear at the beginning of each chapter or subchapter.

Following the text of the code section, you may find a series of annotations with additional information about the statute. **Figure 7.6** describes some of the types of information you can find in the annotations in U.S.C.A.

Not all statutes have annotations. Those that do may not contain all of the information in **Figure 7.6** or may have additional information. The information provided depends on the research references that are appropriate for that statute. If a statute has any annotations, they will always follow the text of the code section. **Figure 7.7** shows the annotations accompanying 18 U.S.C.A. § 2725.

(iii) Updating statutory research using pocket parts

Like other hardcover books used in legal research, U.S.C.A. volumes are updated with pocket parts. If the pocket part gets too big to fit in the back of the book, you should find a separate softcover pamphlet on the shelf next to the hardcover volume.

The pocket part is organized in the same way as the main volume. Therefore, to update your research, you need only look up the section numbers you located in the main volume. The pocket part will show any revisions to the statute, as well as additional annotations if, for example, new cases interpreting the section have been decided. If the pocket part shows new statutory language, the text in the pocket part supersedes the text in the main volume. If no reference to the section appears in the pocket part, the statute has not been amended, and no new research references are available. **Figure 7.8** shows a portion of the pocket part update to 18 U.S.C.A. § 2725.

(iv) Updating statutory research using supplementary pamphlets

The pocket part for each volume is published only once a year. Congress may change a statute after the pocket part is printed, however, and cases interpreting a statute can be issued at any time. Therefore, to update your research, you need to check an additional source.

---

[2] If the statute was enacted after the main volume was published, you will not find it in the hardcover book. More recent statutes will appear in the pocket part or noncumulative supplements, which are explained in the next section.

FIGURE 7.6   INFORMATION CONTAINED IN U.S.C.A. ANNOTATIONS

CATEGORIES OF INFORMATION IN ANNOTATIONS	CONTENTS
Historical Note Sometimes this section is called Historical and Statutory Notes.	Contains the history of the section, including summaries of amendments and the public law numbers and *Statutes at Large* citations for the laws containing the revisions. This section can also refer to the legislative history of the statute (for more discussion of legislative history, see Chapter 8).
Cross-References	Contains cross-references to related provisions of the code.
Library References Sometimes this section is subdivided into categories for Administrative Law, American Digest System, Encyclopedias, Law Reviews, Texts and Treatises, and Forms.	Contains references to related topics and key numbers in the West digest system, as well as references to legal encyclopedia sections with information on the subject (see Chapter 5 for more discussion of the digest system and Chapter 4 for more discussion of legal encyclopedias).
Code of Federal Regulations Sometimes this appears as a separate section, and sometimes it is included with Library References, under the Administrative Law category.	Contains references to administrative agency regulations implementing the statute (for more discussion of administrative regulations, see Chapter 9).
Law Review Articles Sometimes this appears as a separate section, and sometimes it is included with Library References, under the Law Reviews category.	Contains references to relevant law review articles (for more discussion of law reviews and other legal periodicals, see Chapter 4).
Notes of Decisions	Contains summaries of cases interpreting the statute. If the statute has been discussed in a large number of cases, the Notes of Decisions will be divided into subject categories, and each category will be assigned a number. Cases on each subject will be listed under the appropriate number. *Note that these subject and number categories do not correspond to the topics and key numbers within the West digest system.*

FIGURE 7.7 ANNOTATIONS ACCOMPANYING 18 U.S.C.A. § 2725

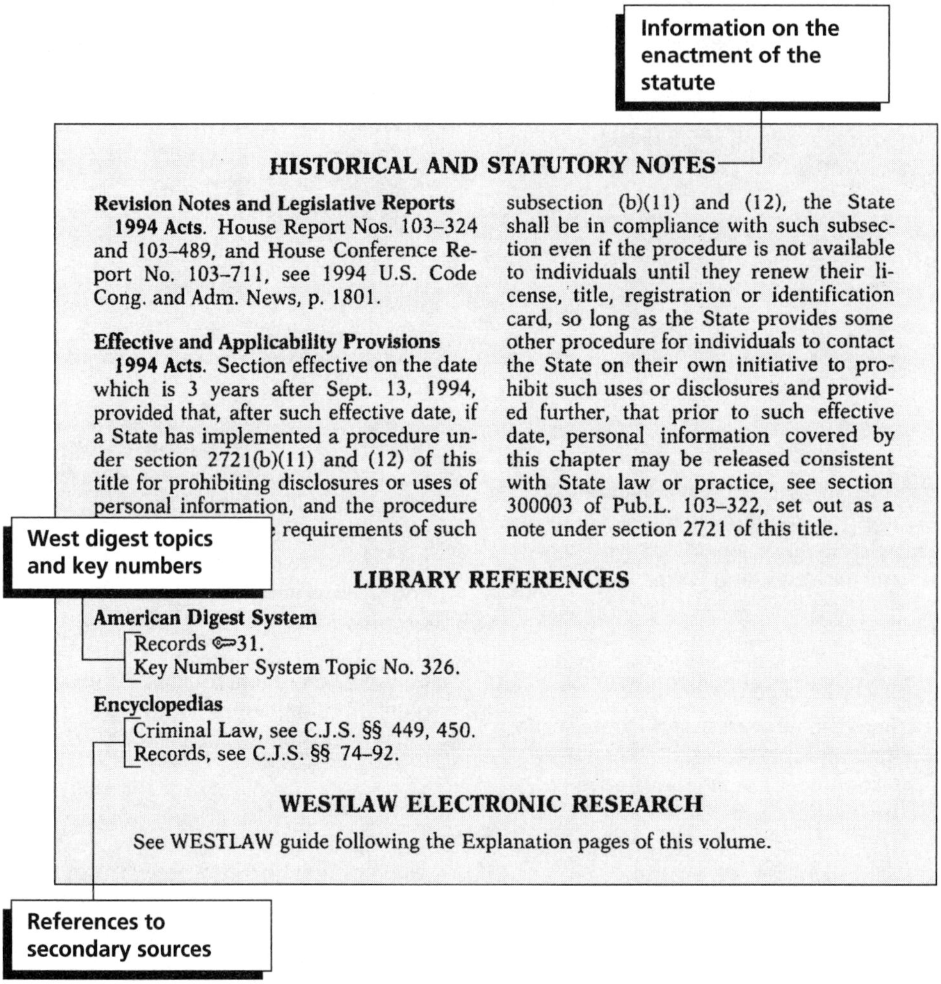

Information on the enactment of the statute

HISTORICAL AND STATUTORY NOTES

Revision Notes and Legislative Reports
 1994 Acts. House Report Nos. 103–324 and 103–489, and House Conference Report No. 103–711, see 1994 U.S. Code Cong. and Adm. News, p. 1801.

Effective and Applicability Provisions
 1994 Acts. Section effective on the date which is 3 years after Sept. 13, 1994, provided that, after such effective date, if a State has implemented a procedure under section 2721(b)(11) and (12) of this title for prohibiting disclosures or uses of personal information, and the procedure requirements of such

subsection (b)(11) and (12), the State shall be in compliance with such subsection even if the procedure is not available to individuals until they renew their license, title, registration or identification card, so long as the State provides some other procedure for individuals to contact the State on their own initiative to prohibit such uses or disclosures and provided further, that prior to such effective date, personal information covered by this chapter may be released consistent with State law or practice, see section 300003 of Pub.L. 103–322, set out as a note under section 2721 of this title.

West digest topics and key numbers

LIBRARY REFERENCES

American Digest System
 Records ⇔31.
 Key Number System Topic No. 326.

Encyclopedias
 Criminal Law, see C.J.S. §§ 449, 450.
 Records, see C.J.S. §§ 74–92.

WESTLAW ELECTRONIC RESEARCH

See WESTLAW guide following the Explanation pages of this volume.

References to secondary sources

Reprinted with permission from Thomson Reuters/West, *United States Code Annotated*, Title 18 (2000), p. 340. © 2000 Thomson Reuters/West.

At the end of the U.S.C.A. set, you should find a series of softcover pamphlets. These are supplements that are published after the pocket part. They are noncumulative, meaning that each pamphlet covers a specific time period. The dates of coverage of each pamphlet should appear on the cover. To update your research thoroughly, you must look for your code section in each pamphlet published since the pocket part. If a change to the statute appears in an earlier pamphlet, the later pamphlets will refer back to the earlier pamphlet. Later pamphlets will not, however, refer back to additional annotations. Therefore, to locate all new annotations, you must check each supplementary pamphlet.

FIGURE 7.8   POCKET PART UPDATE FOR 18 U.S.C.A. § 2725

18 § 2725   CRIMES AND CRIMINAL PROCEDURE

§ 2725. Definitions

In this chapter—

[See main volume for text of (1)]

(2) "person" means an individual, organization or entity, but does not include a State or agency thereof;

(3) "personal information" means information that identifies an individual, including an individual's photograph, social security number, driver identification number, name, address (but not the 5-digit zip code), telephone number, and medical or disability information, but does not include information on vehicular accidents, driving violations, and driver's status.[1]

(4) "highly restricted personal information" means an individual's photograph or image, social security number, medical or disability information; and

(5) "express consent" means consent in writing, including consent conveyed electronically that bears an electronic signature as defined in section 106(5) of Public Law 106–229.

(Added Pub.L. 103–322, Title XXX, § 300002(a), Sept. 13, 1994, 108 Stat. 2102, and amended Pub.L. 106–346, § 101(a) [Title III, § 309(b)], Oct. 23, 2000, 114 Stat. 1356, 1356A–24.)

[1] So in original. The period probably should be replaced with a semicolon.

HISTORICAL AND STATUTORY NOTES

Revision Notes and Legislative Reports

2000 Acts. House Report No. 106–940, see 2000 U.S. Code Cong. and Adm. News, p. 1063.

June 30, 2000, 114 Stat. 472, classified to section 7006(5) of Title 15.

Amendments

2000 Amendments. Par. (2). Pub.L. 106–346, [Title III, § 309(b)], struck out "and".

Pars. (4), (5). Pub.L. 106–346, [Title III, § 309(b)], added pars. (4) and (5).

> **New statutory language supersedes the language in the main volume.**

... in Text

06(5) of Public Law 106–229, referred is section 106(5) of Pub.L. 106–229,

LIBRARY REFERENCES

American Digest System

Records ⊚=31.
Key Number System Topic No. 326.

> **New annotations follow the text of the statute.**

Research References

ALR Library

8 ALR, Fed. 2nd Series 611, Application of Local District Court Summary Judgment Rules to Nonmoving Party in Federal Courts--Statements of Facts.

183 ALR, Fed. 37, Validity, Construction, and Application of Federal Driver's Privacy Protection Act, 18 U.S.C.A. §§ . 2721 to 2725.

2 Am. Jur. Trials 409, Locating Public Records.

49 Am. Jur. Trials 281, Liability for Mishandled Computer Information.

82 Am. Jur. Trials 123, Snowmobile Litigation: Practice and Strategy.

Am. Jur. 2d Commerce § 8, Determination as to Character of Commerce as Interstate or Intrastate.

Am. Jur. 2d Commerce § 42, What Constitutes Subjects of Commerce.

Am. Jur. 2d Privacy § 122, Disclosure of Information in Motor Vehicle Records.

Encyclopedias

... Jur. Proof of Facts 3d 237, Govern-
...ility for Liberty or Privacy Depriva-
...ing from Erroneous Information in
...cords.

... Am. Jur. Proof of Facts 3d 159, Invasion of Privacy by Public Disclosure of Private Facts.

Treatises and Practice Aids

West's Federal Administrative Practice § 375, Department of Transportation–Introduction.

> **Cases interpreting the statute are summarized.**

NOTES OF DECISIONS

Generally ½
Exceptions, personal information 3
Obtaining or using information 4
Particular information, personal information 2
Personal information 1-3
 Exceptions 3
 Particular information 2

½. Generally

Driver's Privacy Protection Act (DPPA) did not require that driver histories be excised of all personal information unless requestor had DPPA permitted use; such reading did not comport with legislative history nor plain language of statute. Camara v. Metro-North R. Co.,

128

The noncumulative pamphlets are organized the same way as the rest of the code: by Title and section number. Therefore, you need to look up the Title and section number of the statute you are researching. The pamphlet, like the pocket part, will list any changes to the statute, as well as additional annotations. If no reference to the section appears in the noncumulative pamphlet, then there is no additional information for you to research.

(2) The popular name and conversion tables

Research using a subject-matter index is appropriate when you know the subject you want to research but do not know the exact statute you need to find. Sometimes, however, you will know which statute you need to find. In that situation, the easiest way to find the citation may be through the popular name table or the conversion tables. In U.S.C.A., the popular name table is published as a separate volume accompanying the General Index. The conversion tables appear in separate softcover "Tables" volumes.

The popular name table allows you to locate statutes according to their popular names. For example, if you wanted to research the Driver's Privacy Protection Act of 1994 but did not know its citation, you could look up a variety of topics in the General Index until you found it. An easier way to do this would be to look up the act according to its popular name. The popular name table lists the public law number, the *Statutes at Large* citation, and the Title and section numbers where the act is codified within U.S.C.A. Remember that when a law is passed by a legislature, it may affect many different areas of the law and, therefore, may be codified in many different places within the code. Thus, the popular name table may refer you to a number of different Titles and sections. For many well-known statutes, however, the popular name table is an efficient way to locate the law within the code. **Figure 7.9** shows the popular name table entry for the Driver's Privacy Protection Act.

Another way to locate a statute in U.S.C.A. is through the conversion tables. If you know the public law number for a statute, you can use the tables to find the *Statutes at Large* citation and the Titles and sections where the law has been codified. Once you know the Title and section numbers, you can locate the statute by citation. **Figure 7.10** is an example from the conversion table for Public Law 106-346, which contains amendments to the Driver's Privacy Protection Act, as well as provisions affecting other Titles of the federal code. The table shows where the statute's provisions are codified.

Because the popular name and conversion tables are published annually, there is no pocket part update for the tables. At the end of each noncumulative supplement, however, you will find updates to the tables. Therefore, if you are unable to find the material you want in the General Index or Tables, check for more recent material in the noncumulative supplements.

FIGURE 7.9   DRIVER'S PRIVACY PROTECTION ACT ENTRY, POPULAR NAME TABLE

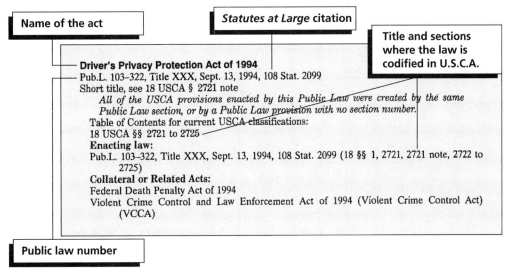

Reprinted with permission from Thomson Reuters/West, *United States Code Annotated*, 2011 Popular Name Table, p. 939. © 2011 Thomson Reuters/West.

FIGURE 7.10   CONVERSION TABLE ENTRY FOR PUB. L. NO. 106-346

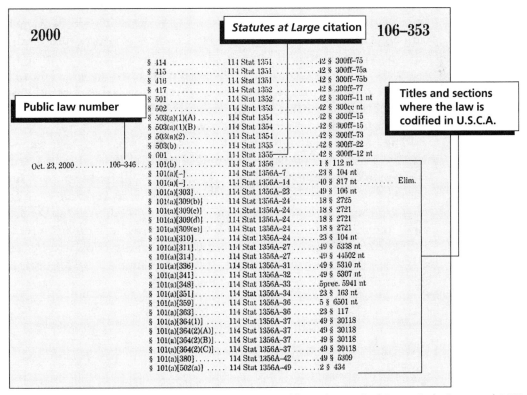

Reprinted with permission from Thomson Reuters/West, Tables Vol. II, *United States Code Annotated*, 2011, p. 1457. © 2011 Thomson Reuters/West.

b. Researching Federal Statutes in *United States Code*

The index, popular name, and conversion table methods of locating statutes are all available with U.S.C. The main difference in researching U.S.C. concerns updating. The index and main volumes of the code are published every six years. In the intervening years, U.S.C. is not updated with pocket parts. Instead, it is updated with hardcover cumulative supplements. A new supplement is issued each year until the next publication of the main set.

In theory, using the supplements should be sufficient to update your research. In practice, however, the system presents some difficulties. Laws can be changed more frequently than the supplements are published, and the government is often two or three years behind in publishing the supplements. To update completely, you would need to research session and slip laws published since the latest supplement. Therefore, U.S.C. is not usually an appropriate source for locating the most current version of a statute, and because it lacks the research references contained in the annotated federal codes, it is not the most useful statutory research tool.

c. Researching Federal Statutes in *United States Code Service*

U.S.C.S. is organized much the same way as U.S.C.A. The index, popular name, and conversion table methods of locating statutes are all available with U.S.C.S. U.S.C.S. often has fewer references to court decisions than the Notes of Decisions in U.S.C.A., but the references to administrative materials are often more comprehensive than those in U.S.C.A.[3] The nature of your research project and the materials available in your library will determine whether it is more appropriate for you to use U.S.C.S. or U.S.C.A. for federal statutory research.

The process of updating U.S.C.S. research is basically the same as that for U.S.C.A. Hardcover main volumes are updated with pocket parts. In addition, at the end of U.S.C.S., you will find softcover supplements to the code as a whole called the Cumulative Later Case and Statutory Service. Unlike the supplements to U.S.C.A., the U.S.C.S. supplements are cumulative, so you only need to check the most recent one. The supplements are organized by Title and section number and will reflect both changes to the statutory language and additional annotations.

---

[3] Chapter 9 explains administrative materials and administrative law research.

2. RESEARCHING STATE CODES, RULES OF PROCEDURE, AND UNIFORM LAWS AND MODEL ACTS

a. State Codes

State codes have many of the same features of U.S.C.A. All have subject indices that can be used to locate statutes. Some also have popular name tables. Most do not, however, have the equivalent of the conversion tables. In addition, the updating process for state statutory research can vary. Virtually all state codes are updated with pocket parts, but some have different or additional updating tools. You may want to check with a reference librarian if you have questions about updating statutory research for a particular state. Sample pages illustrating the process of state statutory research appear in Section E of this chapter.

b. Rules of Procedure

You are probably learning about rules of procedure governing cases filed in court in your Civil Procedure class. Whenever you are preparing to file a document or take some action that a court requires or permits, the court's rules of procedure will tell you how to accomplish your task. The rules of procedure for most courts are published as part of the code for the jurisdiction where the court is located. For example, the Federal Rules of Civil Procedure appear as an appendix to Title 28 in the federal code. In many states, court procedural rules are published in a separate Rules volume.

If you want to locate procedural rules, therefore, one way to find them is through the applicable code. In print, you can locate them using the subject index, or you can go directly to the rules themselves if they are published in a separate volume. Many procedural rules have been interpreted in court opinions, and you need to research those opinions to understand the rules' requirements fully. If you locate rules in an annotated code, summaries of the decisions will follow the rules, just as they do any other provision of the code. You can update your research with the pocket part and any cumulative or noncumulative supplements accompanying the code.

A couple of caveats about locating rules of procedure are in order. First, understanding the rules can be challenging. As with any other type of research, you may want to locate secondary sources for commentary on the rules and citations to cases interpreting the rules to make sure you understand them. For the Federal Rules of Civil Procedure, two helpful treatises are *Moore's Federal Practice* and Wright & Miller's *Federal Practice and Procedure*. For state procedural rules, a state "deskbook," or handbook containing practical information for lawyers practicing in the jurisdiction, may contain both the text of the rules and helpful commentary on them. If you locate the rules through a secondary source, however, be sure to update your research because the rules can be amended at any time.

Second, virtually all jurisdictions have multiple types and levels of courts, and each of these courts may have its own procedural rules. Therefore, be sure you locate the rules for the appropriate court. Determining which court is the appropriate one may require separate research into the jurisdiction of the courts.

Third, many individual districts, circuits, or divisions of courts have local rules with which you must comply. Local rules cannot conflict with the rules of procedure published with the code, but they may add requirements that do not appear in the rules of procedure. Local rules usually are not published with the code, but you can obtain them from a number of sources, including the court itself, a secondary source such as a practice deskbook, or a website, or an online database. To be sure that your work complies with the court's rules, do not neglect any local rules that may add to the requirements spelled out in the rules of procedure.

c. Uniform Laws and Model Acts

Uniform laws and model acts, as explained in Chapter 4, are proposed statutes that can be adopted by legislatures. Technically, they are secondary sources; their provisions do not take on the force of law unless they are adopted by a legislature. If your research project involves a statute based on a uniform law or model act, however, you may want to research these sources.

Many uniform laws and model acts are published in a multivolume set of books entitled *Uniform Laws Annotated, Master Edition* (ULA). The ULA set is organized like an annotated code. It contains the text of the uniform law or model act and annotations summarizing cases from jurisdictions that have adopted the statute. It also provides commentary that can help you interpret the statute. Chapter 4, on secondary sources, explains how to use the ULA set.

3. USING A CITATOR FOR STATUTORY RESEARCH

Chapter 6 discusses citators and how to use them in conducting case research. Citators are also available as research and updating tools for state and federal statutes. Statutory citator entries typically include information about the history of a statute (i.e., whether it has been amended or repealed), as well as lists of citing cases and sources. As noted in Chapter 6, most law libraries no longer carry Shepard's in print. Therefore, specific information about statutory citators appears in the next section on electronic research. As explained in more detail below, Shepard's for statutes is available in Lexis, and KeyCite for statutes is available in Westlaw.

Using a citator in statutory research is useful in two situations. First, citators can provide you with the most complete research references for statutory research. Some print sources (as well as many free Internet databases) provide access only to unannotated versions of codes. If you do not have access to an annotated code, a citator is a useful tool for locating cases interpreting a statute. Even if you are using an annotated code, the statutory annotations often do not list every citing case or source that has cited the statute. If the annotations are too sparse to give you the information you need about a statute, you may find more complete information in a citator.

Second, citators are updated more frequently than print (and some electronic) sources. Therefore, a citator may provide you with the most recent information about the history of the statute (such as any amendments), as well as the most recent research references. Just as you would not want to cite a case that is no longer good law, you would not want to cite a statute that has been repealed or declared unconstitutional. Using a citator, therefore, is the better practice in statutory research.

C. RESEARCHING STATUTES ELECTRONICALLY

Much statutory material is available electronically. This section discusses search options for researching statutes using Westlaw, Lexis, and Internet sources. The features of the electronic statutory citators (Shepard's in Lexis and KeyCite in Westlaw) are also explained in this section.

1. WESTLAW

Westlaw contains annotated versions of the federal code, all 50 state codes, and the District of Columbia code. The annotated version of the federal code in Westlaw is derived from U.S.C.A., although U.S.C. is also available. For most jurisdictions, you will find court rules of procedure included with the code, and for some you will find local court rules as well.

a. Viewing an Individual Code Section

You can retrieve an individual code section using a citation or by executing a search and selecting a code section from the search results. The display for an individual code section begins with a heading containing, among other things, the citation for the section and a **Currentness** link to tell you the date through which the statute has been updated.

In Westlaw.com, the statutory information appears in a single document with the text of the statute followed by annotations like those in a print code. The annotations will include references to secondary sources, summaries of cases that have cited the statute (called "Notes of Decisions"), and other information. See **Figure 7.6** for a description of the types of research references included in U.S.C.A. statutory annotations. Similar information appears in the annotations to other codes.

In WestlawNext, the information you see depends on how you access the statute. If you retrieve the document from its citation, you will see the text of the statute on the opening page, with additional information under accompanying tabs. Information from the annotations appears under the **Notes of Decisions** and **Context & Analysis** tabs. The **Notes of Decisions** tab contains brief summaries of the most important cases that have analyzed the statute. The **Context & Analysis** tab lists secondary sources and other research references that refer to the statute.

The **History** and **Citing References** tabs contain the KeyCite information for the statute. The **History** tab lists amendments and other legislative action affecting the statute, along with legislative history documents if they are available. (Federal legislative history is discussed in Chapter 8.) The **Citing References** tab will list every case or other source that has cited the statute without any summaries. Because KeyCite's **Citing References** list is comprehensive, everything under **Notes of Decisions** and **Context & Analysis** will also appear under **Citing References**, but the reverse is not true. You may find the presentation of the material in **Notes of Decisions** and **Context & Analysis** easier to use.

If you execute a search and select the statute from the search results, the opening page will show the text of the statute and portions of the annotations that contain your search terms. The complete information from the annotations and KeyCite appear under the accompanying tabs.

When you retrieve an individual code section, you can view the table of contents for the statutory chapter and the entire code using the **Table of Contents** link. You can also browse the previous or next section using the links and arrows near the top of the screen. **Figures 7.11** and **7.12** show how a federal statute appears in Westlaw.com and WestlawNext.

b. Searching for Statutes

Westlaw offers several search options for statutory research. If you know you want to research statutes, you should use a source-driven strategy to search within a statutory database. Once you select a database, Westlaw offers several statutory research options, including: **Search**, which allows you to execute a word search; **Find by Citation**; **Table of Contents**; **Statutes Index**; and **Popular Name Table**.

FIGURE 7.11   EXCERPT FROM 18 U.S.C.A. § 2725 IN WESTLAW.COM

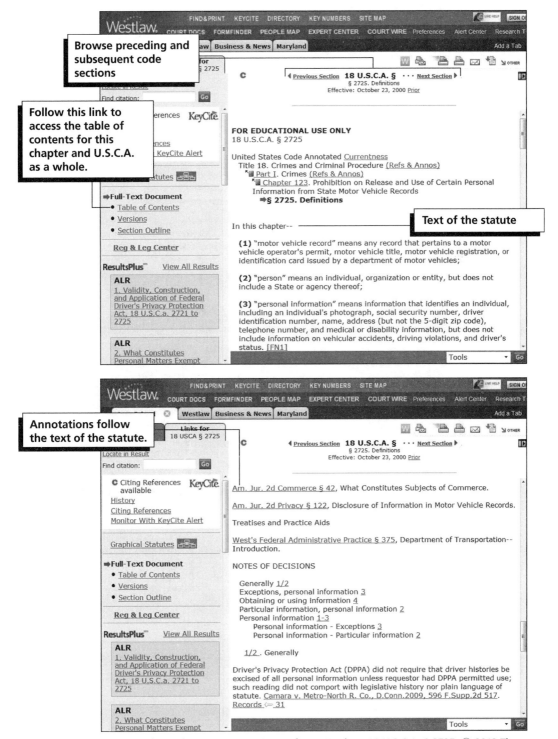

Reprinted with permission from Thomson Reuters/West, from Westlaw, 18 U.S.C.A. § 2725. © 2012 Thomson Reuters/West.

FIGURE 7.12   EXCERPT FROM 18 U.S.C.A. § 2725 IN WESTLAWNEXT

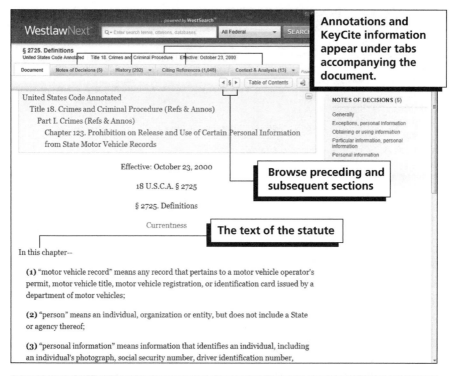

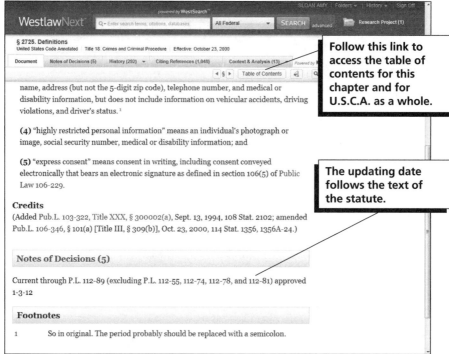

Reprinted with permission from Thomson Reuters/West, from Westlaw, 18 U.S.C.A. § 2725. © 2012 Thomson Reuters/West.

In Westlaw.com, you can select a database in several ways. You can use the **Directory** link at the top of the screen. Under the **Law School** tab, the **Resources** section also lists databases you can select to search. If you have added a tab for a specific jurisdiction, you will find database options for that jurisdiction's statutes listed.

If you select a database using a checkbox, you can execute a word search from the search box at the top of the page. To see the other search options you must select the database a different way. If you follow the links to the statutory table of contents or statutory index or go through the **Directory**, the search screen will show all available search options in the top right corner. **Figure 7.13** shows the Westlaw Statutes Index search screen and the search options available for researching U.S.C.A.

In WestlawNext, you can select a database by drilling down through the menu options on the home page by type of content (statutes and court rules), jurisdiction, or topic. Once you select a database for statutes from a particular jurisdiction, the table of contents for the code will be displayed, and you can execute a search within the code using the search box at the top of the screen. In the **Tools and Resources** section on the right,

FIGURE 7.13   WESTLAW.COM U.S.C.A. STATUTES INDEX SEARCH SCREEN

Reprinted with permission from Thomson Reuters/West, from Westlaw, U.S.C.A. Statutes Index search screen. © 2012 Thomson Reuters/West.

you will see additional search options similar to those in Westlaw.com, including the **Find Template, Statutes Index,** and **Popular Name Table**. **Figure 7.14** shows the table of contents and search options for U.S.C.A.

A word search in a database containing an annotated code will search both the statutory language and the annotations. Thus, it will retrieve documents when the search terms appear in the annotations, such as in a case summary, even if they do not appear in the statutory language, unless you specifically limit your search to words in the statute itself. (Word searching in general and techniques for limiting a search are discussed in Chapter 10, on electronic legal research.) Word searching is useful when you are searching for unique terms that are not likely to be included in the statutory index or table of contents.

The **Find by Citation** and **Find Template** options bring up a list of templates you can use to retrieve statutory citations. You do not have to choose a statutory database to retrieve a statute from its citation, but the

FIGURE 7.14   WESTLAWNEXT U.S.C.A. TABLE OF CONTENTS AND SEARCH OPTIONS

Reprinted with permission from Thomson Reuters/West, from Westlaw, U.S.C.A. Table of Contents screen. © 2012 Thomson Reuters/West.

template may be useful if you are unsure about the citation form for statutes from a particular jurisdiction.

The **Table of Contents** option allows you to browse a code's table of contents. The table of contents will be organized by Title or subject. You can drill down from the main Title or subject headings to chapters and individual code sections. You can also execute a word search within parts of the code by selecting the specific portions you want to search. **Table of Contents** searching is a good option when you are familiar enough with the code to know which subject areas are likely to contain relevant statutes but do not have specific statutory citations. It is also an excellent feature for viewing an entire statutory scheme.

The **Statutes Index** allows you to search the code's subject index just as you would if you were researching in print. Westlaw's statutory indices are identical to West print indices, although West reports that the electronic versions are updated more frequently than the print versions are. The index entries will refer you to statutory provisions the same way a print index would. This is a good research option when you want to search by subject because the index is organized around concepts instead of individual terms in a document and contains cross-references to related terms and concepts. Word searches, by contrast, will search only for the precise terms you specify.

The **Popular Name Table** lists laws by their popular names. It is the electronic version of the print popular name table. Choosing the **Popular Name Table** option displays an alphabetical list of acts by their popular names. The link to an act's popular name will retrieve an entry listing the Title(s) and section(s) where the act is codified. When you know the popular name of a statute but do not have its citation, this is a good research option.

You may also see a reference to **50 State Surveys** among the Westlaw.com search options. In WestlawNext, you can access the same option under the **All Content** tab by selecting **Statutes and Court Rules**. This function accesses a database that West describes as containing "a variety of topical surveys providing references to applicable state laws." It consists mostly of secondary material describing state law on a variety of topics and providing citations to state statutory provisions. It may be useful when you are researching the laws of multiple jurisdictions.

WestlawNext will also allow you to execute a word search without first selecting a database. If you use this content-driven approach, you will ordinarily want to pre-filter the results by jurisdiction. Your search results will include many types of authority, including statutes, which you can view in the **Statutes** section, and again, the results screen will show a variety of options for filtering the search results.

The organization of the results in Westlaw.com and WestlawNext may be by date or relevance depending on the type of searching you do. You have some ability to modify the default sort options, again depending on the type of search.

c. Using KeyCite for Statutory Research

Even though the statutes in Westlaw's databases are usually up to date, you may still want to use KeyCite in your research. You can use KeyCite to update a statute retrieved from another source or to find research references for a statute you obtained from an unannotated code. Even if you used an annotated code, the statutory annotations may not contain information that is useful for your research issue. The KeyCite entry will be more comprehensive because it lists every case that has cited the statute and may be more up to date than the statutory annotations.

In Westlaw.com, the process of using KeyCite for statutes is virtually identical to the process of using it for cases. You can enter a citation or access the service from a statute you are viewing. The KeyCite entry is divided into sections for history and citing references. In WestlawNext, the KeyCite information is automatically included under the **History** and **Citing References** tabs when you view a statutory provision. You can also type *kc:* and a citation to go directly to a statute's KeyCite entry.

KeyCite history lists amendments and other legislative action affecting the statute, along with legislative history documents if they are available. KeyCite citing references will list every case or other source that has cited the statute. You can monitor a statutory KeyCite entry by creating a KeyCite Alert.

2. LEXIS

Lexis contains annotated versions of the federal code, all 50 state codes, and the District of Columbia code. The annotated version of the federal code in Lexis is derived from U.S.C.S. For most jurisdictions, you will find court rules of procedure included with the code, and for some you will find local court rules as well.

a. Viewing an Individual Code Section

The display for an individual code section begins with a heading containing, among other things, the citation for the section and a notation with the date through which it is updated. The text of the statute then appears, followed by annotations like those in a print code containing research references and summaries of cases analyzing the statute. See **Figure 7.6** for a list of items that may appear in statutory annotations.

When you retrieve an individual code section, you have several options for viewing the complete statutory outline. You can view the table of contents for the statutory chapter and the entire code from the

TOC link in Lexis.com and the **Table of Contents** link in Lexis Advance. You can also browse preceding or subsequent code sections using arrows at the top of the document. Choose the option for **Book Browse** in Lexis .com to see the arrows. **Figure 7.15** shows how a federal statute appears in Lexis.com, and **Figure 7.16** shows the same statute in Lexis Advance.

b. Searching for Statutes

Lexis offers several statutory research options. You can retrieve a statute in Lexis from its citation. Lexis also allows source-driven searching by subject or words in the document, and Lexis Advance offers content-driven searching. Because of the differences between the two versions of Lexis, each is addressed separately below. Like Westlaw, Lexis organizes search results in various ways depending on the type of searching you do. You have some ability to modify the default sort options, again depending on the type of search.

(1) Lexis.com

You can retrieve a statute from its citation using the **Get a Document** function. This is the easiest way to locate a statute when you know its citation.

For word or table of contents searches, the first step is selecting a database from the source directory. Once you have selected a statutory source, the search screen will give you the option of executing a word search or browsing the table of contents. If you execute a word search in an annotated code, Lexis.com will look for your search terms in both the statutory language and in any annotations unless you specifically limit your search to words in the statute itself. (Word searching in general and techniques for limiting a search are discussed in Chapter 10, on electronic legal research.)

To browse the table of contents, you can drill down through the main Title or subject headings to individual code sections. You can also restrict your word search to individual Titles, chapters, or sections of the code by checking the box next to each part of the code you want to search. Again, word searching is useful if you are searching for specific statutory terms, and browsing the table of contents is useful for viewing an entire statutory scheme. The table of contents also provides a mechanism for searching statutory subject categories because Lexis does not offer index searching. **Figure 7.17** shows the search screen for searching U.S.C.S.

You can also search the U.S.C.S. Popular Name Table to locate federal statutes by name. As of this writing, you can access the popular name table by following this path: **Federal Legal—U.S., United States Code Service (USCS) Materials, USCS—Popular Name Table**. Once you select this source, you can execute a word search for the name of an act or browse the alphabetical list. Follow the link to an act's popular

FIGURE 7.15 EXCERPT FROM 18 U.S.C.S. § 2725 IN LEXIS.COM

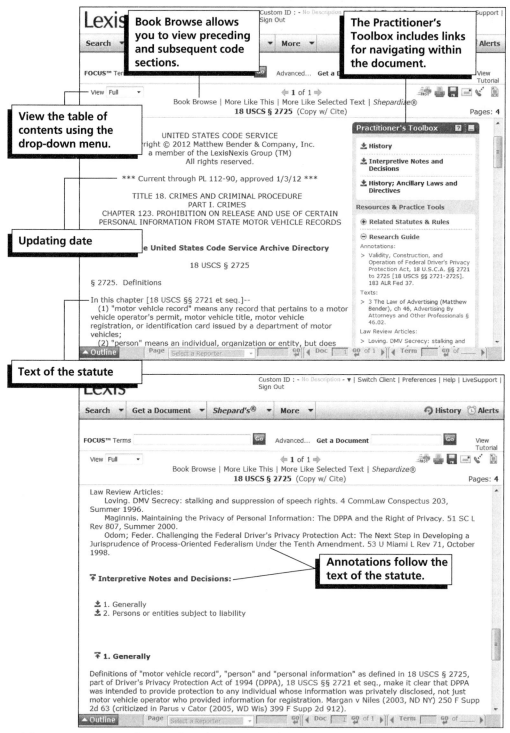

FIGURE 7.16   EXCERPT FROM 18 U.S.C.S. § 2725 IN LEXIS ADVANCE

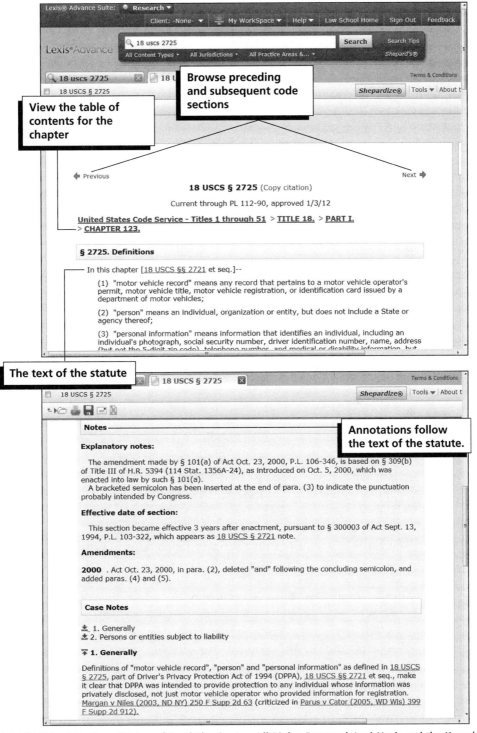

FIGURE 7.17   LEXIS.COM U.S.C.S. SEARCH SCREEN

name to retrieve an entry listing the Title(s) and section(s) where the act is codified. Lexis.com does not allow you to browse state statutes by popular name. If you need to find a state statute by name, you can use the popular name as a word search to locate the act.

(2) Lexis Advance

To retrieve a statute by citation in Lexis Advance, enter the citation in the search box. To conduct a source-driven search for statutes only or a content-driven search for all forms of authority, you will execute a search in the search box, but you will vary the selections from the drop-down menus.

To execute a source-driven word search for statutes only, select **Statutes and Legislation** as the content type. For a content-driven search, choose **All Content** as the content type. With either search, you will usually want to pre-filter the search by jurisdiction. You may want to pre-filter by topic as well, but you do not have to. As this text goes to press, Lexis Advance offers only the broad topic categories listed in the drop-down menu; you cannot drill down to subtopics. After you execute a word search, you will have a variety of options for filtering the search results.

c. Using Shepard's for Statutory Research

Even though the statutes in Lexis's databases are usually up to date, you may still want to use Shepard's in your research. As noted above, using a statutory citator ensures that your research is fully updated. In addition, a citator will provide the most complete research references because it lists every case that has cited the statute and may be more up-to-date than the statutory annotations.

The process of using Shepard's for statutes is virtually identical to the process of using it for cases. You can enter a citation or access the service from a statute you are viewing. A Shepard's entry is divided into three sections: history, citing decisions, and other authorities. In Lexis.com, all three items appear in a single document. In Lexis Advance, each item will appear under a separate sub-tab. The history section shows the history of the statute, indicating, for example, whether the statute has been amended. The citing decisions shows cases that have cited the statute, and the section with other authorities shows law review articles, treatises, and other forms of authority that have cited the statute. You can limit the display to focus on the information most relevant to your research, and you can monitor a statutory Shepard's entry with Shepard's Alert®.

3. INTERNET SOURCES

The federal code, all 50 state codes, and the District of Columbia code are available on the Internet. You can locate them through government websites, such as the website for the House of Representatives, or general legal research websites. Often these sites have search functions that will allow you to retrieve statutes using word, subject, or table of contents searches. As of this writing, index searching is available for only a few states. Cornell Law School's Legal Information Institute site offers a popular name table for the United States Code. Appendix A lists the Internet addresses for websites that may be useful for statutory research. In addition, court rules of procedure, including local court rules, are often available on court websites. If the code or rules of procedure you need to research are available and up-to-date on the Internet, this can be an economical alternative to Lexis and Westlaw research.

Two caveats, however, are important to mention. First, the codes available on the Internet are usually unannotated codes, so you will only find the statutory text, not any additional research references. Second, it is important to check the date of any statutory material you use. Statutory compilations available on the Internet may be updated only as frequently as official print sources. If the material is not up to date, you will need to update your research. Therefore, if you use an Internet source for statutory research, it is especially important to use a citator to obtain research references and update your research.

D. CITING STATUTES

The citation format for statutes is the same using either the *ALWD Manual* (4th ed.) or the *Bluebook* (19th ed.). The general rules for citing statutes can be found in Rule 14 in the *ALWD Manual* and Bluepages B5 in the *Bluebook*.

Citations to statutes can be broken into two components: (a) information identifying the code and code section; and (b) parenthetical information containing the date of the code and any relevant supplements; this section may also include a reference to the publisher of the code. To find out the exact requirements for a citation to a particular code, you must look at Appendix 1 in the *ALWD Manual* or Table T1 in the *Bluebook*, both of which tell you how to cite codes from every jurisdiction in the U.S. Appendix 1 and Table T1 include information on which code to cite if more than one is published, how to abbreviate the name of the code, and whether the name of the publisher must be included with the date in the parenthetical.

In a citation to a Title code, you will ordinarily give the Title number, the abbreviated name of the code, the section symbol, the section number, and a parenthetical containing the date the book was published and, if necessary, the publisher.

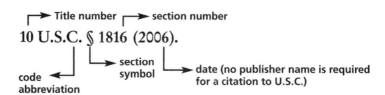

In a citation to a subject-matter code, you will ordinarily list the abbreviated name of the code, the section symbol, the section number, and a parenthetical containing the date the book was published and, if necessary, the publisher.

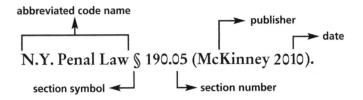

In this example, Appendix 1 and Table T1 provide that citations to McKinney's Consolidated Laws of New York Annotated must include the name of the publisher in the parenthetical, which is why you see the reference to McKinney in this citation. In both examples, note that there is a space between the section symbol (§) and the section number.

Sometimes determining which date or dates to include in the parenthetical can be confusing. The answer is always a function of where a reader would have to look to find the full and up-to-date language of the statute in the print code. If the full statute is contained in the main volume of the code, the date in the parenthetical should refer only to the main volume. If the full statute is contained only in the pocket part, the date should refer only to the pocket part. If the reader must refer both to the main volume and to the pocket part, the parenthetical should list both dates. In making this determination, you should consider *only* the language of the statute itself, not the annotations. If the full text of the statute itself is in the main volume, you do not need to cite the pocket part even if it contains additional annotations. Once you have determined which date to place in the parenthetical, you should then refer to Appendix 1 or Table T1 to determine whether the publisher must also be included. The following are examples of citations with different date information included in the parenthetical.

N.Y. Penal Law § 190.05 (McKinney 2010).

In this example, Appendix 1 and Table T1 require the name of the publisher, and the full text of the statute can be found in the main volume.

N.Y. Penal Law § 190.05 (McKinney Supp. 2012).

In this example, Appendix 1 and Table T1 require the name of the publisher, and the full text of the statute can be found in the pocket part.

N.Y. Penal Law § 190.05 (McKinney 2010 & Supp. 2012).

In this example, Appendix 1 and Table T1 require the name of the publisher, and the reader must refer both to the main volume and to the pocket part to find the full text of the statute.

In citations to a code for which no publisher is required, the only difference would be the omission of the publisher's name, as in the example below.

Haw. Rev. Stat. § 328-1 (2008).

When you look at the entries in Table T1 of the *Bluebook*, you will notice that the names of the codes are in large and small capital letters, e.g., N.Y. PENAL LAW § 190.05 (McKinney 2010). Remember that this is the type style for law review footnotes, not for briefs and memoranda. According to Bluepages B1, large and small capitals are never used in briefs and memoranda. Therefore, in briefs and memoranda, you should use regular type when citing statutes. You should not use all capital letters, nor should you use large and small capital letters.

E. SAMPLE PAGES FOR STATUTORY RESEARCH

Beginning on the next page, **Figures 7.18** through **7.21** contain sample pages from U.S.C.A. The sample pages show the research process you would follow if you were researching the Driver's Privacy Protection Act in print. **Figures 7.22** through **7.26** show ways you could research a Texas statute prohibiting false disparagement of perishable foods in Westlaw and Lexis.

The first step in print U.S.C.A. research is using the most recent General Index to locate relevant code sections. This example shows what you would find if you looked under "Motor Vehicles."

FIGURE 7.18 EXCERPT FROM U.S.C.A. GENERAL INDEX

Index entry

MOTOR

MOTOR VEHICLES—Cont'd
Parts—Cont'd
Exports and imports, fair trade, **15 § 4705 et seq.**
Fair trade, **15 § 4705 et seq.**
Major parts, standards, **49 § 33110 nt**
Origin, small parts, **49 § 32304**
Small parts, origin, **49 § 32304**
Standards, major parts, **49 § 33110 nt**
Passenger motor vehicle equipment, definitions, **49 § 32101**
Passenger motor vehicles,
Automotive fuel economy, ante
Definitions, **49 § 32101**
Safety, generally, post
Standards, generally, post
Passenger restraints. Seat Belts, generally, this index
Passive alcohol sensors, driving while intoxicated or under the influence, **23 § 410**
Peace Corps, **22 § 2514**
Penalties. Fines, penalties and forfeitures, generally, ante
Permits. Licenses and permits, generally, ante
Personal information, States, records and recordation, release, **18 § 2725**
Personal injuries,
Airbags, **49 § 30127 nt**
Database, nontraffic, noncrash incident situations, **49 § 30111 nt**
Insurance, consumer information, **49 § 32303**
Peru, free trade, **19 § 3805 nt**
Petroleum Administration for Defense District, **42 § 7545**
Plans and specifications,
Heritage area, **16 § 461 nt**
Research, **23 § 501 et seq.**
Plug In Electric Drive Vehicles, generally, this index
Political subdivisions,
Fuel economy, preemption, **49 §§ 32918, 32919**
Social Security account numbers, **42 § 405**
Power of attorney, odometers, disclosure, **49 § 32705**
Power windows, safety, **49 § 30111 nt**
Preemption,
Automotive fuel economy, ante
Bumper standards, **49 § 32511**
Country of origin, **49 § 32304**
Larceny, **49 § 33118**
Leases, liability, **49 § 30106**
President-elect and Vice-President-elect, **3 § 102 nt**
President of the United States, this index
Privileges and immunities,
National motor vehicle title information system, **49 § 30502**
National Stolen Passenger Motor Vehicle Information System, **49 § 33109**
Proceedings. Actions and proceedings, generally, ante
Production of books and papers, commercial vehicle safety regulations, **49 § 31133**
Proration, excise tax, **26 § 4481**

MOTOR VEHICLES—Cont'd
Public Buildings and Works, this index
Public Lands, this index
Public policy, automotive fuel economy, **42 § 6201**
Public transit vehicles, maximum axle weight, **23 § 127 nt**
Purchasers and purchasing,
Federal agencies, fuel cell vehicles, **42 § 16121 et seq.**
Maximum prices, **31 § 1343 nt**
Prices, maximum prices, 3
States, fuel cell vehicles,
Qualified clean fuel vehicle
tax, deduction, **26 § 17**
Races. Motor Sports, gene
Rear seatbelts, **49 §§ 30101**
Rearward visibility, safety, 4
Recall, defects, **49 §§ 30111**
Rechargeable batteries, **42 § 14301 et seq.**
Records and recordation,
Bumper standards, **49 §§ 32505, 32506**
Commercial vehicle safety regulations, **49 § 31133**
Consumer Assistance to Recycle and Save Program, **49 § 32901 nt**
Crimes and offenses, privacy, **18 § 2721 et seq.**
Investigations, **49 § 32307**
Larceny, ante
Odometers, **49 § 32706**
State, personal information, privacy, **18 § 2721 et seq.**
Trade-in, Consumer Assistance to Recycle and Save Program, **49 § 32901 nt**
Recreation and Recreational Facilities, this index
Recycling and resource recovery, Consumer Assistance to Recycle and Save Program, **49 § 32901 nt**
Red Cliffs National Conservation Area, **16 § 460www**
Red Rock Canyon National Conservation Area, **16 § 460ccc–2**
Refusal, tests, driving under influence of drugs or alcohol, **18 § 3118**
Registration,
Inauguration ceremonies, **36 § 502**
International Registration Plan and International Fuel Tax Agreement, generally, ante
Social security, account numbers, **42 § 405**
States, post
Registry, National Driver Register, **49 § 30301 et seq.**
Release, trunk lids, **49 § 30**
Renewable fuel program, 42
Rental vehicles, insurance, **§ 6781**
Repairs, **15 § 2301 et seq.**
Asian markets, fair trade, **15 § 4705 et seq.**
Disabling maintenance or support personnel, **18 § 33**
Insurance, consumer information, **49 § 32303**
Odometers, **49 § 32704**

Reference to Title 18, § 2721 and beyond; *et seq.* indicates multiple sections may apply.

Reference to an individual code section

Reprinted with permission from Thomson Reuters/West, *United States Code Annotated*, 2011 General Index J-R p. 453. © 2011 Thomson Reuters/West.

The next step is looking up the statute in the main volume. Because the index indicates that several code provisions may be applicable, you might want to review the chapter outline.

FIGURE 7.19   OUTLINE OF TITLE 18, CHAPTER 123

CHAPTER 123—PROHIBITION ON RELEASE AND USE OF CERTAIN PERSONAL INFORMATION FROM STATE MOTOR VEHICLE RECORDS

Outline of Chapter 123 in Title 18

Sec.
2721. Prohibition on release and use of certain personal information from State motor vehicle records.
2722. Additional unlawful acts.
2723. Penalties.
2724. Civil action.
2725. Definitions.

HISTORICAL AND STATUTORY NOTES

Amendments
  1996 Amendments. Pub.L. 104–294, Title VI, § 604(a)(3), Oct. 11, 1996, 110 Stat. 3506, added items 2721 to 2725, which had previously been editorially supplied. Therefore, no further change was required.

WESTLAW COMPUTER ASSISTED LEGAL RESEARCH

WESTLAW supplements your legal research in many ways. WESTLAW allows you to

● update your research with the most current information
● expand your library with additional resources
● retrieve current, comprehensive history citing references to a case with KeyCite

For more information on using WESTLAW to supplement your research, see the WESTLAW Electronic Research Guide, which follows the Explanation.

§ 2721. Prohibition on release and use of certain personal information from State motor vehicle records

  (a) In general.—Except as provided in subsection (b), a State department of motor vehicles, and any officer, employee, or contractor, thereof, shall not knowingly disclose or otherwise make available to any person or entity personal information about any individual obtained by the department in connection with a motor vehicle record.

  (b) Permissible uses.—Personal information referred to in subsection (a) shall be disclosed for use in connection with matters of motor vehicle or driver safety and theft, motor vehicle emissions, motor vehicle product alterations, recalls, or advisories, performance monitoring of motor vehicles and dealers by motor vehicle manufacturers, and removal of non-owner records from the original owner records

331

Section 2725 contains definitions of the terms used in the statute. The text of the statute is followed by annotations containing research references.

FIGURE 7.20   18 U.S.C.A. § 2725

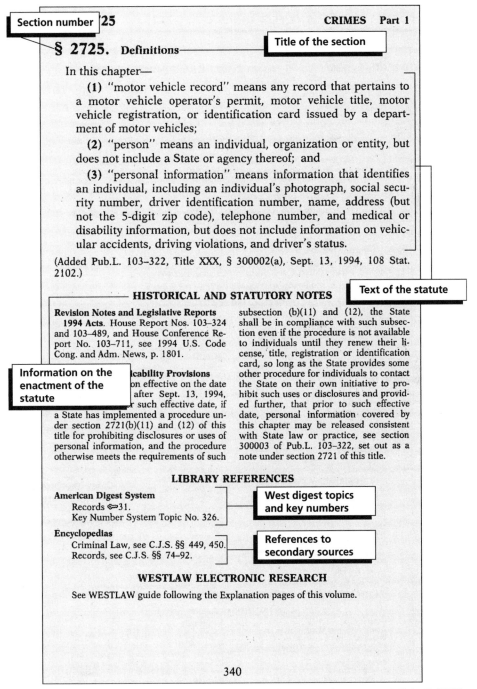

Section number 25   **CRIMES   Part 1**

§ 2725. Definitions——**Title of the section**

In this chapter—

(1) "motor vehicle record" means any record that pertains to a motor vehicle operator's permit, motor vehicle title, motor vehicle registration, or identification card issued by a department of motor vehicles;

(2) "person" means an individual, organization or entity, but does not include a State or agency thereof; and

(3) "personal information" means information that identifies an individual, including an individual's photograph, social security number, driver identification number, name, address (but not the 5-digit zip code), telephone number, and medical or disability information, but does not include information on vehicular accidents, driving violations, and driver's status.

(Added Pub.L. 103–322, Title XXX, § 300002(a), Sept. 13, 1994, 108 Stat. 2102.)

Text of the statute

HISTORICAL AND STATUTORY NOTES

Revision Notes and Legislative Reports
  1994 Acts. House Report Nos. 103–324 and 103–489, and House Conference Report No. 103–711, see 1994 U.S. Code Cong. and Adm. News, p. 1801.

Information on the enactment of the statute icability Provisions
on effective on the date after Sept. 13, 1994, r such effective date, if a State has implemented a procedure under section 2721(b)(11) and (12) of this title for prohibiting disclosures or uses of personal information, and the procedure otherwise meets the requirements of such

subsection (b)(11) and (12), the State shall be in compliance with such subsection even if the procedure is not available to individuals until they renew their license, title, registration or identification card, so long as the State provides some other procedure for individuals to contact the State on their own initiative to prohibit such uses or disclosures and provided further, that prior to such effective date, personal information covered by this chapter may be released consistent with State law or practice, see section 300003 of Pub.L. 103–322, set out as a note under section 2721 of this title.

LIBRARY REFERENCES

American Digest System
  Records ☜31.
  Key Number System Topic No. 326.

West digest topics and key numbers

Encyclopedias
  Criminal Law, see C.J.S. §§ 449, 450.
  Records, see C.J.S. §§ 74–92.

References to secondary sources

WESTLAW ELECTRONIC RESEARCH

See WESTLAW guide following the Explanation pages of this volume.

340

The next step is checking the pocket part. The pocket part entry for § 2725 shows new statutory language that supersedes the language in the main volume. It also shows additional research references. After checking the pocket part, be sure to check any noncumulative supplements. Because the supplements are noncumulative, all supplements published after the pocket part must be checked for amendments to the statute or new annotations.

FIGURE 7.21   POCKET PART ENTRY FOR 18 U.S.C.A. § 2725

---

18 § 2725   CRIMES AND CRIMINAL PROCEDURE

§ 2725. Definitions
   In this chapter—

[See main volume for text of (1)]

   (2) "person" means an individual, organization or entity, but does not include a State or agency thereof;
   (3) "personal information" means information that identifies an individual, including an individual's photograph, social security number, driver identification number, name, address (but not the 5-digit zip code), telephone number, and medical or disability information, but does not include information on vehicular accidents, driving violations, and driver's status.[1]
   (4) "highly restricted personal information" means an individual's photograph or image, social security number, medical or disability information; and
   (5) "express consent" means consent in writing, including consent conveyed electronically that bears an electronic signature as defined in section 106(5) of Public Law 106–229.

(Added Pub.L. 103–322, Title XXX, § 300002(a), Sept. 13, 1994, 108 Stat. 2102, and amended Pub.L. 106–346, § 101(a) [Title III, § 309(b)], Oct. 23, 2000, 114 Stat. 1356, 1356A–24.)

[1] So in original. The period probably should be replaced with a semicolon.

HISTORICAL AND STATUTORY NOTES

Revision Notes and Legislative Reports

   2000 Acts. House Report No. 106–940, see 2000 U.S. Code Cong. and Adm. News, p. 1063.

s in Text

06(5) of Public Law 106–229, referred is section 106(5) of Pub.L. 106–229,

   June 30, 2000, 114 Stat. 472, classified to section 7006(5) of Title 15.

Amendments

   2000 Amendments. Par. (2). Pub.L. 106–346, [Title III, § 309(b)], struck out "and".

   Pars. (4), (5). Pub.L. 106–346, [Title III, § 309(b)], added pars. (4) and (5).

LIBRARY REFERENCES

Digest System
   Records ☞31.
   Key Number System Topic No. 326.

Research References

ALR Library

   8 ALR, Fed. 2nd Series 611, Application of Local District Court Summary Judgment Rules to Nonmoving Party in Federal Courts--Statements of Facts.
   183 ALR, Fed. 37, Validity, Construction, and Application of Federal Driver's Privacy Protection Act, 18 U.S.C.A. §§ . 2721 to 2725.

Encyclopedias

   40 Am. Jur. Proof of Facts 3d 237, Governmental Liability for Liberty or Privacy Deprivation Resulting from Erroneous Information in Agency Records.

   103 Am. Jur. Proof of Facts 3d 159, Invasion of Privacy by Public Disclosure of Private Facts.

   2 Am. Jur. Trials 409, Locating Public Records.

   49 Am. Jur. Trials 281, Liability for Mishandled Computer Information.

   82 Am. Jur. Trials 123, Snow Practice and Strategy.

   Am. Jur. 2d Commerce § 8, to Character of Commerce as trastate.

   Am. Jur. 2d Commerce § 42, What Constitutes Subjects of Commerce.

   Am. Jur. 2d Privacy § 122, Disclosure of Information in Motor Vehicle Records.

Treatises and Practice Aids

   West's Federal Administrative Practice § 375, Department of Transportation—Introduction.

NOTES OF DECISIONS

Generally ½
Exceptions, personal information 3
Obtaining or using information 4
Particular information, personal information 2
Personal information 1-3
   Exceptions 3
   Particular information 2

½. Generally

   Driver's Privacy Protection Act (DPPA) did not require that driver histories be excised of all personal information unless requestor had DPPA permitted use; such reading did not comport with legislative history nor plain language of statute. Camara v. Metro-North R. Co.,

128

Annotation callouts:
New statutory language supersedes the language in the main volume.

New annotations follow the text of the statute.

Cases interpreting the statute are summarized.

FIGURE 7.21   POCKET PART ENTRY FOR 18 U.S.C.A. § 2725 (Continued)

CRIMES AND CRIMINAL PROCEDURE   **18 § 3005**
                                                     Note 4

D.Conn.2009, 596 F.Supp.2d 517. Records ☞ 31

1. Personal information

Driving violations and driver's status were not "personal information" under Driver's Privacy Protection Act (DPPA), and thus public benefit corporation engaged in operation of passenger rail lines, which was wholly owned subsidiary of New York Metropolitan Transportation Authority (MTA), needed neither consent of its employees nor DPPA permitted use to obtain employees' driving violations and driver's status. Camara v. Metro-North R. Co., D.Conn.2009, 596 F.Supp.2d 517. Records ☞ 31

2. —— Particular information, personal information

Name, driver's license number, and license expiration date of employee of public benefit corporation engaged in operation of passenger rail lines, which was wholly owned subsidiary of New York Metropolitan Transportation Authority (MTA), were protected "personal information" under Driver's Privacy Protection Act (DPPA). Camara v. Metro-North R. Co., D.Conn.2009, 596 F.Supp.2d 517. Records ☞ 31

3. —— Exceptions, personal information

Applying interpretive doctrine of expressio unius est exclusio alterius, Driver's Privacy Protection Act (DPPA) provision defining" personal information" as an individual's "photograph, social security number, driver identification number, name, address (but not the 5-digit zip code), telephone number, and medical or disability information" could not be read to apply to an individual's birth date nor his driver's license expiration date. Camara v. Metro-North R. Co., D.Conn.2009, 596 F.Supp.2d 517. Records ☞ 31

4. Obtaining or using information

Acquisition and use of its employees' driving histories by public benefit corporation engaged in operation of passenger rail lines, a wholly owned subsidiary of New York Metropolitan Transportation Authority (MTA), which contained no more "personal information" than corporation had submitted to department of motor vehicles (DMV) in order to obtain those histories, could not be considered obtaining or using personal information from a motor vehicle record, and thus did not implicate protections of Driver's Privacy Protection Act (DPPA). Camara v. Metro-North R. Co., D.Conn.2009, 596 F.Supp.2d 517. Records ☞ 31

PART II—CRIMINAL PROCEDURE

[1] So in original. Only the first word of item should be capitalized.
[2] So in original. Does not conform to chapter heading, and only the first word of item should be capitalized.

HISTORICAL AND STATUTORY NOTES

Amendments

2006 Amendments. Pub.L. 109–164, Title I, § 103(a)(2), Jan. 10, 2006, 119 Stat. 3563, added item for chapter 212A.

2004 Amendments. Pub.L. 108–405, Title IV, § 411(a)(2), Oct. 30, 2004, 118 Stat. 2284, added item for chapter 228A.

Pub.L. 108–405, Title I, § 102(b), Oct. 30, 2004, 118 Stat. 2264, reenacted item for chapter 237, which was formerly repealed.

2000 Amendments. Pub.L. 106–523, § 2(b), Nov. 22, 2000, 114 Stat. 2492, added item for chapter 212.

CHAPTER 201—GENERAL PROVISIONS

§ 3005. Counsel and witnesses in capital cases

Notes of Decisions

4. Death penalty

After government announced that defendant's case would not be certified for death penalty, defendant indicted by grand jury for capital crime was not entitled to continued representation by second appointed counsel learned in capital cases, under statute providing for appointment of learned counsel upon request of defendant indicted for treason or other capital crime, since "capital crime," within meaning of

129

You can research state statutes the same way you research federal statutes. In print, use the index, look up the statute in the main volume, and check the pocket part and other updating tools. To research electronically, you can browse the code's table of contents or execute a word search. In Westlaw, you can also use a statutory index.

To use an index in Westlaw, select the code you want to research. (In Westlaw.com, you also need to open the search screen for the database instead of using the check boxes.) Choose the index option, and search alphabetically through the topics. Figures 7.22 and 7.23 illustrate index searching in Westlaw.com. Although the screen display is different in WestlawNext, the search process is the same in both services.

Figure 7.22 shows the index to Vernon's *Texas Statutes and Codes Annotated*, which you can use to locate the statute that prohibits false disparagement of perishable foods. Under the heading "Food," the index contains an entry for "Perishable food," which directs you to the statute.

FIGURE 7.22 VERNON'S *TEXAS STATUTES AND CODES ANNOTATED* INDEX

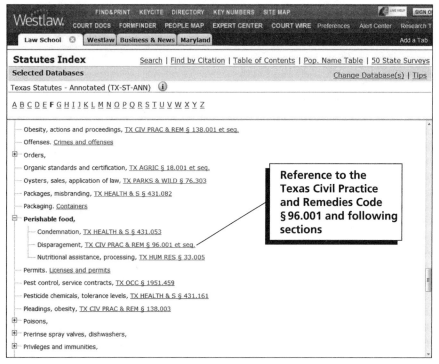

Reprinted with permission from Thomson Reuters/West, from Westlaw, Statutory Index for Vernon's *Texas Statutes and Codes Annotated*. © 2012 Thomson Reuters/West.

Following the link in the index retrieves the first code section in the statute. You can browse preceding or subsequent sections or view the chapter table of contents using the appropriate links.

FIGURE 7.23   TEXAS CIVIL PRACTICE AND REMEDIES CODE § 96.001

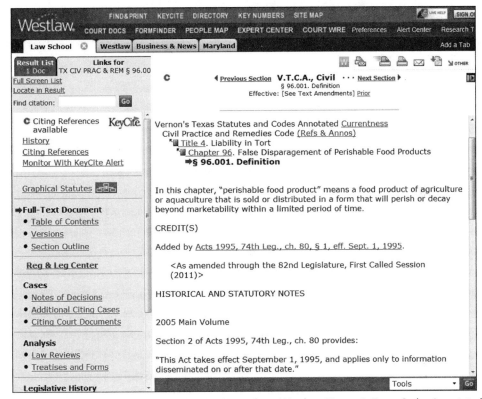

Reprinted with permission from Thomson Reuters/West, from Westlaw, Vernon's *Texas Codes Annotated*, Civil Practice and Remedies Code §96.001. © 2012 Thomson Reuters/West.

Viewing the table of contents allows you to see all of the sections in the statute. To open any section, click on the link.

FIGURE 7.24   OUTLINE OF CHAPTER 96, TEXAS CIVIL PRACTICE AND REMEDIES CODE

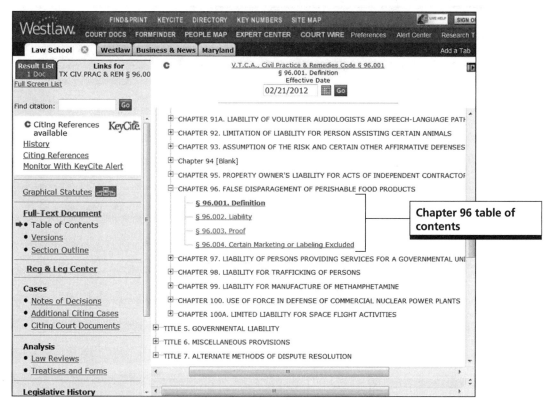

Reprinted with permission from Thomson Reuters/West, from Westlaw, Vernon's *Texas Codes Annotated*, Chapter 96 table of contents. © 2012 Thomson Reuters/West.

Another way to search for statutes is by word searching. In Lexis Advance, you can pre-filter by content type (Statutes and Legislation) and jurisdiction (Texas) before executing a search for *perishable food*. The search retrieves almost 4,000 documents, making it important to use the filtering options and relevancy rankings to target useful information. You can also view the statutory table of contents from the search results.

FIGURE 7.25 LEXIS ADVANCE SEARCH RESULTS

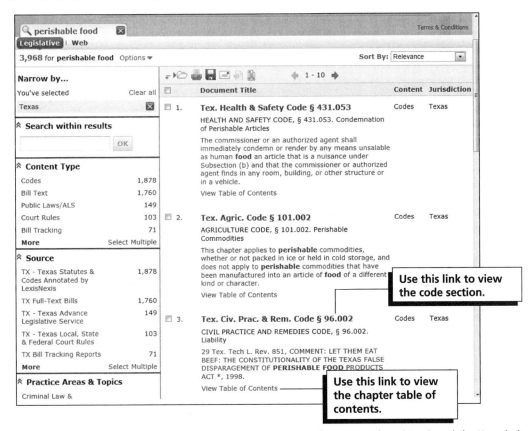

Copyright 2012 LexisNexis, a division of Reed Elsevier Inc. All Rights Reserved. LexisNexis and the Knowledge Burst logo are registered trademarks of Reed Elsevier Properties Inc. and are used with the permission of LexisNexis. From Lexis Advance, statutory search results.

Following the link to Texas Civil Practice and Remedies Code § 96.002 retrieves the code section. You can browse preceding or subsequent sections or view the chapter table of contents using the appropriate links.

FIGURE 7.26 TEXAS CIVIL PRACTICE AND REMEDIES CODE § 96.002

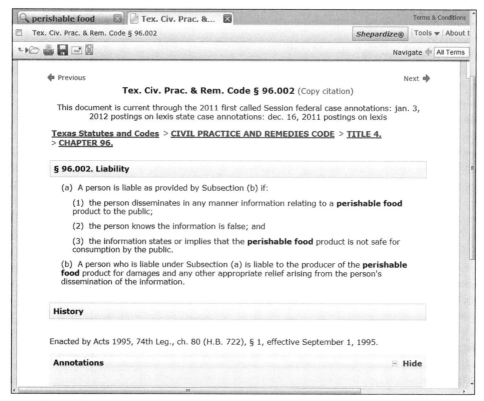

Copyright 2012 LexisNexis, a division of Reed Elsevier Inc. All Rights Reserved. LexisNexis and the Knowledge Burst logo are registered trademarks of Reed Elsevier Properties Inc. and are used with the permission of LexisNexis. Texas Annotated Statutes, Texas Civil Practice and Remedies Code § 96.002.

F. CHECKLIST FOR STATUTORY RESEARCH

1. LOCATE A STATUTE

❐ In print:

- Use an index to search by subject.
- Use the popular name table to locate a statute from its popular name.
- For federal statutes, use the conversion tables to locate a statute using its public law number.

❐ In Westlaw:

- In Westlaw.com and WestlawNext, select a database to search for statutes from a specific jurisdiction; search by popular name, browse the statutory index or table of contents, or execute a word search.
- In WestlawNext, pre-filter by jurisdiction and execute a content-driven search to retrieve statutes and other authorities; filter the results to target appropriate statutes.

❐ In Lexis.com, select a database to search for statutes from a specific jurisdiction; browse the table of contents or execute a word search.

❐ In Lexis Advance, pre-filter by content type (statutes), jurisdiction, and/or topic and execute a search; filter the results to target appropriate statutes.

❐ On the Internet, locate statutes on government or general legal research websites.

2. READ THE STATUTE AND ACCOMPANYING ANNOTATIONS

❐ Use research references to find cases, secondary sources, and other research materials interpreting the statute.

3. UPDATE YOUR RESEARCH

❐ With print research, check the pocket part accompanying the main volume and any cumulative or noncumulative supplements accompanying the code.

- In U.S.C.A., update entries to the popular name and conversion tables with the noncumulative supplements.
- In state codes, check for additional updating tools.

❐ With state or federal statutory research, update your research or find additional research references using a statutory citator such as Shepard's in Lexis or KeyCite in Westlaw.

❐ With Internet research, check the date of the statute and update your research accordingly; consider using a statutory citator to update your research and find additional research references.

FEDERAL LEGISLATIVE HISTORY RESEARCH

A. Introduction to federal legislative history

B. Researching federal legislative history in print

C. Researching federal legislative history electronically

D. Citing federal legislative history

E. Sample pages for federal legislative history research

F. Checklist for federal legislative history research

A. INTRODUCTION TO FEDERAL LEGISLATIVE HISTORY

When a legislature passes a statute, it does so with a goal in mind, such as prohibiting or regulating certain types of conduct. Despite their best efforts, however, legislators do not always draft statutes that express their intentions clearly, and it is almost impossible to draft a statute that contemplates every possible situation that may arise under it. Accordingly, lawyers and judges are often called upon to determine the meaning of an ambiguous statute. Lawyers must provide guidance about what the statute permits or requires their clients to do. In deciding cases, judges must determine what the legislature intended when it passed the statute.

If you are asked to analyze an ambiguous statute, you have a number of tools available to help with the task. If the courts have already resolved the ambiguity, secondary sources, statutory annotations, citators, or other research resources can lead you to cases that explain the meaning of the statute.

If the ambiguity has not yet been resolved, however, you face a bigger challenge. You could research similar statutes to see if they shed light on the provision you are interpreting. You could also look to the language of the statute itself for guidance. You may have studied what are called "canons of construction" in some of your other classes. These canons are principles used to determine the meaning of a statute. For example, one canon provides that statutory terms are to be construed according to their ordinary and plain meaning. Another states that remedial statutes are to be broadly construed, while criminal statutes are to be narrowly construed.[1] Although these tools can be helpful in interpreting statutes, they rarely provide the complete answer to determining the legislature's intent.

One of the best ways to determine legislative intent is to research the paper trail of documents that legislators create during the legislative process. These documents are known as the legislative history of the statute. This chapter discusses various types of documents that make up a statute's legislative history and explains how to locate and use them. At the state level, the types of legislative history documents produced and their ease of accessibility vary widely; therefore, this chapter discusses only federal legislative history.

1. THE PROCESS OF ENACTING A LAW

"Legislative history" is a generic term used to refer to a variety of documents produced during the legislative process; it does not refer to a single document or research tool. Courts consider some legislative history documents more important than others, depending on the type of information in the document and the point in the legislative process when the document was created. Understanding what legislative history consists of, as well as the value of different legislative history documents, requires an understanding of the legislative process. **Figure 8.1** illustrates this process.

The legislative process begins when a bill is introduced into the House of Representatives or the Senate by a member of Congress. After the bill is introduced, it is usually referred to a committee. The committee can hold hearings on the bill to obtain the views of experts and interested parties, or it can refer the bill to a subcommittee to hold hearings. If the committee is not in favor of the bill, it usually takes no action. This ordinarily causes the bill to expire in the committee, although the sponsor is free to reintroduce the bill in a later session of Congress. If the committee is in favor of the bill, it will recommend passage to the full chamber of the House or Senate. The recommendation is presented in a committee report that contains the full text of the bill and an analysis of each provision. Because the committee presents its views in a report, this process is called "reporting out" the bill.

The bill then goes before the full House or Senate, where it is debated and may be amended. The members of the House or Senate vote on the bill. If it is passed, the bill goes before the other chamber of Congress,

---

[1] *See generally* Abner J. Mikva & Eric Lane, AN INTRODUCTION TO STATUTORY INTERPRETATION AND THE LEGISLATIVE PROCESS 114-119 (Aspen Publishers 2d ed. 2002).

FIGURE 8.1 HOW A BILL BECOMES A LAW

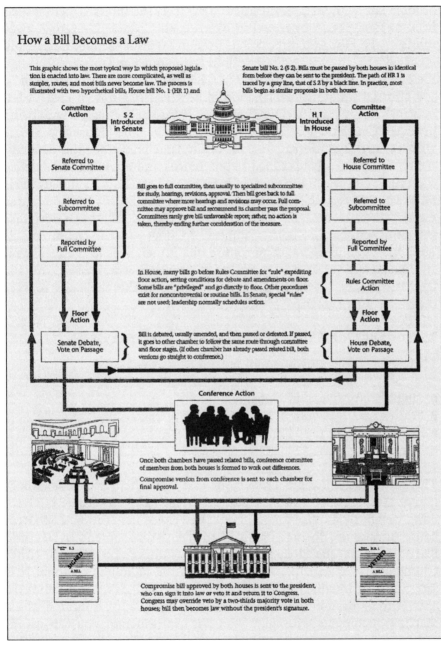

Reprinted with permission from Congressional Quarterly Inc., *Congressional Quarterly's Guide to Congress*, CQ Press, 5th Ed. (2000), p. 1093. Copyright © 2000 CQ Press, a division of SAGE Publications, Inc.

where the same process is repeated. If both chambers pass the bill, it goes to the President. The President can sign the bill into law, allow it to become law without a signature, or veto it. If the bill is vetoed, it goes back to Congress. Congress can override the President's veto if two-thirds of the House and the Senate vote in favor of the bill. Once a bill is passed into law, it is assigned a public law number and proceeds through the publication process described in Chapter 7, on statutory research.

This is a simplified explanation of how legislation is enacted. A bill may make many detours along this path before becoming a law or being defeated. One situation that often occurs is that the House and Senate will pass slightly different versions of the same bill. When this happens, the bill is sent to what is called a conference committee. The conference committee consists of members of both houses of Congress, and its job is to attempt to reconcile the two versions of the bill. If the committee members are able to agree on the provisions of the bill, the compromise version is sent back to both chambers of Congress to be reapproved. If both houses approve the compromise bill, it then goes to the President.

Documents created at each stage of this process constitute the legislative history of a law. The next section describes the major sources that make up a legislative history.

2. SOURCES OF FEDERAL LEGISLATIVE HISTORY

There are four major sources of federal legislative history:

- the bills introduced in Congress;
- hearings before committees or subcommittees;
- floor debates in the House and the Senate;
- committee reports.

These sources are listed in order from least authoritative to most authoritative. Although some of these sources are generally considered to have more weight than others, none should be viewed in isolation. Each item contributes to the documentation of the legislature's intent. In fact, you may find that the documents contain information that is either contradictory or equally as ambiguous as the underlying statute. It is rare when an inquiry into legislative history will give you a definitive answer to a question of statutory interpretation. What is more likely is that the documents will equip you with information you can use to support your arguments for the proper interpretation of the statute.

a. Bills

The bill as introduced into Congress, and any later versions of the bill, can be helpful in determining congressional intent. Changes in language and addition or deletion of specific provisions may shed light on the goal the legislature was attempting to accomplish with the bill. Analysis of changes to a bill, however, requires speculation about the reasons behind the changes. Consequently, this is often considered an insufficient indication of legislative intent unless it is combined with other materials indicating intent to achieve a particular objective.

b. Hearings

Hearings before committees and subcommittees consist of the testimony of experts and interested parties called to give their views on the bill. Documents from these hearings may contain transcripts of testimony, reports, studies, or any other information requested by or submitted to the hearing committee. Unlike interpretation of different versions of a bill, interpretation of hearings does not require speculation. The individuals or groups providing information usually give detailed explanations and justifications for their positions.

Congress uses hearings to gather information. As a consequence, individuals or groups with opposing views are often represented, and their goal is to persuade Congress to act in a particular way. This results in the inclusion of information both for and against the legislation in the hearing documents. Sometimes it is possible to ascertain whether material from a particular source motivated Congress to act in a particular way, but this is not always the case. Therefore, hearing documents must be used carefully in determining congressional intent.

c. Floor Debates

Floor debates are another source of legislative history. They are published in a daily record of congressional proceedings called the *Congressional Record*. Unlike hearings, which include commentary that may or may not have been persuasive to the committee, floor debates consist of statements by the legislators themselves. Thus, the debates can be a source of information about Congress's intent in passing a bill. Debates may consist of transcripts of comments or exchanges taking place on the floor of Congress. In addition, members of Congress are permitted to submit prepared statements setting forth their views. Statements by a bill's sponsors may be especially useful in determining legislative intent. Different members of Congress may give different reasons for supporting legislation, however, and they are permitted to amend or supplement their statements after the fact. As a consequence, floor debates are not a definitive source for determining legislative intent.

d. Committee Reports

Committee reports are generally considered to be the most authoritative legislative history documents. They usually contain the committee's reasons for recommending the bill, a section-by-section analysis of the bill, and the views of any committee members who dissent from the committee's conclusions. If a bill is sent to a conference committee to work out compromise language, the conference committee usually prepares a report. This report discusses only the provisions that differed before the House and the Senate. It usually contains the agreed-upon language of the bill and an explanation of the compromise.

3. METHODS OF LOCATING FEDERAL LEGISLATIVE HISTORY DOCUMENTS

You can locate federal legislative history documents the same ways you locate most other forms of legal authority: by citation; by subject; and, for documents available electronically, by words in the document. Although federal legislative history documents have their own citations, those created in conjunction with legislation that is enacted into law are often organized by the bill number, public law number, or *Statutes at Large* citation associated with the legislation. Not all federal legislative history documents, however, are associated with legislation enacted into law. As a consequence, the methods you choose to research federal legislative history will depend on the type of material you need. If you are researching the history of an individual statute, your approach will be different than if you are looking for legislative activity on a particular subject without regard for whether a statute was passed on the topic.

If you are researching the history of an individual statute, it is important to remember that not all legislation is accompanied by all of the documents described above. A committee might elect not to hold hearings. Or the bill could be amended during floor debate, in which case the amendment would not have any history to be documented elsewhere. In addition, you may not always need to look at all of these documents to resolve your research question. If you are trying to determine Congress's intent in enacting a specific provision within a statute, and a committee report sets out the goals Congress was attempting to accomplish with that provision, you might not need to go any further in your research. Often, however, the committee reports will not discuss the provision you need to interpret. In that case, you may need to delve further into the legislative history, reviewing floor debates or hearings to see if the provision was discussed in either of those sources. In other instances, you may need to compile a complete legislative history.

Your research path will depend largely on the scope of your assignment. You will almost always begin with the statute itself. From there, you should be able to use the bill number, public law number, or *Statutes at Large* citation to locate documents relating to the statute. In most cases, you will probably want to begin by reviewing committee reports. If the committee reports do not address your question, you will then need to assess which other sources of legislative history are likely to assist you and which research tools provide the most efficient means of accessing those documents. If your research takes you beyond readily accessible committee reports, you may want to consult with a reference librarian for assistance in compiling the relevant documents. Remember also that a statute may be amended after its original enactment. Legislative history documents relevant to any amendments will be associated with the bill numbers, public law numbers, or *Statutes at Large* citations of the amending legislation.

If you are trying to find out about legislative activity on a specific topic, rather than the history of an individual statute, you will need to conduct subject or word searches. Because most bills are not passed into law, you may find documents relating to bills that have expired. In addition, you may locate documents unrelated to a bill. For example, committees can hold hearings on any subject within their jurisdiction, even if no legislation on the subject has been introduced.

Some research tools lend themselves more easily than others to subject and word searching, and some are more comprehensive in their coverage than others. Therefore, you will need to determine how much information you need, such as whether you need information on bills that have expired as well as existing legislation, and how far back in time you want to search. Again, you would be well advised to consult with a reference librarian for assistance in developing your research plan for this type of research.

The remainder of this chapter discusses methods for locating legislative history documents. The next section discusses print research tools that are accessible at many law libraries. Legislative history, however, is often easiest to research electronically. In particular, using government websites and commercial subscription services may be the most economical and user-friendly ways to locate federal legislative history.

B. RESEARCHING FEDERAL LEGISLATIVE HISTORY IN PRINT

Two print sources of legislative history are available in many law libraries:

1. compiled legislative histories containing all of the legislative history documents on a statute;
2. *United States Code Congressional and Administrative News*, or U.S.C.C.A.N., which contains selected committee reports on bills passed into law.

1. COMPILED LEGISLATIVE HISTORIES

Legislative histories for major pieces of legislation are sometimes compiled and published as separate volumes. In this situation, an author or publisher collects all of the legislative history documents on the legislation and publishes them in a single place. If a legislative history on the statute you are researching has already been compiled, your work has been done for you. Therefore, if you are researching a major piece of legislation, you should begin by looking for a compiled legislative history.

There are two ways to locate a compiled legislative history. The first is to look in the online catalog in your library. Compiled legislative histories can be published as individual books that are assigned call numbers and placed on the shelves. The second is to look for the statute in a reference source listing compiled legislative histories. One example of this type of reference book is *Sources of Compiled Legislative Histories: A Bibliography of Government Documents, Periodical Articles, and Books*, by Nancy P. Johnson. This book will refer you to books, government documents, and periodical articles that either reprint the legislative history for the statute or, at a minimum, contain citations to and discussion of the legislative history. This book is organized by public law number, so you would need to know the public law number of the statute to get started. You should be able to find the public law number following code sections in U.S.C. or an annotated code. HeinOnline, an electronic subscription service discussed more fully below, has an online directory of compiled legislative histories derived from Professor Johnson's book. Another good reference for compiled legislative histories is *Federal Legislative Histories: An Annotated Bibliography and Index to Officially Published Sources*, by Bernard D. Reams, Jr.

In addition, Congressional Information Service (CIS) compiles legislative history documents and produces them on microfiche. This set has comprehensive coverage, but the microfiche format can be difficult to use. If you are conducting extensive legislative history research and need material unavailable in other forms, you may want to consider using the CIS legislative history set. The indices and other finding tools for this set are published in print, and instructions for using the set accompany the print volumes.

2. UNITED STATES CODE CONGRESSIONAL AND ADMINISTRATIVE NEWS

United States Code Congressional and Administrative News, or U.S.C.C.A.N., is a readily available source of committee reports on bills passed into law. For each session of Congress, U.S.C.C.A.N. publishes a series of volumes containing, among other things, the text of laws passed by Congress (organized by *Statutes at Large* citation) and selected committee reports. References to reports in U.S.C.C.A.N. usually include the year the book was published and the starting page of the document. Thus, to find a report cited as 1996 U.S.C.C.A.N. 2166, you would need to locate the 1996 edition of U.S.C.C.A.N., find the volumes labeled "Legislative History," and turn to page 2166. U.S.C.C.A.N. does not reprint all committee reports for all legislation. Nevertheless, U.S.C.C.A.N. is often a good starting place for research into committee reports because it is available at many law libraries and is fairly easy to use.

U.S.C.C.A.N. is a West publication; therefore, you can find cross-references to it in the annotations in U.S.C.A. The cross-references are usually listed in the Historical and Statutory Notes section of the annotations. If the statute has been amended, the Historical and Statutory Notes section will explain the major changes resulting from later enactments, and the legislative history section of the Historical and Statutory Notes will refer you to the year and page number of any committee reports reprinted in U.S.C.C.A.N. **Figure 8.2** shows U.S.C.C.A.N. references in U.S.C.A., and **Figure 8.3** shows the starting page of a committee report in U.S.C.C.A.N.

FIGURE 8.2   EXCERPT FROM ANNOTATIONS ACCOMPANYING 18 U.S.C.A. § 2441

HISTORICAL AND STATUTORY NOTES

Revision Notes and Legislative Reports

  1996 Acts. House Report No. 104–698, see 1996 U.S. Code Cong. and Adm. News, p. 2166.

  House Report No. 104–788, see 1996 U.S. Code Cong. and Adm. News, p. 4021.

  1997 Acts. House Conference Report No. 105–401, see 1997 U.S. Code Cong. and Adm. News, p. 2896.

References in Text

U.S.C.C.A.N. references ction 101 of the Immigration and nality Act, referred to in subsec. (b), is section 101 of Act June 27, 1952, c. 477, Title I, 66 Stat. 166, which is classified to section 1101 of Title 8, Aliens and Nationality.

Codifications

  Section 584 of Pub.L. 105–118, which directed that section 2401 of title 18 be amended, was executed to section 2441 of Title 18, despite parenthetical refer-

ence to "section 2401 of Title 18", as the probable intent of Congress.

Amendments

  1997   Amendments. Subsec.   (a). Pub.L. 105–118, § 583(1), substituted "war crime" for "grave breach of the Geneva Conventions".

  Subsec. (b). Pub.L. 105–118, § 583(2), substituted "war crime" for "breach" each place it appeared.

  Subsec. (c). Pub.L. 105–118, § 583(3), rewrote subsec. (c). Prior to amendment, subsec. (c) read as follows: "(c) Definitions.—As used in this section, the term 'grave breach of the Geneva Conventions' means conduct defined as a grave breach in any of the international conventions relating to the laws of warfare signed at Geneva 12 August 1949 or any protocol to any such convention, to which the United States is a party."

14

FIGURE 8.3 STARTING PAGE, HOUSE JUDICIARY COMMITTEE REPORT ON THE WAR CRIMES ACT OF 1996

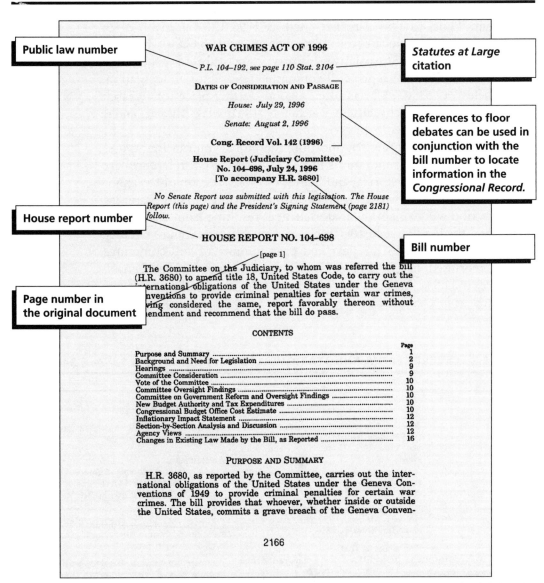

Public law number

Statutes at Large citation

References to floor debates can be used in conjunction with the bill number to locate information in the *Congressional Record*.

House report number

Bill number

Page number in the original document

WAR CRIMES ACT OF 1996

P.L. 104–192, see page 110 Stat. 2104

DATES OF CONSIDERATION AND PASSAGE

House: July 29, 1996

Senate: August 2, 1996

Cong. Record Vol. 142 (1996)

House Report (Judiciary Committee) No. 104–698, July 24, 1996 [To accompany H.R. 3680]

No Senate Report was submitted with this legislation. The House Report (this page) and the President's Signing Statement (page 2181) follow.

HOUSE REPORT NO. 104–698

[page 1]

The Committee on the Judiciary, to whom was referred the bill (H.R. 3680) to amend title 18, United States Code, to carry out the international obligations of the United States under the Geneva Conventions to provide criminal penalties for certain war crimes, having considered the same, report favorably thereon without amendment and recommend that the bill do pass.

CONTENTS

PURPOSE AND SUMMARY

H.R. 3680, as reported by the Committee, carries out the international obligations of the United States under the Geneva Conventions of 1949 to provide criminal penalties for certain war crimes. The bill provides that whoever, whether inside or outside the United States, commits a grave breach of the Geneva Conven-

2166

Reprinted with permission from Thomson Reuters/West, *United States Code Congressional and Administrative News*, 104th Congress—Second Session 1996, Vol. 5 (1997), p. 2166. © 1997 Thomson Reuters/West.

C. RESEARCHING FEDERAL LEGISLATIVE HISTORY ELECTRONICALLY

Most legislative history research is conducted electronically. In particular, government websites can be extremely useful in legislative history research. No matter which electronic source you use, your research strategy will still largely be governed by whether you are looking for information on an individual statute or searching by subject.

As with print research, electronic research into the legislative history of an individual statute is easiest if you have a citation identifying the legislation. Most electronic services will allow you to search using a bill number, public law number, or *Statutes at Large* citation. Conducting a word search using the popular name of an act is also an effective strategy. Simply searching by topic or with general keywords is the least efficient means of researching material on an individual statute. It is possible that you could miss important documents if you do not have the correct terms in the search; in addition, you are likely to retrieve material on other pieces of legislation unrelated to your research. By contrast, topic or keyword searching is most effective when you want to find out about legislative activity on a particular subject.

The scope of your project will also affect which electronic source you choose. Some provide access to the full range of legislative history documents (bill versions, hearings, floor debates, and committee reports). Others are more limited in their coverage. It is important to choose a service that includes the documents you need.

One form of legislative history you can research online is floor debates in the *Congressional Record*. The *Congressional Record* is the record of all activity on the floor of the House and Senate. To research the *Congressional Record* effectively, you need to understand how it is published.

A new volume of the *Congressional Record* is published for each session of Congress. While Congress is in session, the current volume of the *Congressional Record* is published daily in print as a softcover pamphlet; this is called the daily edition. **Figure 8.4** is an excerpt from the daily edition. At the end of each session of Congress, the daily editions are compiled into a hardbound print set; this is called the permanent edition.

The material in these two editions should be identical, but the pages in each are numbered differently. The daily edition is separated into different sections, including sections for House (H) and Senate (S) materials, and the pages within each section are numbered separately. In the permanent edition, all of the pages are numbered consecutively. References to the *Congressional Record* will vary, therefore, depending on whether they are to the permanent or daily edition. References to both

FIGURE 8.4 *CONGRESSIONAL RECORD,* DAILY EDITION

H8620   CONGRESSIONAL RECORD — HOUSE   *July 29, 1996*

> **Comments on the War Crimes Act in the House of Representatives**

Mr. Speaker, H.R. 740, introduced by ⟨gentleman⟩ from New Mexico [Mr. ⟨SCHIFF⟩] and the gentleman from New ⟨Mexico⟩ [Mr. SKEEN] would permit the ⟨Pueblo⟩ of Isleta Indian Tribe to file a ⟨claim⟩ in the U.S. Court of Federal ⟨Claim⟩s for certain aboriginal lands ac⟨quired⟩ from the tribe by the United ⟨State⟩s. The tribe was erroneously ad⟨vised⟩ by the Bureau of Indian Affairs in ⟨regard⟩ to this claim, and as a result ⟨never⟩ filed a claim for aboriginal lands before the expiration of the statute of limitations.

The court's jurisdiction would apply only to claims accruing on or before August 13, 1946, as provided in the Indian Claims Commission Act.

The Pueblo of Isleta Tribe seeks the opportunity to present the merits of its aboriginal land claims, which otherwise would be barred as untimely. The tribe cites numerous precedents for conferring jurisdiction under similar circumstances, such as the case of the Zuni Indian Tribe in 1978.

An identical bill passed the Senate in the 103d Congress, but was not considered by the House. In the 102d Congress, H.R. 1206, amended to the current language, passed the House, but was not considered by the Senate before adjournment. On June 11, 1996, the Judiciary Committee favorably reported this bill by unanimous voice vote.

Mr. Speaker, I reserve the balance of my time.

Mr. SCOTT. Mr. Speaker, I yield myself such time as I may consume.

Mr. Speaker, I think the bill has been explained that was introduced by the gentleman from New Mexico [Mr. SKEEN] and the gentleman from New Mexico [Mr. SCHIFF]. It is a fair bill, and I would just urge colleagues to support it at this time.

Mr. Speaker, I yield back the balance of my time.

Mr. RICHARDSON. Mr. Speaker, I wish to extend my strong support for H.R. 740 which deals with the Pueblo of Isleta Indian land claims. H.R. 740 comes before Congress for a vote which will correct a 45-year-old injustice. In 1951, the Pueblo of Isleta was given erroneous advice by employees of the Bureau of Indian Affairs regarding the nature of the claim the Pueblo could mount under the Indian Claims Commission Act of 1946. This is documented and supported by testimony. The Pueblo was not made aware of the fact that a land claim could be made based upon aboriginal use and occupancy. As a result, it lost the opportunity to make such a claim.

The Pueblo of Isleta was a victim of circumstances beyond its control, and this bill is an opportunity for us to correct this wrong. No expenditure or appropriations of funds are provided for in this bill: only the opportunity for the Pueblo to make a claim for aboriginal lands which the Isletas believe to be rightfully theirs. This bill may be the last chance for the United States to correct an injustice which occurred many years ago because of misinformation from the BIA.

Therefore, I urge my colleagues to support H.R. 740.

Mr. SMITH of Texas. Mr. Speaker, I have no further requests for time, and I yield back the balance of my time.

The SPEAKER pro tempore. The question is on the motion offered by the gentleman from Texas [Mr. SMITH] that the House suspend the rules and pass the bill, H.R. 740.

The question was taken; and (two-thirds having voted in favor thereof) the rules were suspended and the bill was passed.

A motion to reconsider was laid on the table.

WAR CRIMES ACT OF 1996

Mr. SMITH of Texas. Mr. Speaker, I move to suspend the rules and pass the bill (H.R. 3680) to amend title 18, United States Code, to carry out the international obligations of the United States under the Geneva Conventions to provide criminal penalties for certain war crimes.

The Clerk read as follows:

H.R. 3680

Be it enacted by the Senate and House of Representatives of the United States of America in Congress assembled,

SECTION 1. SHORT TITLE.

This Act may be cited as the "War Crimes Act of 1996".

SEC. 2. CRIMINAL PENALTIES FOR CERTAIN WAR CRIMES.

(a) IN GENERAL.—Title 18, United States Code, is amended by inserting after chapter 117 the following:

"CHAPTER 118—WAR CRIMES

"Sec.
"2401. War crimes.

"§ 2401. War crimes

"(a) OFFENSE.—Whoever, whether inside or outside the United States, commits a grave breach of the Geneva Conventions, in any of the circumstances described in subsection (b), shall be fined under this title or imprisoned for life or any term of years, or both, and if death results to the victim, shall also be subject to the penalty of death.

"(b) CIRCUMSTANCES.—The circumstances referred to in subsection (a) are that the person committing such breach or the victim of such breach is a member of the armed forces of the United States or a national of the United States (as defined in section 101 of the Immigration and Nationality Act).

"(c) DEFINITIONS.—As used in this section, the term 'grave breach of the Geneva Conventions' means conduct defined as a grave breach in any of the international conventions relating to the laws of warfare signed at Geneva 12 August 1949 or any protocol to any such convention, to which the United States is a party."

(b) CLERICAL AMENDMENT.—The table of chapters for part I of title 18, United States Code, is amended by inserting after the item relating to chapter 117 the following new item:

"118. War crimes .... 2401".

The SPEAKER pro tempore. Pursuant to the rule, the gentleman from Texas [Mr. SMITH] and the gentleman from Virginia [Mr. SCOTT] each will control 20 minutes.

The Chair recognizes the gentleman from Texas [Mr. SMITH].

GENERAL LEAVE

Mr. SMITH of Texas. Mr. Speaker, I ask unanimous consent that all Members may have 5 legislative days to revise and extend their remarks on the bill under consideration.

The SPEAKER pro tempore. Is there objection to the request of the gentleman from Texas?

There was no objection.

Mr. SMITH of Texas. Mr. Speaker, I yield myself such time as I may consume.

Mr. Speaker, H.R. 3680 is designed to implement the Geneva conventions for the protection of victims of war. Our colleague, the gentleman from North Carolina, WALTER JONES, should be commended for introducing this bill and for his dedication to such a worthy goal.

□ 1445

Mr. Speaker, the Geneva Conventions of 1949 codified rules of conduct for military forces to which we have long adhered. In 1955 Deputy Under Secretary of State Robert Murphy testified to the Senate that—

The Geneva Conventions are another long step forward towards mitigating the severity of war on its helpless victims. They reflect enlightened practices as carried out by the United States and other civilized countries, and they represent largely what the United States would do, whether or not a party to the Conventions. Our own conduct has served to establish higher standards and we can only benefit by having them incorporated in a stronger body of wartime law.

Mr. Speaker, the United States ratified the Conventions in 1955. However, Congress has never passed implementing legislation.

The Conventions state that signatory countries are to enact penal legislation punishing what are called grave breaches, actions such as the deliberate killing of prisoners of war, the subjecting of prisoners to biological experiments, the willful infliction of great suffering or serious injury on civilians in occupied territory.

While offenses covering grave breaches can in certain instances be prosecutable under present Federal law, even if they occur overseas, there are a great number of instances in which no prosecution is possible. Such nonprosecutable crimes might include situations where American prisoners of war are killed, or forced to serve in the Army of their captors, or American doctors on missions of mercy in foreign war zones are kidnapped or murdered. War crimes are a thing of the past, and Americans can all too easily fall victim to them.

H.R. 3680 was introduced in order to implement the Geneva Conventions. It prescribes severe criminal penalties for anyone convicted of committing, whether inside or outside the United States, a grave breach of the Geneva Conventions, where the victim or the perpetrator is a member of our Armed Forces. In future conflicts H.R. 3680 may very well deter acts against Americans that violate the laws of war.

Mr. Speaker, I urge my colleagues to support this legislation, and I reserve the balance of my time.

Mr. SCOTT. Mr. Speaker, I yield myself such time as I may consume.

Mr. Speaker, as the gentleman from Texas has fully explained, H.R. 3680 implements this country's international

editions will give the volume and page number, but the page numbering will differ for each edition. Thus, 142 Cong. Rec. H8620 refers to volume 142 of the *Congressional Record*, page 8,620 of the House section of the daily edition. The "H" before the page number alerts you that the reference is to the daily edition. By contrast, a citation to 142 Cong. Rec. 11,352 refers to volume 142 of the *Congressional Record*, page 11,352 of the permanent edition. Because the page number contains no letter designation, the reference is to the permanent edition.

Some electronic services provide access only to the daily edition. This can affect your research in two ways. First, if you have a citation to a floor debate in the permanent edition of the *Congressional Record*, you may not be able to retrieve it in a service that only provides access to the daily edition. Second, if you locate a floor debate using a word search, the document you retrieve may be from the daily edition even if it is several years old. This may affect your ability to cite the material properly.

Another thing to be aware of when you conduct electronic legislative history research concerns hearings. Some electronic services provide access to testimony provided at hearings, which consists of transcripts of testimony and prepared statements of witnesses, but not to reports, studies, or other documents submitted to the committee. Therefore, if you need the complete content of a congressional hearing, you must choose your research source carefully and may need to obtain the document in print or microfiche.

1. LEXIS AND WESTLAW

Both Lexis and Westlaw provide access to many legislative history documents. Lexis.com, Westlaw.com, and WestlawNext provide access to the full text of bills introduced in Congress, selected committee reports, floor debates in the *Congressional Record*, and congressional testimony, although not complete hearing documents. Additionally, both Lexis.com and Westlaw.com have databases containing compiled legislative histories for certain major pieces of legislation. As this text goes to press, Lexis Advance contains very little legislative history material, although Lexis plans to add this content over time. Search options for legislative history documents, therefore, are likely to evolve as content is added.

In Westlaw, you can retrieve a legislative history document from its citation as long as the document is included in Westlaw's database. If you are searching for the history of an individual statute, the U.S.C.A. annotations will contain links to any congressional reports in Westlaw's database, including those issued in connection with amendments to the statute. The KeyCite history for the statute will also list legislative history documents. Additionally, if you retrieve a statute by public law number, Westlaw provides the legislative history documents associated with the bill.

In Westlaw.com, you can conduct word searches in the databases for individual types of legislative documents or compiled legislative histories. To access these databases, use the Directory, and drill down through federal materials to the Legislative History section.

In Lexis, you can also retrieve a legislative history document from its citation as long as the document is included in the Lexis database. The U.S.C.S. annotations will not link to legislative history documents, however, even if those documents are contained in the Lexis database. Nor will the Shepard's entry list legislative history beyond *Statutes at Large* citations to later enactments affecting the statute.

In Lexis.com, you can conduct word searches in the databases for individual types of legislative documents or compiled legislative histories. With some compiled legislative histories you can view a list of all of the documents in the statute's history, along with other information about the statute. These histories are especially useful when you need to locate the full history of a major piece of legislation.

2. GOVERNMENT WEBSITES

The federal government provides free Internet access to many legislative history documents through Thomas, a website maintained by the Library of Congress, and the Federal Digital System (FDSys), a website maintained by the Government Printing Office (GPO). The Internet addresses for both of these sites are listed in Appendix A.

Thomas will provide you with the text of bills introduced, House and Senate roll call votes, public laws, the text of the *Congressional Record*, committee reports, and other information on the legislative process, although not congressional hearings or testimony. Thomas will also allow you to search in several ways. You can browse or search by public law number, report number, or committee name. Word searching is also available. You can search for documents issued during a particular session of Congress, or you can search multiple sessions simultaneously. To access the *Congressional Record*, you can browse the contents of individual issues or search by subject using the *Congressional Record* index. The introductory screen for Thomas appears in **Figure 8.5**.

An effective way to locate the history of an individual piece of legislation in Thomas is with the public law or bill number. You can browse public laws by number for a particular session of Congress or use the bill number to retrieve a Bill Summary and Status report. This report will provide links to the text of the statute and to all of the legislative history documents in Thomas's database, including congressional reports and floor debates in the *Congressional Record*.

FDSys is another source for legislative history documents. **Figure 8.6** shows some of the search options on the FDSys home page. FDSys

FIGURE 8.5   INTRODUCTORY SCREEN FOR THOMAS

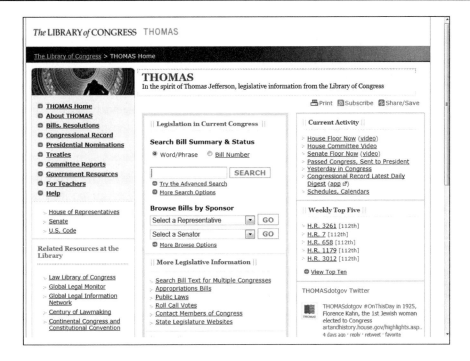

FIGURE 8.6   INTRODUCTORY SCREEN FOR FDSYS

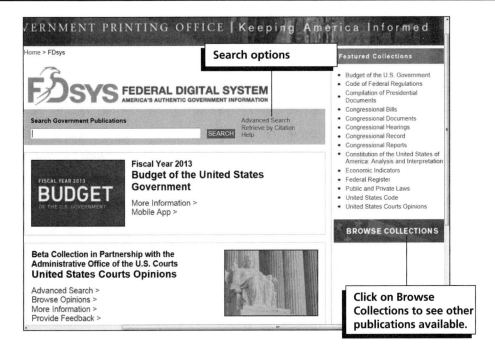

provides access to the text of bills introduced into Congress, selected reports and hearings, and the *Congressional Record*. If you retrieve the record for a public law, using the **More Information** link retrieves a page with a summary of legislative history documents. Another option is using the **History of Bills** database to search by bill number. You can access **History of Bills** from the **Advanced Search** option or by browsing the collections. Searching **History of Bills** will retrieve a record with a link to a file listing legislative history documents. You will then need to use the information provided to retrieve the documents individually in the appropriate database for each publication.

FDSys is a good source to use to access congressional hearings. The hearing documents in FDSys are .pdf versions of the print documents. Thus, unlike most other electronic sources, FDSys provides the complete hearing content, including attachments and other documents, not just testimony.

Word searching in FDSys can be cumbersome. If you do not have a public law or bill number for a statute, you will have the most success if you know the type of document you want and can retrieve it by citation or by browsing by session of Congress.

Both Thomas and FDSys add documents to their databases regularly, but neither provides complete historical access to legislative documents. For some types of information, coverage extends to the early 1970s, but for others, only to the early 1990s. If you are researching fairly recent legislative documents, however, Thomas and FDSys are excellent tools to use.

3. Subscription Services

HeinOnline and ProQuest Congressional are two subscription services available at many law libraries that you can use for federal legislative history research. HeinOnline is best known for its comprehensive database of legal periodicals, but it also contains many other types of information, including legislative documents. HeinOnline has a database of compiled legislative histories derived from Nancy P. Johnson's reference book, *Sources of Compiled Legislative Histories: A Bibliography of Government Documents, Periodical Articles, and Books*. This database provides citations to many compiled legislative histories and full-text access to some. **Figure 8.7** shows an entry from this directory. HeinOnline also has its own collection of compiled legislative histories, the U.S. Federal Legislative History Title Collection. This is a database containing full-text legislative histories on major pieces of legislation. Many of these compiled legislative histories contain complete .pdf versions of the legislative documents, including hearings.

FIGURE 8.7   HEINONLINE *SOURCES OF COMPILED LEGISLATIVE HISTORIES* **ENTRY**

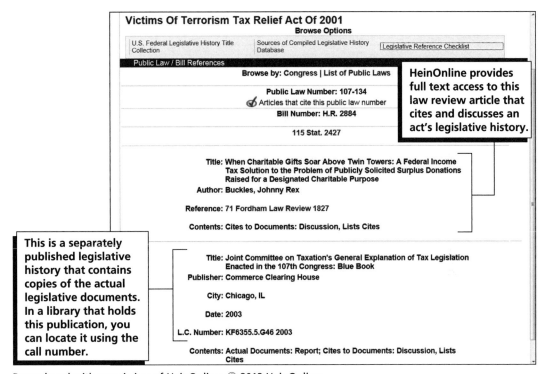

Reproduced with permission of HeinOnline. © 2012 HeinOnline.

ProQuest Congressional (formerly known as Congressional Universe and LexisNexis Congressional) is a commercial research service that provides electronic access to a comprehensive set of legislative documents. Its database includes committee reports, hearing testimony (but not complete hearing documents), bills, and the *Congressional Record.* Within ProQuest Congressional, you can search the full text of the documents in its database, or you can search by number. The easiest way to locate all of the available documents on a piece of legislation is to search by number using the bill number, public law number, or *Statutes at Large* citation. Searching this way retrieves an entry that lists the legislative history documents associated with the statute. The links in the document will retrieve abstracts (summaries) of the documents available. From the abstract, you can retrieve the full text of a document by following the appropriate link. Full-text searching is also an option and is a good way to search for legislative information by topic. You can search for multiple types of documents, such as reports or hearings, simultaneously, although floor debates are in a separate database containing the *Congressional Record.* **Figure 8.8** shows some of the search options for congressional documents.

FIGURE 8.8   SEARCH OPTIONS FOR CONGRESSIONAL PUBLICATIONS IN PROQUEST CONGRESSIONAL

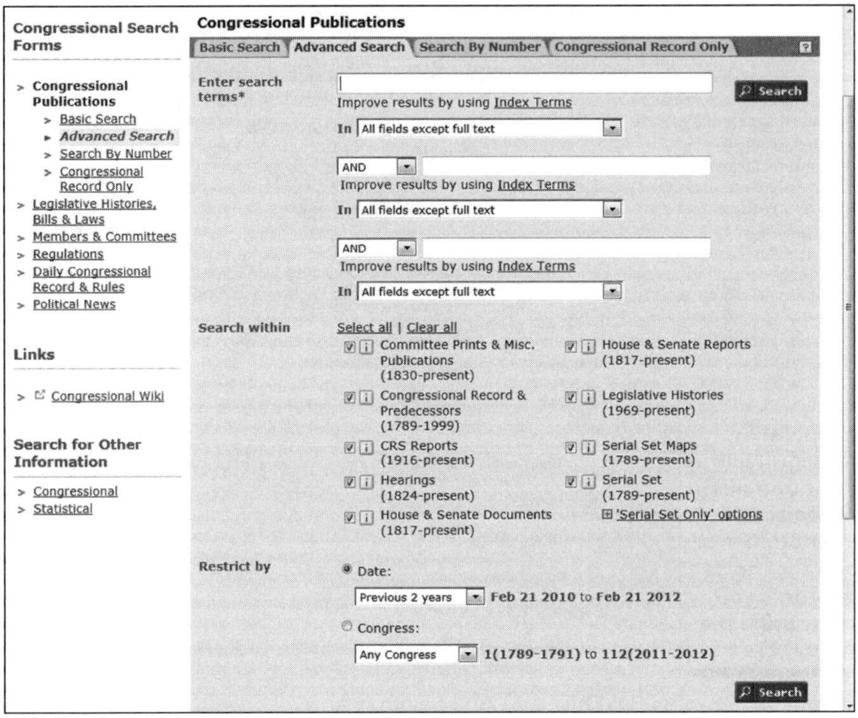

Reprinted with permission of ProQuest, ProQuest Congressional search options. © 2012 ProQuest Congressional.

D. CITING FEDERAL LEGISLATIVE HISTORY

Citations to legislative history documents are covered in the *ALWD Manual* (4th ed.) in Rule 15 and the *Bluebook* (19th ed.) in Bluepages B5.1.6 and Rule 13. This chapter discusses citations to committee reports and floor debates because those are the sources you are most likely to cite in a brief or memorandum.

In the *Bluebook*, the examples contained in Rule 13 show some of the congressional document abbreviations in large and small capital letters. According to Bluepages B1, however, legislative documents in briefs and memoranda should appear in ordinary type.

1. COMMITTEE REPORTS

Using either the *ALWD Manual* or the *Bluebook*, a citation to a committee report consists of four elements: (1) the abbreviation for the type of document; (2) the report number; (3) the pinpoint reference to the cited material; and (4) a parenthetical containing the date of the report.

Although citations to reports in both formats contain the same elements, the document abbreviations, report number, and date differ in their presentation, as illustrated in the following examples. Here is an example of a citation to a report issued by the House of Representatives in *ALWD Manual* format:

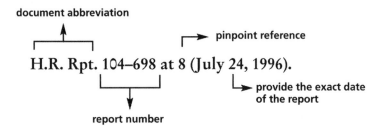

Here is an example in *Bluebook* format:

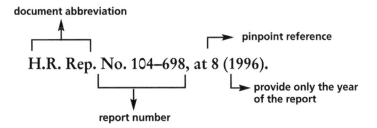

The *ALWD Manual* permits and the *Bluebook* requires a parallel citation to U.S.C.C.A.N. if the report is reprinted there. A citation to a report reprinted in U.S.C.C.A.N. consists of six elements: (1) the report citation, as discussed above; (2) a notation that the citation is to a reprint of the document; (3) the year of the U.S.C.C.A.N. volume; (4) the publication name (U.S.C.C.A.N.); (5) the starting page of the report in U.S.C.C.A.N.; and (6) the pinpoint reference to the page in U.S.C.C.A.N. containing the cited material.

Although the elements of a U.S.C.C.A.N. citation in either *ALWD Manual* or *Bluebook* format are the same, the presentation of the citation varies slightly depending on which format you use. Here is an example in *ALWD Manual* format:

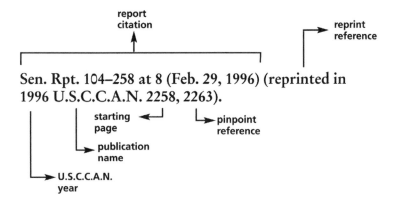

Here is an example in *Bluebook* format:

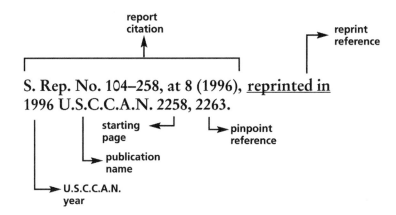

If you locate a report in U.S.C.C.A.N., you can still find the page numbers for the original document. Throughout the report, U.S.C.C.A.N. provides the page numbers of the original document in brackets.

2. FLOOR DEBATES

Floor debates are published in the *Congressional Record*. As explained earlier in this chapter, two versions of the *Congressional Record* are published. The daily edition is published during the current session of Congress, and the permanent edition is published at the close of the session. Both the *ALWD Manual* and the *Bluebook* require citation to the permanent edition if possible. A citation to the permanent edition using either the *ALWD Manual* or the *Bluebook* consists of four elements: (1) the volume number of the *Congressional Record*; (2) the abbreviation Cong. Rec.; (3) the page number with the information cited; and (4) a parenthetical containing the year.

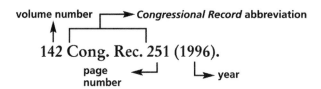

A citation to the daily edition contains the same elements, except that the parenthetical must indicate that the citation is to the daily edition and provide the exact date of the daily edition.

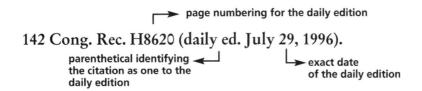

page numbering for the daily edition

142 Cong. Rec. H8620 (daily ed. July 29, 1996).

parenthetical identifying the citation as one to the daily edition

exact date of the daily edition

E. SAMPLE PAGES FOR FEDERAL LEGISLATIVE HISTORY RESEARCH

Beginning below, **Figures 8.9** through **8.13** contain sample pages illustrating what you would find if you researched legislative history documents associated with the War Crimes Act of 1996 using Thomas and FDSys.

Legislative history documents associated with the War Crimes Act of 1996 are available in Thomas. Browsing by public law number retrieves the Bill Summary and Status report.

FIGURE 8.9   BILL SUMMARY AND STATUS REPORT IN THOMAS

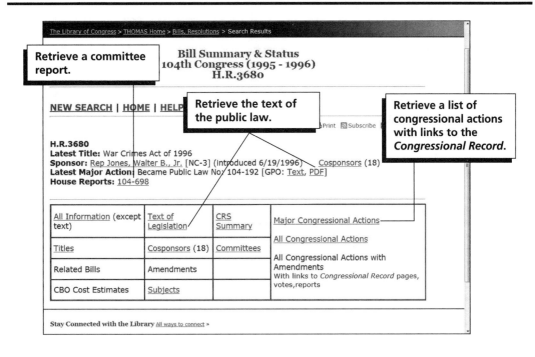

Following the link to House Report 104-698 retrieves the House Judiciary Committee report. Figure 8.10 shows the text view. You can also view the report in .pdf format.

FIGURE 8.10   HOUSE JUDICIARY COMMITTEE REPORT IN THOMAS

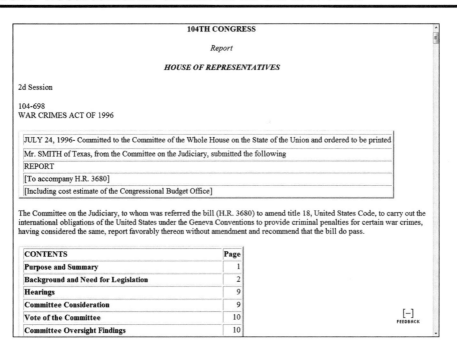

To locate legislative documents in FDSys, use the public law number in the search box on the introductory screen (see Figure 8.6) to search all collections. Searching for *"public law 104-192"* retrieves the results below.

FIGURE 8.11   SEARCH RESULTS IN FDSYS

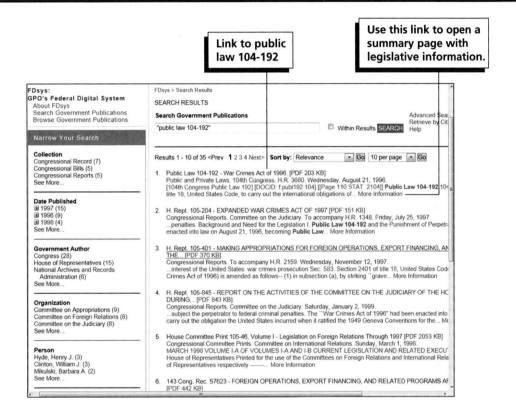

Using the More information link retrieves a summary page with information about legislative history documents. You could retrieve each of the documents listed by going to the database for the type of document and using the information provided to execute a search.

FIGURE 8.12   SEARCH RESULTS IN FDSYS

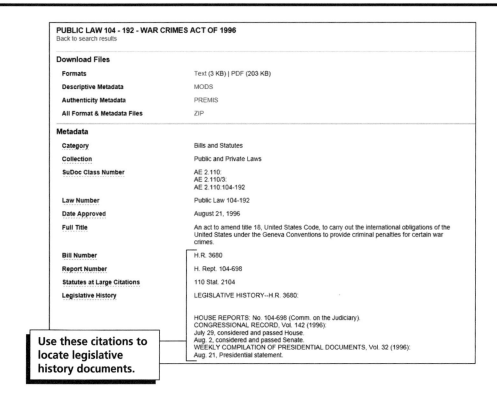

PUBLIC LAW 104 - 192 - WAR CRIMES ACT OF 1996
Back to search results

Download Files

Formats	Text (3 KB)	PDF (203 KB)
Descriptive Metadata	MODS
Authenticity Metadata	PREMIS
All Format & Metadata Files	ZIP

Metadata

Category	Bills and Statutes
Collection	Public and Private Laws
SuDoc Class Number	AE 2.110: AE 2.110/3: AE 2.110:104-192
Law Number	Public Law 104-192
Date Approved	August 21, 1996
Full Title	An act to amend title 18, United States Code, to carry out the international obligations of the United States under the Geneva Conventions to provide criminal penalties for certain war crimes.
Bill Number	H.R. 3680
Report Number	H. Rept. 104-698
Statutes at Large Citations	110 Stat. 2104
Legislative History	LEGISLATIVE HISTORY--H.R. 3680:

HOUSE REPORTS: No. 104-698 (Comm. on the Judiciary).
CONGRESSIONAL RECORD, Vol. 142 (1996):
July 29, considered and passed House.
Aug. 2, considered and passed Senate.
WEEKLY COMPILATION OF PRESIDENTIAL DOCUMENTS, Vol. 32 (1996):
Aug. 21, Presidential statement.

Use these citations to locate legislative history documents.

You can retrieve the same information using the bill number and the History of Bills **database. Access** History of Bills **using the** Advanced Search **option or by browsing the collection. Browse by session of Congress and bill number to retrieve the history report. The report links to a file that lists legislative history documents for many bills. Scroll through the list to locate the legislative history documents for the bill you are researching. You can use the information provided to retrieve the individual documents in the bill's legislative history.**

FIGURE 8.13 HISTORY OF BILLS REPORT IN FDSYS

HISTORY OF H.R. 3680 - A BILL TO AMEND TITLE 18, UNITED STATES CODE, TO CARRY OUT THE INTERNATIONAL OBLIGATIONS OF THE UNITED STATES UNDER THE GENEVA CONVENTIONS TO PROVIDE CRIMINAL PENALTIES FOR CERTAIN WAR CRIMES

Download Files

Formats	Text (1 KB)
Descriptive Metadata	MODS
Authenticity Metadata	PREMIS
All Format & Metadata Files	ZIP file

Metadata

Category	Proceedings of Congress and General Congressional Publications
Collection	History of Bills
SuDoc Class Number	X 1.1/A:
Congress Number	104th Congress
Congress Session	2nd Session
Full Title	A bill to amend title 18, United States Code, to carry out the international obligations of the United States under the Geneva Conventions to provide criminal penalties for certain war crimes
Bill Number	H.R. 3680
Sponsors	Walter B. Jones
Cosponsors	Martin R. Hoke, Bob Stump, Gerald B. H. Solomon, Paul McHale, Duncan Hunter, G. V. (Sonny) Montgomery, Ron Lewis, Peter G. Torkildsen, J. C. Watts Jr., Terry Everett, John M. McHugh, Solomon P. Ortiz, John N. Hostettler, Tillie Fowler, James B. Longley Jr., Jim Kolbe
Last Action	Presented to the President (August 9, September 4, 1996, 142 Cong. Rec. H10019

Document in Context

View Entire History of Bills   Text | More

Use this link to open a history report.

F. CHECKLIST FOR FEDERAL LEGISLATIVE HISTORY RESEARCH

1. IDENTIFY THE SCOPE OF YOUR RESEARCH

❏ Determine whether you need the history of an individual statute or material on a general subject.

❏ To research the history of an individual statute, begin by locating the statute.

- The public law number should follow the statute in U.S.C. or an annotated code.
- To determine congressional intent, start with committee reports; use U.S.C.C.A.N., a compiled legislative history, or an electronic source to locate committee reports.
- For more comprehensive legislative history research, locate floor debates, hearings, and prior versions of the bill in addition to committee reports; use a compiled legislative history or an electronic source to locate a statute's complete legislative history.

❏ To research material on a general subject, use an electronic source to search by subject or keyword.

❏ If necessary, consult a reference librarian for assistance in determining the appropriate scope of your research and locating necessary documents.

2. LOCATE A COMPILED LEGISLATIVE HISTORY FOR A SPECIFIC STATUTE

❏ Search the library's online catalog for separately published legislative histories.

❏ Locate compiled legislative histories for major pieces of legislation in Lexis.com or Westlaw.com.

❏ Use Johnson, *Sources of Compiled Legislative Histories*, U.S. Federal Legislative History Title Collection in HeinOnline, or Reams, *Federal Legislative Histories*.

❏ Search for legislative history by bill number, public law number, or *Statutes at Large* citation to collect all legislative history documents on an individual statute.

3. LOCATE COMMITTEE REPORTS, *CONGRESSIONAL RECORD* FLOOR DEBATES, AND OTHER LEGISLATIVE HISTORY DOCUMENTS FOR A SPECIFIC STATUTE

❏ In print, use annotations in U.S.C.A. to locate cross-references to committee reports reprinted in U.S.C.C.A.N.

❏ In Westlaw, retrieve the public law to locate selected legislative history documents for the statute.

❏ In Lexis.com, use the public law number to search in databases for individual types of legislative history documents.

❐ In Thomas, search by bill number or public law number to retrieve a status and summary report of legislative history documents related to the statute; use the links to retrieve the documents.

❐ In FDSys, search by bill number or public law number to locate a summary of legislative history documents related to the statute, especially for the full text of congressional hearings; use the information provided to retrieve an individual document from the appropriate database.

❐ In ProQuest Congressional, search by bill number, public law number, or *Statutes at Large* citation to locate a summary of documents related to the statute; use the links to retrieve the documents.

CHAPTER 9

FEDERAL ADMINISTRATIVE LAW RESEARCH

- A. Introduction to federal administrative law
- B. Researching federal regulations in print
- C. Researching federal regulations electronically
- D. Citing federal regulations
- E. Sample pages for federal administrative law research
- F. Checklist for federal administrative law research

A. INTRODUCTION TO FEDERAL ADMINISTRATIVE LAW

1. ADMINISTRATIVE AGENCIES AND REGULATIONS

Administrative agencies exist at all levels of government. Examples of federal administrative agencies include the Food and Drug Administration (FDA), the Environmental Protection Agency (EPA), and the Federal Communications Commission (FCC). Agencies are created by statute, but they are part of the executive branch because they "enforce" or implement a legislatively created scheme. In creating an agency, a legislature will pass what is known as "enabling" legislation. Enabling legislation defines the scope of the agency's mission and "enables" it to perform its functions, which may include promulgating regulations and adjudicating controversies, among other functions. If an agency is empowered to create regulations, those regulations cannot exceed the authority granted by the legislature. Thus, for example, while the FCC may be able to establish regulations concerning television licenses, it would not be able to promulgate regulations concerning the labeling of drugs because that would exceed the authority granted to it by Congress in its enabling legislation.

Federal agencies often create regulations to implement statutes passed by Congress. Sometimes Congress cannot legislate with the level of detail necessary to implement a complex legislative scheme. In those circumstances, Congress charges an agency with enforcing the statute, and the agency will develop procedures for implementing more general legislative mandates. In the Family and Medical Leave Act, for instance, Congress mandated that an employer allow an employee with a "serious health condition" to take unpaid medical leave. Pursuant to the statute, the Department of Labor has promulgated more specific regulations defining what "serious health condition" means.

In format, a regulation looks like a statute. It is, in essence, a rule created by a government entity, and many times administrative regulations are called "rules." In operation, they are indistinguishable from statutes, although the methods used to create, modify, and repeal them are different from those applicable to statutes. Federal administrative agencies are required to conform to the procedures set out in the Administrative Procedure Act (APA) in promulgating regulations. State agencies may be required to comply with similar statutes at the state level. Without going into too much detail, the APA frequently requires agencies to undertake the following steps: (1) notify the public when they plan to promulgate new regulations or change existing ones; (2) publish proposed regulations and solicit comments on them before the regulations become final; and (3) publish final regulations before they go into effect to notify the public of the new requirements.

At the federal level, regulations and proposed regulations are published in the *Federal Register*. The *Federal Register* is a daily publication reporting the activities of the executive branch of government. A new volume is published each year. It begins on the first business day of the new year with page one and is consecutively paginated from that point on until the last business day of the year.

After final regulations are published in the *Federal Register*, they are codified in the *Code of Federal Regulations* (C.F.R.). The C.F.R. is divided into 50 "Titles." The C.F.R. Titles are subdivided into chapters, which are usually named for the agencies issuing the regulations. Chapters are subdivided into Parts covering specific regulatory areas, and Parts are further subdivided into sections. To find a regulation, you would need to know its Title, Part, and section number. Thus, a citation to 7 C.F.R. § 210.1 tells you that the regulation is published in Title 7 of the C.F.R. in Part 210, section number 210.1. **Figure 9.1** illustrates what federal regulations look like.

The C.F.R. is updated once a year in four separate installments. Titles 1 through 16 are updated on January 1 of each year, Titles 17 through 27 on April 1, Titles 28 through 41 on July 1, and Titles 42 through 50 on October 1. Because a new set of C.F.R. volumes is published annually, the C.F.R. is not updated with pocket parts. Instead, new or amended regulations are published in the *Federal Register*. They are not codified within the C.F.R. until a new set is published.

FIGURE 9.1 REGULATIONS IN 7 C.F.R. PART 210

Outline of the Part

Statutory authority for promulgating the regulations

Citation to the *Federal Register* where the regulations were originally published

SUBCHAPTER A—CHILD NUTRITION PROGRAMS

PART 210—NATIONAL SCHOOL LUNCH PROGRAM

Subpart A—General

Sec.
210.1 General purpose and scope.
210.2 Definitions.
210.3 Administration.

Subpart B—Reimbursement Process for States and School Food Authorities

210.4 Cash and donated food assistance to States.
210.5 Payment process to States.
210.6 Use of Federal funds.
210.7 Reimbursement for school food authorities.
210.8 Claims for reimbursement.

Subpart C—Requirements for School Food Authority Participation

210.9 Agreement with State agency.
210.10 Nutrition standards and menu planning approaches for lunches and requirements for afterschool snacks.
210.11 Competitive food services.
210.12 Student, parent and community involvement.
210.13 Facilities management.
210.14 Resource management.
210.15 Reporting and recordkeeping.
210.16 Food service management companies.

Subpart D—Requirements for State Agency Participation

210.17 Matching Federal funds.
210.18 Administrative reviews.
210.19 Additional responsibilities.
210.20 Reporting and recordkeeping.

Subpart E—State Agency and School Food Authority Responsibilities

210.21 Procurement.
210.22 Audits.
210.23 Other responsibilities.

Subpart F—Additional Provisions

210.24 Withholding payments.
210.25 Suspension, termination and grant closeout procedures.
210.26 Penalties.
210.27 Educational prohibitions.
210.28 Pilot project exemptions.
210.29 Management evaluations.
210.30 Regional office addresses.
210.31 OMB control numbers.

APPENDIX A TO PART 210—ALTERNATE FOODS FOR MEALS
APPENDIX B TO PART 210—CATEGORIES OF FOODS OF MINIMAL NUTRITIONAL VALUE
APPENDIX C TO PART 210—CHILD NUTRITION LABELING PROGRAM

AUTHORITY: 42 U.S.C. 1751–1760, 1779.

SOURCE: 53 FR 29147, Aug. 2, 1988, unless otherwise noted.

Subpart A—General

§ 210.1 General purpose and scope.

(a) *Purpose of the program.* Section 2 of the National School Lunch Act (42 U.S.C. 1751), states: "It is declared to be the policy of Congress, as a measure of national security, to safeguard the health and well-being of the Nation's children and to encourage the domestic consumption of nutritious agricultural commodities and other food, by assisting the States, through grants-in-aid and other means, in providing an adequate supply of food and other facilities for the establishment, maintenance, operation, and expansion of nonprofit school lunch programs." Pursuant to this act, the Department provides States with general and special cash assistance and donations of foods acquired by the Department to be used to assist schools in serving nutritious lunches to children each school day. In furtherance of Program objectives, participating schools shall serve lunches that are nutritionally adequate, as set forth in these regulations, and shall to the extent practicable, ensure that participating children gain a full understanding of the relationship between proper eating and good health.

(b) *Scope of the regulations.* This part sets forth the requirements for participation in the National School Lunch and Commodity School Programs. It specifies Program responsibilities of State and local officials in the areas of program administration, preparation and service of nutritious lunches, payment of funds, use of program funds, program monitoring, and reporting and recordkeeping requirements.

§ 210.2 Definitions.

For the purpose of this part:

An individual regulation

2. METHODS OF LOCATING REGULATIONS

You can locate federal regulations in several ways. Three common techniques are searching by citation, by subject, or by words in the document. Once you know the Title and Part or section number of a regulation, you can locate it in the C.F.R. in print or electronically. An easy way to find citations to relevant regulations is through an annotated code. Because regulations implement statutory schemes, you will often begin regulatory research by consulting the enabling statute, and the statute's annotations may include citations to regulations. The annotations will not ordinarily direct you to a specific regulation; instead, they will direct you to the Title and Part of the C.F.R. with regulations applicable to the area of law you are researching.

Researching by subject is another useful way to locate regulations. You can search by subject in print using the index to the C.F.R. If you are searching electronically, you may or may not have access to the index. Each Title and Part of the C.F.R. has a table of contents, which you can view in print or electronically to browse by subject. Reviewing the table of contents can be a difficult way to begin your research unless you know which agency promulgated the regulations you are trying to find. Once you find a relevant regulation, however, viewing the table of contents can help you find related regulations, as described more fully below.

Word searching is another way to locate regulations electronically. You can do a source-driven word search in a database limited to federal regulations. You can also do a content-driven search in WestlawNext or Lexis Advance. As long as the search includes federal materials, federal regulations will appear in the search results. Because regulators often use technical terms in regulations, however, word searching can be more difficult than subject searching if you are not already familiar with the regulatory terminology.

Two additional avenues for regulatory research are the telephone and e-mail. Agency staff can be an invaluable resource for understanding the agency's operations, as well as for staying up to date on the agency's activities. If you practice in an area of law subject to agency regulation, do not hesitate to contact agency staff for information. Regulatory notices published in the *Federal Register* typically provide the name and contact information of an agency staff member who can provide additional information about the regulations.

Regulatory research is similar to statutory research in that you will often need to research interrelated regulations, not individual sections of the C.F.R., to answer your research question. Therefore, regardless of the search method you use initially to locate a relevant regulation, you should plan to expand your search to consider the entire regulatory scheme. Because electronic sources often retrieve individual regulations as separate documents, it is especially easy to lose sight of the need to research multiple sections when you are working online. Whether you use print or electronic sources, you can view the detailed outline of sections at the beginning of the Part, as illustrated in **Figure 9.1**, and browse preceding and subsequent sections of the C.F.R. to ensure that you consider all potentially applicable regulations.

Sections B and C, below, explain how to research regulations in print and electronically. Because the federal government has made much regulatory material available on the Internet, most researchers conduct C.F.R. research electronically. The electronic versions of official government sources, however, are updated on the same schedule as the print versions, and the process of updating regulations with official government sources, whether print or electronic, is the same. Therefore, information on updating regulatory research with official government sources appears in Section C, on electronic research. If you are updating federal regulations in print, you can follow the same steps using the print versions of the updating tools.

B. RESEARCHING FEDERAL REGULATIONS IN PRINT

1. LOCATING AND UPDATING REGULATIONS IN PRINT

Researching federal regulations entails two steps:

a. locating regulations;
b. updating your research.

This section describes how to complete these steps using print research resources.

a. Locating Regulations

The C.F.R. is published as a set of softcover books. Once you locate the C.F.R. set, the next question is how to find regulations relevant to your research issue. There are two ways to accomplish this. One way is to use the cross-references to the C.F.R. in U.S.C.S. or U.S.C.A. The other is to go directly to the C.F.R. itself, using a subject index to refer you to relevant C.F.R. provisions.

Because regulations are often used to implement statutory schemes, U.S.C.S. and U.S.C.A. frequently contain cross-references to applicable regulations. Thus, if your research leads you to statutes, the annotations are a useful tool to guide you toward regulations that bear on the area of law you are researching. You may recall from Chapter 7 that U.S.C.S. contains more extensive regulatory annotations than U.S.C.A. does. **Figure 9.2** shows C.F.R. cross-references in U.S.C.S. annotations.

FIGURE 9.2   ANNOTATIONS TO 42 U.S.C.S. § 1751

CODE OF FEDERAL REGULATIONS

Nondiscrimination, 7 CFR Part 15.
National school lunch program, 7 CFR Part 210.
Special milk program for children, 7 CFR Part 215.
School breakfast program, 7 CFR Part 220.
State administrative expense funds, 7 CFR Part 235.
Determining eligibility for free and reduced price lunches, 7 CFR Part 245.

CROSS REFERENCES

This section is referred to in 42 USCS § 1755.

Cross-references to applicable regulations in U.S.C.S. statutory annotations

RESEARCH GUIDE

deral Procedure L Ed:
Fed Proc L Ed, Health, Education, and Welfare § 42:629.

153

Another way to locate regulations is to use the CFR Index and Finding Aids. This is a subject index within the C.F.R. set itself. Like all other C.F.R. volumes, it is a softcover book, and it is published annually.

b. Updating Regulations

As noted above, the C.F.R. is published once a year in four separate installments and is updated through the *Federal Register*, not with pocket parts. Updating C.F.R. research with the *Federal Register* is a two-step process:

■ Use a monthly publication called the List of CFR Sections Affected (LSA) to find any *Federal Register* notices indicating that the regulation has been affected by agency action. Each monthly issue of the LSA is cumulative. Therefore, the current month's LSA will contain updates from the date of the latest C.F.R. volume through the end of the previous month.
■ Use a cumulative table of C.F.R. Parts affected by agency action in the *Federal Register*. This table is published daily. It lists updates for the current month and will update your research from the last day covered by the LSA until the present.

These are the same steps you would follow to update your research using official government sources in electronic form. Therefore, they are explained in more detail in Section C, below.

2. USING A CITATOR FOR REGULATORY RESEARCH

Chapter 6 discusses citators and how to use them in conducting case research. Citators are also available for researching federal regulations. Regulatory citator entries typically contain lists of cases and other sources that have cited a regulation. As noted in Chapter 6, most law libraries no longer carry Shepard's in print. The electronic citators (Shepard's in Lexis and KeyCite in Westlaw) are available for federal regulations, and they are explained in more detail in Section C, below.

Using a citator in regulatory research is useful for locating research references. As of this writing, only Westlaw provides access to a complete annotated version of the C.F.R. Virtually all other sources, whether print or electronic, provide access only to unannotated regulations.[1] Therefore, a citator is a useful tool for locating cases interpreting a regulation. Even if you are using an annotated version of the C.F.R., the regulatory annotations often do not list every citing case or source that has cited the regulation. If the annotations are too sparse to give you the information you need about a regulation, you may find more complete information in a citator.

C. RESEARCHING FEDERAL REGULATIONS ELECTRONICALLY

Lexis, Westlaw, and government websites are all useful sources for regulatory research. This section discusses search options in all three of these sources. It also discusses use of electronic citators for regulatory research.

1. LEXIS AND WESTLAW

The C.F.R. is available in Lexis and Westlaw. Lexis and Westlaw incorporate changes to regulations as they appear in the *Federal Register* so that the version of the C.F.R. you see in these services is ordinarily up to date. You can check the date through which the regulation is updated by checking the updating date at the beginning or end of the document. The *Federal Register* is also available in both services, although the continuous updating of the C.F.R. in Lexis and Westlaw make it unnecessary to use the *Federal Register* for updating regulations. The continuous updates also mean, however, that the versions of the C.F.R. in Lexis and Westlaw are not official sources for regulations. If you need the official source, you must use a print or electronic government source for the C.F.R. and *Federal Register*.

---

[1] Some administrative regulations are reproduced as part of the U.S.C.S. and U.S.C.A. print sets and may have limited annotations; however, the coverage is very limited.

In Lexis.com, you can retrieve federal regulations and *Federal Register* entries from their citations using **Get a Document**. The U.S.C.S. annotations in Lexis also provide links to regulations. To search by subject, you must first select the C.F.R. database from the source directory. The search screen automatically displays the table of contents. You can drill down through the table of contents to search by subject, or you can execute a word search. Once you locate a relevant regulation, you can view the table of contents for the Part from the **TOC** link in the top left corner of the screen.

Similar search options are available in Lexis Advance. You can retrieve a regulation by entering its citation in the red search box. You can use the links to regulations in U.S.C.S. to access regulations. For all other search options, you will execute a search in the search box, but you will vary the selections from the drop-down menus.

To execute a source-driven word search that retrieves only regulations, select **Administrative Codes and Regulations** as the content type. To execute a content-driven word search that retrieves regulations and other types of authority, choose **All Content** as the content type. For either type of search, be sure to limit the jurisdiction to **U.S. Federal**. You can pre-filter by subject area using the **Practice Areas and Topics** drop-down menu, but you do not have to. As this text goes to press, Lexis Advance offers only the broad topic categories listed in the drop-down menu; you cannot drill down to subtopics. After you execute a word search, you will have a variety of options for filtering the search results.

To Shepardize a regulation, you can access Shepard's and enter the citation or access the service from a regulation you are viewing. The Shepard's entry will list cases and other sources that have cited the regulation.

Westlaw also allows you to retrieve administrative regulations and *Federal Register* entries from their citations. As noted above, Westlaw provides access to an annotated version of the C.F.R. Once you access a regulation, Westlaw.com will display a **RegulationsPlus** directory on the left side of the screen with links to annotations. In WestlawNext, the document will be accompanied by tabs with annotations. In addition, the U.S.C.A. annotations in Westlaw also provide some links to regulations, although the references are not as complete as those in U.S.C.S.

In Westlaw.com, you can search by subject by accessing the C.F.R. table of contents or **RegulationsPlus Index** from the **Site Map**. Another way to access these search features is by selecting the C.F.R. database from the **Directory** and following the appropriate links in the top right corner of the screen. You can also execute a word search from the search screen. Once you locate a relevant regulation, you can view the table of contents for the Part from the **Table of Contents** link on the left hand menu. To use KeyCite, you can enter the citation or access the service from a regulation you are viewing. The KeyCite entry will be divided into sections showing the history of the regulation and citing references listing cases and other sources that have cited the regulation.

In WestlawNext, you can select the C.F.R. database using the menu options on the home page. Once you select the database, the table of contents will appear, and you can execute a search within the C.F.R. using the search box at the top of the screen. In the **Tools and Resources** section on the right, you will see additional search options, including the CFR Index. The search results screen will show a variety of options for filtering the search results. The KeyCite history and citing references will be included with the tabs that accompany each regulation.

2. GOVERNMENT SOURCES

Because the C.F.R. and *Federal Register* are government publications, they are widely available on the Internet free of charge. The Government Printing Office's Federal Digital System (FDSys) is one of the best places to research federal regulations, especially because it provides the official version of the C.F.R. in .pdf format. You can enter a citation or search from the FDSys home page or go to the *Code of Federal Regulations* page to browse by Title. **Figure 9.3** shows the main search page for FDSys. Sites for individual agencies can also be good sources for federal regulations. Internet addresses for several useful sites for federal regulatory research are listed in Appendix A.

FIGURE 9.3   FDSYS SEARCH OPTIONS

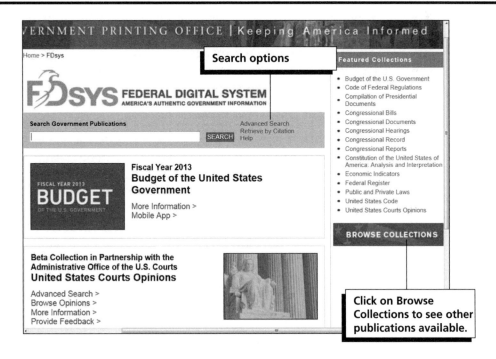

If you use a government source to locate C.F.R. provisions, pay careful attention to the date of the material you are using. Government sources of regulations usually are no more up to date than the print version of the C.F.R. In FDSys, for example, the official C.F.R. database is only updated four times per year as the new print editions of the C.F.R. become available, although the *Federal Register* database is updated daily.

The Government Printing Office offers an unofficial version of the C.F.R. called the *Electronic Code of Federal Regulations* (e-CFR). The e-CFR is updated daily to incorporate changes to regulations as they are published in the *Federal Register*, in the same way that Lexis and Westlaw continually update their C.F.R. databases. Although the e-CFR is not an official source for regulations, it is a useful research tool. By comparing the official C.F.R. text with the e-CFR version, you can determine quickly and easily whether a regulation has been changed since the latest official edition of the C.F.R. was published. If you need an official source and citation for the change, you can then retrieve the *Federal Register* page containing the change by citation in the FDSys *Federal Register* database. You can access the e-CFR by following the link on the FDSys *Code of Federal Regulations* page or by browsing the collection in FDSys.

Although no reason exists to doubt the accuracy of the e-CFR, there may be times when, out of an abundance of caution, you want to double check your research by updating it with official government sources. An alternate method of updating in FDSys requires you to research two sources:

- Use a monthly publication called the List of CFR Sections Affected (LSA) to find any *Federal Register* notices indicating that the regulation has been affected by agency action.
- Use the table of CFR Parts Affected during the current month in the most current *Federal Register* to update from the date of the LSA until the present.

The official updating sources available online are the same as those available in print. Therefore, these are also the steps you must follow to update print research.

The LSA lists each C.F.R. section affected by agency action. It is a cumulative publication. The current month's LSA will contain updates from the date of the latest C.F.R. volume through the end of the previous month. For example, if the latest C.F.R. volume had been published on January 1 and today's date were December 15, the current LSA would be dated November, and it would contain updates from January 1 through November 30.

To locate the LSA, choose the option to **Browse Collections** and locate the **List of CFR Sections Affected** in the publications list. Drill down through the **Monthly LSA** options to the latest LSA and then to the Title of the C.F.R. for the regulation you are updating. Open the document and review the list to see if the C.F.R. provision you are updating appears. If you do not find the section listed in the LSA, there have been no changes to the regulation. If you do find the section listed, the LSA will refer you to the page or pages of the *Federal Register* containing information on the agency's action. **Figure 9.4** is an example of a page from the .pdf version of the November 2011 LSA. It indicates changes to several regulations in 7 C.F.R. Part 210.

The easiest way to find the *Federal Register* page with the change to the regulation is to retrieve it by citation from the search screen on the FDSys home page. You can also browse the *Federal Register* by date to find the page or pages you need. Once you find the page, you can read about the change to the regulation. **Figure 9.5** shows the page from the *Federal Register* with changes to several regulations in 7 C.F.R. Part 210.

The second updating step requires you to use a table of CFR Parts Affected during the month to date. This table lists all of the C.F.R. Parts affected by notices published in the *Federal Register* during the current month and will update your research from the last day covered by the LSA until the present. Thus, if today's date were December 15, the list of CFR Parts Affected During December would contain updates since the November LSA, covering the period from December 1 through December 15.

To access this table, follow the link to the *Federal Register* from the FDSys home page and choose the option to view **Today's issue of the Federal Register**. This will bring up the table of contents of the current issue. Scroll to the bottom and select **Reader Aids**. On this page you will see a table of CFR Parts Affected for the current month. (Note that a different table of CFR Parts Affected appears with the title page of the *Federal Register*. This table is a daily listing that is not cumulative for the month. Be sure to use the monthly table under **Reader Aids**.)

The table lists only the Parts affected by agency action, not individual sections. Therefore, if the table contains a reference to the C.F.R. Part you are researching, you need to retrieve the relevant page from the *Federal Register* to determine the section or sections within the C.F.R. Part affected by agency action. If the table does not list the Part you are researching, your updating is complete. **Figure 9.6** shows an entry for Title 7 of the C.F.R. from the list of CFR Parts Affected During December.

The chart in **Figure 9.7** summarizes the process of updating C.F.R. research with official sources, using the example of a regulation within Title 7 of the C.F.R. published on January 1, 2011, an LSA dated November 30, 2011, and the list of CFR Parts Affected dated December 15, 2011.

FIGURE 9.4   LSA PAGE SHOWING CHANGES TO REGULATIONS

Changes to regulations in Title 7 appear on this page.

Federal Register page with a change to § 210.2

LSA—LIST OF CFR SECTIONS AFFECTED

CHANGES JANUARY 3, 2011 THROUGH NOVEMBER 30, 2011

TITLE 7   Subtitle A—Con.

(a)(47) removed; (a)(113) added 4803

2.66 (a) introductory text, (119) and (121) amended 4802

(a)(49), (56), (116) and (118) removed; (a)(42), (107) and (122) revised 4803

(a)(156) revised.............................52852

2.69 Added......................................10756

2.80 (a)(47) added 4803

6.20—6.37 (Subpart) Appendices 1, 2 and 3 revised 63539

8.2 Amended....................................4803

8.3 Amended....................................4803

8.6 (a) introductory text and (b) amended..4803

8.7 (a)(4) amended...........................4803

8.9 (a)(3) amended...........................4803

12.2 (a) amended..............................4803

12.6 (d) revised................................4804

12.30 (a)(8) removed; (c)(1) amended 22785

23.2 (a) amended..............................4804

23.10 (a) amended 4804

Subtitle B—Regulations of the Department of Agriculture (Parts 27—4299)

Chapter I—Agricultural Marketing Service (Standards, Inspections, Marketing Practices), Department of Agriculture (Parts 27—209)

28.909 (b) republished 25534

28.911 (a) republished in part 25534

35.11 (a) and (b) revised..................14277

46.46 (e)(2) revised; (e)(3) and (4) redesignated as (e)(4) and (5); new (e)(3) added.........................20220

51.1541 (a) revised............................31789

51.1543 (a) revised............................31789

51.1546 (a) revised............................31789

51.1559 Removed...............................31789

51.1560 Revised.................................31789

51.1561 Revised.................................31789

51.1564 Introductory text and Table III amended 31789

51.1565 Introductory text and Table VII amended 31790

52 Policy statement.........................64001

52.54 Revised.....................................253

201.2 introductory text, (f), (h), (i), (w) and (z) amended 31792

201.16 (b) amended 31794

201.20 Revised 31794

201.31a (c)(1) and (2) introductory text amended...........................31794

201.41 (a) amended 31794

201.48 (g) introductory text amended 31794

201.51 (a)(9) added 31794

201.65 Revised 31794

201.74 (a) and (c) amended..............31795

201.75 (c) amended...........................31795

205 Policy statement ...26177, 26927, 46595

205.603 Regulation at 75 FR 51924 confirmed 13504

Chapter II—Food and Nutrition Service, Department of Agriculture (Parts 210—299)

210.2 Amended; interim 35316

Regulation at 72 FR 63790 confirmed......................................66853

210.9 (b)(18) revised; (b)(19) and (20) redesignated as (b)(20) and (21); new (b)(19) added; interim.....................................22797

(b)(1) revised; interim...................35316

Regulation at 72 FR 63791 confirmed......................................66853

210.14 (e) and (f) added; interim 35316

210.15 (a)(6), (7) and (b)(5) amended; (a)(8), (b)(6) and (7) added; interim.....................................35317

210.18 (g)(1)(i)(A)(3) and (4) revised; (g)(1)(i)(B) amended; interim.....................................22797

210.19 (c)(6) introductory text and (ii) amended; interim.........22797

(a)(2) amended; interim...............35317

Regulation at 72 FR 63791 confirmed......................................66853

210.20 (a)(7), (8), (b)(11) and (12) amended; (a)(9), (b)(13) and (14) added; interim..................35318

210.21 (g) added 22607

210.23 (b) amended; interim 22797

(e) added 37982

210.30 (e) amended..........................34569

215.2 Regulation at 72 FR 63791 confirmed 66853

215.3 Regulation at 72 FR 63791 confirmed 66853

215.7 (f) added 37982

215.11 (f) added 37982

215.13a (f) amended; interim 22798

215.14a (e) added..............................22607

FIGURE 9.5   *FEDERAL REGISTER* **PAGE SHOWING REGULATORY CHANGES**

35316   Federal Register / Vol. 76, No. 117 / Friday, June 17, 2011 / Rules and Regulations

ESTIMATED ANNUAL BURDEN FOR 0584–NEW, NATIONAL SCHOOL LUNCH PROGRAM 7 CFR PART 210—Continued

Section	Estimated number of respondents	Frequency of response	Average annual responses	Average burden per response	Annual burden hours
Total Recordkeeping Burden for 0584–0006, Part 210 with Interim Rule.	....	....	....	....	9,593,342

SUMMARY OF BURDEN (OMB #0584–NEW)

Total No. Respondents	20,915
Average No. Responses per Respondent	3.991824
Total Annual Responses	83,489
Average Hours per Response	3.8667
Total Burden Hours for Part 210 With Interim Rule	12,580,591
Current OMB Inventory for Part 210	12,257,764
Difference (New Burden Requested With Interim Rule)	322,827

7 CFR 210.15 and 210.20 require that, in order to participate in the NSLP, SFAs and State agencies must maintain records to demonstrate compliance with Program requirements. 7 CFR 210.23 further requires that State agencies and SFAs maintain records for a period of three years.

E-Government Act Compliance

The Food and Nutrition Service is committed to complying with the E-Government Act of 2002, to promote the use of the Internet and other [...] es to provide [...] for citizen [...] formation and [...] urposes.

[...]—Consultation [...] Indian Tribal [...]

The *Federal Register* entry contains the amendment to the regulation.

Executive Order 13175 requires Federal agencies to consult and coordinate with Tribes on a government-to-government basis on policies that have Tribal implications, including regulations, legislative comments or proposed legislation, and other policy statements or actions that have substantial direct effects on one or more Indian Tribes, on the relationship between the Federal Government and Indian Tribes, or on the distribution of power and responsibilities between the Federal Government and Indian Tribes. In spring 2011, USDA engaged in a series of consultative sessions to obtain input by Tribal officials or their designees concerning the impact of this rule on the Tribe or Indian Tribal governments, or whether this rule may

preempt Tribal law. Reports from these consultations will be made part of the USDA annual reporting on Tribal Consultation and Collaboration. USDA will respond in a timely and meaningful manner to all Tribal government requests for consultation concerning this rule and will provide additional venues, such as webinars and teleconferences, to periodically host collaborative conversations with Tribal officials or their designees concerning ways to improve this rule in Indian country.

List of Subjects in 7 CFR Part 210

Grant programs—education; Grant programs—health; Infants and children; Nutrition; Penalties; Reporting and recordkeeping requirements; School breakfast and lunch programs; Surplus agricultural commodities.

Accordingly, 7 CFR part 210 is amended as follows:

PART 210—NATIONAL SCHOOL LUNCH PROGRAM

■ 1. The authority citation for 7 CFR part 210 continues to read as follows:

Authority: 42 U.S.C. 1751–1760, 1779.

■ 2. In § 210.2:
■ a. The definition of "Nonprofit school food service account" is amended by adding a sentence at the end;
■ b. The definition of "Subsidized lunch (paid lunch)" is removed; and
■ c. The definition of "Paid lunch" added.

The additions read as follows:

Subpart A—General

§ 210.2 Definitions.

*   *   *   *   *

Nonprofit school food service account * * * This account shall include, as appropriate, non-Federal funds used to support paid lunches as provided in § 210.14(e), and proceeds from nonprogram foods as provided in § 210.14(f).

*   *   *   *   *

Paid lunch means a lunch served to children who are either not certified for or elect not to receive the free or reduced price benefits offered under part 245 of this chapter. The Department subsidizes each paid lunch with both

general cash assistance and donated foods. The prices for paid lunches in a school food authority shall be determined in accordance with § 210.14(e).

*   *   *   *   *

Subpart C—Requirements for School Food Authority Participation

■ 3. In § 210.9, paragraph (b)(1) is revised to read as follows:

§ 210.9   Agreement with State agency.

*   *   *   *   *

(b) * * *

(1) Maintain a nonprofit school food service and observe the requirements for and limitations on the use of nonprofit school food service revenues set forth in § 210.14 and the limitations on any competitive school food service as set forth in § 210.11;

*   *   *   *   *

■ 4. In § 210.14, new paragraphs (e) and (f) are added to read as follows:

§ 210.14   Resource management.

*   *   *   *   *

(e) *Pricing paid lunches.* For each school year beginning July 1, 2011, school food authorities shall establish prices for paid lunches in accordance with this paragraph.

(1) *Calculation procedures.* Each school food authority shall:

(i) Determine the average price of paid lunches. The average shall be determined based on the total number of paid lunches claimed for the month of October in the previous school year, at each different price charged by the school food authority.

(ii) Calculate the difference between the per meal Federal reimbursement for paid and free lunches received by the school food authority in the previous school year (*i.e.*, the reimbursement difference);

(iii) Compare the average price of a paid lunch under paragraph (e)(1)(i) of this section to the difference between reimbursement rates under paragraph (e)(1)(ii) of this section.

(2) *Average paid lunch price is equal to/greater than the reimbursement difference.*

When the average paid lunch price from the prior school year is equal to or

FIGURE 9.6 *FEDERAL REGISTER,* CUMULATIVE MONTHLY LIST OF CFR PARTS AFFECTED

Cumulative table of parts affected for the month

i

Reader Aids

Federal Register

Vol. 76, No. 241

Thursday, December 15, 2011

CUSTOMER SERVICE AND INFORMATION

Federal Register/Code of Federal Regulations

General Information, indexes and other finding aids	202–741–6000
Laws	741–6000

Presidential Documents

Executive orders and proclamations	741–6000
The United States Government Manual	741–6000

Other Services

Electronic and on-line services (voice)	741–6020
Privacy Act Compilation	741–6064
Public Laws Update Service (numbers, dates, etc.)	741–6043
TTY for the deaf-and-hard-of-hearing	741–6086

ELECTRONIC RESEARCH

World Wide Web

Full text of the daily Federal Register, CFR and other publications is located at: **www.fdsys.gov.**

Federal Register information and research tools, including Public Inspection List, indexes, and links to GPO Access are located at: **www.ofr.gov.**

E-mail

FEDREGTOC-L (Federal Register Table of Contents LISTSERV) is an open e-mail service that provides subscribers with a digital form of the Federal Register Table of Contents. The digital form of the Federal Register Table of Contents includes HTML and PDF links to the full text of each document.

To join or leave, go to **http://listserv.access.gpo.gov** and select *Online mailing list archives, FEDREGTOC-L, Join or leave the list (or change settings);* then follow the instructions.

PENS (Public Law Electronic Notification Service) is an e-mail service that notifies subscribers of recently enacted laws.

To subscribe, go to **http://listserv.gsa.gov/archives/publaws-l.html** and select *Join or leave the list (or change settings);* then follow the instructions.

FEDREGTOC-L and **PENS** are mailing lists only. We cannot respond to specific inquiries.

Reference questions. Send questions and comments about the Federal Register system to: **fedreg.info@nara.gov**

The Federal Register staff cannot interpret specific documents or regulations.

Reminders. Effective January 1, 2009, the Reminders, including Rules Going Into Effect and Comments Due Next Week, no longer appear in the Reader Aids section of the Federal Register. This information can be found online at **http://www.regulations.gov.**

CFR Checklist. Effective January 1, 2009, the CFR Checklist no longer appears in the Federal Register. This information can be found online at **http://bookstore.gpo.gov/.**

FEDERAL REGISTER PAGES AND DATE, DECEMBER

74625–75426	1
75427–75770	2
75771–76020	5
76021–76292	6
76293–76600	7
76601–76872	8
76873–77106	9
77107–77362	12
77363–77668	13
77669–77894	14
77895–78092	15

CFR PARTS AFFECTED DURING DECEMBER

At the end of each month the Office of the Federal Register publishes separately a List of CFR Sections Affected (LSA), which lists parts and sections affected by documents published since the revision date of each title.

2 CFR

421	76609

3 CFR

Proclamations:

8760	76021
8761	76023
8762	76025
8763	76601
8764	76871
8765	77363
8766	77365

Executive Orders:

13592	76603

Administrative Orders:

Memorandums:

Memorandum of July 19, 2011	76869
Memorandum of November 28, 2011	75423

4 CFR

28	76873

5 CFR

Proposed Rules:

Ch. XXIII	75798

7 CFR

761	75427
763	75427
764	75427
3021	76609

Proposed Rules:

331	77914
400	75799
457	75805
1700	76905

8 CFR

280	74625
1280	74625

9 CFR

201	76874
317	76890
381	76890

Proposed Rules:

121	77914
316	75809
317	75809
320	75809
331	75809
354	75809
355	75809
381	75809
412	75809
424	75809

10 CFR

50	74630, 75771

52	74630, 75771

Proposed Rules:

20	77431
30	77431
32	76625
40	77431
50	76322, 77431
70	77431
72	77431
73	76327
Ch. II	75798
Ch. III	75798
429	76328, 77914
430	76328
431	77914
900	77432
Ch. X	75798

12 CFR

225	
912	
997	
1780	
1781	74648
1782	74648
1783	74648
1784	74648
1785	74648
1786	74648
1787	74648
1788	74648
1789	74648
1790	74648
1791	74648
1792	74648
1793	74648
1794	74648
1795	74648
1796	74648
1797	74648
1798	74648
1799	74648

Proposed Rules:

5	76905
362	78086, 78090
380	77442
Ch. X	75825, 76628

13 CFR

Proposed Rules:

107	76907
121	74749
125	74749
300	76492
301	76492
302	76492
303	76492
304	76492
305	76492
306	76492
307	76492
308	76492
310	76492

No changes to 7 C.F.R. Part 210 are listed.

FIGURE 9.7 UPDATING C.F.R. RESEARCH USING OFFICIAL SOURCES

DATE	JANUARY 1, 2011	JANUARY 1, 2011–NOVEMBER 30, 2011	DECEMBER 1, 2011–DECEMBER 15, 2011
Source	Title 7, C.F.R.	November 2011 List of CFR Sections Affected (LSA)	List of CFR Parts Affected During December
Use	Locate regulations in the C.F.R. Note the date of the C.F.R.	Use the latest monthly issue. Look up the Title and section number of the regulation. If it is listed, look up the page in the *Federal Register* to locate the change.	Use the cumulative table in the Reader Aids section in back of the latest daily issue of the *Federal Register*. If the C.F.R. Part is not listed, no changes have taken place during the month to date. If the C.F.R. Part is listed, each page reference must be checked to see which individual sections have been affected.

D. CITING FEDERAL REGULATIONS

Citations to administrative materials are governed by Rule 19 in the *ALWD Manual* (4th ed.) and Bluepages B5.1.4 and Rule 14.2 in the *Bluebook* (19th ed.). The citations are the same using either format.

A citation to the C.F.R. is very similar to a citation to a federal statute. It consists of the Title number, the abbreviation C.F.R., the pinpoint reference to the Part or section number, and a parenthetical containing the year. Here are two examples:

Title ◄─┐ ┌─► abbreviated name ┌─► year of the C.F.R. volume
      7 C.F.R. pt. 210 (2012).
abbreviation for Part ◄─┘ └─► Part number

Title ◄─┐ ┌─► abbreviated name ┌─► year of the C.F.R. volume
      7 C.F.R. § 210.15 (2012).
                 └─► section number

Citations to the *Federal Register* are also fairly simple and are the same using either the *ALWD Manual* or the *Bluebook*. They require the volume number, the abbreviation Fed. Reg., the page number, and a parenthetical containing the exact date.

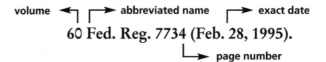

If appropriate, you should also provide a pinpoint reference to the specific page or pages containing the cited material.

E. SAMPLE PAGES FOR FEDERAL ADMINISTRATIVE LAW RESEARCH

Beginning on the next page, **Figures 9.8** through **9.12** contain sample pages from the C.F.R. showing the process of researching regulations pertaining to the national school lunch program in FDSys and the e-CFR.

The first step is locating relevant regulations. You could use a subject index such as the CFR Index and Finding Aids, cross-references in statutory annotations, or a word search to locate relevant regulations. FDSys allows you to view regulations in .pdf format. Once you know the relevant Part, you can use the outline of the Part to review the regulatory scheme.

FIGURE 9.8   7 C.F.R. PART 210 TABLE OF CONTENTS

SUBCHAPTER A—CHILD NUTRITION PROGRAMS

PART 210—NATIONAL SCHOOL LUNCH PROGRAM

Subpart A—General

Sec.
210.1   General purpose and scope.
210.2   Definitions.
210.3   Administration.

Subpart B—Reimbursement Process for States and School Food Authorities

210.4   Cash and donated food assistance to States.
210.5   Payment process to States.
210.6   Use of Federal funds.
210.7   Reimbursement for school food authorities.
210.8   Claims for reimbursement.

Subpart C—Requirements for School Food Authority Participation

210.9   Agreement with State agency.
210.10 Nutrition standards and menu planning approaches for lunches and requirements for afterschool snacks.
210.11 Competitive food services.
210.12 Student, parent and community involvement.
210.13 Facilities management.
210.14 Resource management.
210.15 Reporting and recordkeeping.
210.16 Food service management companies.

Subpart D—Requirements for State Agency Participation

210.17 Matching Federal funds.
210.18 Administrative reviews.
210.19 Additional responsibilities.
210.20 Reporting and recordkeeping.

Subpart E—State Agency and School Food Authority Responsibilities

210.21 Procurement.
210.22 Audits.
210.23 Other responsibilities.

Subpart F—Additional Provisions

210.24 Withholding payments.
210.25 Suspension, termination and grant closeout procedures.
210.26 Penalties.
210.27 Educational prohibitions.
210.28 Pilot project exemptions.
210.29 Management evaluations.
210.30 Regional office addresses.
210.31 OMB control numbers.

APPENDIX A TO PART 210—ALTERNATE FOODS FOR MEALS
APPENDIX B TO PART 210—CATEGORIES OF FOODS OF MINIMAL NUTRITIONAL VALUE
APPENDIX C TO PART 210—CHILD NUTRITION LABELING PROGRAM

AUTHORITY: 42 U.S.C. 1751–1760, 1779.

SOURCE: 53 FR 29147, Aug. 2, 1988, unless otherwise noted.

Subpart A—General

§ 210.1   General purpose and scope.

(a) *Purpose of the program.* Section 2 of the National School Lunch Act (42 U.S.C. 1751), states: "It is declared to be the policy of Congress, as a measure of national security, to safeguard the health and well-being of the Nation's children and to encourage the domestic consumption of nutritious agricultural commodities and other food, by assisting the States, through grants-in-aid and other means, in providing an adequate supply of food and other facilities for the establishment, maintenance, operation, and expansion of nonprofit school lunch programs." Pursuant to this act, the Department provides States with general and special cash assistance and donations of foods acquired by the Department to be used to assist schools in serving nutritious lunches to children each school day. In furtherance of Program objectives, participating schools shall serve lunches that are nutritionally adequate, as set forth in these regulations, and shall to the extent practicable, ensure that participating children gain a full understanding of the relationship between proper eating and good health.

(b) *Scope of the regulations.* This part sets forth the requirements for participation in the National School Lunch and Commodity School Programs. It specifies Program responsibilities of State and local officials in the areas of program administration, preparation and service of nutritious lunches, payment of funds, use of program funds, program monitoring, and reporting and recordkeeping requirements.

§ 210.2   Definitions.

For the purpose of this part:

> The table of contents refers to a specific regulation on reporting and recordkeeping.

7

The outline of the Part will direct you to specific regulations.

FIGURE 9.9   7 C.F.R. § 210.15

Food and Nutrition Service, USDA   **§ 210.16**

(c) *Financial assurances*. The school food authority shall meet the requirements of the State agency for compliance with § 210.19(a) including any separation of records of nonprofit school food service from records of any other food service which may be operated by the school food authority as provided in paragraph (a) of this section.

(d) *Use of donated foods*. The school food authority shall enter into an agreement with the distributing agency to receive donated foods as required by part 250 of this chapter. In addition, the school food authority shall accept [as large quantities as may] [...tly utilized in its nonprofit] [...d service, such foods as may] [...be offered] as a donation by the Department.

[53 FR 29147, Aug. 2, 1988, as amended at 60 FR 31215, June 13, 1995]

§ 210.15   Reporting and recordkeeping.

(a) *Reporting summary*. Participating school food authorities are required to submit forms and reports to the State agency or the distributing agency, as appropriate, to demonstrate compliance with Program requirements. These reports include, but are not limited to:

(1) A Claim for Reimbursement and, for the month of October and as otherwise specified by the State agency, supporting data as specified in accordance with § 210.8 of this part;

(2) An application and agreement for Program operations between the school food authority and the State agency, and a Free and Reduced Price Policy Statement as required under § 210.9;

(3) A written response to reviews pertaining to corrective action taken for Program deficiencies;

(4) A commodity school's preference whether to receive part of its donated food allocation in cash for processing and handling of donated foods as required under § 210.19(b);

(5) A written response to audit findings pertaining to the school food authority's operation as required under § 210.22;

(6) Information on civil rights complaints, if any, and their resolution as required under § 210.23; and

(7) The number of food safety inspections obtained per school year by each school under its jurisdiction.

(b) *Recordkeeping summary*. In order to participate in the Program, a school food authority or a school, as applicable, must maintain records to demonstrate compliance with Program requirements. These records include but are not limited to:

(1) Documentation of participation data by school in support of the Claim for Reimbursement and data used in the claims review process, as required under § 210.8(a), (b), and (c) of this part;

(2) Production and menu records and, if appropriate, nutrition analysis records as required under § 210.10, whichever is applicable.

(3) Participation records to demonstrate positive action toward providing one lunch per child per day as required under § 210.10(a)(2), whichever is applicable;

(4) Currently approved and denied applications for free and reduced price lunches and a description of the verification activities, including verified applications, and any accompanying source documentation in accordance with 7 CFR 245.6a of this Title; and

(5) Records from the food safety program for a period of six months following a month's temperature records to demonstrate compliance with § 210.13(c), and records from the most recent food safety inspection to demonstrate compliance with § 210.13(b).

[53 FR 29147, Aug. 2, 1988, as amended at 54 FR 12582, Mar. 28, 1989; 56 FR 32941, July 17, 1991; 60 FR 31215, June 13, 1995; 65 FR 26912, 26922, May 9, 2000; 70 FR 34630, June 15, 2005; 74 FR 66216, Dec. 15, 2009]

§ 210.16   Food service management companies.

(a) *General*. Any school food authority (including a State agency acting in the capacity of a school food authority) may contract with a food service management company to manage its food service operation in one or more of its schools. However, no school or school food authority may contract with a food service management company to operate an a la carte food service unless the company agrees to offer free, reduced price and paid reimbursable

39

> Regulation referenced in the table of contents

You can update C.F.R. research in FDSys using the LSA and the *Federal Register*. You can also use the unofficial e-CFR to find regulatory changes.

FIGURE 9.10 e-CFR SEARCH SCREEN AND RESULTS

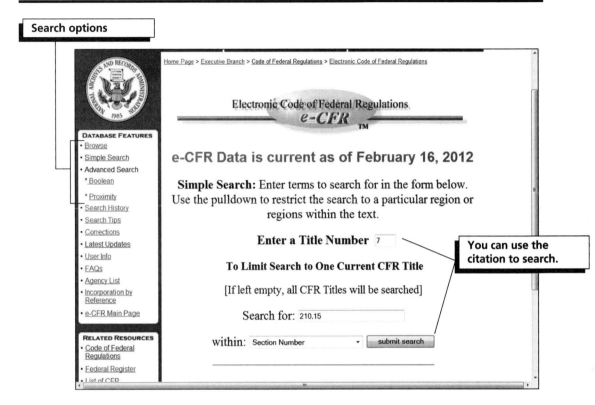

The regulation is displayed in textual form. At the end of the regulation, you will find a reference to the page of the *Federal Register* that contains a change to the regulation.

FIGURE 9.11   e-CFR VERSION OF 7 C.F.R. § 210.15

---

§ 210.15   Reporting and recordkeeping.

⬆ top

(a) *Reporting summary.* Participating school food authorities are required to submit forms and reports to the State agency or the distributing agency, as appropriate, to demonstrate compliance with Program requirements. These reports include, but are not limited to:

(1) A Claim for Reimbursement and, for the month of October and as otherwise specified by the State agency, supporting data as specified in accordance with §210.8 of this part;

(2) An application and agreement for Program operations between the school food authority and the State agency, and a Free and Reduced Price Policy Statement as required under §210.9;

(3) A written response to reviews pertaining to corrective action taken for Program deficiencies;

(4) A commodity school's preference whether to receive part of its donated food allocation in cash for processing and handling of donated foods as required under §210.19(b);

(5) A written response to audit findings pertaining to the school food authority's operation as required under §210.22;

(6) Information on civil rights complaints, if any, and their resolution as required under §210.23;

(7) The number of food safety inspections obtained per school year by each school under its jurisdiction; and

(8) The prices of paid lunches charged by the school food authority.

(b) *Recordkeeping summary.* In order to participate in the Program, a school food authority or a school, as applicable, must maintain records to demonstrate compliance with Program requirements. These records include but are not limited to:

(1) Documentation of participation data by school in support of the Claim for Reimbursement and data used in the claims review process, as required under §210.8(a), (b), and (c) of this part;

---

(2) Production and menu records and, if appropriate, nutrition analysis records as required under §210.10, whichever is applicable.

(3) Participation records to demonstrate positive action toward providing one lunch per child per day as required under §210.10(a)(2), whichever is applicable;

(4) Currently approved and denied applications for free and reduced price lunches and a description of the verification activities, including verified applications, and any accompanying source documentation in accordance with 7 CFR 245.6a of this Title; and

(5) Records from the food safety program for a period of six months following a month's temperature records to demonstrate compliance with §210.13(c), and records from the most recent food safety inspection to demonstrate compliance with §210.13(b);

(6) Records to document compliance with the requirements in §210.14(e); and

(7) Records to document compliance with the requirements in §210.14(f).

[53 FR 29147, Aug. 2, 1988, as amended at 54 FR 12582, Mar. 28, 1989; 56 FR 32941, July 17, 1991; 60 FR 31215, June 13, 1995; 65 FR 26912, 26922, May 9, 2000; 70 FR 34630, June 15, 2005; 74 FR 66216, Dec. 15, 2009; 76 FR 35317, June 17, 2011]

> *Federal Register* reference indicating a change to the regulation on June 17, 2011

§ 210.16   Food service management companies.

⬆ top

(a) *General.* Any school food authority (including a State agency acting in the capacity of [school food] authority) may contract with a food service management company to manage its food service operation in one or more of its schools. However, no school or school food authority may contract with a food service management company to operate an a la carte food service unless the company agrees to offer free, reduced price and paid reimbursable lunches to all eligible children. Any school food authority that employs a food service management company in the operation of its nonprofit school food service shall:

(1) Adhere to the procurement standards specified in §210.21 when contracting with the food service management company;

Using the citation to the *Federal Register* from the e-CFR, you can see the change to the regulation. You can use this reference along with the official version of the C.F.R. if you need to cite an official source for the regulation.

FIGURE 9.12 *FEDERAL REGISTER* PAGE SHOWING CHANGES TO 7 C.F.R. § 210.15

Federal Register / Vol. 76, No. 117 / Friday, June 17, 2011 / Rules and Regulations **35317**

---

greater than the difference in reimbursement rates as determined in paragraph (e)(1)(iii) of this section, the school food authority shall establish an average paid lunch price for the current school year that is not less than the difference identified in (e)(1)(iii) of this section; except that, the school food authority may use the procedure in paragraph (e)(4)(ii) of this section when establishing prices of paid lunches.

(3) *Average lunch price is lower than the reimbursement difference.* When the average price from the prior school year is lower than the difference in reimbursement rates as determined in paragraph (e)(1)(iii) of this section, the school food authority shall establish an average price for the current school year that is not less than the average price charged in the previous school year as adjusted by a percentage equal to the sum obtained by adding:

(i) 2 percent; and

(ii) The percentage change in the Consumers Price Index for All Urban Consumers used to increase the Federal reimbursement rate under section 11 of the Act for the most recent school year for which data are available. The percentage to be used is found in the annual notice published in the **Federal Register** announcing the national average payment rates, from the prior year.

(4) *Price Adjustments.* (i) *Maximum required price increase.* The maximum annual average price increase required under this paragraph shall not exceed ten cents.

(ii) *Rounding of paid lunch prices.* Any school food authority may round the adjusted price of the paid lunches down to the nearest five cents.

(iii) *Optional price increases.* A school food authority may increase the average price by more than ten cents.

(5) *Reduction in average price for paid lunches.* (i) Any school food authority may reduce the average price of paid lunches as established under this paragraph if the State agency ensures that funds are added to the nonprofit school food service account in accordance with this paragraph.

The minimum that must be added is the product of:

(A) The number of paid lunches claimed by the school food authority in the previous school year multiplied by

(B) The amount required under paragraph (e)(3) of this section, as adjusted under paragraph (e)(4) of this section, minus the average price charged.

(ii) *Prohibitions.* The following shall not be used to reduce the average price charged for paid lunches:

(A) Federal sources of revenue;

(B) Revenue from foods sold in competition with lunches or with breakfasts offered under the School Breakfast Program authorized in 7 CFR part 220. Requirements concerning foods sold in competition with lunches or breakfasts are found in § 210.11 and § 220.12 of this chapter, respectively;

(C) In-kind contributions;

(D) Any in-kind contributions converted to direct cash expenditures after July 1, 2011; and

(E) Per-meal reimbursements (non-Federal) specifically provided for support of programs other than the school lunch program.

(iii) *Allowable non-Federal revenue sources.* Any contribution that is for the direct support of paid lunches that is not prohibited under paragraph (e)(5)(ii) of this section may be used as revenue for this purpose. Such contributions include, but are not limited to:

(A) Per-lunch reimbursements for paid lunches provided by State or local governments;

(B) Funds provided by organizations, such as school-related or community groups, to support paid lunches;

(C) Any portion of State revenue matching funds that exceeds the minimum requirement, as provided in § 210.17, and is provided for paid lunches; and

(D) A proportion attributable to paid lunches from direct payments made from school district funds to support the lunch service.

(6) *Additional considerations.* (i) In any given year, if a school food authority with an average price lower than the reimbursement difference is not required by paragraph (e)(4)(i) of this section to increase its average price for paid lunches, the school food authority shall use the unrounded average price as the basis for calculations to meet paragraph (e)(3) of this section for the next school year.

(ii) If a school food authority has an average price lower than the reimbursement difference and chooses to increase its average price for paid lunches in any school year more than is required by this section, the amount attributable to the additional voluntary increase may be carried forward to the next school year(s) to meet the requirements of this section.

(iii) For the school year beginning July 1, 2011 only, the limitations for non-Federal contributions in paragraph (e)(5)(iii) of this section do not apply.

(7) *Reporting lunch prices.* In accordance with guidelines provided by FNS:

(i) School food authorities shall report prices charged for paid lunches to the State agency; and

(ii) State agencies shall report these prices to FNS.

(f) *Revenue from nonprogram foods.* Beginning July 1, 2011, school food authorities shall ensure that the revenue generated from the sale of nonprogram foods complies with the requirements in this paragraph.

(1) *Definition of nonprogram foods.* For the purposes of this paragraph, nonprogram foods are those foods and beverages:

(i) Sold in a participating school other than reimbursable meals and meal supplements; and

(ii) Purchased using funds from the nonprofit school food service account.

(2) *Revenue from nonprogram foods.* The proportion of total revenue from the sale of nonprogram foods to total revenue of the school food service account shall be equal to or greater than:

(i) The proportion of total food costs associated with obtaining nonprogram foods to

(ii) The total costs associated with obtaining program and nonprogram foods from the account.

(3) All revenue from the sale of nonprogram foods shall accrue to the nonprofit school food service account of a participating school food authority.

■ 5. In § 210.15:

■ a. Amend paragraph (a)(6) by removing the word "and" at the end of paragraph;

■ b. Amend paragraph (a)(7) by removing "." at the end of the paragraph and adding "; and" in its place;

■ c. Add a new paragraph (a)(8);

■ d. Amend paragraph (b)(5) by removing "." at the end of the paragraph and adding ";" in its place;

■ e. Add new paragraphs (b)(6) and (b)(7).

The additions read as follows:

§ 210.15 Reporting and recordkeeping.

(a) * * *

(8) The prices of paid lunches charged by the school food authority.

(b) * * *

(6) Records to document compliance with the requirements in § 210.14(e); and

(7) Records to document compliance with the requirements in § 210.14(f).

■ 6. In § 210.19, paragraph (a)(2) is amended by adding a sentence at the end to read as follows:

Subpart D—Requirements for State Agency Participation

§ 210.19 Additional responsibilities.

(a) * * *

(2) * * * Each State agency shall ensure that school food authorities comply with the requirements for

Changes to 7 C.F.R. § 210.15

F. CHECKLIST FOR FEDERAL ADMINISTRATIVE LAW RESEARCH

1. LOCATE PERTINENT REGULATIONS

❏ Use the cross-references to the C.F.R. in the annotations in U.S.C.S. and U.S.C.A.

❏ Use a subject index, such as the CFR Index and Finding Aids.

❏ In Westlaw

- Browse the CFR Index or table of contents.
- Select the CFR database and execute a word search.
- Execute a content-driven search for federal law in WestlawNext, which will include regulations in the **Regulations** section.
- Review regulatory annotations or use KeyCite for regulatory history and research references.

❏ In Lexis

- In Lexis.com, select the CFR database to execute a word search or browse the table of contents.
- In Lexis Advance, execute a source-driven search by selecting **Administrative Codes and Regulations** as the content type or view the results of a content-driven search under the **Administrative Codes and Regulations** tab.
- Use Shepard's for regulatory history and research references.

❏ In the Federal Digital System (FDSys), search by word or citation or browse the table of contents.

2. UPDATE FDSYS RESEARCH WITH THE e-CFR

❏ Compare the official C.F.R. text with the e-CFR version to determine whether the regulation has been amended; locate *Federal Register* notices as necessary for an official citation or additional information.

3. UPDATE C.F.R. RESEARCH USING OFFICIAL SOURCES

❏ Use the same process to update official sources in print or electronically.

❏ To update from the date of the C.F.R. volume through the end of the prior month, look up the regulation in the most recent **List of CFR Sections Affected (LSA)** to locate page numbers in the *Federal Register* reflecting changes to the regulation.

- Look up the *Federal Register* page containing the change and read the information to see how it affects the regulation.

❐ To update from the end of the prior month to the present, use the most current issue of the *Federal Register.*

■ Use the table of **CFR Parts Affected** during the current month in the **Reader Aids** section in the back of the *Federal Register.*

■ If the Part in which the section appears is listed, look up each page number referenced in the table to see if the section has been affected.

4. CONTACT THE AGENCY FOR ADDITIONAL INFORMATION ON RECENT OR PROPOSED REGULATORY CHANGES

ELECTRONIC LEGAL RESEARCH

As Chapter 1 explains, legal research can be accomplished using both print and electronic research tools. Frequently, you will use some combination of these tools in completing a research project. Although print and electronic resources are often used together, this chapter introduces you to some search techniques unique to electronic research. Earlier chapters discussed both print and electronic research in the context of individual types of authority, such as cases or statutes. This chapter explains some of the basics of electronic searching that can be used effectively in a number of services, regardless of the type of authority you need to locate. In doing so, it focuses on research in Westlaw and Lexis, two of the most commonly available commercial services containing a wide variety of legal authority. Although Westlaw and Lexis are featured in this chapter, they are only two of many electronic research services available, and you should be able to adapt the techniques described here to other electronic research services.

This chapter describes electronic search techniques in general terms and provides few specific commands for executing them. Electronic research providers update their services regularly, thus making it impossible to describe commands with any accuracy. In fact, you will likely receive training through your law school on the use of at least Westlaw and Lexis, if not other electronic services, and those training sessions will cover the commands necessary to execute the functions in those services.

Legal research providers strive to make their services as user-friendly as possible. Because most of us search the Internet regularly, legal research providers have tried to make their services feel as familiar as general Internet search engines. Legal research, however, is different from routine Google searching, and it is important to keep those differences in mind when you conduct electronic legal research.

In daily life, you might use the Internet to search for a specific item of information, such as an address or a phone number. You might use one of several largely interchangeable sources to locate generally available information, such as national news or sports scores. You might shop for something by comparing prices and shipping options from a universe of sellers that are largely already familiar to you, such as Amazon.com and BN.com.

These types of searching are different from legal research. The searching you do on a daily basis is often intended to locate a single item of information that meets your needs. In legal research, by contrast, it is rare for a single piece of information to answer your research question. Usually your goal is to identify a relevant group of authorities that you use together to analyze a legal issue. Additionally, the sources of authority in legal research usually are not interchangeable; one case or statute will not be as good as another, and it may be difficult to tell at the beginning of your research process which sources you need to analyze your research issue accurately. You must continue the research process until you know enough to isolate the most relevant authorities, not just any authorities.

The experience you already have with electronic searching will inform your legal research, but it will not transfer completely to legal research. This chapter will explain search techniques and options that will help you build on the search skills you already have so that you can complete your legal research tasks thoroughly and accurately.

A. INTRODUCTION TO ELECTRONIC LEGAL RESEARCH

1. OVERVIEW OF ELECTRONIC LEGAL RESEARCH SERVICES

Electronic legal research services can be divided into three categories. Fee-based services charge individual users a fee every time the service is used. Subscription services charge the subscriber for access, but individual users ordinarily are not charged for researching with the service. Publicly available services are those available for free on the Internet. Appendix A contains the Internet addresses for a number of publicly available research sites, including those discussed in this chapter and elsewhere in this text. A brief overview of some popular electronic legal research services follows.

a. Fee-Based Services

WESTLAW AND LEXIS. Westlaw and Lexis are two of the most commonly available electronic services for conducting legal research. Both of these services contain the full text of a broad range of primary and secondary authorities. As this text goes to press, both are available in two versions: Westlaw.com and WestlawNext, Lexis.com and Lexis Advance.

BLOOMBERG LAW. Bloomberg Law is a relatively new legal research service that provides access to the full text of a range of legal authorities as well as business information. It can be a cost-effective alternative to Westlaw and Lexis. Its coverage of legal information is also less comprehensive than the coverage of Westlaw and Lexis. Bloomberg Law is available on the Internet.

LOISLAWCONNECT. LoislawConnect is similar to Westlaw and Lexis, in that it contains the full text of many legal authorities. It also contains treatises on a number of subjects and has its own citator service, Global-Cite. Although LoislawConnect has less comprehensive coverage than either Westlaw or Lexis, it can be a cost-effective alternative to those services if it contains the information you need. LoislawConnect is available on the Internet.

VERSUSLAW. VersusLaw is similar to LoislawConnect. It also offers access to the full text of a range of legal authorities, and like Loislaw-Connect, it can be a cost-effective alternative to Westlaw and Lexis. Its coverage is also less comprehensive than that of Westlaw and Lexis. VersusLaw is available on the Internet.

FASTCASE AND CASEMAKER. These research services are made available through bar associations and provide access to the full text of a range of legal authorities. One or the other of them may be available through your state bar association.

b. Subscription Services

INDEX TO LEGAL PERIODICALS AND LEGALTRAC. These are index services, meaning that they will generate lists of citations to authorities. Although they primarily provide citations to legal periodicals, they also provide access to the full text of selected documents. These services are described in more detail in Chapter 4.

HEINONLINE. This service provides access to a wide range of authorities, including legal periodicals and other secondary sources; legislative documents, including compiled legislative histories; administrative materials, including the C.F.R. and *Federal Register*; and some international materials. HeinOnline's databases go back further in time than those of some other services. In addition, it provides access to documents in .pdf format. This service is described in more detail in Chapter 4, on secondary source research, and Chapter 8, on federal legislative history research.

PROQUEST CONGRESSIONAL. This service is available at many law libraries. ProQuest Congressional contains a wealth of legislative information, including federal statutes, congressional documents generated during the legislative process, administrative regulations, and news about activities taking place on Capitol Hill. This service is described in more detail in Chapter 8, on federal legislative history research.

SUBJECT-MATTER SERVICES. Some specialty electronic services are devoted to specific areas of the law such as employment law, tax, bankruptcy, and patent law. These providers include Bureau of National Affairs (BNA), CCH, Inc. (CCH), Clark Boardman Callaghan (CBC), Matthew Bender (MB), Pike & Fischer (P & F), and Research Institute of America (RIA). Most originated as print services that were published in three-ring binders and updated with new looseleaf pages, so they are still sometimes called looseleaf services. If you are researching or practicing in a specialized field of law, these services are invaluable resources because they integrate case law, statutes, regulations, and secondary material into a single source. Even as a student, you may be able to subscribe to their news services to obtain regular updates on developments in a field of law. If your law school subscribes to these services, you can access them through the library's portal.

c. Publicly Available Services

WEBSITES OPERATED BY GOVERNMENT OR PRIVATE ENTITIES. Government websites can provide access to local, state, and federal legal information. Some examples of useful sites for federal law include Thomas, which is maintained by the Library of Congress, and the Federal Digital System (FDSys), a site operated by the Government Printing Office. These services are described in Chapters 8 and 9. Many courts also maintain websites where they publish the full text of opinions, local court rules, and other useful information. In addition, websites operated by trade, civic, educational, or other groups may provide useful information in their specialized fields.

LEGAL RESEARCH WEBSITES. A number of Internet sites collect legal information, and these can be useful research sources. Examples of legal research websites include Google Scholar and FindLaw. In addition, several law schools have developed "virtual law library" sites, such as Cornell Law School's Legal Information Institute.

2. OVERVIEW OF THE ELECTRONIC SEARCH PROCESS

When you use electronic research services, you need to follow an organized plan to research effectively. Effective electronic searching usually involves the following four steps.

a. Selecting a Service

You want to choose the service or services most likely to contain the information you need. You need to consider the type of information you need and the scope of coverage of the services available to you. In addition, although you may not be concerned with the cost of research while you are in law school, in practice, selecting a cost-effective service is also an important consideration.

b. Selecting a Search Technique

Once you have selected a service, you will probably have several options for searching for authority. As Chapter 1 explains, most research tools, including most electronic services, organize their content by jurisdiction and type of authority and require you to use a source-driven approach to your research. You may be able to search by subject or execute a word search to locate information within each database. Lexis Advance and WestlawNext also offer the option of content-driven searching, which allows you to search for content before selecting a jurisdiction or type of authority. To search effectively, you must decide which approach is most likely to retrieve the information you need. Chapter 3 describes these two research approaches in more detail.

c. Planning and Executing a Search

After you select a search technique, you need to plan your search. If you use a source-driven approach, you must select a database to search or identify the subject headings you want to research. If you use a content-driven approach, you should determine any criteria by which you can pre-filter your choices (e.g., by jurisdiction). If you use word searching, you must draft a query to search for information. Chapter 2 discusses how to generate and prioritize your search terms. Word searching options are discussed below. Once you have completed the planning process, you are ready to sign on to a service and execute the search.

d. Reviewing and Filtering the Search Results

After you execute a search, you need to manipulate the results in a way that allows you to determine whether the search has been successful. You may need to view a list of documents retrieved, read the text of individual documents, find specific terms within a document, or use links to other documents. You may also need to filter the results to focus on the information most relevant to your research task. Content-driven searching in particular is likely to retrieve a large number of documents. Filtering the results according to the available criteria is critical to analyzing the effectiveness of your search.

In reviewing search results, it is important to pay attention to how the results are displayed. The default display may be by relevance, which means the documents with the best match to your search criteria appear first. "Relevance," however, is a relative concept. A document is likely to be deemed more relevant if the search terms appear frequently in the document or close to each other. The precise criteria for determining relevance varies by service, and the relevancy ranking of documents retrieved from the same search may vary depending on which service you use. You should treat the rankings as an approximation that cannot substitute for your own judgment about the relevance of the documents the search retrieves.

Depending on the service and search technique you use, your search results may not be ranked by relevance. It is common for cases to be listed in reverse date order, statutes in numerical order, and secondary sources in alphabetical order. Because most Internet search engines use relevancy rankings, most of us have been conditioned to review only the first few items in the results to assess the effectiveness of a search. If your results are displayed in a different way, however, the best information from your search could be in the middle or at the end of the search.

The most useful order for displaying search results will depend on your research task. Relevancy ranking is useful when the search retrieves a large number of documents. Reverse date order may be better if you are looking for the most recent authority on an issue. Often you will have the option to change the default order (from date to relevance or from relevance to alphabetical, depending on the source). Regardless of whether you can change the default setting, you must be aware of the order in which the results are listed to assess the effectiveness of the search.

Following these four steps is not always a linear process. You might decide first on your search technique, which could influence the service you select. Even if you follow the steps in order initially, you may repeat some of them based on the search results. For example, after reviewing your search results, you might go back to the second step and select a different search technique. A single search is unlikely to retrieve exactly the desired information, except when you are retrieving a document you need from its citation. One provider offers the following explanation of the search process in the context of word searching:

> Searching is a process, not an event. This should be your mantra when using [electronic research services]. Searching . . . is not about spending time and mental energy formulating the "golden query" that retrieves your desired information in a single stroke. In practice, good online searching involves formulating a succession of queries until you are satisfied with the results. As you view results from one search, you will come across additional leads that

you did not identify in your original search. You can incorporate these new terms into your existing query or create a new one. After each query, evaluate its success by asking:

- Did I find what I was looking for?
- What better information could still be out there?
- How can I refine my query to find better information?

Issuing multiple queries can be frustrating or rewarding, depending on how long it takes you to identify the key material you need to answer your research problem.[1]

3. COST-EFFECTIVE SEARCHING

The cost of electronic research is something you might not notice as a law student because most, if not all, of the cost is subsidized. In practice, however, cost is an important consideration. You cannot use research services for which your client cannot or will not pay. Even if your client is willing and able to pay for some electronic research, you may not have unlimited ability to use fee-based services.

Of course, just because a service is fee-based does not mean it is a bad research option. It can be less expensive to locate authority through a fee-based service than it is to purchase books that would rarely be used, and some tasks can be accomplished more quickly through electronic research. In those situations, increased efficiency can justify the cost of using a fee-based service. You should not shy away from fee-based services simply because using them costs money. You should, however, be aware of cost issues and select the most cost-effective research options for your client, whether they are print or electronic, fee-based or free of charge.

It is difficult to generalize about the cost of fee-based services because many pricing options exist. Generally speaking, use of Westlaw and Lexis will result in the most direct expense to your client. Some large organizations negotiate flat rates for use of these services. But rates are based on the amount of usage, and law firms still pass on the costs to clients. Charges can also be based on the amount of time spent online, the number of searches executed, or both. Premiums may be charged for accessing certain sources, especially those containing multiple types of authority, and separate charges for printing or downloading information also may apply. You can view pricing information in WestlawNext by reviewing the **Subscriber Pricing Guide** under the **Tools** tab. In Lexis

---

[1] VersusLaw, Inc. Research Manual, Part 1, Electronic Searching Strategy, www.versuslaw.com; *select* FAQ/Help, Research Manual, Research Manual Part 1—Search Basics (accessed January 29, 2012).

Advance, pricing information is available from the **Help** link at the top of the screen. Other fee-based services charge for use of their services as well, but their rates are generally lower than those for Westlaw and Lexis. You can view pricing information for these services on their websites.

Because pricing varies widely among fee-based services, it is important to investigate cost issues before you get online. When you work in a law office, you may be required to use a service such as Fastcase or Casemaker before you are permitted to research with Westlaw or Lexis. If the office has a large print collection, you may be required to use some material in print instead of accessing it from a fee-based service.

Subscription and publicly available services are economical choices for your client if they will give you the information you need. Although charges for access to subscription services are usually paid by the subscriber rather than the user, users can be charged for printing or downloading information. Publicly available services on the Internet are the least expensive option because they involve only the cost of access to the Internet.

The following strategies can help you conduct cost-effective research:

a. Generate Search Terms and Plan Your Research Path in Advance

One of the best ways to cut costs is to draft your word searches and plan your research path before you get online. No matter how you are being billed, a thoughtful search strategy defined before you sign on is more likely to lead to useful results. This involves thinking about your search terms and deciding which databases to search or how to pre-filter your search.

Most electronic services require you to select a database before you execute a search. Deciding in advance which databases you plan to search will allow you to search quickly and efficiently. Searching the narrowest database that meets your research needs makes evaluating your search results easier, which in turn reduces the amount of time you spend online. In addition, Westlaw.com and Lexis.com charge a premium for access to databases that contain multiple types of authority, such as those containing all federal or state cases. Determining which databases have the most appropriate information for your search, instead of automatically searching in the premium databases, will make your research more cost effective.

b. Use Research Assistance

Another way to cut costs is to use the research assistance provided by the service. For example, Westlaw and Lexis employ research attorneys to provide assistance to users. You can obtain live help online or telephone assistance through their toll-free numbers. If you are unsure about whether your strategy is likely to be effective, you may want to contact the provider for assistance. The research attorneys will help you create searches to maximize the effectiveness of your research.

c. Execute Searches to Account for the Billing Structure

Once you have signed on to a research service some search options may be more cost effective than others. If you are being charged by the amount of time you spend online, you want to work as quickly as possible to minimize your costs. In that situation, it is especially important that you plan your research before you sign on because you do not want to spend time thinking up your search once you have started accruing charges.

If you are being charged by the number of searches you execute, you will often be able to modify your initial search at no additional cost. In that case, you may want to devise relatively broad searches, along with potential narrowing modifications. You can then execute the broad searches, browse the results, and execute modifications to narrow the results if necessary. This will be more cost effective than executing a series of new searches.

d. Determine Charges for Printing or Downloading Information

Separate charges may apply to downloading or printing documents. Even while you are in law school, there may be limits to the amount of printing you can do without charge. Therefore, whether you are at work or at school, be sure to investigate printing and downloading costs before you get online.

B. EFFECTIVE WORD SEARCHING

Most electronic research providers offer multiple ways to locate information. Citation and subject searching are discussed in more detail in the chapters devoted to individual types of authority. This section explains techniques for effective word searching that you can use to search for many kinds of authority.

Effective word searching requires an understanding of the types of word searches you can conduct. Understanding these options will help you select the type of word searching best suited to your research task, modify the default result display to highlight the most relevant information, and filter the results of the search effectively.

1. TYPES OF WORD SEARCHES

When you execute a word search, the search engine searches a database of documents and retrieves the documents that meet the criteria you set for the search. To do this, the search engine uses an algorithm, or set of rules, to evaluate the search criteria and the documents in the database. A literal search algorithm searches for documents that contain the specific terms in your word search. A non-literal search algorithm also searches for documents that contain the search terms, but it does not limit the result to those documents. It uses the search terms to search background information or meta-data and includes in the results documents that appear relevant to the search terms even though they do not contain those terms. Legal research services use three types of search algorithms: terms and connectors (also called Boolean), natural language, and descriptive term.

A terms and connectors search is a literal search. It identifies documents containing the precise terms you identify, in the precise relationships you request. For example, you could search for documents that contain both the phrase *"ice cream"* and the term *sundae*. Alternatively, you could search for documents that contain either the phrase *"ice cream"* or the term *sundae*, but not necessarily both. AND and OR are examples of connectors, which are the commands that define the relationships among the search terms. A list of the most commonly used commands appears in **Figure 10.1**.

Because you use commands to steer the search logic, you can control the search results more precisely than you can with other search algorithms. If you search for *"ice cream" /s sundae*, the search will retrieve only documents that contain the phrase "ice cream" in the same sentence as sundae; if a document contains "ice cream" and sundae but not within the same sentence, that document will not appear in the search results. The search may retrieve any number of documents, or no documents at all, depending on the number of documents that meet the search criteria. Lexis, Westlaw, and most other legal research providers offer the option of terms and connectors searching. More information on specific terms and connectors commands appears below.

A natural language search is also a literal search. Unlike a terms and connectors search, a natural language search does not require you to specify the relationships among the terms in the documents retrieved. Instead, a natural language search uses embedded rules to evaluate the relationships among the search terms, which it then uses to determine which documents meet the search criteria. A natural language search for *ice cream sundae* will retrieve documents that contain all or some of those terms and will rank the results by relevance. Documents in which the terms appear frequently or close together will be ranked higher than documents that contain only one of the search terms.

FIGURE 10.1   COMMON TERMS AND CONNECTORS COMMANDS

Alternative terms	Term1 **or** Term2
All terms	Term1 **and** Term2
Terms with grammatical proximity	Term1 **/p** Term2 (Term1 appears within the same paragraph as Term2) Term1 **/s** Term2 (Term1 appears within the same sentence as Term2)
Terms with numerical proximity	Term1 **/n** Term2 (Term1 appears within a certain number of words of Term2; **n**= a specific number)
Exclude terms	Term1 **but not** Term2 (Westlaw) Term1 **and not** Term2 (Lexis)
Expand terms	Exclamation point (**!**) for variable word endings (Term! retrieves Term, Terms, Termed, Terming, Terminal, Terminable, and all other variations of the word) (Westlaw and Lexis) Asterisk (*****) for variable letters (Te*m retrieves Term, Team, and Teem) (Westlaw and Lexis)

A natural language search often (but not always) retrieves a predetermined number of documents. For example, if the search is set up to retrieve 100 documents, the results will include 100 documents as long as each document contains at least one of the search terms. If only 75 documents contain the search terms, the search will retrieve 75 documents. It would be unusual for a natural language search to retrieve no documents, although this can happen when your search consists of terms that do not appear in any documents in the database. Lexis, Westlaw, and most other legal research providers offer the option of natural language searching, and natural language searching is often the default search option. Lexis.com also offers a simplified form of natural language searching called Easy Search.

A descriptive term search, as that term is used in this text, refers to a variation of natural language searching that is non-literal. It uses embedded rules to evaluate which documents meet the search criteria, but it searches both the text of the documents in the database and meta-data associated with the documents. In addition to retrieving documents that contain the search terms, therefore, it can also retrieve documents that appear relevant according to the embedded search rules even though they do not contain the search terms. It is extremely rare for a descriptive terms search to retrieve no documents. WestlawNext and Google Scholar have descriptive term search engines. To identify relevant documents, a Westlaw Next descriptive terms search looks for your search terms within document text, but then it also searches West topics and key numbers (described in Chapter 5), KeyCite data (described in Chapter 6), and retrieval data from other users who have executed similar searches.

2. COMPARING WORD SEARCH OPTIONS

Your search results can vary substantially depending on whether you use terms and connectors, natural language, or descriptive terms searching. Understanding the results each type of search produces will help you choose the search method best suited to your research task. The research scenario introduced in Chapter 2 provides an example to illustrate the differences among the search methods:

> Your client recently ended a long-term relationship with her partner. She and her partner never participated in a formal marriage ceremony, but they had always planned to get married "someday." They lived together for five years and referred to each other as husband and wife. Your client and her former partner orally agreed to provide support for each other, and your client's former partner repeatedly made statements like, "What's mine is yours." Your client wants to know if she is entitled to part of the value of the assets her former partner acquired during their relationship or to any support payments.

One legal theory you might want to investigate in connection with this scenario is palimony, which is a claim for support made by an unmarried partner after the dissolution of a romantic relationship. It is similar to alimony granted after a divorce. If you execute a search for the term *palimony* in Florida case law, the results will vary depending on the type of word search you conduct. The results of the searches are summarized in **Figure 10.2**.[2]

A terms and connectors search for *palimony* in Westlaw retrieves the five cases listed in **Figure 10.2**. The same search in Lexis retrieves the same five cases, plus an additional unpublished opinion. All of these cases contain the term *palimony*.

---

[2] The search results described in this section are current as of February 1, 2012. The results you get if you execute these searches may vary somewhat over time as new Florida cases are decided. Additionally, the Lexis Advance search engine is relatively new. Its search capabilities have evolved since it was first introduced, and changes to its functionality after this text is published could affect the search results.

FIGURE 10.2 PALIMONY SEARCH RESULTS COMPARISON

Service	Westlaw.com and WestlawNext	Lexis.com and Lexis Advance	WestlawNext	Google Scholar
Search Type	terms and connectors and natural language	terms and connectors and natural language	descriptive term	descriptive term
Results (listed by relevance according to the search service's criteria)	1. Crossen v. Feldman 2. Evans v. Wall 3. Lowry v. Lowry 4. Gilvary v. Gilvary 5. Posik v. Layton	1. Crossen v. Feldman 2. Evans v. Wall 3. Posik v. Layton 4. Gilvary v. Gilvary 5. Lowry v. Lowry 6. Evans v. Wall (unpublished opinion)	1. Posik v. Layton 2. Crossen v. Feldman 3. Evans v. Wall 4. Poe v. Levy's Estate* 5. Dietrich v. Winters* 6. Bashaway v. Cheney Bros., Inc.* 7. Collier v. Brooks* 8. Lowry v. Lowry 9. Forrest v. Ron* 10. Gilvary v. Gilvary 11. Harrison v. Pritchett* 12. McLane v. Musick* 13. Stevens v. Muse* 14. Tobin & Tobin Ins. Agency, Inc. v. Zeskind* 15. Addison v. Brown* 16. Tyson v. State* 17. Hoffman v. Kohns* 18. Campo v. Tafur* 19. Jarrell v. Jarrell* 20. Newberger v. Newberger*	1. Crossen v. Feldman 2. Evans v. Wall 3. Posik v. Layton 4. Stevens v. Muse* 5. Poe v. Levy's Estate* 6. Gilvary v. Gilvary 7. Lowry v. Lowry 8. Eberhardt v. Eberhardt*

Marked cases (*) do not contain the search term *palimony*.

You get the same results from a natural language search in Westlaw .com, Lexis Advance, or Lexis.com, as well as from an Easy Search search in Lexis.com (although the relevancy rankings differ slightly). This is because the search consists of only one term, and the literal natural language search retrieves only documents that contain the search term. Adding even one additional term (e.g., *palimony support*) increases the search results in Westlaw.com and Lexis.com to the predetermined number of results, usually 100 cases. All of the additional cases retrieved contain only the term *support*, not the term *palimony*. In Lexis Advance, the revised search—*palimony support*—retrieves almost 70,000 cases because there is no limit on the number of documents in the search result, but again, all of the additional cases contain only the term *support*, not *palimony*.

A descriptive term search for the term *palimony* in WestlawNext retrieves 20 cases: five that contain the term *palimony* (and were in the Westlaw.com search results) plus 15 more that do not contain the term *palimony*. The cases are listed in **Figure 10.2**. WestlawNext retrieved the additional 15 cases because the meta-data they contain indicated that they met the embedded rules for relevance to the search term. A review of the cases reveals that several of them share a common topic heading on informal or invalid marriage, and several of them cite or are cited by the cases that contain the term *palimony*. WestlawNext used these and other criteria to connect the cases to the search term, and most of the additional 15 cases are, in fact, indirectly related to palimony. Several of them concern parties seeking property or support from a former partner or discuss doctrines that have some overlap with palimony, such as constructive trust. A few simply are not relevant.

When only a few documents contain your search terms, documents that do not contain the search terms but that nevertheless meet certain relevancy criteria appear in the WestlawNext search results. The relevance of documents that do not contain any of your search terms may be low, however, so WestlawNext limits these search results to 20 documents. If more than 20 documents had contained the term *palimony*, WestlawNext would not have limited the results to 20 documents. But WestlawNext does place some limits on the number of documents it retrieves. One limit is based on relevance. This limit is not a set number. Once the relevance of the documents containing the search terms gets too low, WestlawNext eliminates them from the search results. WestlawNext also places an outer limit on the number of documents in the search results. It will not retrieve more than 10,000 documents in any single category of authority (e.g., cases, statutes, secondary sources).

A descriptive term search in Google Scholar retrieves the eight cases listed in **Figure 10.2**. The results include the same five cases the literal searches retrieved and three additional cases that do not contain the search term but that contain meta-data connecting them to the search term. Google Scholar does not search the same meta-data that Westlaw-Next does and its coverage of state cases does not go back as far in time. This is why it retrieves fewer cases than WestlawNext even though it uses a non-literal search algorithm. Google Scholar does not appear to limit the search results for cases that meet the relevancy criteria based only on meta-data.

Which results are best? The answer depends on your research task. If you only want to retrieve cases that discuss palimony, the literal search results are better suited to your task because you will not have to sort through cases that do not specifically discuss palimony. If you are interested in learning about any claims the client might bring, the non-literal search results may suit your needs better because they may point you toward other legal theories that you had not considered. In a sense, the non-literal search results mimic the results you might get if you looked up a term in a print index and used cross-references to direct you to related topics.

The results in **Figure 10.2** are listed by relevance. You can see that different services ranked the relevance of the documents differently. If the results were listed in reverse date order, they would appear as follows: *Posik v. Layton*; *Crossen v. Feldman*; *Givalry v. Givalry*; *Evans v. Wall*; *Lowry v. Lowry*. These differences do not matter much in a search that retrieves only a few documents, but they can matter a lot in a search that retrieves 50, 100, or 1,000 documents. This simply serves to emphasize the importance of being aware of the way the results are ordered and of treating the relevancy rankings as approximate, rather than definitive.

3. EXECUTING, NARROWING, AND REVIEWING WORD SEARCHES IN LEXIS AND WESTLAW

Lexis and Westlaw allow you to execute a word search as your initial search for documents or as a narrowing search within your initial search results. This section discusses specific features of word searches in each of these services.

a. Lexis.com

In Lexis.com, the options for executing your initial search as a terms and connectors, natural language, or Easy Search search appear on the search screen. In a terms and connectors search, words typed in a sequence with no connector will be treated as a search phrase. Thus, a search for *ice cream* is a search for the exact phrase *ice cream*. The results of a terms and connectors search will be listed in reverse date order for cases, numerical order for statutes, and alphabetical order for many secondary sources. Natural language and Easy Search results are listed according to relevance. You can change these default settings using the **Sort by** options.

Once you execute your initial search, you can narrow the results with the **FOCUS™ Terms** function, which allows you to execute a search within the results. A **FOCUS™ Terms** search will be a terms and connectors search even if your initial search was natural language or Easy Search.

b. Lexis Advance

Lexis Advance will ordinarily treat a search typed into the search box as a natural language search. Lexis Advance automatically interprets many common legal phrases as phrases, rather than as individual search terms. For words that Lexis Advance does not recognize as a phrase, the search algorithm searches each term separately as an individual word. Thus, it treats a search for *ice cream* as a search for *ice OR cream*, which is why a Lexis Advance search can retreive tens of thousands or even hundreds of thousands of documents. You can create a search phrase by putting the search terms in quotation marks.

Although Lexis Advance treats most searches as natural language searches, terms and connectors searching is also an option. Entering a search that incorporates terms and connectors search commands (such as the */p*, or */s* conectors) will cause Lexis Advance to execute the search as a terms and connectors search. The **Search Tips** link in the search box shows the connectors Lexis Advance recognizes. **Search Tips** also contains a template you can use to create a terms and connectors search.

The default display for the search results is by relevance. You can change the default display setting using the **Sort by** options.

Once you execute your initial search, you can re-run it as a terms and connectors search by selecting that choice in the **Options** menu. You can also narrow the search results using the criteria in the **Narrow by** menu. If you use **Search within results**, the search will be a terms and connectors search even if your initial search was a natural language search.

c. Westlaw.com

In Westlaw.com, the options for executing your initial search as a terms and connectors or natural language search appear in the tabs above the search box. In a terms and connectors search, Westlaw.com inserts the *or* connector between words typed in a sequence. Thus, it treats a search for *ice cream* as a search for *ice OR cream*. To create a search phrase, place the terms in quotation marks. The results of a terms and connectors search will be listed in reverse date order for cases, numerical order for statutes, and alphabetical order for many secondary sources. You can change the default setting on the **Preferences** page under **Search**. Natural language results are listed according to relevance.

Once you execute your initial search, you can narrow the results with the **Locate** function, which allows you to execute a search within the results. A **Locate** search will be a terms and connectors search even if your initial search was a natural language search.

d. WestlawNext

WestlawNext will ordinarily treat a search typed into the search box as a descriptive term search. Even when you put your search terms in quotation marks, the search algorithm searches each term separately. Thus, it treats the search for both *ice cream* and *"ice cream"* the same way. The search algorithm recognizes many common legal phrases. If you search for a common legal phrase, the results may show only documents containing the phrase (as opposed to documents that contain one or more of the terms separately) because the results displayed are subject to relevancy limitations. In other words, although the search for *"ice cream"* searches each term separately, the search results may only display documents that contain the phrase *ice cream* and omit documents that contain only the term *ice* or only the term *cream* if the algorithm recognizes *ice cream* as a phrase.

Although WestlawNext treats most searches as descriptive terms searches, terms and connectors searching is also an option. Entering a search that incorporates a grammatical, numerical, or exclusion connector or a term expander (see **Figure 10.1**) will automatically cause WestlawNext to execute the search as a terms and connectors search. In a terms and connectors search, placing words in quotation marks creates a search phrase. The **Advanced** link in the search box brings up a template you can use to create a terms and connectors search, or you can type *advanced:* followed by a search to execute it as a terms and connectors search. The search results are ranked by relevance, but you can change the default setting using the **Sort by** options.

Once you execute your initial search, you can narrow the search results using the filtering options in the **View** menu. If you use **Search within results**, the search will be a terms and connectors search even if your initial search was a descriptive term search.

4. TERMS AND CONNECTORS SEARCH COMMANDS

Terms and connectors searching is useful as an initial search strategy when you want to control the relationships among the search terms. It is also the form of searching you must use when you execute a narrowing search within the initial search results. Therefore, you need to understand how to use terms and connectors searching.

a. Terms and Connectors Search Logic

In terms and connectors searching, you define the relationships among the terms in the search using connectors and other commands. **Figure 10.1** lists the most commonly used commands.

Most searches contain several terms and may contain multiple connectors. When the search is executed, Boolean logic will process the connectors in a specific sequence. In Westlaw and Lexis, the OR connector is processed first, followed by the numerical and grammatical proximity connectors (/N, /P, /S), the AND connector, and finally, the exclusion connectors (AND NOT, BUT NOT). It is important to understand this hierarchy of connectors to create an effective search.

If you executed a search for *ice AND cream OR sundae*, the search for the terms *cream or sundae* would be processed first. After documents with one or the other of those terms were identified, the search for the term *ice* would begin. In effect, the query would be processed as a search for *ice and cream or ice and sundae*. If this was not the intended search, it could miss documents containing the terms you want or retrieve irrelevant documents.

There are two ways to modify this search so that it searches for the phrase *"ice cream"* or the individual term *sundae*. One is by searching for *"ice cream"* as a phrase instead of connecting the words with AND.

Another way to vary the search would be to segregate the *ice AND cream* portion of the search. In Westlaw or Lexis, you can accomplish this by placing a portion of the search in parentheses: *(ice AND cream) OR sundae*. The terms within parentheses would be treated as a separate unit. Thus, the AND connector would apply only to the terms within the parentheses. In this example, adding parentheses would result in a search for the terms *ice AND cream* as a unit, and then in the alternative, for the individual term *sundae*.

b. Using Terms and Connectors for an Initial Search

When you use terms and connectors searching for your initial search, you will want to follow three steps:

- developing the initial search terms;
- expanding the breadth and depth of the search;
- adding connectors to clarify the relationships among the search terms.

In developing the initial search terms, you should use the process described in Chapter 2. Think about the problem in terms of the parties, any places or things, potential claims and defenses, and the relief sought.

Having identified the relevant terms, your next step would be expanding the search. Recall that a terms and connectors search is a literal search. If an object, idea, concept, or action is expressed in a document using terms different from your search terms, a terms and connectors search will not locate the document. Unless you are searching for terms of art that need to appear precisely for a document to be useful, you need to expand the breadth and depth of the search, as explained in Chapter 2.

Expanding the breadth of the search involves generating synonyms and terms related to the initial search terms. You can also expand the breadth of an individual term by using a term expander, such as the asterisk (*) to substitute for individual letters and the exclamation point (!) to substitute for variable word endings. (Although many services use term expander characters, the functions of the characters are not standard. For example, the asterisk (*) in some services is used for variable word endings, not the exclamation point (!). You should review the search commands in any service with which you are unfamiliar.) Expanding the depth involves expressing the terms with varying degrees of abstraction.

Once you have developed and expanded the search terms, the next step is identifying the appropriate relationships among the terms using connectors. The closer the connections you require among the terms, the more restrictive the search will be, and the broader the connections, the more open the search will be. For example, the AND connector, which requires only that both words appear somewhere within the same document, will retrieve more documents than a proximity connector such as /P, which requires the words to appear within the same paragraph. Be sure to take the hierarchy of connectors into account as you consider the relationships among the search terms. If necessary, use parentheses to group categories of terms that you want to search together.

In addition to allowing you to search for terms within the body of a document, many services will allow you to limit your search to individual components of the document, such as words in the title or the name of the author. Although you will not always use this search option, it is an important feature to understand.

In Westlaw, the document components are called "fields"; in Lexis .com, they are called "segments." Westlaw.com, WestlawNext, and Lexis .com will allow you to add field or segment restrictions using menu options or by typing commands into the search. As this text goes to press, Lexis Advance does not offer a segment searching option, although it may be added in the future.

Although you can make a terms and connectors search very specific by using multiple search commands, an effective terms and connectors search does not have to use all or even most of the available commands. The structure and complexity of any search will depend on the nature of the information you need. The important thing is to know what the commands are so you can use them to steer the search engine to retrieve information relevant to your research task.

c. Using Terms and Connectors as a Narrowing Search

Even if you use natural language or descriptive term searching for your initial search, a search within the search results in Westlaw or Lexis will be a terms and connectors search. The way you draft the narrowing search will depend on how you want to filter the search results. Three ways you may want to narrow the search results include:

- adding terms that were not part of the initial search;
- focusing on terms that were part of the initial search;
- changing the relationships among terms that were part of the initial search.

The results of your initial search will depend in part on the level of abstraction of your search terms. If you execute a broad search for a general concept, you will likely retrieve many documents. You may want to narrow the results by adding more specific terms. For example, the doctrine of assumption of risk is a defense to a negligence claim. If you were researching assumption of risk in the context of rock climbing accidents, you might begin your research by looking more abstractly for material related to assumption of risk in sports or recreation. If that search retrieved too many documents to be useful, you could then execute a narrowing search for authority that specifically discusses rock climbing.

To use terms and connectors commands effectively in this context, the narrowing search could include *"rock climbing"* as a search phrase. You could also search for the terms in proximity to one another with a term expander to capture variations on the word *climb*. Thus, the narrowing search might look like this: *rock /5 climb!* This search would retrieve documents in which the term *rock* appears within five words before or after any variation of the word *climb* (climb, climbs, climber, climbed, climbing).

Another way to narrow the search results is by focusing on terms that were part of your initial search. If you execute a search for several alternative terms and retrieve too many documents, narrowing the search to focus on one or two specific terms will limit the search results.

A third way to narrow the search results is to use terms and connectors commands to change the relationships among the words in the search. The AND connector will limit the results by identifying documents that contain all of the specific terms instead of only one. Using the grammatical or numerical connectors (/P, /S, /N) to target documents that contain the terms close together is another good strategy. The exclusion connectors (AND NOT, BUT NOT) are useful when you have a term that is relevant when used in one context but not relevant in others. By excluding documents that contain terms associated with the irrelevant context, you can target more relevant documents.

C. ADDITIONAL ELECTRONIC RESEARCH RESOURCES

1. ALERT OR CLIPPING SERVICES

Sometimes your work on a research project will be done in a few days, but other times it will extend over a longer period of time. In law school, you might work on a moot court brief or scholarly paper for several weeks or even an entire semester. In legal practice, work on individual cases often extends over months or years. When you are working on an issue over a period of time, one electronic resource that may be useful to you is an alert or clipping service. These services automatically run searches through electronic databases and notify you when relevant new information is added to a database. These services allow you to stay up-to-date on developments affecting your research while you are working on a project.

Many news services offer automatic updates on general news topics and current events. Providers of legal information also frequently offer alert or clipping services. Free services, such as Law.com, offer free daily updates on top legal stories. Fee-based services will often allow you to draft specific queries to update your research on a schedule you specify. You can specify the database(s) in which to run the search, the frequency with which the search is to be run, and the manner in which the search results will be delivered to you. Once you access the service, a menu of options will set out the choices available to you.

Westlaw offers several alert services. The two that are most likely to be of use to you in law school are KeyCite Alert and WestClip. KeyCite Alert, which is described in Chapter 6 on citators, notifies you when new information is added to the KeyCite entries for cases, statutes, federal regulations, or certain federal administrative agency decisions. WestClip allows you to draft a word search to be run periodically in the database(s) you specify and delivers the search results to you. In Westlaw.com, you can create a WestClip entry after you run a search by clicking on the **Add Search to WestClip** link at the top of the list of citations. You can access WestClip without first running a search from the **Alert Center** link in the top right corner of the screen or from the **Site Map**. In WestlawNext, use the **Alert Center** link under the **Tools** tab. Note, however, that WestClip works only with terms and connectors searches, not natural language or descriptive term searches.

Lexis also has two alert services. Shepard's Alert® is similar to Key-Cite Alert and is also described in Chapter 6. It notifies you when new information is added to the Shepard's entries for cases, statutes, or federal regulations. After you Shepardize a document use the **Save as Shepard's Alert** link in Lexis.com or the **Create an Alert** link in Lexis Advance. Lexis also has a service similar to WestClip that is called simply Alerts. It runs your search at specified intervals and delivers the search results to you. You must run a search before you can save it as an Alerts entry. In Lexis.com, run a search and click on the **Save as Alert** link at the top of the screen. In Lexis Advance, run a search, use the **Options** link, and select **Create an Alert**. In Lexis.com, the Alert function works only with terms and connectors searches, not natural language or Easy Search queries.

Other services also offer clipping services. You should look for alert or clipping services in any electronic resource you use.

2. PUBLICLY AVAILABLE INTERNET SOURCES

Legal research used to be accomplished primarily, if not exclusively, in a limited universe of research sources produced by legal publishers. As more and more information becomes available via the Internet, however, the range of sources available for researching legal issues continues to grow. Government, educational, non-profit, trade, and civic organizations that are engaged in public education efforts make useful information on many areas of the law available via their websites. In addition, blogs are becoming an increasingly important source of information both in our culture as a whole and in legal research. Law-related blogs are sometimes called blawgs.

Publicly available Internet sources are most likely to be useful to you when you are looking for information on a specific topic. If you find a relevant website or blog, it may provide you with background information on the topic, references to significant legal authorities, news about legislative initiatives pending at the local, state, or federal level, and links to other sites with useful information.

Publicly available Internet sources are simply new types of secondary sources. When viewed this way, their role in legal research becomes clear. The caveats described in Chapter 4, on secondary source research in more traditional legal sources, also apply to publicly available websites: Use them to obtain background information on an area of law and to obtain citations to primary authority. Do not rely on them as authoritative sources of legal rules or as official sources of primary authority.

To make sure you use publicly available Internet sources appropriately, you should follow four steps: (1) locate useful information; (2) assess the credibility of the source of the information; (3) save or print a copy of the information you are using; and (4) verify and update any legal authorities you locate through the source. In the following discussion of these four steps, you will find references to Internet sites that may be useful to you. The Internet addresses for all these sites appear in Appendix A at the end of this text.

To locate useful information, you could use a general search engine, such as Google, or a specialized search engine, such as Google Scholar for scholarly publications or LawCrawler for law-related websites. You can also use a directory such as Blawg, a directory of law-related blogs.

Once you have located useful information, you must assess the credibility of the source. Anyone can post information on the Internet. Much information available on the Internet is inaccurate or out of date. Many individuals and groups post information on the Internet to advance their social or policy agendas. Therefore, you need to make a separate assessment of how much weight to give to information posted on an individual's or organization's website. The sites you visit should contain information you can use to assess the sources' credibility. Most sites sponsored by organizations or entities include information about the group, such as its history and mission. The authors of many blogs will provide biographical information to help you assess their expertise.

If you find useful information on the Internet, be sure to save or print a copy of the page. Internet sites can change at any moment; the information most helpful to you could change or disappear altogether at any time. If you find that information you accessed earlier is no longer available, you can try to find it in an Internet archive, such as the Internet Archive Wayback Machine, which stores copies of sites for future reference. The University of North Texas library system also hosts the Cybercemetery of Former Federal Web Sites. Although these sites provide limited historical records of Internet sites, you cannot count on finding an archived version of a web page that has been changed, moved, or deleted. The better practice, therefore, is to save or print useful information as you locate it.

If you find references to legal authorities through publicly available websites, the last step is verifying and updating your research. You should not assume that the authorities you have located are correct, complete, or up-to-date. Use the information you have found as a springboard into more traditional avenues of legal research to make sure that you have located all pertinent information and that the legal authority you cite is authoritative.

D. CITING AUTHORITY OBTAINED FROM ELECTRONIC LEGAL RESEARCH SERVICES

Much of the information you locate through electronic services will also be available in print format. Both the *ALWD Manual* (4th ed.) and the *Bluebook* (19th ed.) require that you cite the print format if possible. This is not as difficult as it might seem. Many electronic services provide all the information you need for a print citation, including page numbers. For cases, statutes, and other materials available only in electronic format, the following rules apply. This chapter does not contain complete explanations about citing cases, statutes, and other authorities. More information about citing each of these types of authority is included in the chapters devoted to those sources.

1. CASES

Citations to cases available only in Westlaw or Lexis are similar, but not identical, in *ALWD Manual* and *Bluebook* format. *ALWD Manual* Rule 12.12 provides that the citation must contain the following three components: (1) the case name; (2) the database identifier, including the year, the name of the database, and the unique document number; and (3) a parenthetical containing the jurisdiction and court abbreviations and the full date. A pinpoint reference can be provided with "at *" and the page number. The *ALWD Manual* permits, but does not require, the docket number. Here is an example:

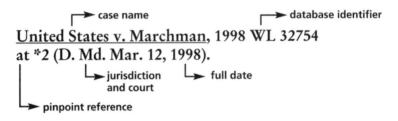

A *Bluebook* citation is the same, except that Bluepages B4.1.4 requires the docket number for the case and a comma before the pinpoint reference. Here is an example:

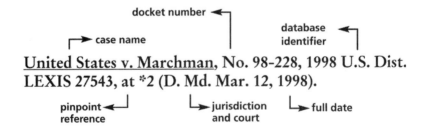

2. STATUTES

Statutory provisions retrieved from Westlaw or Lexis should be cited the same way print materials are cited, with additional information in the parenthetical indicating which electronic service was accessed and the date through which the service was updated. Electronic statutory citations are covered in *ALWD Manual* Rule 14.5 and *Bluebook* Rules 12.5 and 18.3.2. The examples in the *Bluebook* and the *ALWD Manual* use slightly different wording to convey the updating information. Also, the *Bluebook* examples spell out Westlaw, whereas the *ALWD Manual* abbreviates it WL. Otherwise, the citations are the same using either format. Here is an example in *ALWD Manual* format:

18 U.S.C.A. § 2725 (West, WL current through Pub. L. No. 112-71).

Here is an example in *Bluebook* format:

N.Y. Penal Law § 190.05 (McKinney, LEXIS through 2011 released Chapters 1-54, 57-596).

3. MATERIALS AVAILABLE ON THE INTERNET

Both the *ALWD Manual* and the *Bluebook* discourage citations to information on the Internet if it is available in print form because of the transient nature of many Internet sites. If you are citing something available in both print and electronic form that you obtained from an electronic source, both the *ALWD Manual* and the *Bluebook* generally require that you provide the print citation, supplemented with additional information indicating the electronic source.

In the *ALWD Manual*, Rule 38 provides general guidance on citing electronic sources, and Rule 40 covers citations to information available only on the Internet. According to Rule 40, a citation to an authority available only via the Internet consists of up to five components: (1) the author of the item or owner of the website; (2) the title of the item, underlined or italicized; (3) a pinpoint reference if one is available; (4) the URL; and (5) the date, which could be the date of the item, the date the site was updated, or the date you accessed the site, depending on the material you are citing. Here is an example of a citation to a news report in *ALWD Manual* format:

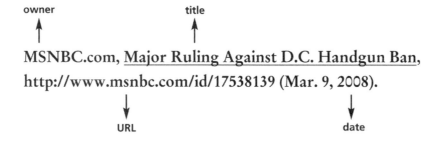

In the *Bluebook*, information on Internet citations appears in Rule 18.2. Rule 18.2.1 provides general guidance on citing information

available on the Internet. The rest of Rule 18.2 discusses how to construct different types of Internet citations. To cite a source available only via the Internet in *Bluebook* format, you must combine the requirements of Rule 18.2.1 with those in 18.2.2-18.2.3. The *Bluebook* does not provide specific formats for Internet citations to all forms of authority. In many cases, you will need to format the citation by analogizing to the rules applicable to similar print sources.

For example, an Internet news report is analogous to a print newspaper article. Applying the principles in Rule 18.2, as well as those for newspaper articles in Bluepages B9.1.4, you could cite the news report this way:

E. CHECKLIST FOR ELECTRONIC LEGAL RESEARCH

1. SELECT AN ELECTRONIC RESEARCH SERVICE

❏ Consider the scope of coverage of the service.
❏ Consider the cost of the service.

2. SELECT A SEARCH TECHNIQUE

❏ Retrieve a document from its citation.
❏ Execute a source-driven search by selecting a database and executing a word search or searching by subject.
❏ Execute a content-driven search by pre-filtering by jurisdiction (if possible), executing a word search, and filtering the results.

3. PLAN AND EXECUTE A SEARCH

❏ For word searches, consider the search options:

- Terms and connectors (Boolean) searching is literal and uses specific commands to define the relationships among search terms.
- Natural language searching is literal and uses embedded rules to define the relationships among search terms.
- Descriptive term searching is non-literal and uses embedded rules both to define the relationships among search terms and to search document meta-data.

❏ In Westlaw and Lexis, be aware of the differences among search algorithms and default search options and tailor your search approach accordingly.
❏ Use terms and connectors searching effectively in an initial search:

- Develop the initial search terms.
- Expand the breadth and depth of the search.
- Specify the relationships among the terms using connectors.
- Use a field or segment restriction to target useful authorities.

4. REVIEW AND FILTER SEARCH RESULTS

❏ Relevance, date, or other result ranking choices affect which documents appear at the top of the search results.
❏ Narrowing searches will be terms and connectors searches even if the initial search is not; use terms and connectors commands to:

- Add search terms.
- Focus on terms in the initial search.
- Change the relationships among terms in the initial search.

5. USE ADDITIONAL TOOLS FOR EFFECTIVE ELECTRONIC RESEARCH

❑ Use an alert or clipping service to keep research up to date.

- In Westlaw, use KeyCite Alert and WestClip.
- In Lexis, use Shepard's Alert® and Alerts.

❑ Use publicly available Internet sources.

- Locate useful sites to obtain background information on a topic or citations to primary authority.
- Assess the credibility of the source.
- Save or print copies of useful pages.
- Verify and update any legal authorities you locate.

CHAPTER 11

DEVELOPING A RESEARCH PLAN

A. INTRODUCTION TO RESEARCH PLANNING

When you get a research assignment, you might be tempted to begin the project by jumping directly into your research to see what authority you can find. In fact, searching for authority right away is not the best way to start. Thought and planning before you begin researching will help you in several ways. You will research more efficiently if you have a coherent research plan to follow. You will also research more accurately. Searching haphazardly can cause you to miss important authorities, and nothing is more disconcerting than feeling as though you came across relevant authority by accident. Following an organized plan will help ensure that you check all the appropriate places for authority on your issue and will give you confidence that your research is correct and complete.

B. CREATING A RESEARCH PLAN

Creating a research plan requires three steps: (1) obtaining preliminary information about the problem; (2) planning the steps in your research; and (3) working effectively in the library and online. Each of these steps is discussed in turn.

1. OBTAINING PRELIMINARY INFORMATION

When you first receive a research assignment, you might feel like you do not know enough to ask very many questions about it. While this might be true as far as the substance of the problem is concerned, you need to determine the scope of your project by obtaining some preliminary information from the person making the assignment. Specifically:

■ **HOW MUCH TIME DO I HAVE FOR THIS ASSIGNMENT?**
The amount of time you have affects your overall approach, as well as your time management with other projects you have been assigned.

■ **WHAT FINAL WORK PRODUCT SHOULD I PRODUCE?**
You should determine whether you are expected to produce a memorandum, pleading, brief, or informal report of your research results. To a certain extent, this also will be a function of the amount of time you have for the project.

■ **ARE THERE ANY LIMITS ON THE RESEARCH MATERIALS I AM PERMITTED TO USE?**
As a matter of academic integrity, you want to make sure you use only authorized research tools in a law school assignment. In practice, some clients might be unable or unwilling to pay for research completed with tools requiring additional fees, such as Lexis or Westlaw.

■ **WHICH JURISDICTION'S LAW APPLIES?**
This is a question the person giving you the assignment might not be able to answer. There will be times when the controlling jurisdiction will be known. In other cases, it will be up to you to determine whether an issue is controlled by federal or state law, and if it is a question of state law, which state's law applies.

■ **SHOULD I RESEARCH PERSUASIVE AUTHORITY?**
Again, the person making the assignment might not be able to answer this question. You could be asked to focus exclusively on the law of the controlling jurisdiction to answer your research question, or you could be asked specifically to research multiple jurisdictions. If either of those requirements applies to your research, you certainly want to know that before you begin your research. What is more likely, however, is that you will simply be asked to find the answer to a question. If the law of the controlling jurisdiction answers the question, you might not need to go further. If not, you will need to research persuasive authority. Understanding the scope of the assignment will help you focus your efforts appropriately.

In your research class, there will be many parts of the assignment that your professor will expect you to figure out on your own as part of learning about the process of research. In a practice setting, however, you might also ask the following questions:

■ **DO YOU KNOW OF ANY SOURCES THAT ARE PARTICULARLY GOOD FOR RESEARCHING IN THIS AREA OF LAW?**
Practitioners who are experienced in a particular field might know of research sources that are especially helpful for the type of research you are doing, including looseleaf or other subject-matter services.

■ **WHAT BACKGROUND ON THE LAW OR TERMS OF ART SHOULD I KNOW AS I BEGIN MY RESEARCH?**
In a law school assignment, you might be expected to identify terms of art on your own. In practice, however, the person giving you the research assignment might be able to give you some background on the area of law and important terms of art to help you get started on your research.

■ **SHOULD I CONSULT ANY WRITTEN MATERIALS OR INDIVIDUALS WITHIN THE OFFICE BEFORE BEGINNING MY RESEARCH?**
Again, in law school, it would be inappropriate to use another person's research instead of completing the assignment on your own. In practice, however, reviewing briefs or memoranda on the same or a similar issue can give you a leg up on your research. In addition, another person within the office might be considered the "resident expert" on the subject and might be willing to act as a resource for you.

2. PLANNING THE STEPS IN YOUR RESEARCH

Once you have preliminary information on your research project, you are ready to start planning the steps in your research process. The plan should have the following components:

- an initial issue statement
- a list of potential search terms
- an outline of your search strategy

a. Developing an Initial Issue Statement and Generating Search Terms

The starting points for your plan are developing an initial issue statement and generating possible search terms. The issue statement does not need to be a formal statement like one that would appear at the beginning of a brief or memorandum. Rather, it should be a preliminary assessment of the problem that helps define the scope of your research. For example, an initial issue statement might say something like, "Can the plaintiff recover from the defendant for destroying her garden?" This issue statement would be incomplete in a brief or memorandum because it does not identify a specific legal question and might not contain enough information about the facts. At this point, however, you do not know which legal theory or theories might be successful, nor do you know for certain which facts are most important. What this question tells you is that you will need to research all possible claims that would support recovery.

Alternatively, you might be asked to research a narrower question such as, "Can the plaintiff recover from the defendant *in negligence* for destroying her garden?" This issue statement again might be insufficient in a brief or memorandum, but for purposes of your research plan, it gives you valuable information. Your research should be limited to liability in negligence; intentional torts or contract claims are beyond the scope of this project.

Although this might seem like an exercise in the obvious, the discipline of writing a preliminary issue statement can help you focus your efforts in the right direction. If you are unable to write a preliminary issue statement, that is an indication that you are not sure about the scope of the assignment and may need to ask more questions about what you should be trying to accomplish.

Once you have written your initial issue statement, you are ready to generate a list of possible search terms. Chapter 2 discusses how to do this, and the techniques described in that chapter should be employed to develop search terms in your research plan.

b. Outlining Your Search Strategy

Once you have a preliminary view of the problem, the next step in creating an effective research plan is mapping out your search strategy. Unless you have access to WestlawNext or Lexis Advance, you will need to use a source-driven approach. With a source-driven approach, you need to determine which research sources are likely to have relevant information. Then, you must determine the order in which you want to research those sources. If you have access to WestlawNext or Lexis Advance, you must decide whether a source-driven or content-driven approach is best for your project. Considerations affecting this assessment are discussed in Chapter 3.

Chapter 1 discusses three general categories of authority: mandatory primary authority, persuasive primary authority, and secondary authority. With source-driven research, you need to decide which of these categories of authority provides a good starting point for your research, and then, within each category, which specific authorities you should consult.

With content-driven research, you must decide how to pre-filter a search for multiple types of authority.

The best way to approach these tasks is to begin with what you know, identify what you do not yet know, and determine the best ways to fill in the blanks. Your goal should be to use the information you already have to begin narrowing the field of all legal information before you begin looking for authority. This will determine the level of generality at which to begin your research and set the framework for the research steps you need to follow. By answering a series of questions about your knowledge of the research issue, you can determine the best starting point for your research. **Figures 11.1** and **11.2** are flowcharts you can use to guide your inquiry and plan your research steps.

For many research projects, your ultimate goal will be to produce a written document, such as a brief or memorandum, describing and applying primary mandatory authority relevant to the issue. If this type of authority does not exist or does not fully resolve the question, then you probably will also need to discuss primary persuasive authority, secondary authority, or both. Although this is not what you will be asked to do in every research project, this section will illustrate the process of outlining your research path based on this goal. As you will see, this process can be adapted for other types of research projects that you might be asked to complete.

The process of identifying what you know, identifying what you do not yet know, and determining how best to fill in the blanks can be applied to two components of the project: the search for primary mandatory authority, and the search for persuasive authority. You might not be able to map out a complete research plan for both components of the project before beginning your research. At a minimum, however, you should try to plan your search for primary mandatory authority. If a search for persuasive authority becomes necessary, you can then rework your plan to include those sources.

(1) Searching for primary mandatory authority
Beginning with the search for primary mandatory authority, the flowchart in **Figure 11.1** illustrates the process you might undertake.

As you can see from the flowchart, the more you can narrow the field of legal information at the start, the further down the process you can begin. If you know nothing about the subject, you will probably need to begin by reading secondary sources, either by choosing a particular secondary source or by reviewing the secondary sources retrieved from a content-driven search. If you already have a citation to an authority on point, you can use that as a starting point.

Once you have a sense of the applicable legal doctrine, you should also have a sense of whether the issue is a common-law issue governed by

FIGURE 11.1   FLOWCHART FOR DETERMINING YOUR RESEARCH PATH

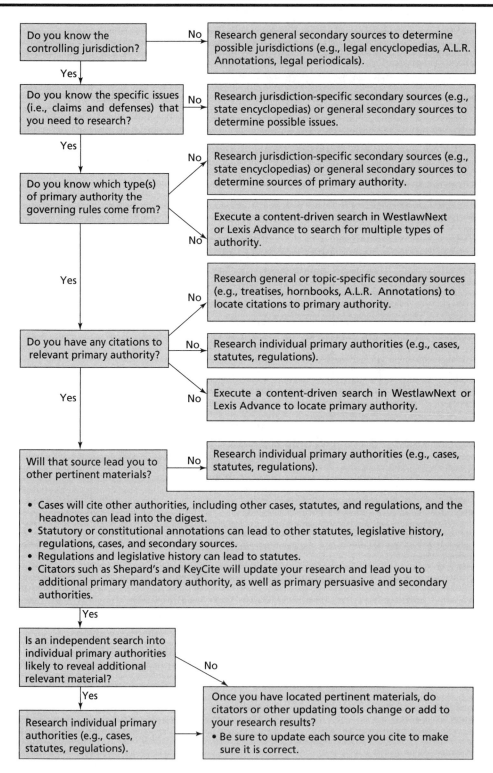

case law or an issue to which statutes, regulations, and other types of authority might apply. You can use this information to determine the best starting point for researching individual primary authorities or filtering the results of a content-driven search.

Once you have identified some primary mandatory authority on the issue, whether through secondary sources or some other avenue, you can use the information within individual authorities as a springboard to other primary authorities. As noted in the flowchart, for example, a case will contain headnotes that can lead you to other cases. The cases should also cite relevant statutory and regulatory provisions. Statutory annotations can lead you to legislative history, regulations, secondary sources, and cases. Of course, it is possible that the sources you consult initially will not lead you to other primary authorities. In that case, you might want to research individual primary sources independently to make sure you have located all of the relevant authority.

(2) Searching for persuasive authority

As you conduct your research, you might determine that you need to search for persuasive authority to analyze your research issue thoroughly. As in your search for primary mandatory authority, in your search for persuasive authority, you should begin with what you know, identify what you do not yet know, and determine the best ways to fill in the blanks.

The first thing you need to know is why you are searching for persuasive authority. Persuasive authority can serve a variety of purposes in your analysis of a research question. Here are four common reasons why you would want to research persuasive authority:

- When you want to buttress an analysis largely resolved by primary mandatory authority.
- When the applicable legal rules are clearly defined by primary mandatory authority, but the specific factual situation has not arisen in the controlling jurisdiction. You might want to try to locate factually analogous cases from other jurisdictions.
- When the applicable rule is unclear and you want to make an analogy to another area of law to support your analysis.
- When the issue is one of first impression in the controlling jurisdiction for which no governing rule exists. In this case, you might want to find out how other jurisdictions have addressed the issue, or if no jurisdiction has faced the question, whether any commentators have analyzed the issue.

In each of these situations, you might want to research persuasive authority consisting of non-mandatory primary authority from within the controlling jurisdiction, such as cases or statutes in an analogous area of law, primary authority from other jurisdictions, or secondary authority analyzing the law.

Once you have determined why you need to research persuasive authority, you should review the material you have already located. In your search for primary mandatory authority, you might already have identified some useful persuasive authority. Secondary sources consulted at the beginning of your research could contain persuasive analysis or useful citations to primary persuasive authority. Secondary sources often identify key or leading authorities in an area of law, and that might be enough to meet your needs. A citator might also have identified useful persuasive authority. If the authorities you have already located prove sufficient, you should update your research to make sure everything you cite remains authoritative and, if appropriate, end your search for persuasive authority.

On the other hand, you might review the results of your research and determine that you need to undertake a separate search for persuasive authority. When you first reviewed secondary sources and used citators, it might not have been with an eye toward locating persuasive authority. Therefore, you might want to take a second pass at these sources. In addition, the persuasive authority you ran across early in your research might not be the best material for you to cite; a more focused research effort could yield more pertinent material.

If you determine that you need to conduct a separate search for persuasive authority, your next step will be deciding the best research path to follow. The flowchart in **Figure 11.2** illustrates several research avenues for locating persuasive authority. Your research path will vary according to a number of factors, including the amount of time you have, the resources available to you, and the type of work product you are expected to produce. Therefore, the flowchart is intended simply to illustrate options that would be available to you, not to establish a definitive path for locating each type of authority.

One thing you might notice as you review the flowchart is that secondary sources play an important role in locating persuasive authority. Unless you know the precise jurisdiction from which you plan to cite persuasive authority, beginning your search for persuasive authority in primary sources is not likely to be efficient in most cases. Secondary sources are key to determining which jurisdictions are likely to have relevant authority and which types of authority are likely to be helpful to you.

c. Deciding Between Print and Electronic Sources

One additional decision you will need to make in formulating a research plan is whether to conduct your research using print research tools, electronic tools, or both. Most students gravitate toward electronic sources,

FIGURE 11.2 FLOWCHART FOR RESEARCHING PERSUASIVE AUTHORITY

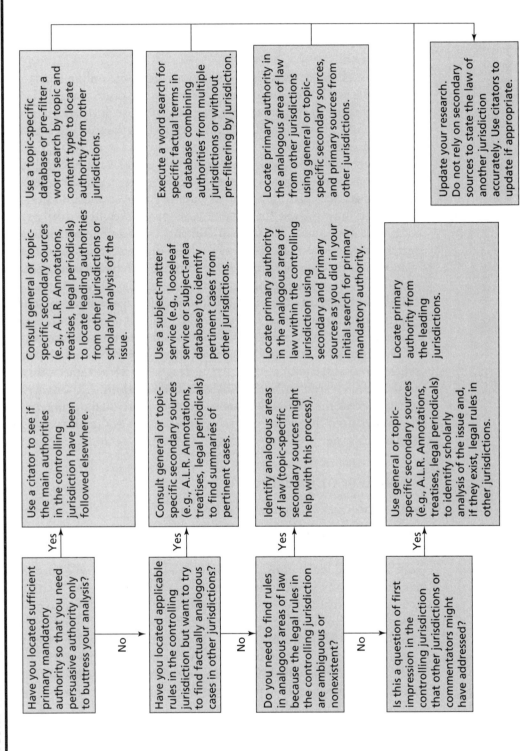

and much legal authority is available online. Some libraries no longer maintain extensive print collections. For certain tasks, however, you should consider print research. Libraries continue to hold secondary sources and statutes in print because those are sources lawyers continue to find useful.

Although many secondary sources are available online, many others are not. In particular, a number of treatises are only available in print, especially those in specialized areas of law or those devoted to the law of an individual jurisdiction. If you limit yourself to the treatises available in Lexis and Westlaw, you may miss important sources. A trip to the library to investigate treatises will often be a good use of your research time.

Print can also offer advantages in statutory research. Although some electronic services provide access to statutory indices, most do not, which means you must browse the table of contents or execute a word search to locate statutes online. The table of contents can be a cumbersome way to search unless you already know which titles or subject areas to search. Legislation is not always organized in an intuitive fashion. Further, legislation often contains terminology that might not be familiar to you. A word search that does not include the precise statutory language will not be effective. A print index, by contrast, is organized by subject and will contain cross-references that can help direct you to the correct terms or concepts.

Additionally, you will often need to review the complete statutory scheme to analyze your research issue. It is easy to lose sight of this when an electronic search retrieves individual code sections. Although you can usually access the table of contents from an individual document, some researchers find that working in the books makes evaluating related code provisions easier.

3. WORKING EFFECTIVELY

a. Keeping Track: Effective Note Taking

Once you have outlined your path, you are ready to begin executing your search plan. Keeping effective notes as you work is important for several reasons. It will make your research more efficient. You will know where you have already looked, so you can avoid repeating research steps. This is especially critical if you will be working on the project for an extended period of time or if you are working with other people in completing the research. You will also have all of the information you need for proper citations. Moreover, if it happens that your project presents novel or complex issues for which there are no definitive answers, careful note taking will allow you to demonstrate that you undertook comprehensive research to try to resolve those issues.

Note taking is an individualized process, and there is no single right way to do it. Some electronic research services will keep track of your research by collecting a list of searches you run and documents you view. You may be able to name and save a record of your searches. This is useful, but unless you conduct all of your research with a single service, it will not be a complete record of your search process, especially if you do some research in print. You may be able to download your search history so that you can integrate information from multiple services into a single record of your own, which you can then annotate with your own notes about steps that did and did not lead to useful information.

Once you begin locating specific sources, you will need to organize what you find. Electronic providers may allow you to create folders for research projects. You can also create your own folders outside of any research service to collect information on your project. You can create a folder on your computer or use a service such as Dropbox to access documents on multiple devices.

When you save or download information, you may want to add notes to it. Electronic research services may have functions that allow you to add "sticky notes" with notes about the document as a whole. You may also be able to highlight or mark text and append notes at a particular location within a document. You can also do these things without using a research service's tools. Free and inexpensive "sticky note" software is available, and many programs have commenting functions you can use to add notes to documents.

When you find useful information, you must decide how to organize your research, which documents or snippets to save, and what notes to add to what you have saved. You will probably want to begin by making a folder for all material related to the project as a whole. Sub-folders for research material, your notes, and any factual documents related to the project may be useful. With respect to research material, you may want to segregate content by issue if you are researching multiple issues or by type of authority if you are researching a single issue.

When it comes to saving documents, there is a constant tension between reading what you find and saving the material itself. Most people save more than they need, and many students use collecting and saving documents as a procrastination technique, promising themselves that they will read the information later. Excessive downloading or copying will not improve your research. Certainly, having access to key authorities is important for accurate analysis, quotation, and citation. Facing a huge, disorganized collection of information, however, can be demoralizing, especially because most of the information will probably prove to be irrelevant in the end if you have not made thoughtful choices about what to save or copy.

The fact is that you will not know for certain at the beginning of your research which sources should be saved and which should not. Only as you begin to understand the contours of the legal issue will the relevance (or irrelevance) of individual legal authorities become apparent to you. Therefore, you should conduct some research before you begin saving material. As you delve into the research, you may find that you need to go back to materials you bypassed originally. You may also find it helpful to have a "maybe" folder for your research where you can collect sources that you are not sure will be helpful. If you do this, however, it is important to return to that information periodically to assess its usefulness.

When you find information you want to save, you may be able to choose between saving the entire document or just a snippet. The benefit of saving a snippet is that you have the precise content that appears relevant.

Saving snippets also presents several potential pitfalls. The passage that seemed most relevant to you at one time may not turn out to be the best part of the document upon later reflection. You also run the risk of taking a passage out of context and representing it inaccurately in your analysis. If you save only snippets, you may be tempted to use a collection of snippets pasted into a document as a substitute for analysis and synthesis of the authorities. This can also lead to inadvertent plagiarism if each snippet is not properly cited.

There are times when just a snippet will do, such as when only a few pages out of a 50-page law review article are relevant to your research. You should be cautious, however, when choosing to save only snippets of documents. Often the better practice is saving the entire document even if you do not plan to use the entire document to analyze your research issue.

The next step in documenting your research is deciding which notes to add to the item you save. For most items you will want to note the following information:

The database or source for the item	If you use a folder in an electronic service, you may not need to note this. If you generate your own folder or import content from another source into a folder housed in an electronic research service, you should note where you located the item.
Citation	This does not need to be in proper citation form, but enough information for a proper citation should be included here. Some electronic services will include this information automatically when you save information within that service. If you are doing your own cutting and pasting, however, you need to take the extra step of noting the source and the citation information. Note that citations provided by publishers often do not conform to *ALWD Manual* or *Bluebook* format.
Method of locating the source	This could include references to a secondary source that led you to this authority or the search terms you used in an index or database. Noting this information will help you assess which search approaches are most effective. A sticky note or comment at the beginning of the document is a good place to record this information.

Summary of relevant information	This might be a few sentences or a few paragraphs, depending on the source and its relevance. Making a note about why you saved the item may jog your memory about its relevance when you go back to review it later.
Updating information	Note whether the source has been updated and the method of updating. If you are researching in print, you might note the date of any pocket part or supplement. For electronic research, you should note the updating date for a statute or secondary source. If appropriate, you should also note which citator you use to verify the validity of the source.

This might not be the only information you need to note. For example, in case research, you may also want to note separately the topics and key numbers in the most important cases. You also may want to make notes or highlight text within the body of a document to make the relevant portions easy for you to find. At a minimum, however, you should keep track of the pieces of information listed above.

Although many people keep electronic notes and download most of their research material, some people still do better with hard copy. The physical acts of printing important sources, organizing them under tabs in a binder or stacking them in piles on the floor, and marking key portions with a highlighter and sticky notes can give you a different perspective on what you have found. If you have trouble visualizing the big picture of your project with an electronic filing system, consider working with at least some of your research in hard copy as an alternative.

b. Deciding When to Stop

Deciding when your research is complete can be difficult. The more research you do, the more comfortable you will be with the process, and the more you will develop an internal sense of when a project is complete. In your first few research assignments in law school, however, you will probably feel uncertain about when to stop because you will have little prior experience to draw upon in making that decision.

One issue that affects a person's sense of when to stop is personal work style. Some people are anxious to begin writing and therefore stop researching after they locate a few sources that seem relevant. Others put off writing by continuing to research, thinking that the answer will become apparent if they just keep looking a little bit more. Being aware of your work style will help you determine whether you have stopped too soon or are continuing your research beyond what is necessary for the assignment.

Of course, the amount of time you have and the work product you are expected to produce will affect the ending point for your research. If you are instructed to report back in half an hour with your research results, you know when you will need to stop. In general, however, you will know that you have come full circle in your research when, after following a comprehensive research path through a variety of sources, the authorities you locate start to refer back to each other and the new sources you consult fail to reveal significant new information.

The fact that a few of the sources you have located appear relevant does not mean it is time to stop researching. Until you have explored other potential research avenues, you should continue your work. It might be that the authorities you initially locate will turn out to be the most relevant, but you cannot have confidence in that result until you research additional authorities. On the other hand, you can always keep looking for one more case or one more article to support your analysis, but at some point the benefit of continuing to research will be too small to justify the additional effort. It is unlikely that one magical source exists that is going to resolve your research issue. If the issue were clear, you probably would not have been asked to research it. If you developed a comprehensive research strategy and followed it until you came full circle in your research, it is probably time to stop.

C. FINDING HELP

Even if you follow all of the steps outlined in this chapter, from time to time, you will not be able to find what you need. The two most common situations that arise are not being able to find any authority on an issue and finding an overwhelming amount of information.

1. WHAT TO DO IF YOU ARE UNABLE TO FIND ANYTHING

If you have researched several different sources and are unable to find anything, it is time to take a different approach. You should not expect the material you need to appear effortlessly, and blind alleys are inevitable if you approach a problem creatively. Nevertheless, if you find that you really cannot locate any information on an issue, consider the following possibilities:

■ MAKE SURE YOU UNDERSTAND THE PROBLEM
One possibility is that you have misunderstood a critical aspect of the problem. If diligent research truly yields nothing, you might want to go back to the person who gave you the assignment to make sure you correctly noted all of the factual information you need and have understood the assignment correctly.

■ **RETHINK YOUR SEARCH TERMS**

Have you expanded the breadth and depth of your search terms? You might be researching the right concepts but not have expressed them in a way that yields information in an index or from a word search. Expanding your search terms will allow you to look not only more widely for information, but also more narrowly. For example, if you have searched unsuccessfully using *moving vehicle* as a search term for authority involving transportation equipment, you might need to move to more concrete terms, such as *automobile* or *car*.

In addition, you might need to rethink search terms directed to applicable legal theories. If you have focused on a theory of recovery for which you have not been able to locate authority, you might need to think about other ways to approach the problem. Try not to become so wedded to a legal theory that you pursue it to the exclusion of other viable claims or defenses.

■ **GO BACK TO SECONDARY SOURCES**

If you did not consult secondary sources originally, you might want to take that route to find the information you need. The material on the issue might be scattered through many subject areas or statutory sections so that it is difficult to compile the relevant subset of information without secondary sources that tie disparate threads of authority together. In addition, the search terms that seemed applicable when you started your research might, in fact, not be helpful. Secondary sources can help point you in the right direction.

Another difficulty is that you might be looking for the wrong type of authority. Are you sure this is a question of state law? Although a content-driven search will retrieve multiple types of authority, pre-filtering by the wrong jurisdiction will take you in the wrong direction. If you are using source-driven searching, you may need to look in other sources if, for example, statutes as well as cases apply to the situation. Secondary sources can help you determine what type of primary authority is likely to be relevant to the situation.

Finally, secondary sources can help you determine whether you are facing a question of first impression. If the controlling jurisdiction simply has not faced this question yet, secondary sources should direct you to jurisdictions that have. If no jurisdiction has resolved the issue, legal periodicals might direct you to arguments and analogies that could be made.

2. WHAT TO DO IF YOU FIND AN OVERWHELMING AMOUNT OF MATERIAL

The same strategies that will help you if you are unable to find any material will also help if you find an overwhelming amount of material. Making sure you understand the problem, of course, is critical. Rethinking your search terms to narrow your approach can also help. If you located information primarily using word searches, you might want to try searching by subject, using either print or electronic research tools, because searching by subject instead of by terms in the document might help you focus on relevant authority. Consulting secondary sources, however, is probably the most useful strategy. Synthesizing large amounts of authority is difficult. Secondary sources can help you identify the key authorities and otherwise limit the scope of the information on the issue.

Another consideration here is the scope of your research. If much of the authority you have located is secondary authority or primary persuasive authority, you might need to refocus on primary mandatory authority from the controlling jurisdiction. If the controlling jurisdiction has a sufficient amount of authority for thorough analysis of the issue, you might not need to cite persuasive authority. You might also need to narrow your scope by limiting the legal theories you are considering. If some are clearly more viable than others and you already have an overwhelming amount of authority, you might want to focus on the theories that seem to provide your client with the best chances of prevailing.

Even when you take these steps, finding an overwhelming amount of material is not uncommon with content-driven searching. Because the results include many types of authority and because of the way the search algorithms work, it is not unusual for a content-driven search to return thousands or tens of thousands of documents. This is obviously too much information to be useful.

With content-driven searching, using the relevancy rankings and filtering the search results are critical. Although you should not assume that the very best authority will be the first item in the search results, you must rely to some extent on the relevancy rankings when a search retrieves 10,000 documents. Those at the bottom of the list are not likely to be very relevant; they may contain only one reference to only one of your search terms. Post-search filtering is also important. Even when you pre-filter by jurisdiction, you may retrieve both state and related federal information or cases from all levels of court within the state. Limiting the results to the controlling tribunal or a specific publication, using a date restriction, and searching for terms within the initial results are all good strategies for focusing on the most relevant information.

D. SAMPLE RESEARCH PLANS

The research plans in **Figures 11.3** through **11.6** are intended to help you develop a coherent research strategy for four common types of research: state common-law research, state statutory research, federal statutory research, and federal and state procedural research. These plans are representative samples of how you could approach the research process and may provide a useful starting point for your own research planning.

1. STATE COMMON-LAW RESEARCH

FIGURE 11.3 FLOWCHART FOR STATE COMMON-LAW RESEARCH

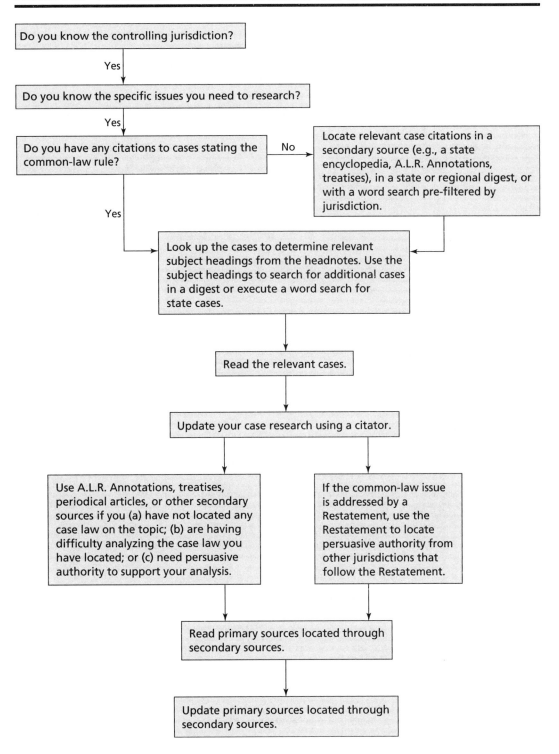

2. STATE STATUTORY RESEARCH

FIGURE 11.4   FLOWCHART FOR STATE STATUTORY RESEARCH

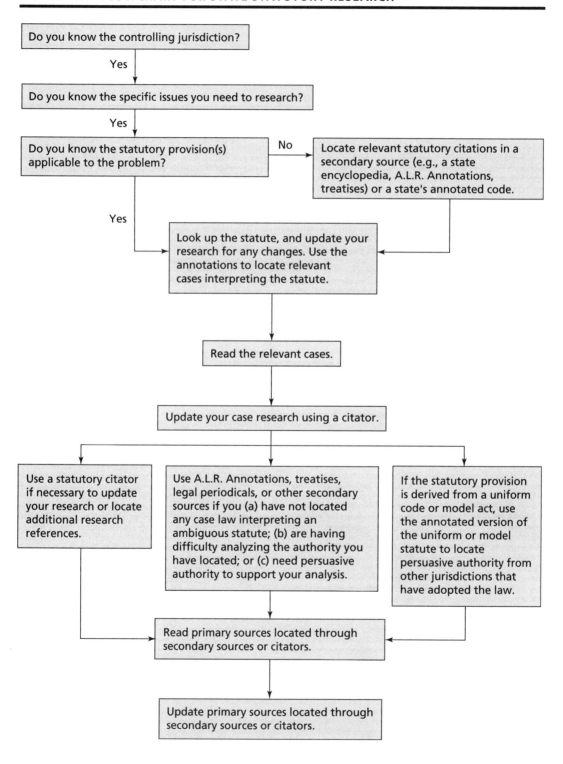

3. Federal Statutory Research

FIGURE 11.5 FLOWCHART FOR FEDERAL STATUTORY RESEARCH

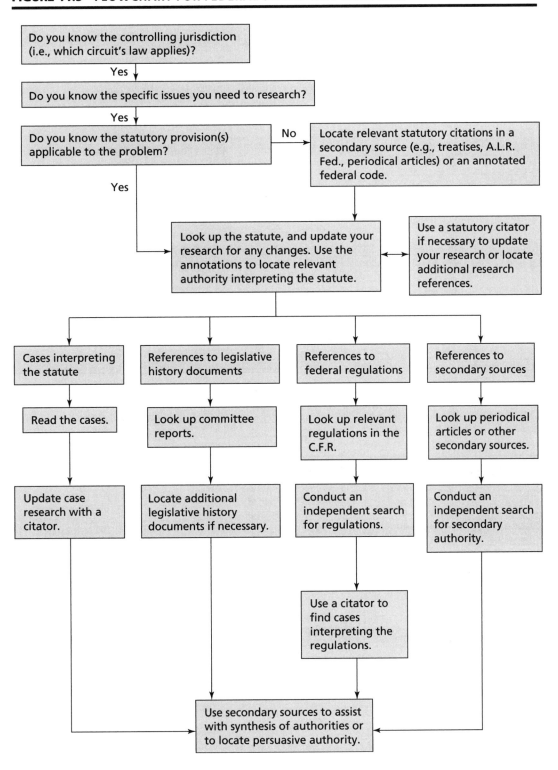

4. FEDERAL OR STATE PROCEDURAL RESEARCH

FIGURE 11.6   FLOWCHART FOR RESEARCHING RULES OF PROCEDURE

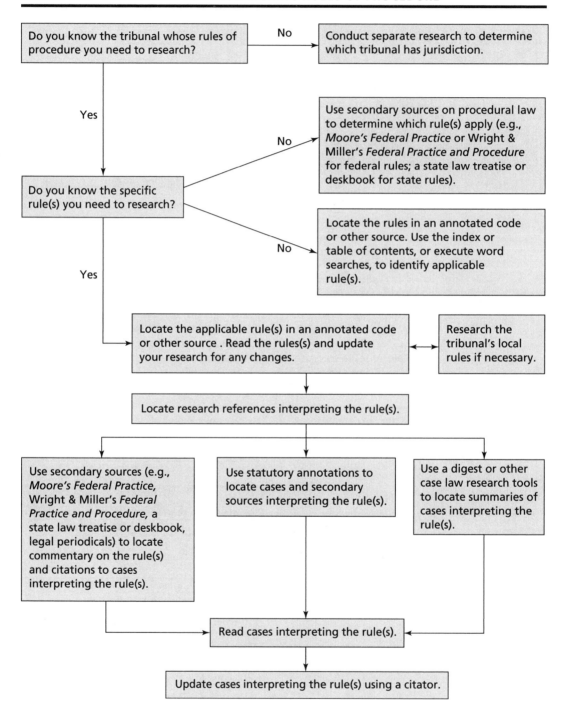

E. RESEARCH CHECKLISTS

1. CHECKLIST FOR DEVELOPING AN EFFECTIVE RESEARCH PLAN

1. OBTAIN PRELIMINARY INFORMATION ON THE PROBLEM

- ❏ Determine the due date, work product expected, limits on research tools to be used, controlling jurisdiction (if known), and whether persuasive authority should be located (if known).
- ❏ If permitted, find out useful research tools, background on the law or terms of art, and whether other written materials or individuals with special expertise should be consulted.

2. PLAN THE STEPS IN YOUR RESEARCH

- ❏ Develop a preliminary issue statement.
- ❏ Generate a list of search terms.
- ❏ Identify the type and sequence of research tasks by identifying what you know, what you do not yet know, and how best to fill in the blanks.

  - ▪ Narrow the field of legal information using what you already know about the research issue (e.g., jurisdiction).
  - ▪ Use the information you already know to determine whether source- or content-driven searching is most efficient for your task.
  - ▪ Use secondary sources to narrow the field further.
  - ▪ When you are ready to review primary authority, focus on mandatory authority first.
  - ▪ Locate persuasive authority later, if necessary:

    - ▪ to buttress an analysis largely resolved by primary mandatory authority;
    - ▪ to locate factually analogous cases from other jurisdictions;
    - ▪ to make an analogy to another area of law when the applicable rule is unclear;
    - ▪ to locate commentary or applicable rules from other jurisdictions on an issue of first impression.

  - ▪ Determine the best mix of print and electronic research tools for your research project.

3. WORK EFFECTIVELY

- ❏ Keep effective notes.
- ❏ Stop researching when your research has come full circle.
- ❏ Find help if you need it.

  - ▪ If you are unable to find anything or find too much material, make sure you understand the problem, rethink your search terms, consult secondary sources, and reevaluate the legal theories you are pursuing.

2. Master Checklist of Research Sources

The following is an abbreviated collection of the research checklists that appear at the end of the preceding chapters in this text. This master checklist may help you develop your research plan. It may also be useful to you as you conduct research.

Secondary Source Research

1. LEGAL ENCYCLOPEDIAS

- ❏ Use for very general background information and limited citations to primary authority, but not for in-depth analysis of a topic.
- ❏ Locate information in print by using the subject index or table of contents, locating relevant sections in the main volumes, and updating with the pocket part.
- ❏ Use word or table of contents searches in Lexis and Westlaw.
- ❏ Use content-driven searching in WestlawNext and Lexis Advance by executing a search, reviewing results for secondary sources, and filtering the content by source or other appropriate criteria.

2. TREATISES

- ❏ Use for an in-depth discussion and some analysis of an area of law and for citations to primary authority.
- ❏ Locate treatises in print through the online catalog; locate information within a treatise by using the subject index or table of contents, locating material in the main volumes, and updating with the pocket part.
- ❏ Use word or table of contents searches in Lexis and Westlaw to access selected treatises.
- ❏ Use content-driven searching in WestlawNext and Lexis Advance by executing a search, reviewing results for secondary sources, and filtering the content by source or other appropriate criteria.

3. LEGAL PERIODICALS

- ❏ Use for background information, citations to primary authority, in-depth analysis of a narrow topic, or information on a conflict in the law or an undeveloped area of the law.
- ❏ Use the LegalTrac and ILP electronic indices to locate citations to legal periodicals and full text of selected articles.
- ❏ Use Lexis and Westlaw to access legal periodicals.
- ❏ Use HeinOnline and SSRN to locate legal periodicals in .pdf format.
- ❏ Locate selected legal periodicals using a law-related website or general Internet search engine.

4. *AMERICAN LAW REPORTS*

❏ Use A.L.R. Annotations for an overview of an area of law and citations to primary authority.

❏ Locate material in A.L.R. by using the A.L.R. Index, locating material in the main volumes, and updating with the pocket part.

❏ Use word or table of contents searches in Lexis and Westlaw to access A.L.R. Annotations; use Westlaw for the first series of A.L.R. and for e-annos.

❏ Use content-driven searching in WestlawNext by executing a search, reviewing results for secondary sources, and filtering the content by source or other appropriate criteria. Use a similar process in Lexis Advance when its coverage includes A.L.R. Annotations.

5. RESTATEMENTS

❏ Use for research into common-law subjects and to locate mandatory and persuasive authority from jurisdictions that have adopted a Restatement.

❏ Locate information within a print Restatement by using the subject index or table of contents to find Restatement sections in the Restatement volumes, locating case summaries in the noncumulative Appendix volumes, and updating the Appendix volumes with the pocket part.

❏ Use Lexis.com and Westlaw to access Restatement rules and case annotations; coverage may be limited in Lexis Advance but is expected to increase over time.

6. UNIFORM LAWS AND MODEL ACTS

❏ Use to interpret a law adopted by a legislature and to locate persuasive authority from other jurisdictions that have adopted the law.

❏ Locate in print using *Uniform Laws Annotated, Master Edition* (ULA).

❏ Locate information in the ULA set by using the *Directory of Uniform Acts and Codes: Tables and Index*, locating relevant provisions in the main volumes, and updating with the pocket part.

❏ Use Lexis.com and Westlaw to access selected uniform laws and model acts; coverage may be limited in Lexis Advance but is expected to increase over time.

Case Research

1. SELECT A PRINT DIGEST

❏ Use federal, state, regional, or combined digests.

2. LOCATE TOPICS AND KEY NUMBERS IN A PRINT DIGEST

❐ Work from a case on point, the Descriptive-Word Index, or the topic entry.

3. READ THE CASE SUMMARIES IN THE PRINT DIGEST

❐ Use the court and date abbreviations to target appropriate cases.

4. UPDATE PRINT DIGEST RESEARCH

❐ Check the pocket part and any cumulative or noncumulative interim pamphlets.
❐ If necessary, check the closing table and mini-digests.

5. ELECTRONIC CASE RESEARCH—SEARCHING BY SUBJECT

❐ In Westlaw, search for cases by subject using the **West Key Number** (Custom Digest) function or from a case on point.
❐ In Lexis.com, search for cases by subject using the **Topic or Headnote** search function or from a case on point.

6. ELECTRONIC CASE RESEARCH—WORD SEARCHING

❐ In Westlaw and Lexis, execute word searches within a specific database; in WestlawNext and Lexis Advance, pre-filter by jurisdiction or content type, execute a search, and filter the results to target appropriate cases.
❐ Use Google Scholar or websites for courts or other tribunals to search for cases.

Research with Citators

1. USE SHEPARD'S IN LEXIS

❐ Access Shepard's by entering a citation or using the link in a relevant case.
❐ Interpret the entry.

■ Direct history appears first, followed by citing cases organized by jurisdiction and secondary sources.
■ Use history and treatment codes and headnote references to identify the most relevant citing cases.
■ Filter the display to focus on the most relevant information.
■ In Lexis Advance, use the **Map** view for a snapshot of case history in chart form and the **Grid** view for a snapshot of treatment by later citing cases in chart form.

2. USE KEYCITE IN WESTLAW

☐ Access KeyCite by entering a citation or from a relevant case.

☐ Interpret the entry in Westlaw.com.

- ■ View the **Full History** of the original case to see direct history and negative indirect history or the **Direct History (Graphical View)** to see the history of the original case in chart form.
- ■ View the **Citing References** to see indirect history and citing sources; negative cases appear first, followed by positive cases (divided by depth of treatment and then by jurisdiction) and citing sources.

☐ Interpret the entry in WestlawNext using the **Negative Treatment, History,** and **Citing References** tabs; filter the display to focus on the most relevant information.

☐ Use the descriptions of the history and treatment and headnote references to identify the most relevant cases.

☐ Customize the display to focus on the most relevant information.

Statutory Research

1. LOCATE A STATUTE

☐ Use a subject index, popular name table, or for federal statutes, the conversion tables in print.

☐ Use Lexis and Westlaw to access state and federal statutes electronically using word, table of contents, or popular name searches; in Westlaw, use the statutory index.

☐ In WestlawNext and Lexis Advance, pre-filter by jurisdiction and execute a content-driven search to retrieve statutes and other authorities; filter the results to target appropriate statutes.

☐ On the Internet, locate statutes on government or general legal research websites.

2. READ THE STATUTE AND ACCOMPANYING ANNOTATIONS

3. UPDATE YOUR RESEARCH

☐ With print research, check the pocket part accompanying the main volume and any cumulative or noncumulative supplements accompanying the code.

- ■ In U.S.C.A., update entries to the popular name and conversion tables with the noncumulative supplements.
- ■ In state codes, check for additional updating tools.

❐ With state or federal statutory research, update your research or find additional research references using a statutory citator such as Shepard's in Lexis or KeyCite in Westlaw.

❐ With Internet research, check the date of the statute and update your research accordingly; consider using a statutory citator to update your research and find additional research references.

Federal Legislative History Research

1. IDENTIFY THE SCOPE OF YOUR RESEARCH

❐ Determine whether you need to find the history of a particular statute or material on a general subject.

2. LOCATE A COMPILED LEGISLATIVE HISTORY

❐ Use the library's online catalog; Johnson, *Sources of Compiled Legislative Histories*; Reams, *Federal Legislative Histories*; Hein-Online's U.S. Federal Legislative History Title Collection; or compiled legislative histories in Lexis.com and Westlaw.com.

3. LOCATE COMMITTEE REPORTS, *CONGRESSIONAL RECORD* FLOOR DEBATES, AND OTHER LEGISLATIVE HISTORY DOCUMENTS FOR A SPECIFIC STATUTE

❐ Use annotations in U.S.C.A. to locate cross-references to U.S.C.C.A.N.

❐ In Westlaw, retrieve the public law and use links to legislative history documents.

❐ In Lexis.com, use the public law number to search in databases for individual types of legislative history documents.

❐ In Thomas and FDSys, search by bill number or public law number to retrieve legislative history documents.

❐ In ProQuest Congressional, search by bill number, public law number, or *Statutes at Large* citation to locate legislative history documents.

Federal Administrative Law Research

1. LOCATE PERTINENT REGULATIONS

❐ Use statutory cross-references or a subject index to locate federal regulations in the C.F.R. in print.

❐ Use Lexis, FDSys, or other Internet sites to locate unannotated C.F.R. provisions.

❐ Use Westlaw to locate an annotated version of the C.F.R.

2. UPDATE FDSYS RESEARCH WITH THE e-CFR

3. UPDATE C.F.R. RESEARCH WITH OFFICIAL SOURCES

- ❏ Update from the date of the C.F.R. volume through the end of the prior month by using the most recent LSA to find *Federal Register* references affecting the regulation.
- ❏ Update from the end of the prior month to the present by using the cumulative table of CFR Parts Affected for the current month in the Reader Aids section in the back of the most recent issue of the *Federal Register*.

4. CONTACT THE AGENCY FOR ADDITIONAL INFORMATION ON RECENT OR PROPOSED REGULATORY CHANGES

Electronic Legal Research

1. SELECT AN ELECTRONIC RESEARCH SERVICE

- ❏ Consider the scope of coverage and cost.

2. SELECT A SEARCH TECHNIQUE

- ❏ Retrieve a document from its citation.
- ❏ Execute a source-driven search by selecting a database before executing a search.
- ❏ Execute a content-driven search by pre-filtering by jurisdiction, executing a word search, and filtering the results.

3. PLAN AND EXECUTE A SEARCH

- ❏ For word searches, consider the search options: terms and connectors, natural language, and descriptive term.
- ❏ In Westlaw and Lexis, be aware of the differences among search algorithms and default search options.
- ❏ Use terms and connectors searching effectively in an initial search by developing the initial search terms, expanding the breadth and depth of the search, specifying the relationships among the terms, and using a field or segment search if appropriate.

4. REVIEW AND FILTER SEARCH RESULTS

- ❏ Relevance, date, or other result ranking choices affect which documents appear at the top of the search results.
- ❏ Narrowing searches will be terms and connectors searches even if the initial search is not; use terms and connectors commands to add search terms, focus on terms in the initial search, or change the relationships among terms in the initial search.

5. USE ADDITIONAL TOOLS FOR EFFECTIVE ELECTRONIC RESEARCH

❏ Use an alert or clipping service to keep research up to date.
❏ Use publicly available Internet sources.

  ■ Locate useful sites to obtain background information on a topic or citations to primary authority.
  ■ Assess the credibility of the source.
  ■ Save or print copies of useful pages.
  ■ Verify and update any legal authorities you locate.

Selected Internet Research Resources

FEDERAL GOVERNMENT WEBSITES

Federal Digital System
http://www.fdsys.gov
> The federal government's source for many government publications, including the *Code of Federal Regulations* and the *Federal Register*. Provides access to a wide range of legislative history documents. Links to the e-CFR for updating federal regulatory research and the CyberCemetery of Former Federal Web Sites for locating archived versions of federal websites.

Library of Congress
http://www.loc.gov
> Search the online catalog of the Library of Congress, and locate a wealth of legal and general information.

Thomas
http://thomas.loc.gov
> The Library of Congress's online source for legislative information. This site contains committee reports, the *Congressional Record*, and other legislative history documents.

United States House of Representatives Office of the Law Revision Counsel
http://uscode.house.gov
> This site contains an electronic version of the United States Code.

United States Supreme Court
http://www.supremecourtus.gov
> The site for the U.S. Supreme Court.

USA.gov
http://www.usa.gov
> The U.S. government's official portal to a wide range of governmental resources.

United States Courts of Appeals
http://www.[identifier].uscourts.gov
> Each federal circuit court of appeals has its own website; insert *ca* and the number of the circuit as the identifier in the URL above to access a numbered circuit's site, e.g., *ca1* for the First Circuit; *ca2* for the Second Circuit, etc. The Federal Circuit is identified as *cafc*, and the District of Columbia Circuit is identified as *cadc*.

STATE GOVERNMENT WEBSITES

National Center for State Courts
http://www.ncsc.org
> Provides links to court websites for each state.

Every state government has a portal that provides access to legal information for the state. You can locate a state's website using a search engine or through the library websites listed below.

LIBRARY WEBSITES

Law library sites can be used to search for a wide range of legal authorities, including state and federal cases and statutes, administrative materials, secondary sources, and legal news. Those listed here are good starting points for research, but many other library sites are also useful for legal research.

Cornell Law School's Legal Information Institute
http://www.law.cornell.edu

Georgetown Law Library
http://www.ll.georgetown.edu

Washburn University School of Law WashLaw Legal Research on the Web
http://www.washlaw.edu

GENERAL LEGAL RESEARCH WEBSITES

Like the law library websites, these sites provide access to a wide range of legal materials. Some can be accessed free of charge; others are fee-based services.

Free Services

All Law
http://www.alllaw.com

American Bar Association: The Lawlink Legal Research Jumpstation
http://www.abanet.org
    Search for *lawlink jumpstation* on the ABA website.

FindLaw
http://lp.findlaw.com

Heiros Gamos
http://www.hg.org

LLRX.com
http://www.llrx.com

Fee-based Services

Bloomberg Law
http://www.bloomberglaw.com

LoislawConnect
http://www.loislaw.com

Lexis Advance
http://advance.lexis.com

Lexis.com
http://www.lexis.com

VersusLaw
http://www.versuslaw.com

Westlaw.com and WestlawNext
http://www.westlaw.com

Internet Search Engines

General Internet search engines can be used to locate legal information. Those listed here are specialized search engines.

Google Scholar
http://www.scholar.google.com
    Searches case law and scholarly literature.

LawCrawler
http://lawcrawler.findlaw.com
    Searches for legal information.

MetaCrawler
http://www.metacrawler.com
    Allows you to excute a search through multiple search engines simultaneously.

Other Websites of Interest

ALWD Citation Manual
http://www.alwdmanual.com or
http://www.aspenlawschool.com/books/dickerson_alwd
    Contains updates and information on the *ALWD Citation Manual*.

Blawg
http://www.blawg.com
    Contains a directory of law-related blogs.

The Bluebook
http://www.legalbluebook.com
    Contains the electronic version of the *Bluebook*, along with tips and updates available without a subscription.

Introduction to Basic Legal Citation
http://www.law.cornell.edu/citation
    Provides tips on using the *Bluebook* and *ALWD Citation Manual*.

Internet Archive Wayback Machine
http://www.archive.org
    Contains archived web pages. To see what a website displayed on a date in the past, enter the URL for the site, and select the date.

Martindale-Hubbell
http://www.martindale.com
>   Search for individual lawyers, firms, or government agencies employing attorneys.

Social Science Research Network (SSRN), Legal Scholarship Network (LSN)
http://www.ssrn.com
>   Provides full-text access to published and forthcoming legal periodical articles.

Subscription Services

This list of subscription services does not include their web addresses because individual users cannot access these services' search features from their websites. Your library may subscribe to the services listed below. If so, you may be able to access them through the library's portal.

Casemaker
>   A full-text research service providing access to a range of primary authorities that is available through some state bar associations.

Fastcase
>   A full-text research service providing access to a range of primary authorities that is available through some state bar associations.

HeinOnline
>   A service providing access to legal periodicals, legislative history documents, and other publications.

Index to Legal Periodicals
>   A periodical index that also provides full text of selected articles.

LegalTrac
>   A periodical index that also provides full text of selected articles.

ProQuest Congressional
>   A service that provides full-text access to federal legislative history documents.

Index

Bold page numbers indicate reprinted examples.